A SHORT CHRONOLOGY
OF AMERICAN HISTORY

A SHORT CHRONOLOGY

RUTGERS UNIVERSITY PRESS

NEW BRUNSWICK, N.J.

1952

OF American
History
1492
1950

Irving S. and Nell M. Kull

To Blaisdell, Robert, and Martha

ACKNOWLEDGMENTS

For a book such as this, obligations are due to the large company of historians who have contributed through the years to the picture of America's past.

Special gratitude goes to colleagues on the faculties of history and political science at Rutgers University who have read various sections of the manuscript and given valuable suggestions. It is a pleasure to name them: Ardath Burks, L. Ethan Ellis, John J. George, Samuel McCulloch, Sidney Ratner, Bennett Rich, Norman Stamps, and Henry Winkler. Needless to say, none is held responsible for errors of commission or omission. The research assistance of Stanley Friedelbaum and Beulah Van Riper established many a date. Page Spencer, guiding the book through the press, is commended for her skill and patience.

Particular gratitude is extended to the Research Council of Rutgers University for aid when research pressures were greatest.

INTRODUCTION

This short chronology is a selection of some ten thousand events in American history, arranged in sequence from 1492 through 1950. The book is designed to serve two purposes: by means of a complete index, to provide a quick reference to the date of any one of the events included; and to give the reader a sense of the developing pattern of history by placing the events in their chronological relationship to each other.

The chronology of any single thread of American history could well outstretch this volume. Therefore, the items included were selected to give as complete a picture as possible. Many readers will find omissions in their fields, while others may wonder at the inclusion of certain items. Major emphasis has been given to social, economic, and political history. The large field of cultural and intellectual history has been reserved for a supplementary volume. However, a few of the items belonging to that volume have escaped the blue pencil, and now and then some event stands, defended only by a whim of the authors.

Thomas Prince, author of the first critical historical work produced in America, *Chronological History of New England*, 1736, wrote in his preface, "I . . . quickly found . . . chronology to be vastly more difficult than one can imagine, who has not applied himself to the study." And he added, "I have labored after accuracy; and yet I dare not say that I am without mistake; nor do I desire the reader to conceal any he may possibly find." The authors hope this chronology may be so useful as to warrant revision and, with Thomas Prince, shall welcome suggestions as well as corrections.

Contents

CHRONOLOGY 1

The dates in italics at the top of each page indicate the year or years covered on that page.

INDEX 299

"Without a trustworthy chronology, history would be but a darksome chaos."

FRANÇOIS CLÉMENT

CHRONOLOGY

NOTES TO THE READER

Calendar: Much confusion in the dating of events has resulted from the continued use of the Julian Calendar by the Protestant countries after the Gregorian Calendar had been adopted by the Catholic countries in 1582. Not until 1752 did Great Britain and her colonies officially adopt the Gregorian Calendar. In the meantime, for practical purposes the so-called Historical Year came into use. Beginning the year on January 1, it used the Gregorian (New Style) year-dates but continued the Julian (Old Style) month-dates. This chronology follows the Historical Year usage for dates prior to 1752.

Local time is used in the dates assigned to events unless otherwise indicated.

Election day: For Presidential election years from 1792 to 1844, the first Wednesday in December has been designated as election day, when electors cast their ballots for President (Act of Mar. 1, 1792). From 1848 on, the Tuesday following the first Monday in November, when electors are chosen, has been designated as election day (Act of Jan. 23, 1845). Although technically inaccurate, the party commitments of the electors justify this procedure. The subsequent electoral vote has been included in the election day item. Popular vote is not regularly given until 1872, when all electors were for the first time chosen by popular vote.

Acts of Congress: Dates of acts of Congress are the dates of the President's signature.

Brackets are used to indicate subsequent but related material.

1492

"The discovery of America, and that of a passage to the East Indies by the Cape of Good Hope, are the two greatest and most important events recorded in the history of mankind." Adam Smith in *Wealth of Nations*, 1776.

Aug 3 Columbus sets sail from Palos, Spain, in the *Santa Maria*, with Pinzon brothers in command of the *Niña* and the *Pinta*.

Oct 12 At early morning one of the Bahama Islands, probably Watling's Island, is sighted from the *Pinta*. Landing, Columbus takes possession in name of Ferdinand and Isabella, calling island San Salvador. Subsequently, he discovers Cuba and Haiti which he calls Española. Builds fort La Navidad on northern coast of Española.

1493

Mar 15 Columbus reaches Palos, Spain, completing his first voyage.

May 4 Papal line of demarcation drawn by Alexander VI 100 leagues west of Azores and Cape Verde Islands, lands west of line to belong to Spain, and east of it to Portugal.

Sept 25 Columbus sails from Cadiz, Spain, upon second voyage to America. Discovers Jamaica and Puerto Rico and, on Haiti, finding fort La Navidad destroyed, builds new settlement, Isabella. Leaving his brother Bartholomew in charge, he returns to Spain, arriving June 11, 1496.

1497

John Cabot, Venetian navigator, sails west under patent from King Henry VII of England. Reaches coast of North America, north of New England, sails southward 300 leagues and returns to England. This voyage and one in 1498, made with his son Sebastian, as far south as South Carolina, become base for England's claim to North America.

1498

May 30 Columbus sails from Spain on third voyage, reaching continent of South America, at mouth of the Orinoco, Aug. 1. Finds revolt at settlement in Haiti. He and his brother Bartholomew are returned to Spain in chains.

1499

Amerigo Vespucci, Florentine merchant, probably visits South America with Alonzo de Ojéda (Spanish).

1

1500

French, English, Portuguese and Spanish fishing fleets, from this date, are making yearly trips to Newfoundland for cod. Considerable international barter occurs among the fishermen.

1501

Amerigo Vespucci accompanies Portuguese expedition to South America, which he says is his second voyage to this "new world."

1502–1504

Columbus makes fourth voyage during which he coasts between Honduras and Panama still seeking a passage to India.

1507

Name "America" given to the new land by Martin Waldseemuller, geographer, who, having read letters of Amerigo Vespucci, believes him to be discoverer.

1511

Diego de Velasquez begins conquest of Cuba.

1513

Apr   Juan Ponce de León, governor of Puerto Rico, discovers Florida, landing near St. Augustine.

Sept 25   Vasco Nuñez de Balboa, after crossing Isthmus of Darien, beholds Pacific Ocean, first European to see it.

1517

Francisco Hernández de Córdoba explores Yucatan, finding remnants of great cities and wealth, and visits coast of Florida.

1519

Alonzo Alvarez de Pineda completes exploration of Gulf of Mexico from Florida to Vera Cruz. Discovers what some believe is Mississippi River, possibly Mobile Bay.

Hernando Cortés begins conquest of the Aztecs of Mexico.

Ferdinand Magellan, Portuguese navigator, sails with royal patent from Spanish king to find a western passage to the Indies.

1520

Oct 21   Magellan enters strait which now bears his name, his fleet taking 38 days to pass through it to the Pacific.

1521

Francisco Gordillo, sent by Lucas Vásquez de Ayllón, sails from Santo Domingo up the Atlantic coast as far as Carolina at 33° 30'.

Ponce de León comes a second time to Florida with patent to colonize lands on west coast, this time with 200 settlers. They are dispersed by Indians.

1522

First circumnavigation of globe completed by one of Magellan's vessels, under Juan Sebastian del Cano, arriving in Spain by way of India and Cape of Good Hope. Magellan had been killed by natives in Philippine Islands.

Hernando Cortés, after his conquest of Mexico, is recognized as its ruler by King of Spain.

1524

Giovanni da Verrazano, Florentine mariner, with commission from Francis I of France, seeking new route to Asia, skirts North American coast from North Carolina to Newfoundland. Exploit establishes original claim of France to North America.

1525

Estevan Gomez, Portuguese under Spanish auspices, sails down Atlantic coast from Nova Scotia to Florida. Completes Spanish exploration of entire Atlantic coast from Strait of Magellan to Nova Scotia.

1526

Ayllón, official at Santo Domingo, with 500 men and women, founds San Miguel de Gualdape, somewhere between Cape Fear and James rivers. Beset with difficulties, settlement is abandoned.

1528

Pánfilo de Narváez, with royal patent from Spain and 600 settlers, arrives at Tampa Bay on Florida coast. After ill luck, they embark for Mexico, are shipwrecked on coast of Texas.

1533

Lower California discovered by Gonzalo Jiménez de Quesada, sent out by Cortés.

1534

Jacques Cartier, Breton pilot financed by Francis I, explores Gulf of St. Lawrence, taking possession of region in name of King of France.

1535

Cartier makes second voyage to the St. Lawrence, ascending it to La Chine rapids and naming mountain at their foot "Mount Royal" (Montreal).

1536

The Institutes by John Calvin, fundamental in colonial Protestant theology, first published.

Alvar Núñez Cabeza de Vaca, with 3 other survivors of Narváez expedition, reaches Gulf of California after long journey from Mississippi River region.

1539–1543

Hernando de Soto, with royal patent from Spain, arrives at Tampa Bay to colonize Florida. Begins 4-year expedition leading to Savannah River, across North Carolina piedmont, south toward Mobile Bay, northwest where he discovers Mississippi River near present-day Memphis (1541), westward across Arkansas and Oklahoma, down Arkansas River to the Mississippi where he dies and is secretly buried in the river.

1539

Friar Marcos de Niza, Franciscan monk inspired by tales of de Vaca, sent by Don Antonio de Mendoza, viceroy of New Spain in Mexico City to Zuni pueblos of New Mexico, reports he sees at distance one of the 7 cities of legendary Cibolo.

1541

Francisco Vásquez Coronado, sent by Mendoza on expedition from Mexico in search of the 7 cities of Cibolo, discovers the Grand Canyon, crosses Texas, where he is first European to see a herd of buffalo, and continues as far as Quivira in central Kansas.

De Soto discovers Mississippi River.

Cartier, in third expedition to the St. Lawrence, establishes settlement at Quebec, abandoned after much hardship.

1542–1543

Juan Rodriguez Cabrillo of Spain explores the coast of California, but misses San Francisco Bay. His pilot, Bartolomé Ferrelo, continues nearly to Columbia River.

1553

Muscovy Company of London merchants formed, first of great English trading companies.

1555

Richard Eden's translation of Peter Martyr's *Decades of the Newe World* stimulates English interest in America.

1558

Elizabeth becomes Queen of England, patroness of English explorers.

1562

Jean Ribaut, backed by Gaspard de Chatillon Coligny in French Huguenot venture, explores northern coast of Florida and establishes settlement near present site of Beaufort, S. C., which he calls Port Royal. Settlement deserted after his return to France for reinforcements.

John Hawkins, first of great English seadogs, carries 300 Negroes from coast of Guinea to Haiti, trades them for ginger, sugar and pearls at large profit. Returning to England, brings news of Florida country. Makes similar expeditions 1564 and 1567. Knighted 1565 for prowess.

1563

Thomas Stucley receives warrant from Queen Elizabeth to colonize Florida, but expedition resolves into one of piracy.

The Book of Martyrs by John Foxe published by John Day press in London. Much read by Puritans of 17th century.

1564

French Huguenots under René Goulaine de Laudonnière, sent by Coligny, establish Fort Caroline on St. John's River in Florida.

1565

Pedro Menéndez de Avilés, with 600 settlers, establishes St. Augustine, Fla., first permanent European settlement in future United States.

Menéndez destroys Laudonnière settlement at Fort Caroline.

1572

Francis Drake makes his first voyage to America against the Spanish. Crosses Isthmus of Panama and beholds the Pacific.

1574

An estimated 152,500 Spanish settlers are in the Americas.

1576

Martin Frobisher sails from England in search of a northwest passage to Cathay. Enters bay subsequently named for him, discovers Baffin's Land and returns to England with an Eskimo and ore believed to contain gold. Makes similar voyages 1577 and 1578.

1577

Dec 13 Drake sails from Plymouth, England, to plunder the Spanish on Pacific coast. Passes through Strait of Magellan, up west coast of Americas as far as Oregon, takes California region in name of Queen Elizabeth, naming it Nova Albion, returns to England (Sept. 1580) by way of the Pacific and Cape of Good Hope with plunder worth thousands of pounds, is knighted by the queen. First Englishman to sail the Pacific or circumnavigate the globe.

1578

June 11 Sir Humphrey Gilbert receives patent from Queen Elizabeth giving him right to "inhabit and possess at his choice all remote and heathen lands not in the actual possession of any Christian prince." His first expedition ends in disaster.

1581

Negro slaves of Spanish king sent to St. Augustine, Fla.

1582

Gregorian Calendar introduced in Catholic European countries.

Richard Hakluyt, Oxford clergyman, publishes *Divers Voyages Touching the Discovery of America.*

1583

June 11 Sir Humphrey Gilbert sails second time from England to plant colony in America. Takes possession of Newfoundland in name of the queen. Is lost on return voyage and later his colonists disappear.

1584

Walter Raleigh, with royal patent similar to that of Gilbert (but confirmed by Parliament, 1585), sends exploring expedition to America. Explorers discover island of Roanoke, off North Carolina, and return with glowing account of the land. Queen Elizabeth knights Raleigh for discovery and names new land Virginia.

Hakluyt presents to the queen his essay *Discourse on Western Planting*, arguments for encouraging colonies.

1585

Raleigh's second expedition, in command of Sir Richard Grenville and Ralph Lane, plants colony on Roanoke Island. Grenville returns to England, leaving Lane as governor.

John Davis makes first of 3 voyages to America in 3 successive years. Strait bearing his name is discovered.

C.1585

The potato introduced into Spain from South America.

1586

Thomas Cavendish sails from England to South America. With rich plunder of Spanish treasure, he returns to England by way of Cape of Good Hope, second Englishman to circumnavigate the globe.

Sir Francis Drake burns Spanish fort at St. Augustine. Stopping at Roanoke Island, he picks up Raleigh's low-spirited colonists and takes them back to England.

Tobacco carried from Roanoke to England by Drake.

Sir Richard Grenville arrives at Roanoke Island from England with more settlers after the first settlers have left with Drake. Grenville returns to England.

1587

Raleigh's third expedition to Roanoke, in command of John White, brings 150 colonists, including 25 women and chil-

dren, first to come from England to America. Arriving at Roanoke in July, they find no trace of Grenville's settlers of the year before. White returns to England for supplies.

Aug 18 Birth of Virginia Dare, granddaughter of John White, first white child of English parents born in North America.

1588

Guinea Company organized in England to carry on traffic in Negro slaves from west coast of Africa.

Destruction of Spanish Armada in English Channel gives England control of the seas.

1589

Raleigh assigns right of settling and trading in Virginia to group of London merchants, Sir Thomas Smith, John White, Richard Hakluyt and others.

1591

John White, after absence of 4 years, returns to Roanoke Island to find all settlers, including his family, have disappeared.

1598

Marquis de la Roche, with patent from French king to found colony on the St. Lawrence, lands 2 shiploads of vagabonds on Sable Island, east of Nova Scotia. Settlement abandoned 5 years later.

1598-1608

Juan de Oñate of Spain secures submission of New Mexico and sends out expeditions which explore from Kansas to Gulf of California. Founds Santa Fe.

1600

East India Company (English) chartered, Sir Thomas Smith first governor.

Commercial partnership formed in France between Sieur de Pontgrave, Pierre Chauvin, and Pierre du Guast, Sieur de Monts. Given monopoly of fur trade in New World, they make 2 successful voyages to mouth of the Saguenay on St. Lawrence River, where they make small settlement.

1602

Bartholomew Gosnold makes expedition to America. First Englishman to step on New England coast, he sails from Maine to Cape Cod, obtaining furs from Indians.

Dutch East India Company chartered in Holland.

1603

Martin Pring, sent out by Richard Hakluyt, makes expedition of trade and exploration to New England.

Samuel de Champlain, appointed pilot and geographer by the king, accompanies Pontgrave to New France. They explore St. Lawrence River as far as La Chine Rapids.

Pierre du Guast, Sieur de Monts, appointed lieutenant-governor of Acadia, the region between 40th and 46th parallels, by Henry IV, is granted fur

monopoly of that region. His commission directs founding of settlements, teaching Catholicism to Indians, and religious freedom for Huguenots.

1604

End of long wars with Spain, after which England turns to American colonization.

Champlain accompanies Sieur de Monts to America. Leaving de Monts and his company to settle on St. Croix Island at head of Passamaquoddy Bay, Champlain begins exploration of New England coast, from Maine to Cape Cod.

1605

Sieur de Monts, after hard winter, moves colony from St. Croix and settles Port Royal on Nova Scotia.

George Weymouth, sent out by Henry Wriothesley, Earl of Southampton, and Lord Thomas Arundel, visits the Maine coast. Returns to England with several Indians and favorable report of country.

1606

Separatist congregation organized at Scrooby, England, with John Robinson, pastor, future Pilgrim Fathers of Plymouth Colony.

Apr 10 London and Plymouth Com-panies chartered by James I. London Company given right to colonize somewhere on coast between 34th and 41st parallels, Plymouth Company between 38th and 45th, and neither settlement to be within 100 miles of the other.

Aug 12 Plymouth Company sends out ship under Henry Challons to explore its new domain in America. Ship and crew captured by Spaniards, fail to reach destination.

Oct Plymouth Company sends second vessel under Thomas Hanham and Martin Pring who reach coast of Maine in safety and return with glowing accounts of country.

Dec 20 London Company sends out 144 men for Virginia in 3 ships, the *Sarah Constant,* the *Goodspeed* and the *Discovery,* under Captain Christopher Newport.

1607

Henry Hudson, commissioned by Muscovy Company (English) to find northeast passage to Orient, reaches Greenland and discovers bay named for him.

Apr 26 London Company's ships enter Chesapeake Bay.

May 14 First permanent English settlement in America begun at Jamestown, Va.

June 15 Fort at Jamestown completed.

June 22 Captain Newport sails from Jamestown for England, carrying load of shining ore, thinking it gold, and leaving colonists confronted with discord.

Aug 18 Sagadahoc, at mouth of Kennebec River in Maine, settled by George Popham, sent over with 2 vessels by Plymouth Company. Settlement abandoned after winter of suffering.

Autumn Sickness and starvation attack Jamestown.

Dec Captain John Smith goes up Chickahominy River to trade for corn with Algonquins. Captured by Indians, life is saved by Pocahontas, daughter of chief Powhatan, as Smith later tells story.

1608

Scrooby congregation slips by stealth from England to Amsterdam, Holland.

Glass workers sent by London Company build glass furnaces at Jamestown.

Jan 2 Captain Newport arrives at Jamestown with food and 110 new settlers, the First Supply. Finds colony reduced to 40.

Jan 2 John Smith, returning from captivity by Indians, seized and condemned to death by enemies in Jamestown council, is released by Captain Newport, just arrived from England.

Jan 7 Jamestown fort consumed by fire.

Apr 9 Captain Newport sails from Jamestown, ship loaded with worthless mica.

Summer John Smith explores Chesapeake Bay and Potomac River, seeking South Sea.

July 3 Quebec founded by Champlain, lieutenant-governor of New France.

Aug Disease and famine again attack Jamestown.

Aug 13 John Smith's *A True Relation of Such Occurrences and Accidents of Noate as Hath Hapned in Virginia Since the First Planting of That Collony,* in form of letter, entered for publication at Stationers' Hall, London. First account of Virginia to be published, it was brought by Captain Francis Nelson in the *Phoenix,* sailing from Jamestown, June 2.

Sept 10 John Smith elected president of council at Jamestown. Rules without assistants.

Sept 29 Second Supply ship, under Captain Newport, arrives at Jamestown.

Dec Captain Newport leaves Jamestown for England with cargo of pitch, tar, iron ore, soap ashes and clapboards, and with John Smith's report on colony and map of Chesapeake Bay and its rivers.

1609

Scrooby congregation moves to Leyden from Amsterdam.

Spring   John Smith gets 40 acres into cultivation. Raising of corn learned from Indians.

May 5   Samuel Argall sails from Ports- mouth, sent by London Company to find shorter route to Virginia. Arrives with news and provisions July 14.

May 23   London Company obtains new royal charter, incorporating London patentees as a joint stock company and bestowing upon them land and rights of government hitherto reserved to the king. Henceforth, commonly known as Virginia Company. Sir Thomas Smith appointed treasurer.

June 8   Nine ships with 800 persons, the Third Supply, sails from Falmouth, England for Jamestown. Deputy governor-elect Sir Thomas Gates, Sir George Somers and Captain Newport wrecked in Bermudas, remaining there a year. Seven of the vessels reach Jamestown during August.

July   Champlain, accompanied by Algonquins and Hurons, ascends Richelieu River and discovers lake now bearing his name.

July 30   Champlain puts to flight band of Iroquois near Ticonderoga, beginning of long strife between Iroquois and French.

Sept 12   Henry Hudson, employed by Dutch East India Company to seek a northeast passage to the Orient, after changing course and exploring North American coast from Newfoundland to Virginia, enters river named for him and follows it to site of Albany.

Oct 5   John Smith, badly burned in powder explosion and deposed from presidency of Jamestown by enemies, sent back to England in one of Sir Thomas Gates' ships.

Winter   "Starving time" in James- town by spring 1610 reduces population from 500 to 60.

1610

Feb 28   Thomas West, Lord De la **Warr,** commissioned by Virginia Company first lord-governor and captain-general of Virginia with absolute rule, with or without a council.

May 23   Deputy-governor Sir Thomas Gates, Sir George Somers and Captain Newport, shipwrecked in Bermudas July 1609, arrive at Jamestown to find colony in sad state.

June 6   Lord De la Warr, with 3 ships, settlers and supplies, arrives in Chesapeake Bay, learns of Gates' arrival at Jamestown and his plan to abandon it.

June 8   Deputy-governor   Gates,   al- ready embarked with discouraged colonists for fishing stations in Newfoundland, meets Lord De la Warr in James River and is ordered by him to return.

June 10   Lord De la Warr arrives at Jamestown. [Captain Samuel Argall and Sir George Somers sent by Lord De la Warr to Bermudas for pork and fish. Stockade at Point Comfort built for defense.]

Sept 10   Sir Thomas Gates sails for England.

1611

Henry Hudson set adrift to perish by mutinous crew in bay named for him.

Three Spaniards, spies for Philip III, enter James River in their caravel. Held prisoners for 5 years at Jamestown, continue secret communication with Spain urging destruction of colony.

Henrico, settlement on present-day Farrar's Island 40 miles north of Jamestown, made by Sir Thomas Dale. First expansion of Jamestown colony.

Mar 28   Lord De la Warr, ill, returns to England.

May 10   Sir Thomas Dale arrives in Virginia with settlers and supplies.

Aug 1 Sir Thomas Gates, deputy-governor, arrives in Virginia bringing 200 men and 20 women.

1612

Dale's Laws, published in London as *Laws Divine Morall and Martiall,* drawn up by William Strachey, Sir Thomas Gates and Sir Thomas Dale, are enforced in Virginia. Severe code, in effect until 1619.

A Map of Virginia by Captain John Smith published in London.

John Rolfe begins cultivation of tobacco in Virginia.

Mar 12 Virginia Company receives third charter, giving members increased power and extending its jurisdiction to Bermuda Islands.

1613

Dutch fur-trading post established on Manhattan Island by Hendrick Christianson and Adriaen Block.

Bermuda Hundred, Va., founded by Sir Thomas Dale.

Champlain explores Ottawa River to about 100 miles above present city of Ottawa.

Apr Sir Samuel Argall captures Pocahontas, holds her as hostage in peace negotiations with Powhatan.

July Argall, sent by Sir Thomas Dale, expels French and burns buildings at Port Royal and Jesuit settlement on Mount Desert Island, returning with 15 prisoners.

Nov Argall returning from Mount Desert stops at Manhattan Island, forces Christianson to haul down Dutch flag and raise that of England.

1614

Captain John Smith explores New England coast, naming and charting it.

Sir Thomas Dale allots 3-acre holdings to settlers in Virginia, beginning of system of private holdings.

Tobacco first exported to England on the *Elizabeth* by John Rolfe.

Mar 27 Ordinance of 1614. Dutch congress promises trade monopoly to discoverers of new countries. [Cornelius May from Holland explores coast from Long Island to Delaware Bay. Cape May, N. J., named for him.]

Apr 5 Pocahontas marries John Rolfe.

Oct 1 Adriaen Block, Dutch fur trader, arrives in Amsterdam with map and story of exploration in America. Has explored East River, Long Island Sound, Connecticut River as far as Hartford, and New England coast as far as Salem. His name remains on Block Island.

Oct 11 New Netherland Company chartered, giving Amsterdam merchants 3-year monopoly of fur trade along coasts and rivers they explore in America.

1615

Four Recollet friars of Franciscan order arrive at Quebec with Champlain, beginning of French missionary activity among Indians.

Champlain explores Ottawa River to Lake Nipissing, thence to Lake Huron, first of Great Lakes to be discovered, establishing fur traders' route into interior.

1616

Deputy-governor Sir Thomas Dale, with Pocahontas and John Rolfe, returns to England from Jamestown. Pocahontas presented at court.

A Description of New England by Captain John Smith published in London.

1617

Plague nearly wipes out Indians along New England coast between Penobscot River and Narragansett Bay.

Samuel Argall, new deputy-governor of Virginia, begins 2 years of exploitation of Company for himself and friends.

Ten tons of Virginia leaf tobacco dispatched in the *George* for England.

1618

Lord De la Warr, governor, sails for Virginia with supplies and settlers. Dies on outward voyage.

Nov 18 Charter of privileges, orders, and laws granted Virginia settlers by Virginia Company in London, giving them voice in making of laws.

1619

First iron works in America set up on Falling Creek, Va.

Shipload of marriageable girls, to be sold to planters at 120 pounds of tobacco each, sent to Virginia by Virginia Company.

One hundred children from London slums sent as apprentices to Virginia.

Apr 19 Sir George Yeardley, new governor, arrives in Virginia, bringing the charter of privileges and a commission to establish a council and general assembly.

New land policy set up. A hundred acres of land, promised in Charter of 1609, now granted to each colonist who arrived before 1616, and the head right,

50 acres for every colonist transported, is introduced.

Apr 28 Sir Edwin Sandys, liberal, elected treasurer of Virginia Company in London, replacing Thomas Smith.

July 30 First representative assembly in America convenes in Jamestown, 2 burgesses coming from each of 11 plantations.

Aug First Negroes brought to Virginia, possibly in the *Treasurer,* a ship of Robert Rich, Earl of Warwick, possibly in a Dutch vessel. Sold as servants, they are beginning of slavery in English colonies.

1620

Sickness returns to Virginia, over 1000 die.

Feb 20 Pilgrims, the Leyden Separatists, granted patent by Virginia Company, through Thomas Weston, permitting them to settle within its territory in America.

June 18 Henry Wriothesley, Earl of Southampton, liberal and friend of Sandys, elected treasurer of Virginia Company. Treasurer until charter is annulled, 1624.

July 22 Pilgrims sail from Delft-Haven, Holland, in the *Speedwell* for Southampton to join the *Mayflower* for voyage to America.

Sept 6 The *Mayflower*, with 149 on board, sails from Plymouth, the *Speedwell* left behind as unseaworthy.

Nov 3 Council for New England established by royal charter in reorganization of Plymouth Company, with title to all territory in North America between 40th and 48th parallels from sea to sea.

Nov 9 The *Mayflower* sights Cape Cod; drops anchor in Provincetown harbor, within territory of Council for New England.

Nov 11 **Mayflower Compact signed in** Provincetown harbor, basis for government of colony.

Peregrine White born to Susanna Fuller White, first child of English parents to be born in New England.

Dec 11 **Exploring party from the** *Mayflower* **lands at Plymouth.**

Dec 16 **The** *Mayflower* **brings Pilgrims to Plymouth from Provincetown.**

Dec 25 **First house for common use at** Plymouth is begun.

1621

Congregational system of church government introduced at Plymouth by Pilgrims.

Jan 21 *Mayflower* company gathers on shore for first preaching service.

Mar 21 Last of *Mayflower* passengers come ashore to live.

Mar 22 **Massassoit, war chief of Wampanoags, comes to Plymouth and "they** treat of peace."

Apr 5 The *Mayflower* sails for England.

Apr 21 **William Bradford chosen governor of Plymouth colony upon death** of John Carver.

May 12 **Edward Winslow and Susanna** Fuller White married in Plymouth colony's first wedding.

June 1 **Pilgrims through their London promoters obtain land grant from** Council for New England, having settled in its territory.

June 3 **Dutch West India Company** chartered in Holland.

July 24 **Ordinance and Constitution** for Virginia government granted by Virginia Company.

Oct   **Sir Francis Wyatt arrives in** Jamestown as governor, bringing the Ordinance and Constitution.

Oct 24 **English monopoly of all Virginia tobacco claimed in king's order.**

Nov 10 **The** *Fortune* **arrives at Plymouth with 35 settlers but no supplies.**

Dec 13 **The** *Fortune,* **freighted at** Plymouth with clapboards and beaver skins, sails for England. Captured by French on voyage.

1622

A Relation or Journall of the Beginning and Proceedings of the English Plantation at Plimoth published by George Morton (Mourt) in England.

Jan   **Narragansett tribe sends to** Plymouth colony bundle of arrows tied with snake skin, challenge of war. Bradford returns skin filled with bullets.

Mar 22 **Massacre of over 350 colonists** in Virginia, led by Opechancanough.

Aug   **Colony sent out by Thomas** Weston, with no known grant, settles Wessagusset, later Weymouth, on Massachusetts Bay. Many starve in ill-provided winter following.

Aug 10 **John Mason and Sir Ferdinando Gorges granted by Council for** New England territory extending 60 miles inland between Merrimac and Kennebec rivers.

Nov 6 **Royal proclamation forbids unlicensed fur trading and fishing on** North Atlantic coast within Council for New England grant. Part of Council's conflict with Virginia Company.

Dec 30 **Robert Gorges, son of Ferdinando Gorges, commissioned lieutenant-general of New England by Council for** New England and granted 10-mile frontage along coast of Boston Bay, extending 30 miles inland.

1623

Fishing settlement on Cape Ann (Gloucester) established by merchants of

Dorchester, England, with grant from Council for New England.

Settlements at Piscataqua (Portsmouth) and Cocheco (Dover), N. H., and Casco Bay and Saco Bay, Maine, made under auspices of Gorges and Mason.

First sawmill in Maine erected near York.

Salt works set up at Piscataqua, N. H.

Silk culture encouraged in Virginia by assembly, which directs planting of mulberry trees.

Mar Myles Standish of Plymouth rescues Wessagusset settlers from Indians and starts them off for England.

June 29 Council for New England divides North Atlantic coast from Bay of Fundy to Narragansett Bay among its 20 patentees.

Sept Robert Gorges plants settlement for fishing and trading at Wessagusset, where Weston's colony was. Settlers return to England after hard winter.

1624

By this year nearly 13,000 of the 14,000 who came to Virginia have died of disease and exposure.

Population of Plymouth numbers 180.

Good News from New England by Edward Winslow published in London.

A General Historie of Virginia, New England and the Summer Isles by Captain John Smith published in London.

At Plymouth each family is given one acre to till as its own.

Edward Winslow brings 3 cows and a bull to Plymouth from England.

First permanent settlers from Holland, chiefly French-speaking Walloons, arrive at Manhattan Island on the *New Netherland* under Dutch West India Company. A small number is left on the island. Fort Nassau on east shore of Delaware River, opposite present-day Phil-

adelphia, and Fort Orange (Albany) up Hudson River, founded by groups from the *New Netherland*.

June 16 Virginia becomes royal colony when charter of Virginia Company is revoked after long conflict with liberal elements in Company.

July 15 Commission of 40 men appointed by Privy Council in London to take charge of affairs in Virginia in place of defunct Virginia Company.

1625

Death of James I; Charles becomes king.

Three Jesuits arrive at Quebec from France to convert all North American Indians to Christianity.

Sarah de Rapaelje, daughter of Joris de Rapaelje, a Walloon, born at Breuckelen (Brooklyn), first child of European parents to be born in New Netherland.

1626

Peter Minuit made director-general of New Netherland by Dutch West India Company, purchases Manhattan Island from Indians for 24 dollars and founds settlement of New Amsterdam.

First flour mill in colonies built at New Amsterdam.

Naumkeag (Salem) founded by settlers from Cape Ann (Gloucester) under leadership of Roger Conant, when Dorchester promoters withdraw support.

Nov 15 Pilgrims at Plymouth, through agent Isaac Allerton in London, agree to buy out London partners for 1,800 pounds to be paid in 9 annual installments.

1627

Company of New France organized by Cardinal Richelieu and given perpetual monopoly of fur trade and absolute title to all territory between Florida and Arctic Circle.

Thomas Morton sets up maypole at Merrymount (Quincy) in mockery of Pilgrims. Merrymount suppressed next year by Captain Myles Standish.

New Amsterdam and Plymouth open friendly trade relations. Plymouth, with patent from Council for New England, sets up trading post on the Kennebec.

1628

Reformed Church in America founded by Dutch settlers in New Amsterdam as Reformed Protestant Dutch Church.

Mar 19 New England Company formed to take over interests of moribund Dorchester Company. Obtains from Council for New England patent for all New England from 3 miles north of the Merrimac to 3 miles south of the Charles and from sea to sea.

Mar 26 Virginia House of Burgesses restored after interval of 4 years.

Sept 6 Beginning of Massachusetts Bay Colony: John Endecott, with some 40 colonists, arrives at Naumkeag (Salem) under patent from New England Company, finding there Roger Conant and group of "Old Planters."

1629

First brick kiln in colonies set up at Naumkeag (Salem).

First tannery in New England set up at Lynn, Mass.

Quebec taken from French by Scotch-English adventurers led by David Kirke.

Acadia resettled and named Nova Scotia by Scotch settlers sent by Sir William Alexander.

Sir Robert Heath granted by Charles I all land between 31st and 36th parallels, naming it Carolina. No settlement made.

Mar 4 New England Company transformed by royal charter into Massachusetts Bay Company and its patent of March 19, 1628, confirmed.

Mar 10 Parliament dissolved. Charles I rules without it until 1640, period of Great Migration.

June 7 Patroon system of large landed estates in New Netherland established by Charter of Privileges adopted by Dutch West India Company.

June 29 Five ships and 400 settlers sent by New England Company arrive in Salem harbor, met by John Endecott.

Aug 6 Congregational form of church government modeled after that of Plymouth established at Salem.

Aug 26 Cambridge Agreement signed by 12 members of Massachusetts Bay Company, pledging themselves to migrate to New England if the charter may be taken with them.

Oct 20 John Winthrop elected governor of Massachusetts Bay Company.

Nov 7 New Hampshire, between Merrimac and Piscataqua rivers, granted John Mason by Council for New England. Divides Mason-Gorges grant of 1622.

Nov 17 Laconia, region bordering on Lake Champlain, granted to Sir Ferdinando Gorges and John Mason by Council for New England.

1630

Population: 4,000 in British West Indies, 3,000 in Virginia, 300 in Plymouth.

The Great Migration (1630–1640) to Massachusetts Bay colony begins. 16,000 settlers arrive from England in 198 ships during the decade.

William Bradford begins writing *History of Plymouth Plantation*.

Rensselaerwyck established on upper Hudson River by Killian van Rensselaer, first patroon.

Jan 13 Plymouth Patent granted to William Bradford and others by Council for New England, defining limits of grant of June 1, 1621.

Mar   Sir John Harvey arrives in Vir-ginia as governor.

Mar 29   Puritans with John Winthrop, governor of Massachusetts Bay Company, sail from Southampton for New England in 11 ships, carrying the Company's charter with them. John Cotton's farewell sermon: "2 Sam. 7:10. Moreover I will appoint a place for my people Israel, and will plant them, that they may dwell in a place of their own, and move no more."

Mar 29   John Winthrop, after embark-ing for Massachusetts, begins his diary, 1630–1649. Published 1790 as *The History of New England.*

June 12   John Winthrop in the *Ar-bella*, first of Puritan ships, enters Salem harbor.

July 30   Puritans establish Congrega-tional church at Charlestown.

Aug 23   Governor Winthrop and his court of assistants hold first session at Charlestown.

Aug 23   Winthrop's court of assistants orders wage ceiling of 2 shillings a day in building trades. First legislation in America to affect free labor.

Oct 19   A general court, first in New England, held in Boston; 108 settlers appear before it demanding admission as freemen of Massachusetts Bay Company.

1631

Swannendael, first settlement in Delaware, established by group of stockholders of Dutch West India Company with grant to shores of Delaware River. Soon abandoned.

Feb 5   The *Lyon* arrives at Salem with supplies, Roger Williams a passenger.

May 16   William   Claiborne   and group of Virginia merchants receive royal grant for fur trade. Establish trading post on Kent Island in Chesapeake Bay, August.

May 18   Massachusetts Bay General Court declares that none but members of approved Puritan churches shall be freemen, and only freemen may vote for officials of the Company.

May 18   Massachusetts Bay General Court admits 118 new members to rights of freemen.

May 24   Charles I appoints special commission headed by Sir Edward Sackville, Lord Dorset, to advise him upon "the advancement of the plantation of Virginia."

July 4   The   *Blessing   of   the   Bay* launched, a small bark built for Governor Winthrop.

1632

Feb 3   Watertown settlers protest tax-ation to fortify Newtown, imposed by court of assistants at Boston in which they have no voice.

Mar 19   Lord Saye and Sele and Lord Brooke, with 9 other Puritans, obtain from Earl of Warwick, president of Council for New England, large tract of land at mouth of Connecticut River.

Mar 29   Treaty of St. Germain-en-Laye restores to France Acadia and Quebec taken by English, 1629.

May 9   Massachusetts Bay General Court orders that a board composed of 2 delegates from each town shall guide governor and assistants in laying taxes. Result of Watertown protest.

June 20   Maryland by royal charter granted to Cecilius Calvert, Lord Baltimore. Carved out of original grant to Virginia, named for Queen Henrietta Maria.

Oct 3 Public use of tobacco forbidden by Massachusetts Bay General Court.

1633

First watermill for grinding corn erected at Dorchester.

Wouter van Twiller succeeds Peter Minuit as director-general of New Netherland.

Adam Roelantsen arrives in New Amsterdam to act as voorlezer in the church and to start a school, beginning of education in settlement.

June 8 Dutch build fortified trading post, Fort Good Hope, on land purchased from Pequots, where Hartford now stands.

July 3 Virginia's claim to lands of Lord Baltimore's grant, cut out of original Virginia lands, disallowed by Privy Council.

Sept 4 John Cotton and Thomas Hooker, eminent ministers, arrive in Boston from England.

Oct   William Holmes, with settlers from Plymouth, establishes trading post at Windsor on Connecticut River.

Oct 8 Dorchester in Massachusetts Bay colony organizes first town government.

Nov 22 Maryland settlers sail from Cowes, England, in the *Ark* and the *Dove* under Leonard Calvert.

1634

Jean Nicolet, sent by Champlain, enters Wisconsin region by way of Green Bay and Fox River and establishes trade with Indians.

Virginia divided into 8 shires or counties, in each of which is to be held a monthly court.

Mar 27 Maryland colonists under Governor Leonard Calvert, brother of

Lord Baltimore, found settlement of St. Mary's on St. Charles River.

Apr 28 Commission for Foreign Plantations appointed by Charles I to make laws for all English colonies, regulate religion, appoint judges, and remove governors when necessary. (William Laud, Archbishop of Canterbury, head of Commission.)

May 14 Massachusetts Bay colony establishes representative system of government after deputies from its towns demand to see charter of Company.

Sept 4 Seizure of Kent Island in the Chesapeake, in dispute between Maryland and Virginia, and arrest of William Claiborne ordered by Lord Baltimore.

Sept 18 Mrs. Anne Hutchinson arrives in Boston from England.

1635

Symms Free School, established by legacy of Benjamin Symms in Elizabeth City County, is Virginia's first school.

Boston Latin School founded.

Feb 3 New England re-divided among 8 patentees by Council for New England, through Sir Ferdinando Gorges. Only that of Gorges ever confirmed by king.

Feb 26 Maryland assembly of all freemen of colony convenes without authority of Lord Baltimore and drafts code which he disallows.

Apr   Governor John Harvey of Virginia deposed by council and sent to England, because of his support of Lord Baltimore in controversy with Claiborne and his disregard of privileges of Virginia assembly.

Spring   Inhabitants of Watertown, Roxbury and Dorchester granted permission to move to Connecticut Valley by Massachusetts Bay General Court.

June 7 Council for New England surrenders charter to king.

Oct   Connecticut River towns of Windsor, Wethersfield and Hartford settled by Massachusetts Bay families.

Oct 9 Roger Williams, preaching separation of church and state, banished from Massachusetts Bay by General Court.

Nov   Fort Saybrook built at mouth of Connecticut River by John Winthrop, Jr., authorized by Lord Saye and Sele, Lord Brooke and other Puritans, patentees of Warwick grant of 1632.

1636

Mar 3 Township Act, passed by General Court of Massachusetts Bay, grants powers of government to freemen of the towns.

Mar 3 Majority vote of both assistants and deputies required for all acts by Massachusetts Bay General Court.

Mar 3 Establishment of new churches only with consent of General Court is enacted by Massachusetts Bay.

May 25 Sir Henry Vane elected governor of Massachusetts Bay.

June   Roger Williams founds first Rhode Island settlement, Providence, on Narragansett Bay.

June   Thomas Hooker leads his Newtown congregation to settle at Hartford on Connecticut River.

Aug 8 Lord Baltimore in his Conditions for Plantations directs formation of 1,000-acre manors in Maryland.

Oct 28 Harvard College founded by vote of General Court of Massachusetts Bay which appropriates 400 pounds for it.

Nov 15 Plymouth colony adopts code of laws, first in New England.

1637

Pequot War waged by Connecticut Valley settlers nearly extinguishes Pequot tribe, establishing 40-year peace on New England frontier.

New English Canaan by Thomas Morton, satire on Pilgrims, published, Amsterdam.

Mar 9 Reverend John Wheelwright, brother-in-law of Anne Hutchinson, goes on trial for preaching seditious sermon.

May 1 Connecticut towns of Hartford, Wethersfield and Windsor hold first general court at Hartford. Determine upon offensive warfare against Pequots, 90 men to be raised.

May 17 John Winthrop elected governor of Massachusetts Bay, succeeding Sir Henry Vane, a partisan of Anne Hutchinson and the Antinomians.

July 23 Sir Ferdinando Gorges appointed governor-general of Massachusetts Bay by the king. Appointment never accepted.

Aug 3 Sir Henry Vane leaves for England.

Nov 4 Reverend John Wheelwright banished from Boston.

Nov 7–8 Trial and conviction of Mrs. Anne Hutchinson for Antinomian heresy. Governor Winthrop presides at trial as both prosecutor and judge. Mrs. Hutchinson sentenced to banishment.

1638

Representative government adopted by Plymouth colony.

William Kieft succeeds Wouter van Twiller as director-general of New Netherland.

Reverend John Wheelwright founds settlement of Exeter, N. H.

New Sweden Company (Swedish West India Company) sends to Delaware River 50 settlers under Peter Minuit to build Fort Christina (Wilmington, Delaware).

Mar 7 Hutchinsonians, while at Providence, sign a civil compact based upon

Old Testament. William Coddington elected "judge."

Mar 22 Anne Hutchinson banished from Massachusetts Bay. Finds refuge on Aquidneck Island and helps found Portsmouth.

Mar 24 Aquidneck Island in Narra-gansett Bay purchased from Narragansetts by Hutchinsonians.

Apr 4 Kent Island given to Maryland by Commission for Foreign Plantations.

Apr 4 Surrender of Massachusetts Bay charter demanded by Commission for Foreign Plantations. Not enforced.

Apr 15 New Haven founded by The-ophilus Eaton and John Davenport, without charter or land grant.

Aug 28 John Winthrop writes to Thomas Hooker on democracy: ". . . it is unsafe to refer matters of counsel to the body of the people, *quia* the best part is always the least, and of that best part the wiser part is always the lesser."

Sept 21 Treaty of Hartford gives Pe-quot country to Connecticut Valley towns and disperses remaining Pequots among Narragansetts and Mohicans.

1639

Baptist Church in America founded by Roger Williams at Providence, R. I.

Stephen Day sets up first printing press in English colonies, at Cambridge, Mass.

First post office established by Massachusetts Bay General Court in house of Richard Fairbank in Boston.

Each town in Massachusetts Bay ordered by General Court to lay out roads connecting it with the next.

Newport, R. I., founded by William Coddington, seceding from Anne Hutchinson's settlement at Portsmouth.

Jan 14 Fundamental Orders of Con-necticut adopted by freemen of Windsor, Wethersfield and Hartford, first written constitution in history detailing functions of government.

Apr 3 Sir Fernando Gorges receives royal charter, confirming grant from Council for New England in division of 1635 and making him governor and proprietor of Maine.

June 4 Fundamental Articles of New Haven, proposed by Rev. John Davenport and based upon Scriptures, adopted by 70 "free planters" as a constitution.

Nov   Sir Francis Wyatt reappointed governor of Virginia with order from king to restore House of Burgesses.

1640

Population of English colonies estimated at 28,000; of New England, 22,500.

Bay Psalm Book published by Stephen Day at Cambridge, first book published in America.

First general court of province of Maine held at Saco.

Southold on Long Island settled by English from New Haven, beginning of English encroachment upon Dutch claims.

Nov 3 Long Parliament convenes in London. Great Puritan Migration to New England soon ends.

1641

An estimated 300,000 cod exported from New England this year.

Glass factory established at Salem, Mass.

Lord Baltimore extends to Maryland English statute of mortmain to curb land acquisitions by Jesuits.

Mar 2 William Bradford deeds to freemen of Plymouth land patent of 1630 granted to him as trustee by Council for New England.

June 2 **General Court of Massachu-setts Bay** grants the towns power to regulate prices of commodities and wages.

June 14 **Proprietors of Dover and Portsmouth, N. H.,** surrender jurisdiction to Massachusetts Bay colony, reserving land rights. No religious requirement for citizenship in New Hampshire made by Massachusetts.

Dec 10 **Body of Liberties, a code of laws,** adopted by General Court of Massachusetts Bay colony.

1642

Civil War in England, 1642–1649.

Sir William Berkeley becomes royal governor of Virginia, succeeding Sir Francis Wyatt.

New Haven settlers, who purchased lands from Indians on the Delaware, driven from trading post there by Dutch and Swedes.

Care of the poor by each town enacted by Plymouth colony.

June 14 **Massachusetts law of 1642** empowers town authorities to punish parents and guardians who fail to train their children in reading and principles of religion.

1643

Thomas Mayhew establishes first Indian mission on Martha's Vineyard.

Iron workers imported from England by John Winthrop, Jr., who sets up first successful iron works in colonies at Lynn, Mass.

Woolen and fulling mill set up in Rowley, Mass., by 20 families of skilled cloth workers from Yorkshire, England.

Lord Baltimore, to attract settlers, sends notice to New England that all creeds will be protected in Maryland.

Feb 15 **Johan Printz, third governor,** arrives in New Sweden with Swedish settlers.

Feb 25 **William Kieft, director-general** of New Netherland, assents to massacre by the Dutch of a band of trusting Algonquins. Begins 2 years of Indian disturbance, leaving 2,000 settlers slain and New Netherland exhausted.

Mar 2 **Virginia adopts act denying** right of governor and council to impose taxes without consent of assembly.

Mar 2 **Virginia assembly enacts banishment** of non-conformist ministers.

Apr **New Haven colony formed by** union of New Haven and surrounding towns.

May 19 **New England Confederation** formed by colonies of Massachusetts Bay, Plymouth, Connecticut and New Haven, a league for offense and defense.

Oct 27 **New Haven colony drafts constitution** for representative government.

Nov 24 **Commission to Control Plantation Affairs,** headed by Robert Rich, Earl of Warwick, appointed by Long Parliament.

1644

The Keyes of the Kingdom of Heaven by John Cotton published, London.

The Bloudy Tenent of Persecution for the Cause of Conscience by Roger Williams published, London.

Puritans, persecuted by Governor Berkeley in Virginia, begin migration to Maryland.

Mar 7 **Bi-cameral system of legislature** adopted by Massachusetts Bay.

Mar 14 **Patent of Providence Plantations,** authorizing union of towns of Providence, Newport and Portsmouth, obtained by Roger Williams from Long Parliament.

Apr 18   Opechancanough begins 2-year war against Virginians, massacring 300 settlers. After he is killed in 1646, tidewater Virginia lives in peace.

May 29   John Winthrop defeated in re-election for governor by popular party in Massachusetts Bay.

Nov 13   Banishment of all Baptists en- acted by Massachusetts Bay General Court.

Nov 13   Massachusetts Bay General Court directs county courts to have Indians in their shires instructed in knowledge and worship of God.

Dec 5   Town of Saybrook joined to Colony of Connecticut.

1645

Aug 30   Treaty with Narragansetts made at Boston by commissioners of New England Confederation.

1646

Milk for Babes, drawn out of the Breast of Both Testaments by John Cotton published, London.

Joseph Jenks improves the scythe and the sawmill, for which he is given Massachusetts patents.

May 6   John Winthrop again elected governor of Massachusetts Bay, remaining in office until his death in 1649.

May 6   Dr. Robert Child and 6 friends petition General Court of Massachusetts Bay for toleration of Presbyterianism. After long controversy, Child is banished from colony.

Oct 28   John Eliot preaches first ser- mon to Indians, at falls of Charles River in Watertown.

Winter   "No snow all winter long nor sharp weather," writes John Eliot.

1647

Fatal pestilence spreads over New England.

The Simple Cobler of Aggawam by Nathaniel Ward published, London.

First witch executed in America is hanged in Hartford; 14 hanged in Massachusetts and Connecticut, 1647–1662.

May   Freemen from towns of Ports- mouth, Newport and Providence, the Providence Plantations, meet at Providence to make laws under Charter of 1644 and form a union to which Warwick is admitted.

May 11   Peter Stuyvesant, last director- general of New Netherland, arrives at New Amsterdam.

Nov 11   Massachusetts Law of 1647 requires every town of 50 householders to employ a teacher of reading and writing, and every town of 100 families to establish a grammar school.

1648

The Way of the Congregational Churches Cleared by John Cotton published, London.

The Survey of the Summe of Church Discipline by Thomas Hooker published, London.

Boston shoemakers and coopers granted charters, similar to those of mediaeval guilds, by general court.

Laws and Liberties of Massachusetts published. A revision of Body of Liberties of 1641.

Jan   Margaret Brent, executrix of estate of Governor Leonard Calvert, demands place and voice in Maryland assembly, but in vain.

June   Margaret Jones adjudged a witch by General Court of Massachusetts Bay and hanged in Boston.

Aug   Cambridge Platform framed for church management and discipline by synod of Congregational churches of New England.

Aug 6 William Stone of Virginia, a Protestant, appointed governor of Maryland by Lord Baltimore. [Several hundred Puritans under Richard Bennett leave Virginia for Maryland. Welcomed by Governor Stone, they settle Providence near present Annapolis.]

1 6 4 9

The Glorious Progress of the Gospel among the Indians in New England by Edward Winslow published.

Adrian Van der Donck, leader of liberals in New Amsterdam, journeys to Holland and asks that New Netherland be taken over from Company and ruled by Dutch government.

English colonial trade has largely passed into hands of the Dutch by this date.

Jan 30 King Charles I beheaded; the Commonwealth begins. Cavaliers begin migrating to Virginia after execution of Charles I.

Apr 21 Toleration Act of Maryland passed, granting protection to all Christians.

May 19 Parliament declares it has supreme authority over the colonies.

July 19 Society for the Propagation of the Gospel in New England incorporated in England by effort of Edward Winslow.

Oct 10 Virginia assembly condemns execution of Charles I and declares Charles II rightful ruler. Gains for Virginia title of Old Dominion.

1 6 5 0

Population of English colonies in North America estimated at 52,000.

The Tenth Muse, Lately Sprung Up in America, poems by Anne Bradstreet published, London.

Apr 6 Maryland granted by Lord Baltimore a two-house assembly, lower house of delegates and upper house of councillors.

May   Laws of Connecticut codified, modeled upon Body of Liberties of Massachusetts Bay.

Sept 19 Treaty of Hartford allows the Dutch to hold lands in their possession at Hartford and divides Long Island between English and Dutch.

Oct 3 Act of Parliament, sometimes called a navigation act, to punish rebellious colonies of Virginia, Barbados, Bermuda and Antigua, forbids their trade with foreign nations.

1 6 5 1

July 19 Dutch from New Netherland settle Fort Casimir (New Castle) on Delaware River.

Oct 9 Navigation Act, sometimes called "first," defines England's commercial policy in terms of mercantile system. Goods from Asia, Africa or America to be carried into England or her colonies only in English vessels, manned chiefly by Englishmen. Act precipitates Anglo-Dutch War, 1652–1654.

Oct 14 Persons of "mean condition" forbidden by Massachusetts Bay General Court to dress in the style of the upper classes.

1 6 5 2

Anglo-Dutch war, 1652–1654.

Boston's first book store opened.

Mar 12 Virginia submits to authority of the Commonwealth. Sir William Berkeley removed from governorship.

Mar 29 Maryland submits to authority of the Commonwealth. Lord Baltimore temporarily deprived of governmental powers.

Apr 30 Virginia assembly elects Richard Bennett governor and William Claiborne secretary of state. Enters 8 years of almost complete self-government.

May 18 First law against slavery in North America enacted by Rhode Island.

May 27 Mint established in Boston by general court. Pine-tree shillings and smaller pieces coined until 1684.

Nov Massachusetts Bay runs her northern boundary line, claiming that 3 miles north of the Merrimac means 3 miles north of its source, thus including Gorges' settlements as far as Saco Bay in Maine.

Nov 20 Kittery, Maine, submits to jurisdiction of Massachusetts Bay, first settlement in Gorges' province to do so.

1653

First settlement in Carolina made on Chowan River, near Albemarle Sound, by adventurers from Virginia. Becomes nucleus of North Carolina.

New England Confederation votes to declare war against Dutch of New Netherland, rumored to be conspiring with the Nyantics against Connecticut settlers. Massachusetts refuses to abide by decision, June 2.

Dec 10 First representative assembly of New Netherland convened in New Amsterdam, with representatives from 4 Dutch and 4 English towns to protest against arbitrary government of New Netherland.

1654

Wonder-Working Providences of Zion's Saviour in New England by Captain

Edward Johnson published, London, an average man's description of Puritan life.

Mar 7 Plymouth, obtaining confirmation from Parliament of grant on Kennebec River, sends Thomas Prince to organize local government.

Apr Fort Good Hope (Dutch) taken by Connecticut colonists, England and Holland being at war.

June 20 Recruits enlisted in New England to proceed against New Amsterdam are about to leave Boston when word comes of peace between England and Holland.

Sept First Sephardic Jews, 23 men, women and children, arrive in New Amsterdam, refugees from Brazil.

Fall Port Royal and St. John on Nova Scotia taken from the French by New England force under Major Robert Sedgwick, Cromwellian soldier.

1655

Lady Deborah Moody, Long Island, allowed to vote in town meeting, the one known instance of woman suffrage in colonies.

Mar 25 Governor William Stone, appointee of Lord Baltimore, deposed by Puritans in civil war in Maryland.

Sept New Sweden (Delaware) captured by the Dutch under command of Peter Stuyvesant and becomes part of New Netherland.

1656

Leah and Rachel, or, The Two Fruitful Sisters, Virginia and Maryland by John Hammond published, London.

Quakers arrive at Boston from England, are imprisoned or banished without trial.

A library in which the public may read opened in Boston.

May 14 **"One spinner to a family,"** requirement made by Massachusetts Bay General Court.

June 19 **Ann Hibbins hanged for a** witch. "She had more wit than her neighbors," said Rev. John Norton.

Oct 2 **Connecticut passes law to fine** and banish Quakers.

1657

Connecticut limits franchise to property owners.

The Scots' Charitable Society of Boston for relief of poor established.

Aug **Five Quakers arrive in New** Amsterdam. Severely punished by Governor Stuyvesant and banished to Rhode Island.

Nov 30 **Lord Baltimore's authority re-**stored in Maryland.

1658

Plymouth colony adopts workhouse program, providing work for vagrants, rebellious children and stubborn servants.

May 26 **Consolidation of Rhode Is-**land now completed. Massachusetts Bay resigns all jurisdiction.

July 13 **Massachusetts Bay takes over** jurisdiction of Casco Bay (Falmouth), last of Maine settlements.

Fall **New England Confederation** orders expulsion of Quakers and death if they return.

1659

Christian Commonwealth by John Eliot published, London.

Latin School in New Amsterdam opened by Alexander Carolus Curtius, as provided by Dutch West India Company.

1660

Population of English and Dutch continental colonies estimated at 85,000.

Boston establishes an almshouse.

Indians of North America by this date have become greatly dependent upon traffic in furs.

Colonists from New England settle near mouth of Cape Fear River, N. C. Settlement short-lived.

Mar 13 **Sir William Berkeley recalled** by assembly to governorship of Virginia.

May 8 **Stuarts restored to English** throne with accession of Charles II.

June 1 **Mary Dyer, Quaker, returning** to Boston after banishment, is hanged.

July 27 **Edward Whalley and William** Goffe, regicide judges of Charles I, arrive in Boston.

Sept 13 **First Navigation Act, re-enact-**ing and expanding Navigation Act of 1651, becomes cornerstone of British navigation system. Lists colonial exports which may be shipped only to British Isles and English possessions—the "enumerated" articles.

Dec 1 **Council for Foreign Plantations,** Edward Hyde, earl of Clarendon, president, organized in London.

1661

Lord Baltimore sends Charles Calvert, his oldest son, to Maryland as governor.

Virginia gives legal recognition to slavery: "Negroes are incapable of making satisfaction [for time lost in running away] by addition of time."

Aug 8 **Charles II formally proclaimed** king in Massachusetts, after some delay as in Rhode Island and New Haven.

Sept   Royal order against putting Quakers to death sent to Massachusetts.

1662

The Day of Doom by Michael Wigglesworth published, Cambridge.

Massachusetts Bay receives from crown confirmation of charter upon conditions of liberty of worship for Anglicans and franchise for property holders.

King Philip, chief of Wampanoags, renews pledges of friendship with Plymouth.

English law passed authorizing justices of the peace to send "rogues, vagabonds, and sturdy beggars" to the colonies.

Mar 23   Virginia passes severe laws against Quakers.

Mar 23   Virginia adopts a digest of her former laws concerning Indians.

Apr 23   Connecticut granted a charter by Charles II upon application of John Winthrop, Jr., first governor. Territory extends from Massachusetts on the north to the Atlantic and from Narragansett Bay to the Pacific.

Sept   Halfway Covenant adopted by Massachusetts synod. Baptized persons of good character, although not church members, may present their children for baptism.

Oct 8   Halfway Covenant adopted by Massachusetts Bay General Court and ordered published.

Oct 8   Two   licensers   of   printing presses, who must approve everything to be printed, appointed by Massachusetts Bay General Court.

1663

John Eliot completes translation of Bible into Algonquin language.

Mar 24   Carolina, region between the 31st and 36th parallels and extending to the Pacific, granted to 8 of his favorites by Charles II.

July 8   Rhode   Island   given   royal charter by Charles II, continued as its constitution until 1842.

July 27   Second Navigation Act, known as Staple Act, passed by Parliament: colonial imports from Europe must pass through England.

1664

Jan 29   Committee of Lord Berkeley, Sir George Carteret and William Coventry, appointed by Council for Foreign Plantations, reports possibility of an early overthrow of New Netherland.

Mar 12   Charles II grants to his broth- er, the Duke of York, region between Connecticut and Delaware rivers, including Dutch colony of New Netherland.

Apr 2   Richard Nicolls named by Duke of York deputy-governor of New Netherland, still claimed by Dutch.

Apr 10   First Assembly of delegates from all localities in New Netherland convenes at New Amsterdam to ask government protection against English and Indians, without effect.

Apr 21   Parliament   receives   report from committee of trade that merchants consider the Dutch greatest enemy to English trade.

June 24   Duke of York grants to John, Lord Berkeley and to Sir George Carteret region between Hudson and Delaware rivers, from about 40th parallel to Cape May, to be called Nova Caesarea or New Jersey.

July 23   Four   royal   commissioners headed by Richard Nicolls arrive at Boston from England to reduce Dutch colony of New Netherland and investigate governments of New England.

Aug 2σ New Netherland surrenders to the English with fall of New Amsterdam, which becomes New York.

Summer Governor Nicolls proclaims liberal offers to settlers. Large settlement of New Jersey by Puritans from New England and Long Island begins.

Sept 24 Fort Orange capitulates to English, is named Albany.

Oct William Drummond is appointed governor of Albemarle settlement on Chowan River [North Carolina] by Governor Berkeley of Virginia, authorized by Carolina proprietors in London.

Oct 1 Dutch and Swedes on the Delaware surrender to England. Conquest of New Netherland complete.

Oct 19 Printing presses allowed only in Cambridge by Massachusetts Bay General Court.

Nov 20 Long Island Sound designated as Connecticut's southern boundary by royal commission.

Dec 4 "A great and dreadful comet" seen in New England.

1665

Second Anglo-Dutch War, 1665–1667.

Sir John Yeamans and large number of colonists from Barbados make settlement of "Charles Town" at mouth of Cape Fear River [North Carolina]. Endures for 2 years.

First Baptist church in Massachusetts organized at Charlestown.

Elizabethtown, settled from Long Island, made capital of East Jersey by Governor Philip Carteret.

Governor Richard Nicolls opens Newmarket Course at Hempstead, Long Island, for horse racing.

Jan 5 New Haven formally submits to union with Connecticut.

Jan 7 Concessions and Agreements adopted as plan of government by proprietors of Carolina.

Feb 10 Concessions and Agreement, patterned after plan for Carolina, issued by New Jersey proprietors Berkeley and Carteret for their colony, providing for governor, council and representative assembly.

Mar 1 Duke's Laws ratified, introduced by Governor Nicolls before convention of deputies from Westchester and Long Island towns.

June 12 Governor Nicolls grants charter to city of New York, with monopoly of trade to freemen, but denial of self-government.

June 30 New charter for Carolina issued, extending boundaries from parallel 36° 30′ on the north to 29° on the south.

1666

The Character of the Province of Maryland, written in verse by George Alsop, published, London.

Governor Nicolls of New York says of democracy: "It hath taken so deep a root in these parts that the very name of Justice of the Peace is an abomination."

New Haven emigrants with land grants from Governor Carteret arrive in region of Newark, N. J., there to establish a model of New England.

May 3 Maryland assembly prohibits planting of tobacco for one year, market being glutted. Disallowed by Lord Baltimore Nov. 24.

Oct 11 Massachusetts Bay colony refuses to send representatives to England to answer charges brought against her by the royal commissioners, who recommended annulment of her charter.

1667

June 5 Five Dutch men-of-war attack shipping in James River, carrying off 18 merchant ships.

July 21 New Netherland finally surrendered by the Dutch to the English by Treaty of Breda; Acadia restored to France.

Sept 23 Virginia enacts that legal status of a slave is not changed by baptism.

1668

May 25 First representative assembly in New Jersey meets at Elizabethtown.

1669

Indian Primer by John Eliot published, Cambridge.

Meat out of the Eater, discussing necessity of afflictions upon God's children, by Michael Wigglesworth, published, Cambridge.

July 21 Fundamental Constitutions adopted, plan of government for Carolina believed drafted by John Locke. Substituted for Concessions and Agreements of 1665.

1670

East Jersey colonists with land titles from Governor Nicolls oppose quit-rents to proprietors.

Ten thousand persons spirited from England this year for sale in colonies.

Mar 1 Fundamental Constitutions, second draft, the one generally cited, adopted for Carolina.

April First permanent settlement in South Carolina made at Charles Town on Albemarle Point, on Ashley River, by Englishmen under William Sayle.

Apr 20 Virginia assembly votes against "bringing in of felons."

May 2 Hudson Bay Company chartered by Charles II.

July 8 England and Spain in Treaty of Madrid agree to recognize each other's rights in territory now occupied.

Oct 3 Assembly in Virginia limits suffrage to freeholders.

Dec 18 Suffrage in Maryland limited to property owners by Lord Baltimore.

1671

Population of Virginia estimated by Governor Berkeley as 45,000, including 6,000 indentured and 2,000 slaves.

Thomas Batts and Robert Fallam from Virginia travel into the West and discover Falls of the Great Kanawha.

Cinchona bark is in use in Virginia as cure for malaria.

Governor Berkeley of Virginia, in his Report to Council for Foreign Plantations, says, "I thank God that we have no free schools nor printing presses, and I hope we shall not have for a hundred years, for learning has brought disobedience and heresy and sects into the world; and printing has divulged them and libelled governments. God keep us from both."

French explorers at Sault Sainte Marie lay claim to interior of North America in name of Louis XIV.

June Plymouth passes her first school law.

Summer Father Jacques Marquette, Jesuit missionary, establishes French mission at Michilimackinac.

1672

Third Anglo-Dutch War, 1672–1674.

Count de Frontenac sent to Canada as governor of New France.

George Fox, Quaker, makes missionary journey through colonies.

Council for Trade and Foreign Plantations, under Lord Ashley and his associate John Locke, put in charge of colonial affairs by Charles II.

The Nicolls grants of 1664 to Jersey settlers declared void by Duke of York.

Third Navigation Act passed by Parliament to insure delivery of enumerated articles, particularly tobacco, at English ports. Collectors of customs for colonies soon appointed.

1673

Eight Dutch men-of-war attack and destroy 11 merchant ships in James River.

Fort Frontenac built on Lake Ontario by French.

Feb 25 Virginia granted as proprietary province by Charles II to Lords Arlington and Culpeper for 31 years.

June 17 Father Marquette and Louis Joliet, fur-trader, venturing from Green Bay by way of Fox and Wisconsin rivers, discover Mississippi River, down which they paddle to mouth of Arkansas River. Returning, reach Green Bay, September.

Bituminous coal discovered in Illinois by Marquette and Joliet.

July 30 New York retaken from the English by the Dutch.

1674

La Salle receives from Louis XIV permission to explore the Mississippi to its mouth.

Feb 9 New York restored to England by Treaty of Westminster at end of Third Anglo-Dutch War.

Mar 18 Lord Berkeley sells his inter-est in New Jersey to 2 English Quakers, Edward Byllynge and his agent John Fenwick.

July 1 Sir Edmund Andros appointed governor of New York by Duke of York.

July 29 Carteret's territory in New Jersey confirmed and defined as East Jersey by Duke of York.

1675

First printing press in Boston, allowed by General Court, set up by John Foster, America's earliest engraver.

Salem, first Quaker settlement in New Jersey, founded by John Fenwick.

Lords of Trade, standing committee of Privy Council, established to take over duties of Council for Trade and Foreign Plantations.

Feb 14 Edward Byllynge conveys his West Jersey rights to William Penn, Gawen Lawrie and Nicholas Lucas, Quakers. John Fenwick soon conveys his rights to them.

June   Governor Andros of New York appears at Saybrook, claiming Connecticut west of Connecticut River for Duke of York.

June 24 King Philip's War (1675–1678) begins with attack by Wampanoags on Swansea, R. I. Spreads death and waste throughout New England frontier.

1676

Indian war on frontiers of Virginia and Maryland.

Apr 20 Bacon's Rebellion begins. Na-thaniel Bacon leads unauthorized expedition of Virginia frontiersmen against Indians when Governor Berkeley refuses to take action.

May 29 Governor Berkeley declares Bacon traitor and rebel.

June   Bacon leads revolt of small planters against Governor Berkeley.

June 5 Virginia assembly, supporting Bacon, meets. Passes reform legislation, "Bacon's laws."

June 10 Edward Randolph, commis- sioned to report on Massachusetts Bay, lands in Boston. Oct. 12, reports to Lords of Trade Massachusetts' undue independence of British authority and recommends making her a royal province.

July 1 Quintipartite Deed divides New Jersey, allotting East Jersey to Carteret and West Jersey to Quaker proprietors Byllynge, Penn, Lucas and Lawrie.

Aug 12 King Philip's War ends in New England with death of Philip. Hostilities continue in Maine and New Hampshire until 1678.

Sept 19 Jamestown, Va., burned by Bacon.

Nov   Rebellion begins in Maryland against authority of proprietor. Ends in hanging of 2 malcontents by deputy-governor Thomas Notley.

1677

First medical work printed in America, a pamphlet, *To Guide the Common People of New England how to order Themselves . . . in the Small Pocks,* by Thomas Thacher.

Jan 29 Three commissioners arrive from London to investigate matters in Virginia. In consequence, Governor Berkeley is recalled April 27.

Mar 3 Concessions and Agreements of West Jersey signed in England by proprietors, freeholders and emigrants.

May 6 Massachusetts Bay buys rights of Ferdinando Gorges to southern

Maine when his heirs' claims are upheld by Privy Council, and holds Maine as a proprietary possession until 1684.

Aug   Burlington in West Jersey set- tled by Quakers from England, bringing Concessions and Agreements with them.

Oct 10 Massachusetts Bay passes law enforcing navigation acts.

1678

Severe smallpox epidemic occurs in New England.

Culpeper Rebellion in Carolina led by John Culpeper against navigation act of 1672 and quit-rents.

Apr 12 King Philip's war ends in Maine in a treaty signed at Casco.

1679

Apr 25 Virginia assembly enacts law forbidding importation of Carolina tobacco or its shipment from Virginia ports.

July 24 New Hampshire made a royal colony.

Dec 7 Edward Randolph arrives in New York, collector of customs throughout New England.

1680

Increase Mather preaches sermon, "Heaven's Alarm to the World," inspired by great comet of this year, the "dreadful comett starr." Dutch settlers on the Hudson tremble and petition for "a day of fasting and humiliation."

French Huguenots arrive at Charles Town, Carolina.

Charles Town declared seat of Carolina government by proprietors.

Aug 6 Duke of York confirms rights and titles of Quaker proprietors to West Jersey.

1681

Mar 4 William Penn in charter from Charles II granted region between 40th and 43rd parallels, extending 5 degrees west of Delaware River, which Charles named Pennsylvania.

Apr   Penn sends first colonists to Pennsylvania under William Markham, deputy-governor.

July 11 Conditions and Concessions issued by Penn to regulate land transactions in his colony.

Nov 21 West Jersey assembly first meets in Burlington, with Samuel Jennings governor.

1682

Tobacco-cutting riots on Virginia plantations to raise prices in glutted market.

Jan 12 Fundamental Constitutions for Carolina, new set, issued.

Feb 1 William Penn with 11 other Quakers purchases East New Jersey from Carteret heirs.

Mar 1 Fenwick's grant in West Jersey purchased by Penn and associates.

Apr   Penn sends over Thomas Holme as surveyor-general to lay out Philadelphia.

Apr 9 La Salle, descending Mississippi River to its mouth, claims whole region for Louis XIV of France and names it Louisiana.

Apr 25 Penn issues first Frame of Government, as Pennsylvania's constitution.

Aug   Welsh Quakers arrive and settle Welsh Tract west of Philadelphia.

Aug 24 Newcastle and lower Counties on the Delaware [Delaware] deeded to William Penn by Duke of York.

Sept 28 West Jersey grants Matenicunk Island to Burlington for maintenance of a school, believed to be first school fund in America.

Oct 29 Penn lands on Pennsylvania soil at Upland (Chester).

Dec 4 First Pennsylvania assembly meets at Upland (Chester). Incorporates Delaware settlements with Pennsylvania; adopts a code, the Great Law; naturalizes settlers already there.

1683

Increase Mather organizes in Boston first scientific society in colonies to effect "Improvements in Philosophy and Additions to the Stores of Natural History."

Mar 14 Duke of York confirms rights and title of 24 Quaker proprietors to East Jersey.

Apr 2 Penn signs Pennsylvania and Delaware Frame of Government, superseding Frame of 1682.

June 23 Penn enters into a treaty with the Indians at Shackamaxon under "Treaty Elm," according to tradition.

Oct   Germantown, Pa., founded by Francis Daniel Pastorius and 13 Mennonite families from the Rhineland.

Oct 17 New York holds its first representative assembly under English rule, Thomas Dongan governor. Adopts Charter of Liberties which are disallowed, 1686.

1684

An Essay for the Recording of Illustrious Providences by Increase Mather published, Boston and London.

Perth Amboy settled by proprietors of East Jersey. Becomes its capital and port of entry, 1686.

Penn and Lord Baltimore return to England, each to present his case in dispute over claim to Delaware.

July 24 La Salle sails from France with colonists to settle in Louisiana, in order to control interior fur trade and establish base for attack upon New Spain.

July 30 Iroquois renew peace covenant with English in meeting with Governor Dongan of New York at Albany.

Sept 5 New England Confederation commissioners hold final meeting at Hartford.

Oct 23 Massachusetts charter annulled in court of chancery, to curb her growing independence of royal authority. End of Massachusetts Bay Company.

Oct 23 Massachusetts requirement of church membership for voting ends with annulment of her charter.

1685

La Salle, missing mouth of Mississippi, lands at Matagorda Bay, Texas, and builds Fort St. Louis.

Feb 6 Duke of York succeeds to English throne as James II.

Feb 6 New York becomes a royal province when Duke of York ascends the throne.

Oct 17 Lords of Trade decide in favor of Penn and against Lord Baltimore in claim to Delaware.

Oct 18 Revocation of Edict of Nantes by Louis XIV of France increases Huguenot migration to America, by way of England and Holland, largest number coming to South Carolina.

1686

Eight book shops listed in Boston at this date.

Arkansas Post at mouth of Arkansas River established by Henri de Tonty, earliest French settlement in lower Mississippi Valley.

May 17 Joseph Dudley assumes office as temporary governor of New England.

June 3 Sir Edmund Andros commissioned governor-general of Dominion of New England by James II.

June 15 Anglican church worship first set up in Boston.

Aug 17 Spanish soldiers from Florida attack and destroy Scotch settlement of Stuart Town (Port Royal) [South Carolina].

Dec 20 Andros arrives in Boston as governor-general of Dominion of New England.

1687

Sir Isaac Newton's *Principia* published in England.

Jan 12 Rhode Island government dissolved by Andros and changed to that of an English county.

Mar 19 La Salle, after fruitless wanderings in southwest, assassinated by 2 followers in present Texas.

Aug   Massachusetts towns of Ipswich and Topsfield refuse to pay taxes levied without consent.

Nov 1 Connecticut government dissolved by Andros and changed to that of a county.

1688

Feb 14 Carolina assembly refuses to accept proprietors' letter declaring Fundamentals of 1669 no longer valid. Colony on verge of revolt.

Apr   The Germantown Friends' Protest against Slavery, presented in Monthly Meeting, is earliest anti-slavery document in America.

Apr 7 Increase Mather sails for England, sent by churches of Massachusetts to petition renewal of Massachusetts charter.

Apr 7 Andros given new commission by James II making him governor of all New England colonies, New York and New Jersey.

Apr 8 East Jersey proprietors surrender political authority to crown.

Aug   Andros takes over government of New York and the Jerseys, annexing them to Dominion of New England.

Oct   West Jersey proprietors surrender government to crown.

Dec 11 James II deposed, flees to France.

1689

King William's War, 1689–1697, between French and English colonists, American phase of War of League of Augsburg.

Memorable Providences by Cotton Mather published, Boston.

James Blair appointed Commissary of Virginia by Bishop of London.

Feb 13 William and Mary proclaimed king and queen of England by Parliament, concluding Glorious Revolution.

Feb 16 New Committee of Privy Council on Trade and Foreign Plantations appointed by William and Mary.

Apr 4 News of landing of William of Orange in England arrives in Boston.

Apr 18 Governor Andros overthrown by inhabitants of Boston, New England's counterpart of Glorious Revolution.

Apr 27 Virginia proclaims the new sovereigns, William and Mary.

May 1 Rhode Island resumes govern- ment under old charter.

May 9 Connecticut resumes govern- ment under old charter.

May 24 Toleration Act passed by Parliament, safe-guarding religious liberties of Dissenters.

May 24 Massachusetts re-establishes government according to old charter.

June 1 Jacob Leisler seizes fort of New York in popular uprising. (Opening of Leisler's Rebellion.) Deputy-governor Francis Nicholson overthrown.

July 27 Protestant Association under John Coode seizes St. Mary's, capital of Maryland, in revolt against proprietary government. Organizes new government in name of William and Mary.

Aug 3 Pemaquid fort on Maine border captured in French-Indian raid.

Oct 16 Count Frontenac returns from France as governor of Canada with supplies and plans for conquest of New England.

Dec 11 Leisler seizes control of government of New York province.

Dec 16 English Bill of Rights enacted by Parliament as statute law, a century later to be put into United States Constitution.

1690

Population, estimated: Boston, 7,000; Newport, 2,600; New York, 3,900; Philadelphia, 4,000; Charleston, 1,100.

John Locke's *Two Treatises on Government* published in England.

The New England Primer printed in Boston, about this date.

Paper industry in America introduced in Philadelphia by Dutch immigrant William Rittenhouse.

French Huguenots from Virginia make permanent settlement on Pamlico River [North Carolina].

Jan 22 Iroquois council at Onondaga, N. Y., renews declaration of allegiance to English king, promising aid against French.

Feb 1 Protestant Associates in Maryland continued in power by William and Mary.

Feb 9 Schenectady, N. Y., massacre by French and Indians in Frontenac's attempt to conquer New York.

Mar 12   New Hampshire assembly votes reannexation to Massachusetts.

Mar 27   Salmon Falls, N. H., destroyed in French-Indian raid.

May 1 Intercolonial congress convenes at New York, with delegates from Massachusetts, Plymouth, Connecticut and New York, to plan overland attack upon French at Montreal, and naval attack upon Quebec, both of which fail.

May 11 Sir William Phips captures Port Royal, Nova Scotia.

May 20 Casco (Portland), Maine, de- stroyed by French and Indians, part of Frontenac's plan.

Aug   Land expedition via Lake Champlain to take Montreal, led by Fitz-John Randolph, turns back to Albany from lack of quotas and support.

Sept 25 *Public Occurrences,* a printed sheet, comes out in Boston as first American newspaper. No second issue.

Oct 6 Seth Sothell, popular leader banished from Albemarle, seizes government at Charles Town, Carolina. Results in banishment of Governor James Colleton.

Oct 7   Sir William Phips begins unsuc- cessful siege of Quebec.

Dec   Massachusetts issues her first pa- per currency, to pay soldiers returning from Quebec expedition.

1 6 9 1

Jeremiah Dummer of Boston paints portraits of himself and his wife, probably first native painter of ability.

Francis Nicholson comes to Virginia as deputy-governor.

Apr   Lower Counties on Delaware given separate government by William Penn, who appoints William Markham deputy-governor.

May 13 First assembly in New York under direct authority of English crown re-enacts Charter of Liberties, 1683, and declares for representative government.

May 16   Jacob Leisler executed for his part in Revolution of 1689 in New York.

June 27 Maryland   becomes   royal province.

Oct 7   Massachusetts receives charter as royal colony, enlarged by Plymouth, Maine, Nova Scotia and territory between it and Maine.

Nov 8   North Carolina placed under a deputy of the Carolina governor who remains at Charles Town, S. C. Term "North Carolina" first used.

1 6 9 2

Salem witchcraft mania, 19 hanged, 1 pressed to death.

New Jersey restored to government of proprietors.

Feb 17 Thomas Neale receives patent from William and Mary, authorizing him to establish post offices in colonies for 21 years.

Apr 4 Andrew Hamilton appointed Thomas Neale's deputy to set up colonial post offices.

May 10 Anglican Church established as state church of Maryland. Disallowed by Parliament 1696.

Aug 13 New Hampshire again be- comes royal colony.

Oct 21 Benjamin Fletcher, governor of New York, commissioned governor of Pennsylvania by William and Mary. Pennsylvania made a royal province and William Penn deprived of proprietorship.

1693

Wonders of the Invisible World by Cotton Mather published, Boston, defending execution of witches.

Power to initiate laws granted by proprietors of Carolina to its assembly as well as to governor and council.

East Jersey assembly authorizes tax-support of public schools.

Feb 8   College of William and Mary in Virginia chartered. [James Blair first president.]

Oct 4   Conference of deputies from colonies to plan for war against French meets on call of Governor Fletcher of New York. Results negligible.

1694

Maryland capital moved from St. Mary's to Providence (Annapolis).

Massachusetts law to discourage excessive drinking requires tavern keepers to sell no liquors to any on "list of common tiplers."

Rice cultivation introduced in South Carolina.

Feb 10   Francis Nicholson becomes governor of Maryland.

Aug 15   Treaty between Iroquois and delegates from Massachusetts, Connecticut, New York and New Jersey signed at Albany to forestall Iroquois peace with French.

Aug 20   Penn reinstated proprietor of Pennsylvania by William and Mary.

1695

First Episcopal church, Christ Church, built in Philadelphia.

1696

Pensacola, Fla., settlement planted by Spain as defense against French.

King William's School, provided for by Maryland assembly, opens at Annapolis.

Religious freedom for all Christians except Roman Catholics guaranteed by South Carolina assembly.

Dr. Thomas Bray appointed Commissary of Maryland by Bishop of London. Establishes parish libraries.

Apr 10   Navigation Act, to perfect en-forcement of acts passed under Charles II, enacted by Parliament.

May 15   Board of Trade set up by Wil-liam III, independent of Privy Council, succeeds Lords of Trade.

Aug 15   Pemaquid fort on Maine bor-der retaken by French under Le Moyne d'Iberville.

Nov 7   Pennsylvania's third Frame of Government, submitted by Governor William Markham, accepted by assembly.

1697

Limestone found at Newbury, Mass.

Trinity Church built in New York.

Penn Charter School established in Philadelphia, supported by public money.

Vice-admiralty courts set up in the colonies by Privy Council, implementing Navigation Act of April 10, 1696.

Feb 8   William Penn submits to Board of Trade proposal for colonial congress, with representatives from each colony and a president appointed by the king.

Mar 15   Haverhill, Mass., raided by French and Indians.

Sept 10   Treaty of Ryswick ends King William's War. Territorial *status quo ante bellum* in America restored.

1698

Slave trade opened to private merchants by Parliament, beginning New England's triangular trade: New England-Africa-Caribbean Islands.

Francis Nicholson becomes governor of Virginia.

1699

God's Protecting Providence in the Remarkable Deliverance of Robert Barrow by Jonathan Dickenson, one of best Indian-captivity tracts, published, Philadelphia.

Williamsburg, Va., founded by act of assembly as new capital, following fire at Jamestown 1698.

Pierre Le Moyne d'Iberville, to forestall English, establishes post at Biloxi, beginning of French colony of Louisiana.

Sulpician Mission to Indians set up at Cahokia by French Jesuits in Illinois country. Moves next year to Kaskaskia.

Wool Act passed by Parliament forbidding exportation of wool from American colonies or Ireland, one reason for Scotch-Irish migration to America.

Jan 7 Treaty between Massachusetts and Abenaki Indians at Casco Bay, Maine, ends French and Indian warfare on New England border.

June 29 Massachusetts passes law de-signed to prevent spread of infectious diseases.

July 6 Captain Kidd, pirate, seized in Boston and sent to England, hanged May 23, 1701.

Nov 30 Penn returns to his colony after 15 years in England.

1700

Population of the colonies, estimated, 262,000.

Roman Catholic priests banished by Massachusetts General Court. New York takes similar action.

Piracy Act of Parliament establishes special courts in colonies for trial of pirates.

First library law in colonies enacted by South Carolina assembly for support of library in Charles Town.

Five hundred French Huguenots settle in tidewater Virginia.

June 24 Samuel Sewall publishes tract in Boston, *The Selling of Joseph,* condemning holding of slaves.

1701

New York adopts neutrality toward French in Canada and maintains non-belligerency until 1709.

Yale College founded at Saybrook, Conn., moves to New Haven 1716.

Detroit founded by Lamothe Cadillac, strategic point in chain of French settlements between Canada and Louisiana.

Mar 26 Board of Trade recommends to king that all charter colonies be made royal provinces.

May 8 Connecticut General Court agrees to hold May session in Hartford, October session in New Haven.

June 16 Society for Propagation of the Gospel in Foreign Parts chartered in England.

Aug 4 Iroquois conclude treaty of peace with French and their Indian allies at Montreal.

Oct 28 Charter of Privileges adopted in Pennsylvania, its fundamental law until 1776.

Nov 12 Anglican Church established in North Carolina by first Vestry Act of assembly. Disallowed, 1703, by proprietors.

1702

Queen Anne's War (1702–1713), American phase of War of Spanish Succession.

Anglican Church finally established in Maryland.

Magnalia Christi Americana by Cotton Mather published, London.

Mar 8   Accession of Anne to English throne.

Apr 17   East and West Jersey united as royal province of New Jersey under governor of New York, sessions of assembly to meet alternately at Perth Amboy and Burlington.

June 11   Joseph Dudley, appointed governor of Massachusetts and New Hampshire, arrives in Boston.

Sept   St. Augustine, Fla., plundered and burned by Carolinians under Governor James Moore.

1703

Abenaki, or Eastern Indians, make peace treaty with Governor Dudley of Massachusetts at Casco, Maine. Ten years of Indian war, backed by French, begins within 2 months.

Paper money issued by South Carolina to pay for St. Augustine attack.

May 12   Rhode Island and Connecti-cut agree upon boundary line. Confirmed by king in Council 1728.

1704

French Huguenots plant settlement, Bath, near Pamlico River, N. C.

Roman Catholic services in Maryland restricted to private homes from this date until Revolution.

Feb 29   Deerfield massacre by French and Indians, worst disaster of Queen Anne's War in colonies.

Apr 24 *The Boston News-Letter* begins publication; first regularly issued newspaper in America, continuing until Revolution.

May 6   Non-Anglicans excluded from membership in South Carolina assembly by act of assembly. Annulled by royal order June 10, 1706.

June 18   The piece of eight shall not be valued at over 6 shillings in any colony, by royal proclamation.

Nov 22   First independent assembly of Delaware, "Lower Counties of Pennsylvania," meets at New Castle. Separation from Pennsylvania complete except for common governor.

Winter   Madame Sarah Knight trav-els from Boston to New York and return. Journey described in *The Private Journal.*

1705

The History of Virginia by Robert Beverley published, London.

Fort Vincennes on the Wabash founded by French.

Bounties on importation of naval stores from colonies offered by Parliament.

New York law against runaway slaves provides death penalty for slaves found 40 miles north of Albany.

Rice, West Indies molasses and naval stores added by Parliament to list of enumerated articles to be shipped only to English ports.

Virginia requires by law that an apprenticed orphan shall be taught by his master to read and write.

Virginia slave code, fifth revision, declares slaves to be real estate.

Second Vestry Act of North Carolina reestablishes Anglican as state church.

1706

Mar   Philadelphia Presbytery, first in America, is formed, Francis Makemie moderator.

June 10   Anglican test for membership in South Carolina assembly annulled by royal order.

Aug 24   Charleston attacked by French and Spanish from Havana and St. Augustine. Repulsed by Carolinians.

Nov 30   Anglican Church established in South Carolina by assembly.

1707

Trial and acquittal of Francis Makemie, Presbyterian, by New York court ends prosecution of Protestant dissenters in that colony.

Philadelphia mechanics protest competition of hired Negro slaves.

Mar 6   Act of Union approved by Queen Anne. England, Scotland and Wales become United Kingdom of Great Britain.

1708

Currency Act of Parliament sets penalty for taking foreign coins at rate above legal ratio in colonies.

Sot-Weed Factor by Ebenezer Cook of Maryland published in London.

Aug 29   Massacre at Haverhill, Mass., by French and Indians from Canada.

Oct 14   Saybrook Platform adopted by General Court of Connecticut, changing her church government from Congregational to semi-Presbyterian basis.

1709

Quakers build meeting house in Boston.

New York and New England plan attack on Quebec by sea and Montreal by land. Abandoned when expected British support fails.

Short Introduction to Latin Tongue . . . Accidence Abridged by Ezekiel Cheever, colonial schoolmaster, published, Boston.

1710

Pennsylvania rifle, with spiral bore, is developed among "Pennsylvania Dutch," 1710–1720. Significant in Revolutionary War.

Great German migration to America begins.

Six hundred and fifty Swiss and German Palatines brought by Baron de Graffenried settle New Bern on Neuse River, North Carolina.

Governor Robert Hunter of New York brings 3,000 Germans from Palatinate to settle on Hudson River to produce naval stores.

Five Iroquois chiefs taken by Colonel Peter Schuyler to Queen Anne's court to impress them with might of England.

Bonifacius, or, Essays to Do Good by Cotton Mather published in Boston.

French settlement of Biloxi moved to present site of Mobile.

Apr   Free school founded at Charleston, South Carolina, by act of assembly.

June 21   Colonel Alexander Spotswood, governor of Virginia, arrives at Jamestown, authorized by king to extend right of habeas corpus.

Oct   Port Royal, Acadia, captured from French by British and colonial troops under Colonel Francis Nicholson, and renamed Annapolis.

1711

Post-office Act of Parliament establishes postal system for British colonies with deputy postmaster for America in New York.

Cary's Rebellion in North Carolina against establishment of Anglican Church.

Complaint of too much Latin and Greek in free schools of Boston recorded in town records.

June   New England governors called by Francis Nicholson meet at New London to plan campaign against Canada: Quebec via St. Lawrence River, Montreal via Lake Champlain.

July 30 British fleet with colonial troops sails from Boston to take Quebec. Fails from incompetence of officers.

Sept 22 Tuscarora Indian War (1711– 1713) begins with massacre of settlers on Chowan and Roanoke rivers, North Carolina. New Bern abandoned.

1712

Jan 28 North and South Carolina mi- litia, assisted by friendly Indians, attacks Tuscaroras on Neuse River, killing 300.

Apr   Slave revolt in New York City. Twenty Negroes burned or hanged.

May 9 Carolina finally separated into North and South Carolina, each colony with its own governor. Edward Hyde becomes first governor of North Carolina.

June 7 Pennsylvania passes law pro- hibiting importation of Negroes.

Sept 14 Antoine Crozat granted mo- nopoly of trade in Louisiana by Louis XIV, which he holds until 1717.

1713

Boundary line between Massachusetts and Connecticut run and accepted by legislature of each colony.

The schooner, American type of sailing vessel, first built by Captain Andrew Robinson in Gloucester, Mass.

Churches Quarrel Espoused by John Wise published, New York. Justifies Congregationalism.

Mar 23 Fort   Nohucke,   Tuscarora stronghold in North Carolina, captured by South Carolina force, ending Tuscarora war.

Mar 31 Treaty of Utrecht ends Queen Anne's War. France gives Hudson Bay country, Newfoundland and Nova Scotia to Great Britain, and accepts British protectorate over Iroquois; the Asiente grants Britain 30-year monopoly of slave trade with Spanish colonies.

July 11 Abenaki, or Eastern Indians, make peace with Governor Dudley of Massachusetts at Portsmouth.

1714

Governor Spotswood of Virginia establishes iron furnaces on Rapidan River and brings in German settlers for labor.

First organ in New England installed in King's Chapel, Boston, gift of Thomas Brattle.

Androboros by Governor Robert Hunter of New York published, first play written and printed in this country.

Aug 1 George I succeeds Queen Anne on British throne.

1715

Maryland re-established as proprietary colony when Benedict Leonard Calvert, 4th Lord Baltimore, a Protestant, is restored as proprietor.

Negroes forbidden separate meeting houses in North Carolina.

Apr 15 Yemassee Indians, incited by Spanish, attack settlers in South Carolina, killing some 400. Peace made next year.

1716

Elections for assembly to be held in parishes instead of at Charleston, as enacted by South Carolina.

Boston Light built, first American lighthouse.

First playhouse in America erected at Williamsburg, Va.

Governor Spotswood of Virginia leads expedition across Blue Ridge into Valley of Virginia in interest of westward movement. Companions become known as Knights of Golden Horseshoe.

1717

Great German migration to Pennsylvania—Mennonites, Dunkers, Moravians —begins about this date.

Mississippi Bubble. Origin in grants by Louis XIV of monopoly rights in Louisiana trade to John Law and his Company of the West. Thousands speculate in stocks for development of Mississippi Valley.

Illinois settlements incorporated as part of Louisiana.

Vindication of Government of the New England Churches by John Wise published, Boston.

Religion Professed by the Quakers by William Penn published, Philadelphia.

1718

Great Scotch-Irish migration to America begins about this date.

San Antonio, Tex., founded by Spanish.

Five hundred pounds subscribed in Boston for Christian instruction of Indians.

Tuscaroras make peace with North Carolina. Eventually join Iroquois as Sixth Nation.

New Orleans founded by French under Jean Baptiste le Moyne, Sieur de Bienville, governor of Louisiana.

Edward Teach, "Blackbeard," pirate, killed in North Carolina.

Sept 27 Stede Bonnet, Carolina coast pirate, and crew seized by South Carolina government expedition. Bonnet hanged Dec. 10.

1719

Scotch-Irish from North Ireland settle Londonderry, N. H. Begin cultivation of potatoes in colonies.

Spanish at Pensacola, Fla., surrender to de Bienville and French.

Dec 21 South Carolina made royal colony after revolt against proprietors, who retain land rights.

Dec 21 *The Boston Gazette* first published, James Franklin editor.

Dec 22 *The American Weekly Mercury*, first newspaper in Pennsylvania first published, Andrew Bradford editor.

1720

Lead mined in southeastern Missouri.

Mississippi Bubble bursts in collapse of John Law's Company of the West and ruin of speculators.

Theodorus J. Frelinghuysen arrives in New Jersey as preacher to Dutch on the Raritan.

1721

Sir Robert Walpole appointed British chancellor of exchequer. Pursues policy of "salutary neglect" of American colonies, resulting in slack enforcement of navigation laws (1721–1742).

Marine insurance begun in Philadelphia with John Copson's "Assurances from Losses Happening at Sea, &c."

Cotton Mather and Dr. Zabdiel Boylston introduce inoculation for smallpox in America, with epidemic in Boston.

Gustavus Hesselius, Swedish immigrant to Delaware, commissioned to paint "The Last Supper" for Church of St. Barnabas in Queen Anne Parish, Maryland—first public art commission in colonies.

Governor's censorship of publications in Massachusetts abolished by General Court.

May 29 Francis Nicholson arrives at Charleston as royal governor of South Carolina.

Aug 7 *The New England Courant* first published, James Franklin editor.

1722

Lovewell's War, 1722–1725, with Abenaki Indians, inspired by French Jesuit Rale, begins in Maine.

Daniel Coxe of New Jersey draws up first published plan for political union of colonies. Printed in London.

New Orleans made capital of Louisiana.

Benjamin Franklin publishes *Silence Dogood Papers* anonymously in *New England Courant.*

Iroquois in treaty with Governor Spotswood of Virginia at Albany agree not to cross Potomac River or Blue Ridge without permission of governor of Virginia.

Issue of copper coins in pennies and farthings allowed colonists by Parliament.

Copper, and beaver and other furs put on enumerated list by Parliament.

Hemp, lumber and naval stores freed from import duties by Parliament.

1723

Schools in each county provided for by Maryland assembly.

Benjamin Franklin leaves Boston for Philadelphia.

Brafferton Hall, first important Georgian building in the South, completed at William and Mary College.

1724

Fort Dummer (Brattleboro), first permanent settlement in Vermont, made by Massachusetts to protect her frontier.

Black Code proclaimed in New Orleans by Governor de Bienville for regulation of Negroes and banishment of Jews.

Carpenters' Company of Philadelphia, a craft guild, founded on lines of European guilds.

The Present State of Virginia by Hugh Jones published, London. Advocates study of American history.

Property qualifications for suffrage established in Rhode Island.

1725

Nathaniel Ames, almanac-maker and physician, begins publication of *Astronomical Diary and Almanac* (1725–1775), Boston.

Vitus Bering, Danish navigator sent by Catherine I of Russia in search of passage through northern straits, reaches sea named for him.

New York Gazette, New York's first newspaper, begins publication under William Bradford.

Shipment of North Carolina tobacco from Virginia ports prohibited by Virginia assembly. Disallowed by Board of Trade.

1726

Germans begin to move from Pennsylvania into Valley of Virginia.

Oswego, fort and trading post, established on Lake Ontario by Governor Burnet of New York.

Gilbert Tennent begins preaching to Presbyterians in Raritan Valley, N. J.

Hoop Petticoats, Arraigned and Condemned by the Light of Nature and the Law of God published anonymously, Boston.

1727

Christ Church, second structure, begun in Philadelphia, in style of Christopher Wren.

Junto Club founded by Benjamin Franklin in Philadelphia.

Dr. Cadwallader Colden's _History of the Five Indian Nations_ published.

George II succeeds George I on British throne.

Sept 19 _Maryland Gazette_, first newspaper in Maryland, begins publication at Annapolis.

1728

Colonel William Byrd of Virginia serves as commissioner to run boundary line between Virginia and North Carolina. His _History of the Dividing Line_ published 1841.

"Casket Girls" arrive in New Orleans as wives for settlers. Each presented new gown in small chest.

1729

Benjamin Franklin's _Modest Enquiry into the Nature and Necessity of a Paper-Currency_ published, Philadelphia.

Arithmetick, Vulgar and Decimal by Professor Isaac Greenwood of Harvard published, Boston. First textbook on arithmetic by an American.

George Berkeley, Irish idealist, arrives at Newport, R. I. Is to contribute to American philosophical thought.

Carolina proprietors surrender their charter to crown, Lord Carteret reserving his eighth of the grant.

North and South Carolina made royal provinces by act of Parliament.

Benjamin Franklin becomes owner and publisher of _The Pennsylvania Gazette_.

1730

Alexander Spotswood appointed postmaster-general for the colonies.

Thomas Godfrey, Pennsylvanian, makes improved mariner's quadrant.

Baltimore, Md., settled. Provides seaport for interior.

Tobacco Inspection Law enacted by Virginia provides quality inspection at ports.

Carolina rice may be shipped directly to European ports south of Cape Finisterre, by act of Parliament.

1731

Printing press set up at Charleston, S. C.

John Bartram establishes Botanical Gardens near Philadelphia.

First circulating library in America established in Philadelphia by Franklin.

Natural History of Carolina, Florida and the Bahama Islands by Mark Catesby, scientist, published, London.

Jan 23 **Louisiana** **again** **becomes** French royal province with surrender of charter of John Law's Company of the West.

Dec 30 First public concert in America given "at Mr. Pelham's great room" in Boston.

1732

Scotch-Irish in Pennsylvania begin moving into Valley of Virginia.

Hat Act of Parliament prohibits intercolonial trade in hats and restricts their manufacture.

Almshouse supported by public funds established in Philadelphia, probably first in colonies.

First regular stagecoach service inaugurated in New Jersey between Burlington and Amboy.

Benjamin Franklin begins issue of *Poor Richard's Almanac* (1732–1757).

The Vade Mecum for America: or, A Companion for Traders and Travellers by Thomas Prince published in Boston, America's first guide book.

Seventh-Day Adventist community founded at Ephrata, Pa., by Johann Conrad Beissel.

Jan 8 *The South Carolina Gazette* (Charleston) established, with Benjamin Franklin backing Thomas Whitmarsh, editor.

Feb 28 Lord Carteret sells his eighth of the Carolina grant to promoters of Georgia colony.

June 9 Georgia charter granted by George II to James Edward Oglethorpe and associates, interested in imprisoned debtors, authorizing them to colonize land between Savannah and Altamaha rivers "from the Atlantic to the South Seas."

Sept 27 *The Rhode Island Gazette*, first newspaper in colony, published in Newport, James Franklin editor.

1733

Colonel William Byrd of Westover, Va., writes travel diary, *A Journey to the Land of Eden,* while in search of lands in North Carolina. Published in 1841.

Jan 13 James Edward Oglethorpe arrives at Charleston, S. C., with about 130 settlers and Georgia charter.

Feb 12 Savannah founded by Oglethorpe, after obtaining consent from Creek Indians, first settlement in Georgia, last of the 13 colonies.

May 17 Molasses Act passed by Parliament, following pressure of a West Indian planter lobby, imposing high duties upon sugar, molasses and rum imported into colonies from West Indies.

July 30 First Masonic lodge, under regular charter, established in Boston.

Nov 5 *New York Weekly Journal*, founded by opponents of Governor William Cosby, begins publication, John Peter Zenger editor.

1734

German Lutherans from Salzburg, Bavaria, establish successful settlement at Ebenezer, Ga.

William Bull of South Carolina takes medical degree in Europe, first American to do so.

Great Awakening in American colonies begins at Northampton, Mass., in church of Jonathan Edwards.

Popular party wins aldermanic election in New York City, assisted by Zenger's *New York Weekly Journal.*

Nov 17 John Peter Zenger, editor of *New York Weekly Journal,* arrested for libel of Governor William Cosby.

1735

Severe epidemic of scarlet fever in New England.

Georgia trustees prohibit slavery and importation of rum in colony.

Augusta, Ga., fort and trading post, established on Savannah River.

Feb 18 "Flora, or Hob in the Well," an opera given in Charleston, first recorded performance of opera in America.

Aug   John Peter Zenger's trial for libel. His acquittal a victory for freedom of the press.

1736

John and Charles Wesley arrive at Savannah, Ga.

William Tennent establishes "log-college" on his farm in New Jersey to instruct Presbyterian ministers for frontier settlements.

Scotch settlement of New Inverness made near mouth of the Altamaha in Georgia.

Dr. William Douglass publishes *The Practical History of a New Epidemical Eruptive Miliary Fever . . . in Boston . . . 1735 and 1736.* Earliest clinical description of scarlet fever.

A Chronological History of New-England in the Form of Annals by Rev. Thomas Prince published, Boston.

Aug 6   *The Virginia Gazette,* Virginia's first newspaper, published by William Parks in Williamsburg.

1737

First organ built in America made by Johannes Klemm, Moravian organ builder, for Trinity Church, New York.

John Wesley holds Sunday catechism classes for children in Savannah, Ga.

Boundary line dispute between Massachusetts and New Hampshire begins, not to be settled until 1889.

Narrative of Surprising Conversions by Jonathan Edwards published in Boston. Pictures Great Awakening.

1738

John Winthrop, colonial scientist second to Franklin, begins 41 years of teaching of natural philosophy at Harvard.

New Jersey given own royal governor, Lewis Morris, after joint governorship with New York since 1702.

May 7   George Whitefield, Methodist evangelist, arrives at Savannah from England on his first visit.

Dec 21   Augusta and Frederick coun-ties beyond Blue Ridge established by Virginia legislature.

1739

The War of Jenkin's Ear, 1739–1748, between England and Spain begins, soon merging into War of Austrian Succession, 1740–1748.

Pierre and Paul Mallet, French explorers, first sight Rocky Mountains, near headwaters of the Arkansas.

Caspar Wistar establishes glass factory in Salem County, N. J., bringing glass blowers from Germany. Factory operates for 40 years.

Plunket Fleeson of Philadelphia introduces manufacture of wallpapers.

Governor Oglethorpe of Georgia makes peace treaty with Creek Indians.

Slave insurrection at Stono, S. C.

Sugar taken off enumerated list by Parliament for countries south of Cape Finisterre.

1740

Massachusetts land bank begins operations, issuing notes based on land mortgages. Discontinued by Parliament, 1741.

Governor Oglethorpe makes unsuccessful expedition against Spanish at St. Augustine in defense of English settlements.

George Whitefield establishes orphanage in Savannah, Ga., and begins preaching tour through New England.

Pattison brothers, Edward and William, of Berlin, Conn., begin manufacture of tinware, selling it from house to house, first tin peddlers in colonies.

Naturalization act of Parliament by which a foreigner who becomes citizen of one colony becomes automatically citizen of all.

Aug 5 New Hampshire-Massachusetts boundary confirmed by royal decree.

Aug 5 New Hampshire-Maine bound-ary confirmed by royal decree.

1741

Vitus Bering, Danish navigator under Russian commission, sails along coast of Alaska and Aleutian Islands.

Jonathan Edwards delivers famous brimstone sermon, "Sinners in the Hands of an Angry God," at Enfield, Conn.

Moravian settlement of Bethlehem, Pa., founded.

Sixty fishing vessels go out from Marblehead, Mass., 70 from Gloucester.

Journeymen bakers in New York City go on strike.

Elizabeth Lucas Pinckney introduces indigo in South Carolina.

New Hampshire given own royal governor, Benning Wentworth, after joint governorship with Massachusetts since 1692.

Jan *The American Magazine,* first magazine in colonies, published by Andrew Bradford in Philadelphia. Three issues.

Jan *The General Magazine and Historical Chronicle for all the British Plantations in America,* Benjamin Franklin editor, begins publication in Philadelphia 3 days after appearance of *The American Magazine.* Continues 6 months.

June 1 Presbyterian Church splits into Old Side and New Side over revival methods of Great Awakening. Subsequently organize separate synods. Reunite, 1758.

1742

A "Singstunde" held at Bethlehem, Pa., forerunner of present-day Bach festivals.

Faneuil Hall, gift to city of Boston by Peter Faneuil, completed.

Benjamin Franklin invents a stove. Publishes 2 years later *An Account of the New Invented Pennsylvanian Fire-Places.*

The Compleat Housewife, an English cookbook, reprinted by William Parks, Virginia, America's first published cookbook.

Puppet shows in Philadelphia advertised in *The Pennsylvania-Gazette.*

Spanish attack upon Georgia settlements repulsed by Oglethorpe.

Sugar cane brought to Louisiana from San Domingo by Jesuits.

1743

American Philosophical Society organized in Philadelphia by Benjamin Franklin and Junto Club members.

Governor Oglethorpe leads retaliatory expedition against Spanish in vicinity of St. Augustine.

Seasonable Thoughts on the State of Religion in New England by Charles Chauncy, pastor of First Church in

Boston, published, Boston. Argues against abnormal practices of revivalism.

The American Magazine and Historical Chronicle, Jeremiah Gridley editor, third magazine in colonies, begins publication in Boston. Continues for 3 years.

Pierre Verendrye, French fur trader, sights Bighorn Range of Rocky Mountains.

1744

King George's War, 1744–1748, between England and France, American phase of War of the Austrian Succession, 1740–1748.

David Brainerd begins missionary labors among Indians of Pennsylvania and New Jersey.

Six Nations cede to England their lands in Ohio Valley north of river, in treaty with commissioners from Virginia, Maryland and Pennsylvania, at Lancaster, Pa.

Dr. Alexander Hamilton records his journey from Annapolis, Md., to Portsmouth, N. H., probably earliest recorded pleasure trip in America.

Samuel Richardson's *Pamela* reprinted in Philadelphia by Benjamin Franklin, first novel to be printed in America.

1745

William Logan, Chief Justice of Pennsylvania and friend of William Penn, founds the Loganian Library in Philadelphia.

June 17 Louisburg, on Cape Breton Island, taken from French by British under William Pepperell and Commodore Peter Warren, after 6-week siege.

1746

Princeton University, as College of New Jersey, founded by Presbyterians.

May 28 Massachusetts-Rhode Island boundary confirmed by the king in Council.

1747

Philosophic Solitude; or, The Choice of a Rural Life by William Livingston published, New York.

Indigo, first consignment, shipped from South Carolina to England.

1748

Draper's Meadows, first English settlement west of Allegheny Divide, founded by Virginia frontiersmen.

Loyal Land Company granted 800,000 acres in southwest Virginia by Council of Virginia. Dr. Thomas Walker appointed field agent 1749.

French, to win the Iroquois, found Sulpician mission at present-day Ogdensburg, N. Y.

Essays on Field-Husbandry in New-England by Rev. Jared Eliot published, Boston.

May 13 Bounty of 6 pence per pound on importation of indigo from colonies in America provided by act of Parliament.

Oct 18 Treaty of Aix-la-Chapelle restores Louisburg and Cape Breton Island to the French. End of King George's War.

1749

Academy founded at Philadelphia, Benjamin Franklin president of board of trustees. Later becomes University of Pennsylvania.

Murray-Kean dramatic company opens at Philadelphia, bringing English theater to America.

Great drought occurs this year in New England. They send to Pennsylvania, even to England, for hay.

Celoron de Bienville leads expedition from Lake Erie to assert French claim to Ohio Valley and deposits lead plates so inscribed at mouth of each important river.

Georgia trustees repeal action of 1735 which prohibited slavery in, and importation of rum into, colony.

Jan 1 First Hampshire Grant [Vermont], township of Bennington, made for settlement by Governor Benning Wentworth of New Hampshire, on land claimed by New York.

May 19 Ohio Company, organized by Virginians and Englishmen, chartered by George II, with grant of 500,000 acres on upper Ohio River.

June Halifax founded in Nova Scotia by Lord Halifax and 2,500 settlers from England.

1750

Bituminous coal first mined in America in Richmond Basin, Va.

Jacob Yoder, Pennsylvanian, invents flatboat for inland waters.

Stage performances prohibited in Massachusetts by General Court.

A Discourse Concerning Unlimited Submission and Non-resistance to the Higher Powers by Jonathan Mayhew published.

Iron Act of Parliament prohibits colonial manufacture of iron beyond pig and bar stage, but allows entry of pig and bar iron into England duty free.

Christopher Gist, Indian trader, sent out by Ohio Company to explore Ohio region and select lands for the Company. Builds Fort Cumberland at Will's Creek.

Cumberland Gap named by Thomas Walker as he passes through it on way to Kentucky country.

June 22 Jonathan Edwards dismissed from pastorate at Northampton, Mass., by council of churches. [Goes as missionary to Indians at Stockbridge.]

1751

Currency Act of Parliament prohibits issue of paper money in New England.

John Bartram's *Observations on American Plants* published.

Experiments and Observations in Electricity made at Philadelphia in America by Mr. Benjamin Franklin published in London.

1752

Franklin makes famous kite experiment.

Pennsylvania Hospital, first permanent hospital in America, opens in Philadelphia.

Philadelphia Contributionship for the Insurance of Homes by Loss of Fire established, first fire insurance company.

John Finley, fur trader, descends the Ohio as far as Louisville and explores Kentucky.

Jan 1 Gregorian Calendar officially adopted by Great Britain and her colonies.

June 23 Georgia becomes royal colony.

1753

Moravians from Bethlehem, Pa., purchase and settle large tract in North Carolina piedmont.

Marquis Duquesne de Menneville, new governor of Canada, sends force to Ohio country to erect Fort Presque Isle on Lake Erie, Fort le Boeuf on French

Creek, and to seize British trading post of Venango at junction of French Creek and Allegheny River.

Benjamin Franklin and William Hunter appointed joint postmasters-general of the colonies. Franklin holds this office till 1774.

Oct 31 George Washington commissioned by Governor Dinwiddie of Virginia to demand that French withdraw from Ohio country.

Dec 12 Washington delivers Governor Dinwiddie's demands to French commandant at Fort le Boeuf. Demands ignored.

1754

French and Indian War, 1754–1763, American phase of Seven Years' War.

King's College (Columbia) in New York City chartered by George II. Dr. Samuel Johnson president and first tutor.

Jonathan Edwards' *On the Freedom of the Will* published.

John Woolman publishes *Some Considerations on the Keeping of Negroes Recommended to the Professors of Christianity of Every Denomination.*

Semi-weekly stage and boat line between New York and Philadelphia, "load or no load," operated by James Wells.

Benjamin Franklin makes overland trip from Philadelphia to Portsmouth, N. H., in 18 days.

Susquehanna Company of Connecticut men purchases Wyoming Valley, on upper Susquehanna, from Six Nations. Claimed by Penn family, Valley is center of dispute until 1787.

Jan   Captain William Trent, sent by Governor Dinwiddie, builds fort at junction of Monongahela and Allegheny rivers.

Apr 17 Captain Trent expelled from fort at junction of Monongahela and Allegheny rivers by French who erect Fort Duquesne in its place.

May 28 Washington, dispatched by Dinwiddie to attack French at Fort Duquesne, meets and defeats small French force near Great Meadows, on the Monongahela.

June 19 Albany Congress, with representatives of New York, Pennsylvania, Maryland and New England colonies, meets at Albany to treat with Iroquois.

July 3 Washington, under great odds, surrenders to French at Fort Necessity, which he erected at Great Meadows. French left in possession of Ohio Valley.

July 10 Albany Plan of Union, drafted by Franklin, tentatively adopted by Albany Congress. Not accepted by colonies or Great Britain.

1755

Charles Chauncy of First Church in Boston writes *Benevolence of the Deity*.

Friends withdraw from Pennsylvania assembly, unwilling to vote for military defense.

Feb 20 General Edward Braddock disembarks at Hampton Roads, Va., as commander-in-chief in America, with 2 regiments of British regulars.

Apr 12 *Connecticut Gazette*, first newspaper in colony, published at New Haven.

Apr 14 Braddock meets with governors of New York, Massachusetts, Virginia, North Carolina, Pennsylvania and Maryland at Alexandria, Va., to plan 4-fold attack upon French at forts Duquesne, Crown Point, Niagara and in Nova Scotia.

June   Braddock's Road cut through forest from Fort Cumberland to the Monongahela.

June 16 Fort Beauséjour, Nova Scotia, surrenders to Colonel Robert Monckton after fortnight's siege.

July 9 Braddock defeated and mortally wounded by force of French and

Indians on Monongahela River, 7 miles from Fort Duquesne.

Sept 8   Battle of Lake George in Crown Point expedition. French defeated by English under Sir William Johnson. Crown Point not reached.

Oct 24   Niagara expedition under Gov-ernor Shirley of Massachusetts abandoned at Oswego. Garrison of 700 left at Oswego.

Autumn   About 6,000 French Aca-dians carried from Nova Scotia and distributed among British colonies from Massachusetts to Georgia. Theme of Longfellow's *Evangeline.*

Fall   Fort William Henry at head of Lake George built by Sir William Johnson.

Nov 18   New England shaken by an earthquake.

1756

Rule of 1756 proclaimed by British Admiralty, declaring neutrals in time of war shall not carry on trade legally closed in time of peace.

May   Marquis de Montcalm takes command of Canadian forces.

May 18   Great Britain formally de-clares war on France.

Aug 14   Fort Oswego destroyed by French under General Montcalm after 3-day siege.

Oct 7   *New Hampshire Gazette*, first newspaper in colony, begins publication at Portsmouth.

1757

First exhibition of colonial paintings held in New York.

History of New York by William Smith published in London.

William Pitt, Secretary of State for Southern Department, takes charge of war against France and directs campaign for conquest of Canada.

July 27   Franklin arrives in London as agent of Pennsylvania, remaining 5 years.

Aug 9   Fort William Henry under Colonel George Monroe captured by French under Montcalm.

1758

Jonathan Edwards succeeds his son-in-law, Rev. Aaron Burr, as president of College of New Jersey. Within 2 months, dies of smallpox.

The Great Christian Doctrine of Original Sin Defended by Jonathan Edwards published.

The Way to Wealth by Benjamin Franklin published.

July 8   Battle of Ticonderoga. British under General James Abercrombie defeated by French under Montcalm. British loss, 1,944; French, 377.

July 26   Louisburg on Cape Breton Island falls to British under Generals Jeffrey Amherst and James Wolfe and Admiral Edward Boscawen. French loss, about 1,000; British, 521.

Aug 27   Fort Frontenac (Kingston, On-tario) taken from French by British under Colonel John Bradstreet.

Nov 25   Fort Duquesne taken from French by Brigadier General John Forbes and renamed Fort Pitt. Ohio Valley abandoned to British.

1759

Francis Hopkinson writes "My Days Have Been So Wondrous Free," America's earliest secular musical composition.

Halley's Comet of 1682 appears in first predicted return.

John Winthrop, Harvard professor of Mathematics and Natural Philosophy, delivers 2 lectures on comets.

Rev. Andrew Burnaby begins 2 years' tour; account published in 1775 as *Travels through the Middle Settlements in North America.*

June 26 General James Wolfe and Admiral Charles Saunders with British fleet of nearly 300 ships and craft, ascending the St. Lawrence, anchor below Quebec.

July 25 Fort Niagara captured by British under Sir William Johnson.

July 26 French evacuate fort at Ti- conderoga before advance of Amherst.

Aug 4 Crown Point captured by Brit- ish from French.

Sept 13 Battle on Plains of Abraham overlooking Quebec. Complete victory for British. Both generals, Wolfe and Montcalm, killed. British loss, 58 killed, 597 wounded; French loss, 1,200 killed, wounded and prisoners.

Sept 17 Surrender of Quebec to Brit- ish.

Sept 18 British troops enter Quebec.

Oct Cherokee Indian War, 1759– 1761, in southern colonies begins.

1760

Population of the 13 colonies, estimated, 1,600,000.

Benjamin West of Pennsylvania arrives in Italy, first American to study art in Europe.

Mar 20 Boston swept by disastrous fire.

Apr 28 Second battle on Plains of Abraham. French defeat English.

May 16 French retire from Quebec as English reinforcements arrive.

Sept 8 Montreal surrenders to Gen- eral Jeffrey Amherst. All New France passes into hands of Great Britain.

Oct 26 George III ascends British throne.

1761

Virginia legislative acts raising duty on imported slaves vetoed by crown.

John Winthrop leads expedition to Newfoundland to observe transit of Venus across sun.

Feb 24 James Otis delivers fiery ad- dress before superior court of Massachusetts against use of Writs of Assistance by British customs officers: "An act against the Constitution is void."

May James Otis elected to Massa- chusetts General Court.

Dec 9 Colonial judgeships to be held only during pleasure of king, by royal order.

1762

James Otis publishes his first political pamphlet, *A Vindication of the Conduct of the House of Representatives of the Province of the Massachusetts-Bay,* in contest with governor.

St. Cecelia Society organized in Charleston, S. C., for choral singing.

United Company of Spermaceti Chandlers formed by Sephardic Jews, in Newport, R. I., soon to develop into monopoly of the industry in colonies.

William Shippen, Jr. lectures on anatomy in State House, Philadelphia, first American to make use of dissection to illustrate his subject.

Jan 4 Great Britain declares war on Spain. Occupies Martinique, Cuba and Manila during year.

Sept 29 "The Military Glory of Great Britain," dramatic exercise, performed at commencement of College of New Jersey.

Nov 3 Louis XV secretly cedes Louisiana west of the Mississippi plus Isle d'Orleans to his "dear and beloved cousin," king of Spain.

Nov 3 Preliminaries of peace signed at Fontainebleau by France and Great Britain.

1763

Survey of Mason and Dixon Line, boundary line between Pennsylvania and Maryland, begun by Charles Mason and Jeremiah Dixon. Completed in 1767, it is marked by milestones.

Feb 10 Treaty of Paris ends French and Indian War. France cedes to Great Britain Canada and all her territory east of the Mississippi except Isle d'Orleans, retaining fishing rights on Newfoundland Banks. Spain cedes Florida to Great Britain, who restores Cuba and Philippines to Spain.

Feb 23 Charles Townshend becomes First Lord of Trade with oversight of colonial administration.

May 7 Pontiac's War against British expansion and occupation of French posts in western territory begins with blockade of Detroit.

Oct 7 Royal Proclamation of 1763 prohibits extension of settlement beyond headwaters of streams flowing into the Atlantic, and divides new possessions on continent into 3 royal provinces, Quebec, East Florida and West Florida. Indian affairs placed under royal control.

Dec 1 Patrick Henry, arguing in Parsons' Cause in Virginia, challenges authority of crown to disallow colonial statutes.

1764

Brown University founded as Rhode Island College by Baptists.

James Davenport of Pennsylvania invents spinning and carding machinery.

The History of the Colony of Massachusetts Bay, vol. I, by Thomas Hutchinson, royal governor, published.

St. Louis, Mo., settled by Illinois French.

Employers' association organized in New York.

Mar George Grenville, chancellor of the exchequer, announces intention to impose stamp and other duties upon British colonists.

Apr 5 Sugar Act, replacing Molasses Act of 1733, passed by Parliament, "toward defraying necessary expenses of defending, protecting and securing said colonies." [Colonies dispatch memorials of protest.]

Apr 19 Currency Act of Parliament forbids colonists to issue paper money as legal tender.

July 20 Hampshire Grants (Vermont), west of the Connecticut, declared by king to belong to New York.

July 23 James Otis' pamphlet *The Rights of the British Colonies Asserted and Proved* published in Boston.

Sept Oxenbridge Thacher's *Sentiments of a British American,* following thought of James Otis, published.

Nov 17 Pontiac's War ends with submission to British on the Muskingum, in Ohio country.

Dec 22 Stephen Hopkins, governor of Rhode Island, publishes "The Rights of Colonies Examined," in *Providence Gazette,* by authority of assembly.

1765

Many Acadian refugees arrive in Louisiana (1765–1766).

First medical school in America opens in Philadelphia, later, College of Physicians and Surgeons.

New Jersey assembly appropriates 200 pounds for unemployment relief.

John Bartram appointed royal botanist in America by king.

Henry William Stiegel opens Manheim glassworks in Lancaster County, Pa., first in America to produce successfully table and decorative glass.

History of New Jersey by Samuel Smith published.

Feb   Martin Howard publishes anonymously at Newport *A Letter from a Gentleman at Halifax to his Friend in Rhode Island,* criticising arguments of Thacher, Otis and Hopkins.

Mar 22   Stamp Act becomes law, providing for stamps on newspapers, legal papers, pamphlets, playing cards, etc. Internal tax to raise revenue within colonies. [Sons of Liberty organize throughout colonies to resist enforcement of Stamp Act. Non-importation agreements adopted by colonial merchants.]

May 15   Quartering Act of Parliament orders colonists to provide barracks and supplies to British troops.

May 30   Virginia House of Burgesses passes 5 resolutions proposed by Patrick Henry denouncing Stamp Act.

June 8   Massachusetts General Court adopts circular letter calling representatives from all colonies to a congress to meet in New York in October.

Oct 7   Stamp Act Congress, with delegates from 9 colonies, meets in New York. "A declaration of rights and grievances of the colonists of America" adopted Oct. 19. Petitions to king and House of Lords adopted Oct. 22, to House of Commons Oct. 23.

Nov 1   Stamp Act goes into effect amid tolling of muffled bells and with flags at half mast.

Dec   John Dickinson publishes his pamphlet *The Late Regulations respect-* *ing the British Colonies on the Continent of America, Considered in a Letter from a Gentleman in Philadelphia to his Friend in London.*

1766

John Singleton Copley, American artist, exhibits his "Boy with the Squirrel" in London.

Rutgers University founded at New Brunswick, N. J., as Queen's College by Dutch Reformed Church.

Jan 17   London merchants petition Parliament for repeal of Stamp Act.

Feb 13   Benjamin Franklin declares, in examination before House of Commons, that Stamp Act cannot be enforced.

Mar 5   Don Antonio de Ulloa, first Spanish governor of Louisiana, arrives at New Orleans.

Mar 18   Stamp Act repealed. [New Yorkers in their rejoicing vote statues to George III and William Pitt.]

Mar 18   Declaratory Act of Parliament declares that Parliament has power to bind colonies "in all cases whatsoever."

July   Treaty of Oswego officially ends Pontiac's War.

1767

David Rittenhouse constructs the orrery, a machine reproducing solar system's movements for 5,000 years.

"The Prince of Parthia" by Thomas Godfrey, first American dramatist, performed at Southwark Theatre, Philadelphia. First American drama to be acted.

June 15   New York assembly, refusing to fulfill requirements of Quartering Act, is suspended by Parliament.

June 29   Customs Collecting Act establishes commissioners to administer acts of trade.

June 29 Townshend Revenue Act imposes duties on glass, red and white lead, painters' colors, tea and paper imported into colonies.

July 2 Tea Act provides drawback in favor of East India Company on re-exportation of tea from England to colonies.

Sept 4 Charles Townshend, chancellor of the exchequer, dies. Lord North succeeds him.

Oct 28 Boston town-meeting renews non-importation agreement. Similar action follows in other colonies to compel repeal of Townshend Acts.

Nov 5 Five members of American Board of Commissioners of the Customs, appointed by king, arrive in Boston.

Nov 20 Townshend Revenue Act goes into effect.

Dec 2 John Dickinson's *Letters of a Farmer in Pennsylvania to the Inhabitants of the British Colonies* appear in *Pennsylvania Chronicle*. Reprinted in newspapers throughout colonies. Argument against external taxation.

1768

Adam Kuhn, student of Linnaeus, begins lectures on botany at College of Pennsylvania.

John Witherspoon becomes president of College of New Jersey.

New York Chamber of Commerce founded.

Office of Secretary of State for the Colonies created by the crown and Lord Hillsborough appointed to the post.

War of the Regulation in western North Carolina, a frontier protest against tidewater control (1768–1771), begins.

Feb 11 Massachusetts House of Representatives adopts circular letter prepared by Samuel Adams to be sent to assemblies of other colonies, suggesting united opposition to Great Britain by discussion and petition.

June 10 John Hancock's sloop *Liberty* seized in Boston harbor by customs officials, following smuggling of wine. Riot follows.

June 30 Massachusetts House of Representatives refuses to rescind circular letter, as ordered by Lord Hillsborough. Assembly dissolved by Governor Bernard next day.

July 18 John Dickinson's "Song for American Freedom," patriotic ballad, published in *Boston Gazette*. Reprinted as "The Liberty Song."

Aug 1 Boston merchants in large meeting form non-importation agreement.

Sept 22 Delegates from 26 towns in Massachusetts, called by selectmen of Boston, meet in Faneuil Hall. Draw up statement of grievances. Adjourn Sept. 28.

Oct 1 Two regiments of British soldiers land in Boston from Halifax to enforce customs laws.

Oct 14 Treaty with Cherokees at Hard Labor, S. C., confirms their cessions to crown of land within North and South Carolina and Virginia.

Nov 5 Treaty of Fort Stanwix in which Iroquois cede to crown claims to territory between Ohio and Tennessee rivers.

1769

Anthracite coal first used in a smithy forge. Wilkes-Barre, Pa.

Dartmouth College founded by Congregationalists.

Dr. Benjamin Rush becomes first American professor of chemistry at College of Pennsylvania.

Old Colony Club formed at Plymouth to commemorate landing at Plymouth, 1620.

Daniel Boone begins exploration in Kentucky.

Watauga settlement begun in present eastern Tennessee by emigrants from southwest Virginia.

Feb 9 Trial in England of inciters of rebellion in colonies, reviving act of Henry VIII, urged by Parliament.

May 16 Virginia Resolves, protesting ministerial policy, drawn up by George Mason, adopted by House of Burgesses and ordered sent to other assemblies.

May 18 Virginia Association of ex-Burgesses, following dissolution of the House by governor, agrees upon non-importation of British goods.

June Vandalia Company, syndicate of Englishmen and Americans, petitions Board of Trade for purchase of 2,400,-000 acres in West Virginia and eastern Kentucky. Proposed colony of Vandalia approved by king, 1775.

July 16 San Diego Mission established by Father Junipero Serra, Franciscan, first Spanish mission and settlement in present California.

Nov 2 San Francisco Bay discovered by Governor Gaspar de Portolá of Lower California.

1770

Population of the 13 colonies estimated at 2,205,000.

Jan 31 Lord North becomes prime minister of Great Britain.

Mar 5 Lord North moves repeal of Townshend Revenue Act except tax on tea.

Mar 5 Boston massacre, 3 persons killed, 2 mortally wounded, 6 injured.

Apr 12 Townshend Revenue Act re-pealed.

Oct Captain Preston and some Brit-ish soldiers of Boston massacre episode acquitted, defended in jury trial by John Adams and Josiah Quincy.

1771

Benjamin West, American artist, exhibits his "The Death of Wolfe" at Royal Academy, London.

"The Flying Machine," stagewagon, with help of stageboat, advertised to make trip between New York and Philadelphia in one and a half days.

James Robertson brings family and settlers from North Carolina to Watauga settlement in eastern Tennessee.

May 16 Regulators in western North Carolina overthrown by Governor Tryon in battle at Alamance Creek.

July 12 Virginia House of Burgesses disapproves establishment of Protestant Episcopate in American colonies.

1772

Charles Willson Peale paints first of his 60 portraits of Washington, at Mount Vernon.

Francis Asbury appointed general superintendent of Methodists in America by John Wesley.

Philip Freneau and Hugh Henry Brackenridge deliver as commencement address at College of New Jersey their poem "The Rising Glory of America."

The Progress of Dulness by John Trumbull published. Satire on education and clergy.

Sommersett case. Lord Mansfield, Chief Justice, declares a slave is free the instant he sets foot on soil of England.

Watauga Association, a compact formed by settlers from Virginia and North Carolina in present eastern Tennessee, John Sevier and James Robertson leaders.

June 10 British revenue boat *Gaspee* burned by mob in Narragansett Bay where it ran aground.

Nov 2 Committees of Correspondence first organized in Massachusetts under

Samuel Adams and Joseph Warren, to be followed by similar committees throughout colonies.

1773

Blackstone's Commentaries, vol. I, reprinted at Philadelphia.

Benjamin Franklin's "Rules by which a Great Empire may be reduced to a Small One" published in British newspapers.

Poems on Various Subjects by Phillis Wheatley, young slave girl in Boston, published.

Philip Mazzei brings from Italy men and materials to launch silkworm culture in Virginia.

Colonization by free Negroes in West Africa advocated by President Ezra Stiles of Yale and Dr. Samuel Hopkins.

Mar 12 Virginia House of Burgesses appoints Provincial Committee of Correspondence to keep in touch with other colonies.

May   Regulating Act, passed by Parliament to assist British East India Company, encourages its shipping of tea to America, subject to threepenny tax.

Nov   John Dickinson publishes *Two Letters on the Tea Tax.*

Dec 16 Boston Tea Party. Boston citizens throw tea from ships into harbor. Charleston, Philadelphia and New York also resist landing of tea.

1774

Benjamin Franklin's articles "On the Rise and Progress of the Differences between Great Britain and Her American Colonies" published in *Public Advertiser,* London.

John Woolman's *Journal,* begun 1755, published.

President Myles Cooper of King's College, loyalist, publishes anonymous pamphlet *A Friendly Address to all Reasonable Americans.* Mobbed next year, escapes to England.

Summary View of the Rights of British America . . ., pamphlet by Thomas Jefferson published, Williamsburg and London.

Harrodsburg, first distinct settlement in Kentucky, founded by James Harrod from Pennsylvania.

Rhode Island and Connecticut prohibit importation of slaves.

Mar 31 Boston Port Act, first of coercive acts, receives royal assent.

**May   ** *Observations on the Act of Parliament, commonly called the Boston Port Bill; with Thoughts on Civil Society and Standing Armies,* pamphlet by Josiah Quincy published, Boston.

Considerations on the Nature and Extent of the Legislative Authority of the British Parliament by James Wilson published, following Josiah Quincy's *Observations.*

May 12 Boston Committee of Correspondence recommends to all colonies suspension of trade with Great Britain.

May 13 General Thomas Gage arrives in Boston to supersede Hutchinson as governor and to command British troops. Four regiments arrive shortly.

May 20 Massachusetts   Government Act, nullifying charter, receives royal assent.

May 20 Administration of Justice Act receives royal assent.

May 24 Virginia House of Burgesses sets aside June 1, when Port Act will go into effect, as day of fasting and prayer.

May 26 Virginia House of Burgesses dissolved by Governor Dunmore.

May 27 Virginia Burgesses, meeting unofficially at Raleigh Tavern, Williamsburg, adopt resolution calling for annual intercolonial congress. Copies of resolution sent to other legislatures.

June 1 Boston harbor, where more than 600 vessels entered in previous year, closed to imports and exports by Boston Port Act of March 31.

June 2 Quartering Act passed by Parliament.

June 17 Massachusetts elects delegates to intercolonial congress to meet at Philadelphia. Sets date as Sept. 1.

June 22 Quebec Act of Parliament extends boundary of province of Quebec to Ohio River.

Aug 6 Ann Lee, founder of Shaker movement in America, arrives at New York from Liverpool with 8 followers.

Aug 27 Transylvania Company for land speculation and settlement of Kentucky organized by Judge Richard Henderson and North Carolina friends.

Sept 1 General Gage seizes Massachusetts' stock of powder at Charlestown.

Sept 5 First Continental Congress assembles in Philadelphia, with Peyton Randolph president. All colonies but Georgia represented.

Sept 17 Suffolk Resolves, drawn up by Joseph Warren and adopted by convention in Suffolk County, Mass., protesting against coercive acts of Parliament, laid before Congress and approved.

Sept 28 Joseph Galloway, conservative delegate from Pennsylvania, submits to Congress "Plan of a Proposed Union between Great Britain and the Colonies" and proposes that Congress declare its abhorrence of any idea of independence. Rejected by majority of 1 vote.

Autumn Loyalist party is taking shape.

Oct George Washington writes that independence is not desired by any thinking man in all North America.

Oct 5 Massachusetts assembly, meeting in Salem, reorganized as a provincial congress. Subsequently adjourning to Concord, elects John Hancock president and forms military organization of minute-men.

Oct 10 Battle of Point Pleasant at mouth of the Great Kanawha won by Virginians, ending Lord Dunmore's War against Shawnees. Safeguards settlement in Kentucky and Tennessee.

Oct 14 Declaration of Rights and Grievances adopted by Congress.

Oct 20 The Association adopted by Congress to enforce suspension of trade with Great Britain after Dec. 1. Ratified within 6 months by all colonies except New York and Georgia.

Oct 26 First Continental Congress adjourns until May 10, 1775, if necessary at that date.

Nov 16 Rev. Samuel Seabury, "Westchester Farmer," begins Loyalist pamphlet attack upon Continental Congress. *Free Thoughts on the Proceedings of the Continental Congress* his first blast.

Nov 30 Thomas Paine arrives in Philadelphia from England, introduced by Franklin.

Dec Alexander Hamilton replies to Rev. Samuel Seabury in *A Full Vindication of the Measures of the Congress. . . .*

Dec 12 Daniel Leonard, Tory lawyer, publishes first of series of weekly letters *To the Inhabitants of the Province of Massachusetts* (Dec. 12, 1774–Apr. 3, 1775) under pen name of "Massachusettensis."

1775

United Company of Philadelphia for Promoting American Manufactures organized.

David Bushnell builds the *Turtle,* a submarine for military purposes, in Saybrook, Conn.

Words of "Yankee Doodle" written by Edward Barnes and set to old English tune.

Jan 23 John Adams replies to Daniel Leonard in *Boston Gazette* over signature of "Novanglus" (Jan. 23–Apr.17).

Feb 1 Earl of Chatham's plan for conciliation with colonies presented to Parliament. Rejected at first reading.

Feb 1 Second provincial congress of Massachusetts meets in Cambridge to put province in state of defense.

Feb 27 Lord North's Conciliatory Res- olution agreed to by House of Commons.

Mar 10 Daniel Boone sent with 30 axemen by Transylvania Company to cut road to Kentucky River, the Wilderness Road.

Mar 17 Treaty of Sycamore Shoals. Cherokees for $10,000 in goods cede to Transylvania Company territory between Kentucky River and highlands south of the Cumberland.

Mar 22 Edmund Burke delivers ad- dress on conciliation with America in House of Commons.

Mar 30 New England Restraining Act to restrain trade of New England receives royal assent.

Apr 1 Boonesborough founded by Daniel Boone on Kentucky River.

Apr 14 First abolition society in America organized in Pennsylvania.

Apr 18–19 "Midnight ride" of Paul Revere and William Dawes gives alarm of British approach to Concord.

Apr 19 Battles of Lexington and Concord. British destroy military stores, retreat to Lexington and then to Boston. Beginning of War for Independence.

News of Lexington reaches Philadelphia, April 24; Virginia, April 30; North Carolina, a week later; and Charleston, May 8.

Apr 19 Siege of British in Boston begins, continuing until March 17, 1776.

May 10 Ticonderoga captured from British by Ethan Allen.

May 10 Second Continental Congress meets in Philadelphia.

May 12 Crown Point taken from British by Seth Warner.

May 23 A provincial congress in New York called by committee of 100 to withstand strong Tory party in colony.

May 23 Transylvania settlers, in con- vention, adopt plan of government.

May 24 John Hancock chosen presi- dent of Second Continental Congress.

May 25 British Generals Howe, Bur- goyne and Clinton arrive in Boston with troops.

May 31 Mecklenburg Resolves, adopt- ed by frontiersmen of Charlotte in Mecklenburg County, N. C., declare null and void all laws and commissions from king and Parliament.

June 9 Massachusetts, upon request, advised by Congress to form temporary government.

June 14 Congress resolves to raise 10 companies of riflemen and sets pay for officers and privates for Continental Army.

June 15 George Washington ap- pointed commander-in-chief of Continental Army.

June 17 Battle of Bunker Hill, victory for British, save in heavy losses: British killed and wounded, between 1,000 and 1,500; American, 411. General Joseph Warren, colonial leader, killed.

June 22 Congress resolves to issue $2,000,000 in bills of credit, Continental money.

July 3 Washington takes command of Continental Army at Cambridge after traveling 12 days from Philadelphia.

July 6 Congress adopts "Declaration of the Causes and Necessity of Taking up Arms," prepared by Dickinson and Jefferson.

July 8 Petition to king, offering recon- ciliation, drafted by Dickinson, adopted by Congress.

July 31 Congress adopts reply to Lord North's Conciliatory Resolution which had reached Congress May 26.

Aug "On the Conqueror of America Shut up in Boston" and "General Gage's

Soliloquy," poems of the Revolution by Philip Freneau, published.

Aug   Thomas Paine, editor of *Pennsylvania Magazine,* inserts an essay on females, early plea for underprivileged sex.

Aug 7 John Trumbull's *McFingal,* first canto, satire on General Gage, published in *Connecticut Courant.*

Aug 23 Proclamation of Rebellion issued by order of George III.

Sept 1 Petition of July 8 to king from Congress refused at hearing.

Oct 18 Falmouth (Portland) burned by British.

Nov 12 Montreal taken from British by General Richard Montgomery.

Nov 28 American Navy founded by Congress, adopting rules for its regulation.

Nov 29 Committee on Foreign Corre-spondence appointed by Congress.

Dec 22 Trade and intercourse with colonies prohibited by act of Parliament.

Dec 31 Battle of Quebec. Colonists under Benedict Arnold and General Richard Montgomery repulsed. Canada lost to colonists.

1776

Phi Beta Kappa Society founded at College of William and Mary.

New York Hospital, second in colonies, opened.

Philadelphia Friends' Meeting excludes those holding slaves.

Spanish presidio and mission at San Francisco founded.

Spanish discover mouth of Columbia River while moving north to counter rumored Russian and British activity.

Virginia abolishes entail. Within 10 years all states but 2 have done so.

Devereaux Jarratt writes *A Brief Narrative of the Revival of Religion in Virginia,* account of the great revival.

Thoughts on the Nature of War by Anthony Benezet published.

Jan 1 Norfolk, Va., burned and can-nonaded by order of Lord Dunmore, governor.

Jan 1 Continental flag with 13 stripes raised by Washington before headquarters at Cambridge.

Jan 5 New Hampshire adopts first written state constitution.

Jan 10 *Common Sense* **by Thomas** Paine published in Philadelphia. Converts thousands to idea of independence.

Feb 27 At Moore's Creek Bridge, Scottish loyalists from upper North Carolina crushed by Carolinian patriots, 900 prisoners taken.

Mar 3 Silas Deane appointed com-mercial agent to France by Congress.

Mar 4 Dorchester Heights fortified by Washington.

Mar 14 Congress advises disarming of loyalists.

Mar 17 Boston evacuated by British when General William Howe, with army and 900 loyalists, sails for Nova Scotia.

Mar 23 Congress authorizes privateers to prey upon British commerce.

Mar 26 South Carolina adopts state constitution.

Apr 6 Congress opens ports of colonies to all countries "not subject to the King of Great Britain," but prohibits importation of slaves.

Apr 12 Provincial congress of North Carolina instructs her delegates in Congress to stand for independence, first colony to do so.

Apr 13 Washington arrives in New York from Cambridge with main part of his army.

May 10 Congress adopts resolution urging each colony without a government sufficient to its needs to adopt such a government.

May 15 Virginia Convention instructs Virginia delegates in Congress to propose independence.

May 29 Committee on Mechanics in New York urges New York delegates in Congress to vote for independence.

June 7 Richard Henry Lee, chairman of Virginia delegation, offers resolution in Congress "That these United Colonies are and of right ought to be free and independent states," and that a plan of confederation be submitted to the several colonies.

June 10 Pierre Caron de Beau- marchais arranges French loan to Americans. Consent to loan obtained from Louis XVI by Comte de Vergennes in May.

June 11 Committee to draft a decla- ration of independence appointed by Congress, Thomas Jefferson chairman.

June 12 Committee to draft plan for a confederation appointed by Congress, John Dickinson chairman.

June 12 Virginia Bill of Rights, draft- ed by George Mason, as part of Virginia constitution, adopted by Virginia Convention.

June 28 At Sullivan's Island, Charles- ton, S. C., patriots repulse British fleet under General Clinton and Sir Peter Parker.

June 29 Virginia adopts state consti- tution.

June 30 General William Howe and his troops from Halifax disembark on Staten Island.

July 2 New Jersey adopts state consti- tution.

July 2 Lee's resolution declaring inde- pendence adopted by Congress.

July 4 Declaration of Independence, as drafted by Jefferson and amended, adopted by Congress and signed by John Hancock, president.

July 5 Copies of Declaration of Inde- pendence sent to the several state assemblies.

July 9 Declaration of Independence formally adopted by provincial congress in New York.

July 12 Plan for confederation of the 13 colonies reported to Congress by Dickinson.

July 12 British fleet, Lord Richard Howe in command, arrives from England off Staten Island.

Aug 1 Sir Henry Clinton and his troops arrive at Staten Island from Charleston.

Aug 2 Declaration of Independence signed by members of Congress present.

Aug 27 Battle of Long Island. Patri- ots under General Israel Putnam defeated by General Howe.

Aug 29 Washington retreats during night from Long Island to New York City.

Sept 15 British occupy New York City; Washington retreats to Harlem Heights.

Sept 16 British repulsed at Harlem Heights.

Sept 21 Delaware state constitution proclaimed.

Sept 22 Captain Nathan Hale cap- tured and executed as spy by British.

Sept 26 Benjamin Franklin, Thomas Jefferson and Silas Deane appointed commissioners to France to obtain aid. In December, Arthur Lee takes Jefferson's place.

Sept 28 Pennsylvania adopts state con- stitution by convention.

Oct 3 Congress authorizes domestic loan of $5,000,000 at 4 per cent.

Oct 11 Battle of Island of Valcour on Lake Champlain. Benedict Arnold's fleet, though defeated, delays push toward south by Sir Guy Carleton who soon withdraws to Canada.

Oct 28 White Plains engagement be- tween Washington and Howe narrow victory for British.

Nov 11 Maryland adopts state constitution.

Nov 16 Fort Washington surrendered to British.

Nov 19 Watauga settlement received under jurisdiction of North Carolina as Washington County.

Nov 20 General Nathanael Greene surrenders Fort Lee to British.

Nov 21 Washington begins retreat across New Jersey.

Dec Negotiations for French aid begun in Paris.

Dec 1 Cornwallis reaches Raritan River, hot on trail of Washington.

Dec 6 Transylvania incorporated by Virginia as County of Kentucky.

Dec 8 British take possession of Newport, R. I.

Dec 8 British reach Trenton.

Dec 8 Washington crosses Delaware River near Trenton into Pennsylvania.

Dec 18 North Carolina adopts state constitution by convention.

Dec 19 Thomas Paine's first number of the *American Crisis* printed: "These are the times that try men's souls."

Dec 20 Congress meets at Baltimore, Md.

Dec 25 Washington crosses the Delaware at night for surprise attack upon British at Trenton.

Dec 26 Battle of Trenton. Washington inflicts stinging defeat upon British. Over 1,000 Hessians captured and taken across the Delaware.

Dec 29 Washington occupies Trenton.

1777

Decisive year of the Revolution.

Oliver Evans, Pennsylvania, invents cardmaking machine.

Directions for Preserving the Health of Soldiers by Dr. Benjamin Rush published in *Pennsylvania Packet.*

Jan 3 Battle of Princeton. Three British regiments defeated by Washington. [Washington goes into winter quarters at Morristown. Cornwallis retreats to New Brunswick.]

Jan 15 New Hampshire Grants (Vermont) makes declaration of independence in convention at Westminster and seeks of Congress recognition as state.

Feb 5 Georgia adopts state constitution.

Mar 4 Congress returns to Philadelphia from Baltimore.

Apr 20 New York adopts state constitution by convention.

Apr 26 American stores at Danbury, Conn., destroyed by British.

Apr 27 Benedict Arnold defeats British at Ridgefield, Conn.

June 14 Stars and Stripes adopted by Congress as American flag, 13 stars and 13 stripes.

June 30 General Howe and British troops leave New Jersey for New York and vicinity.

July 1 General Burgoyne's troops appear before Ticonderoga.

July 6 Ticonderoga abandoned to Burgoyne by Americans under General Arthur St. Clair.

July 7 At Hubbartton, Vt., Americans in retreat from Ticonderoga are defeated.

July 8 Vermont by convention adopts written constitution. Provides for manhood suffrage and abolition of slavery.

July 23 General Howe with troops leaves Staten Island for Philadelphia by way of Chesapeake Bay.

July 29 General Philip Schuyler, at approach of Burgoyne, evacuates Fort Edward and retreats down the Hudson.

July 31 Marquis de Lafayette commissioned major-general by Congress.

Aug 4 Command of Continental Army of the North transferred from General Schuyler to General Gates by Congress.

Aug 6 Battle of Oriskany, N.Y., Americans check British invasion down Mohawk Valley. General Nicholas Herkimer killed.

Aug 16 Battle of Bennington. Captain John Stark, reinforced by Colonel Seth Warner, defeats British under Colonel Friedrich Baum.

Aug 22 Colonel Barry St. Leger, British, abandons siege of Fort Stanwix at approach of Benedict Arnold, returns to Canada.

Sept 11 Battle of Brandywine. Washington, severely defeated in flank movement by General Howe, retards Howe's advance upon Philadelphia.

Sept 19 First Battle of Saratoga or Bemis Heights. Burgoyne suffers heavy losses but holds field.

Sept 20 At Paoli, Pa., General Anthony Wayne defeated by British.

Sept 26 British under General Howe occupy Philadelphia.

Sept 27 Congress meets for one day at Lancaster, Pa., and adjourns.

Sept 30 Congress meets at York, Pa. Adjourns immediately.

Oct 4 Washington defeated at Germantown, Pa.

Oct 7 Second battle of Saratoga or Bemis Heights. Burgoyne defeated by General Horatio Gates. Benedict Arnold major inspiration to victory.

Oct 17 Burgoyne surrenders entire force to Gates in "Convention of Saratoga." British army to surrender arms, march to Boston and embark on transports, not to serve again in the war. Victory assures French aid for American cause.

Nov 15 Articles of Confederation adopted by Congress.

Nov 16–20 British take Fort Mifflin and Fort Mercer and gain complete control of the Delaware.

Nov 17 Articles of Confederation submitted to states for ratification.

Nov 22 First requisition upon states, to be paid in paper money, made by Congress. By Oct. 6, 1779, 4 requisitions totalling $95,000,000 are made.

Nov 27 Confiscation of loyalists' estates approved by Congress.

Nov 28 John Adams appointed commissioner to France, succeeding Silas Deane.

Dec Washington goes into winter quarters at Valley Forge.

Dec Conway cabal, to discredit and displace Washington, ends unsuccessfully, early 1778.

Dec 7 Word of Burgoyne's defeat at Saratoga reaches American commissioners in Paris.

1778

Captain James Cook explores Pacific coast from Oregon northward, which becomes basis for English claim to region.

Olmstead case. Pennsylvania court sets at nought decision of commissioners appointed by Congress to hear appeals in privateering captures.

Virginia abolishes slave trade.

Jan 21 "The Battle of the Kegs" by Francis Hopkinson published in *New Jersey Gazette.*

Feb 6 Franco-American Treaty of Commerce and Treaty of Alliance signed in Paris. Ratified by Congress May 4.

Feb 17 Lord North presents to Parliament plan for conciliation with colonies.

Feb 23 Baron Von Steuben (Prussian) arrives at Valley Forge where he assists Washington in drilling of army.

Mar 19 South Carolina adopts state constitution.

May 12 George Rogers Clark, with some 150 Virginia volunteers, sets out for Kaskaskia, major British post in Illinois country.

June 17 Peace offers, brought by commissioners from Parliament, rejected by Congress. Reassured by French alliance, only independence will satisfy.

June 18 Philadelphia evacuated by Sir Henry Clinton, who begins march across New Jersey to New York. Americans enter as British leave.

June 28 Battle of Monmouth won by Washington. British move on to New York.

July 2 Congress returns to Philadelphia.

July 4 Wyoming Valley massacre in Pennsylvania by Tories and Indians.

July 4 Court-martial of General Charles Lee for disobedience at Battle of Monmouth opens at New Brunswick. Found guilty Aug 12.

July 5 Kaskaskia falls to George Rogers Clark, followed by Cahokia and Vincennes.

July 8 Count D'Estaing's French fleet of 18 vessels reaches Delaware Capes to aid Americans, only to learn British have left Philadelphia.

July 9 Delegates in Congress from Massachusetts, Rhode Island, Connecticut, New York, Pennsylvania, Virginia and South Carolina sign Articles of Confederation. North Carolina, July 21; Georgia, July 24; New Hampshire, Aug. 8; New Jersey, Nov. 26; Delaware, May 5, 1779.

July 10 France declares war against Great Britain.

July 29 D'Estaing's French fleet arrives off Newport from New York.

Aug 29 General John Sullivan and Americans leave Newport to British, D'Estaing and fleet having sailed from Newport for Boston.

Sept 14 Benjamin Franklin appointed minister to France.

Nov 11 Massacre of settlers of Cherry Valley, N. Y., by Tories and Iroquois.

Dec 17 Vincennes retaken by British under Colonel Hamilton.

Dec 29 Savannah, Ga., captured by British. Americans retreat across Savannah River.

1779

George Wythe named at William and Mary to first professorship of law in an American college.

First Universalist congregation organized by John Murray, Englishman, at Gloucester, Mass.

Jan 6 British capture Sunbury, Ga.

Jan 29 Augusta, Ga., taken by British under General John Campbell.

Feb 3 General William Moultrie repulses British at Port Royal, S. C.

Feb 14 At Kettle Creek, Ga., British defeated.

Feb 25 Vincennes surrendered by Colonel Henry Hamilton and British to George Rogers Clark.

Mar 3 British victorious at Briar Creek, Ga.

May 31 Stony Point and Verplanck Point, N. Y., taken by British.

June 16 Spain declares war against Great Britain on promise of France to help recover Gibraltar and Floridas. Makes no alliance with America.

July Loyalist expedition led by Governor Tryon of New York raids Connecticut coast, burns Fairfield and Norwalk, and ships in New Haven harbor.

July 16 Stony Point, N. Y., retaken by Anthony Wayne and Americans in midnight attack.

Aug Indian villages in Genesee Valley, N. Y., destroyed by Sullivan and Americans in march against Six Nations.

Aug 19 Americans under Major Henry Lee take British garrison at Paulus Hook (Jersey City), N. J.

Aug 29 Sullivan defeats Tories and Indians in Battle of Newtown near Elmira.

Sept   British ports Manchac, Baton Rouge and Natchez taken by Galvez, Spanish governor of Louisiana.

Sept 16 Siege of Savannah, Ga., begun by Americans under General Benjamin Lincoln and French under Count D'Estaing.

Sept 23 John Paul Jones' naval victory with the *Bonhomme Richard* over the *Serapis* off coast of Scotland.

Sept 27 John Adams appointed to negotiate peace with Great Britain; and John Jay appointed minister to Spain.

Oct 11–25 British evacuate Rhode Island.

Oct 20 Siege of Savannah abandoned by Americans and French. Count Pulaski mortally wounded. D'Estaing sails for France.

Nov 29 Congress issues last paper money, $10,000,140, making total authorized since June, 1775, $241,552,780.

Dec   Washington goes into winter quarters at Morristown, N. J.

1780

Population estimated, 2,781,000.

American Academy of Arts and Sciences organized at Boston.

Professor of modern languages appointed at William and Mary College at suggestion of Thomas Jefferson.

In *Holmes v. Walton* New Jersey Court declares invalid an act of its Legislature, first case of state court declaring a law unconstitutional.

Phillips Academy at Andover, Mass., incorporated. First in New England.

Transylvania College founded in Kentucky.

Jan 15 Court of appeals established by Congress.

Mar 1 Pennsylvania legislature provides for gradual emancipation of slaves.

Mar 14 Mobile taken by Galvez, Spanish governor of Louisiana.

Mar 18 Forty to One Act passed by Congress. Continental bills to be redeemed at 1/40 of face value.

May 12 Charleston, S. C., under General Lincoln surrenders to Sir Henry Clinton and British after month's siege; 2,500 Continental soldiers taken prisoner.

May 19 Uncommonly dark day in most parts of New England, "as dark as it commonly is at one hour after sunset." Some thought it was day of judgment.

June 7 Massachusetts state constitution, first to be adopted by convention specifically called for that purpose, ratified by popular vote. Its Bill of Rights, containing "all men are born free and equal," understood to apply to slavery.

June 23 Battle of Springfield, N. J. General Greene defeats British.

July 10 Count de Rochambeau arrives at Newport with 6,000 French troops. Fleet and troops blockaded there by Clinton for a year.

Aug 3 Benedict Arnold given command of West Point.

Aug 16 Battle of Camden, S. C. Americans under Gates severely defeated by Cornwallis.

Aug 26 First specie requisition upon states, $3,000,000, made by Congress. Three specie requisitions by Mar. 16, 1781, amounting to $10,642,988.

Sept 23 Benedict Arnold's plot to surrender West Point to Sir Henry Clinton revealed through capture of British spy Major André. Arnold escapes to British ship *Vulture*.

Oct 2   Major André hanged as spy.

Oct 5   United States accepts rules of Armed Neutrality Agreement between Russia, Denmark and Sweden: to overturn England's Rule of 1756, principle is "free ships make free goods."

Oct 7   Battle of King's Mountain, N. C. British and Tories under Major Ferguson defeated by mounted backwoodsmen. Turning point in war in South.

Oct 10   Resolution of Congress urges states to cede their western lands to Union and pledges its faith that such lands shall be settled and admitted as states.

Oct 10   Connecticut votes to cede western lands to Union.

Nov 4   Congress asks states for quotas in flour, hay and pork toward war support.

Dec 20   Great Britain declares war on Netherlands.

1781

Pueblo de los Angeles founded in California.

A General History of Connecticut . . . By a Gentleman of the Province by Samuel Peters, loyalist, published, London.

Stanger brothers, former Wistar employees, start glass factory at Glassboro, N. J.

Jan   Fort St. Joseph [Michigan] taken from British by Spanish under Don Eugenio Pourré. Basis for Spanish claim to Illinois country at end of war.

Jan 1   Pennsylvania troops at Morristown break camp and demand back pay. Congress subsequently yields to demands.

Jan 2   Virginia cedes to Union her claims to western lands north of the Ohio, with conditions. Not acceptable to Congress.

Jan 5   Benedict Arnold with British troops plunders and burns Richmond, Va.

Jan 17   Battle of the Cowpens, N. C. Tarleton's British cavalry defeated by General Daniel Morgan's men.

Jan 20   New Jersey troops mutiny. Soon quelled by General Robert Howe from West Point.

Jan 28–Feb 13   General Greene, pursued by Cornwallis, makes masterly retreat through North Carolina into Virginia.

Feb 3   Five per cent duty on imports proposed by Congress. Fails through opposition of one state, Rhode Island.

Feb 20   Robert Morris chosen superintendent of finance by Congress.

Mar 1   New York's deed of cession of western lands presented in Congress.

Mar 1   Articles of Confederation become effective when signed by delegates of last state, Maryland, assured of cession of western lands by New York and Virginia.

Mar 2   United States in Congress assembles, still popularly called Continental Congress.

Mar 12   James Madison in committee report advises authorization of Congress to compel states by force to fulfill their federal obligations.

Mar 15   Battle of Guilford Court House, N. C. Called victory by British, although they are forced to leave North Carolina for Virginia. General Greene turns back to retake South Carolina and Georgia.

Spring   Continental money has ceased to have value. "Not worth a Continental."

Apr 25   Greene and American troops defeated at Hobkirk's Hill, S. C.

May 9   Pensacola surrenders to Spanish, completing their conquest of West Florida.

May 20   Cornwallis joins Benedict Arnold at Petersburg, Va.

June 15 Congress appoints peace commission, John Adams, John Jay, Benjamin Franklin, Henry Laurens and Thomas Jefferson, to treat with Great Britain. Jefferson declines.

June 19 General Greene and Americans repulsed at Fort Ninety-Six, S. C., British stronghold.

July 6 Lafayette repulsed by Cornwallis at Jamestown Ford, Va.

Aug 1 Cornwallis, pressed by Lafayette, retires to Yorktown and Gloucester Point on York River, Va., defensible position.

Aug 10 Robert R. Livingston chosen by Congress secretary for foreign affairs.

Aug 22 Edmund Randolph offers committee report asking more powers for Congress.

Aug 30 Comte De Grasse with French fleet arrives in Chesapeake Bay from West Indies.

Sept 5 De Grasse badly cripples British fleet under Admiral Graves in Chesapeake Bay.

Sept 5 Allied Armies, 16,000 strong, under Washington, Lafayette and Rochambeau, arrive at head of Chesapeake Bay.

Sept 6 Benedict Arnold plunders and burns New London, Conn.

Sept 8 Battle of Eutaw Springs, S. C. Americans under Greene retreat and British retire to Charleston.

Sept 10 De Barras, French commander, arrives with squadron in Chesapeake Bay from Newport and joins De Grasse the next day.

Sept 28 Siege of Yorktown begins.

Oct 19 Siege of Yorktown ends with Cornwallis' surrender. 7,000 British soldiers become prisoners of war.

Oct 24 Washington's dispatch of Oct. 19, announcing victory at Yorktown, read before Congress at Philadelphia. Members repair to Dutch Lutheran Church to give thanks.

Oct 30 General Benjamin Lincoln chosen secretary at war by Congress.

Dec 22 General Lafayette sails from Boston for France.

Dec 31 Bank of North America at Philadelphia incorporated by Congress.

1782

First complete English Bible to be printed in America issued by Robert Aitken, Philadelphia, approved by Congress, Sept. 21.

Letters from an American Farmer by St. Jean de Crevecoeur published.

King's Chapel, Boston, declares for Unitarianism. Adopts revised liturgy 1785.

New York Legislature proposes convention to revise and amend Articles of Confederation. Congress takes no action.

Feb 27 House of Commons urges king to end war against America.

Mar 20 Lord North resigns as prime minister.

Apr 19 The Netherlands recognizes independence of United States.

June 20 Great Seal of United States adopted by Congress.

July 11 Savannah, Ga., evacuated by British.

Oct 29 New York cession of western lands accepted by Congress.

Nov 30 Provisional treaty of peace signed in Paris by American commissioners, Franklin, Jay and Adams, with British negotiator Richard Oswald. Negotiations made independently of France.

Dec 14 Charleston, S. C., evacuated by British.

1783

Post-war depression, 1783–1787.

Dickinson College founded in Pennsylvania.

Timothy Dwight opens school for girls as well as boys at Greenfield Hill, Conn.

Quaco, a slave, declared free by Massachusetts court, interpreting her Bill of Rights. In Federal census, 1790, Massachusetts is only state to report "no slaves."

Spelling Book by Noah Webster published.

Feb 5 Sweden recognizes independence of United States.

Feb 25 Denmark recognizes independence of United States.

Mar 15 Washington at Newburgh, N. Y., urges group of dissatisfied army officers to have confidence in justice of Congress. As a result, Congress votes them full pay for 5 years.

Mar 24 Spain recognizes independence of United States.

Apr 18 Congress urges states to alter Articles of Confederation to give her power to levy import duties for 25 years, duties to be applied on national debt. Fails through opposition of one state, New York, 1786.

Apr 19 End of war proclaimed by Congress just 8 years after battle of Lexington.

May 13 Society of Cincinnati formed by commissioned army officers at time of disbanding.

June 5 *Vermont Gazette*, first newspaper in state, begins publication at Bennington.

June 30 Congress meets in Princeton, following mutiny of unpaid soldiers in Philadelphia.

July Russia recognizes independence of United States.

Sept 3 Definitive treaty of peace signed by Great Britain and United States at Paris.

Sept 3 Great Britain signs peace terms with France and Spain at Versailles. Florida ceded to Spain by Great Britain.

Oct 31 New Hampshire convention proclaims constitution, adopted in popular election.

Nov 2 Washington issues "Farewell Address to the Army" from Rocky Hill, N. J.

Nov 3 Army disbands by congressional order.

Nov 25 Last of British army leaves New York.

Nov 26 Congress meets at Annapolis.

Dec 4 Washington bids farewell to officers of army at Fraunces Tavern, N. Y.

Dec 23 Washington resigns commission as commander-in-chief before Congress at Annapolis.

Dec 31 Foreign debt of U. S. at this date: France, $6,352,500; Spain, $174,017; Holland, $1,304,000.

1784

State of Franklin organized by citizens of Tennessee Valley; John Sevier chosen governor; Congress petitioned for admission as state.

Connecticut and Rhode Island adopt laws for gradual emancipation of slaves.

Reason, the Only Oracle of Man, by Ethan Allen published.

Jeremy Belknap's *History of New-Hampshire,* first of 3 vols., published.

Geography Made Easy by Jedediah Morse published.

Inquiry into the Effects of Ardent Spirits on the Human Body and Mind by Benjamin Rush published.

Notes on Virginia by Thomas Jefferson published in Paris.

Tapping Reeve opens law school at Litchfield, Conn.

First bale of cotton shipped to England. (Cotton centennial, 1884.)

Benjamin Franklin invents bi-focals.

Jan 14 Congress ratifies definitive treaty of peace with Great Britain.

Feb 7 Massachusetts Bank of Boston chartered.

Feb 22 The *Empress of China* sails from New York for Canton by way of Cape Horn, beginning U. S. trade with China.

Mar   John Jacob Astor, German immigrant, lands in Baltimore with 7 flutes, his stock in trade.

Mar 1 Virginia's final cession of western lands to the Union accepted by Congress.

Mar 15 Bank of New York organized. Opens June 9.

Apr 8 Lord Sydney writes Governor-General Haldimand of Canada that U. S. posts on Great Lakes "will not be evacuated until articles of Treaty of Peace are complied with."

Apr 23 Jefferson's first Territorial Ordinance adopted by Congress. Never put into effect, significant as early attempt to organize the West.

Apr 30 Congress requests from states right to pass navigation act to counter British restrictions. Opposed by most of states.

May   John Jay appointed secretary for foreign affairs.

June 2 North Carolina cedes her western lands to Union. Repeals cession Nov. 20, 1784.

June 2 New Hampshire adopts new constitution.

June 26 Spain closes Mississippi River to navigation by Americans.

Sept 1 Washington starts on tour into West in interest of land developments.

Sept 21 The *Pennsylvania Packet and Daily Advertiser* published in Philadelphia, first daily newspaper in America.

Oct 5 Dutch Reformed Church Synod appoints Dr. John Henry Livingston professor of theology, establishing first theological seminary in America, in New York City, subsequently New Brunswick Theological Seminary.

Oct 22 Second Treaty of Fort Stanwix signed with Six Nations. They surrender all claims to Northwest.

Nov 1 Congress meets at Trenton, N. J.

Nov 14 Samuel Seabury of Connecticut consecrated first American bishop of Protestant Episcopal Church.

Dec 24 Methodist Episcopal Church formally organized at Baltimore. Liturgy and discipline, sent over by John Wesley, adopted. Francis Asbury and Thomas Coke chosen superintendents.

1785

Virginia builds turnpike between Alexandria and the Shenandoah Valley, 1785–1786.

Virginia abolishes primogeniture. By 1791, abolished in all states.

Matthew Egerton opens cabinet shop in New Brunswick, N. J., for making of fine furniture.

Oliver Evans, Delaware, invents automatic flour mill.

Philadelphia Society for Promoting Agriculture founded. Earliest agricultural society.

New York City Manumission Society organized by John Jay and Alexander Hamilton.

Sketches of American Policy by Noah Webster published. Stresses need for stronger central government.

Jan 1 *Falmouth Gazette and Weekly Advertiser* published, Maine's first newspaper.

Jan 11 Congress convenes in New York.

Jan 21 Treaty with Ohio Indians at Fort McIntosh. [Fails because Shawnees refuse to sign.]

Jan 27 Georgia charters the first state university.

Feb 24 John Adams appointed minister to England.

Mar 10 Jefferson appointed minister to France to succeed Franklin, retiring.

Mar 28 Commissioners from Virginia and Maryland, meeting at Mount Vernon, draft agreement on navigation of the Potomac. Ratified by both states in autumn, it leads to Virginia's invitation to all states to conference on commerce at Annapolis.

Apr 19 Massachusetts' cession of western lands to the Union accepted by Congress.

May 17 Potomac Company, with charters from Virginia and Maryland for development purposes, organized at Alexandria. Washington made president.

May 20 Land Ordinance of 1785 establishes 6-mile-square system of survey of public lands. Sale of minimum lots of 640 acres at $1 an acre authorized.

July 1 Massachusetts General Court passes resolutions favoring convention to revise Articles of Confederation.

July 2 Don Diego de Gardoqui, minister from Spain, recognized by Congress.

Sept 10 Treaty of commerce made with Prussia. Ratified by Congress May 17, 1786.

Sept 14 Franklin, after absence of 9 years, returns to Philadelphia from France.

Dec 5 Maryland accepts Mount Vernon proposals and suggests Pennsylvania and Delaware be invited to join in commercial agreement with Maryland and Virginia.

1786

Printers of Philadelphia strike for $1 a day wage, are refused.

Pittsburg Gazette, first newspaper west of Alleghenies, established by John Scull and Joseph Hall.

Philadelphia Dispensary, first in America, established.

Agriculture and Practical Husbandry by Metcalf Bowler published.

Philip Freneau's *Poems,* including "The Wild Honeysuckle," published.

Jan 16 Statute for establishing religious freedom adopted by Virginia legislature, Jefferson its author.

Jan 21 Virginia legislature issues call to all states to convention at Annapolis, first Monday in September next, to consider matters of commerce.

Feb 15 Congressional committee reports, recommending improvement of Confederation, especially to provide for collection of taxes. Congress does nothing about it.

Mar 1 Ohio Company, to purchase land and promote settlement in the West, organized in Boston by New England men Rufus Putnam and Samuel H. Parsons, Revolutionary generals, and Rev. Manasseh Cutler.

May 28 Connecticut's final cession of western lands accepted by Congress.

June 17 Charles River toll bridge between Boston and Charlestown opened.

Aug   Shays' Rebellion (Daniel Shays) begins, height of social discontent in central and western Massachusetts during post-war depression. Put down, February 1787, by General Benjamin Lincoln.

Aug   Vermont courts threatened with mob violence at hands of paper money advocates.

Aug   Jay-Gardoqui Agreement, to close the Mississippi to American navigation for 25 years, laid before Congress. Not accepted. Negotiations end.

Aug 8 Spanish milled dollar adopted by Congress as basis of U. S. coinage.

Sept 11 Annapolis Convention meets with delegates from Virginia, Delaware, Pennsylvania, New Jersey and New York to treat of commerce. Adopts proposal (Sept. 14) that convention of all states meet at Philadelphia, second

Monday in May, 1787, to devise provisions necessary "to render the Constitution of the Federal Government adequate to the exigencies of the Union."

Sept 20 Armed mob marches on New Hampshire legislature, attempting to force passage of paper money law.

Sept 21 In *Trevett v. Weeden,* a Rhode Island state court declares a law passed by legislature contrary to state constitution is null and void.

Oct 16 U. S. mint established by Congress.

Oct 23 Congress makes second request of states for power to pass navigation act. Fails of sufficient state support.

Oct 26 *The Anarchiad,* written by 4 members of Hartford group, Joel Barlow, John Trumbull, David Humphreys and Lemuel Hopkins, published in *New Haven Gazette,* continuing serially until Sept. 13, 1787. Political conservatism.

1787

Oliver Evans invents high-pressure steam engine.

Quakers in Philadelphia organize Society for Alleviating the Miseries of Public Prisons, first prison reform society.

The Vision of Columbus by Joel Barlow published. Cultural patriotism.

Defence of the Constitutions of Government of the United States of America, vol. 1, by John Adams, published, London.

Feb 21 Congress officially issues call for delegates to convention in Philadelphia May 14, "for the sole and express purpose of revising the articles of confederation."

Apr 16 *The Contrast* by Royal Tyler performed in New York, first American comedy produced by professional company.

May 25 Federal Convention opens in Independence Hall, Philadelphia. Washington chosen president.

May 29 Virginia, or large-state, plan of constitution introduced by Edmund Randolph.

May 29 Charles Pinckney lays before Convention plan of federal government.

May 30 Convention agrees "that a na-tional government ought to be established consisting of a supreme Legislative, Executive, and Judiciary." New York divided, Connecticut voting no.

May 30 Controversy over proportional representation begins in Convention. Madison moves that congressional representation be proportioned to importance and size of states.

June 6 Convention in committee of the whole decides that members of lower house of legislature be elected by popular vote.

June 7 Convention in committee of the whole votes unanimously that upper house of legislature be chosen by state legislatures.

June 15 New Jersey, or small-state, plan of constitution proposed by William Paterson.

June 18 Hamilton presents his plan of government before Convention.

June 19 Virginia plan reported as preferred by committee of the whole to Convention.

July 5 Compromise proposal of grand committee on representation reported to Convention: proportional representation in first branch of legislature, equal representation in second.

July 5 Manasseh Cutler arrives in New York, talks of buying millions of acres of new land on the Ohio for Ohio Company.

July 13 Northwest Ordinance adopted by Congress, providing for government of Northwest with ultimate statehood. Slavery excluded.

July 16 Compromise on representa-tion adopted by Convention.

July 18 Treaty with Morocco, promising respect for American commerce, ratified by Congress.

Aug 9 South Carolina's cession of western lands accepted by Congress.

tion.

Aug 11 *Kentucky Gazette* published in Lexington by John Bradford. First newspaper in Kentucky.

Aug 22 John Fitch gives successful demonstration of his 12-side-paddle steamboat on Delaware River, to amusement of members of Federal Convention.

Aug 23 Convention adopts provision that the Constitution, and laws and treaties made under its authority, shall be supreme law of states.

Sept 17 Constitution signed by delegates then present at Convention, except Randolph, Mason and Gerry, and resolution adopted to submit it to Congress, in session at New York.

Sept 28 Congress votes to submit proposed Constitution to conventions of the states.

Oct 5 Arthur St. Clair appointed governor of Northwest Territory by Congress.

Oct 27 Ohio Company signs contract for purchase of lands on the Ohio with Treasury Board of Congress.

Oct 27 *The Federalist,* series of essays in defense of Constitution, written by Alexander Hamilton, James Madison and John Jay, begins publication in New York *Independent Journal* over name of "Publius," runs through 7 months.

Dec 3 James Rumsey demonstrates his steamboat on the Potomac.

Dec 7 Delaware ratifies Constitution. Vote unanimous.

Dec 12 Pennsylvania ratifies Constitution, 46–23.

Dec 18 New Jersey ratifies Constitution. Vote unanimous.

Dec 27 "The New Roof and Objections to the Proposed Plan of a Federal Government for the United States on Genuine Principles" by Francis Hopkinson published in *Pennsylvania Packet.*

1788

American states have by this date regained their prosperity, following post-war depression.

James Wilkinson intrigues with Spanish at New Orleans over separation of Kentucky and Tennessee from Union.

An Appeal to the Public with Respect to the Unlawfulness of Divorces by Benjamin Trumbull published.

Letters from the Federal Farmer to the Republican by Richard Henry Lee, opposing ratification of Constitution, published as pamphlet.

Jan 2 Georgia ratifies Constitution. Vote unanimous.

Jan 9 Connecticut ratifies Constitution, 128–40.

Feb 6 Massachusetts ratifies Constitution, 187–168, with recommendation of amendments.

Apr 7 Marietta, at mouth of Muskingum River on the Ohio, settled by Ohio Company, beginning settlement of Northwest.

Apr 28 Maryland ratifies Constitution, 63–11.

May 23 South Carolina ratifies Constitution, 149–73.

June 21 New Hampshire, ninth state, ratifies Constitution, 57–47, placing it in operation.

June 25 Virginia ratifies Constitution, 89–79.

July 2 President of Congress announces that 9 states have ratified Constitution.

July 26 New York ratifies Constitution, 30–27.

Sept 13 Congress orders states to choose Presidential electors first Wednesday in January, to cast their votes on first Wednesday in February, and that new Congress shall meet in New York first Wednesday in March.

Dec 28 Losantiville (Cincinnati), at mouth of Big Miami River on the Ohio, settled by J. C. Symmes, land speculator, with New Jersey colonists.

1789

John Jacob Astor makes first purchase of real estate on the Bowery Road, Manhattan Island.

Execution by hanging of Rachel Wall for highway robbery in Massachusetts.

Anglican Church in America formally becomes Protestant Episcopal Church.

First Presbyterian General Assembly meets in Philadelphia.

History of the American Revolution by Dr. David Ramsey published.

Dissertations on the English Language by Noah Webster published. Plea for national language.

University of North Carolina founded.

Jan 7 First national election for Presidential electors.

Jan 9 Treaty of Fort Harmar, renewing Treaty of Fort McIntosh, signed by Ohio Indians with General Arthur St. Clair.

Feb 4 Presidential electors elect George Washington and John Adams President and Vice-President of U. S.

Mar 4 First Congress under Constitution meets in New York but without quorum.

Apr 1 House of Representatives, with quorum, begins business. Frederick Augustus Muhlenberg elected speaker.

Apr 6 Senate has quorum. First Federal Congress finally organized.

Apr 6 Electoral returns counted. Messengers sent to notify Washington and Adams of election.

Apr 8 The House proceeds to matter of revenue for new government.

Apr 14 Charles Thomson, secretary of Congress, messenger, arrives at Mount Vernon with news of Washington's election.

Apr 15 *The Gazette of the United* *States* begins publication at New York, John Fenno editor. Earliest of administration organs, it becomes Hamiltonian.

Apr 16 George Washington leaves Mount Vernon for New York, arriving Apr. 23.

Apr 21 John Adams arrives in New York, takes oath of office, and is seated as presiding officer of Senate.

Apr 30 George Washington inaugurated at New York as first president of U. S.

June 1 First act of Congress regulates time and manner of administering oaths.

July 4 First Tariff Act, to become effective Aug. 1.

July 14 Fall of Bastille in France. French Revolution begins. Thomas Jefferson, U. S. minister to France, a spectator.

July 20 Tonnage Act levies 50 cents tax per ton on foreign vessels in American ports.

July 27 Department of Foreign Affairs created by Congress. Name changed to Department of State Sept. 15. John Jay acting Secretary until Mar., 1790.

Aug 7 Department of War created by Congress. Henry Knox appointed Secretary of War Sept. 12.

Sept 2 Department of Treasury created by Congress. Alexander Hamilton appointed Secretary of Treasury Sept. 11.

Sept 22 Postmaster General provided for by Congress. Samuel Osgood appointed to office Sept. 26.

Sept 24 Judiciary Act provides for Attorney General and begins Federal system of district, circuit and supreme courts. Edmund Randolph first Attorney General.

Sept 25 Congress submits to states 12 amendments to Constitution. Ten amendments, the Bill of Rights, adopted 1791.

Sept 26 John Jay appointed Chief Justice of Supreme Court.

Sept 29 First Congress under Consti- tution adjourns.

Oct 13 Jefferson offered post of Secre- tary of State in letter of Washington.

Oct 15 Washington begins tour of New England states.

Nov 21 North Carolina ratifies Consti- tution, 184–77, twelfth state to do so.

Nov 26 First national Thanksgiving, by congressional resolution and President's proclamation.

Dec 18 Virginia consents to separation of Kentucky counties from her jurisdiction.

Dec 21 Georgia legislature sells 25,- 400,000 acres, mostly claimed by Spain, to 3 Yazoo land companies for $207,580.

Dec 22 North Carolina finally cedes western lands to Union.

1790

Population of U. S., 3,929,214 (First Census).

National debt, $54,124,464.56.

Samuel Slater from England sets up Arkwright cotton machinery in factory at Pawtucket, R. I., where in 1791 first cotton warp is spun. Industrial Revolution in America begins.

Jacob Perkins, Massachusetts, invents nail cutter and header, effective in single operation.

French royalists, fleeing from the Revolution, begin migration to America.

Six hundred French settlers, encouraged by poet Joel Barlow, found Gallipolis on the Ohio on land of Scioto Company.

The New England Farmer, or, Georgical Dictionary by Rev. Samuel Deane published.

Jan 14 Alexander Hamilton submits first report on public credit to Congress.

Feb 11 First antislavery petitions to Congress are submitted.

Feb 25 North Carolina's final cession of western lands to Union accepted by Congress.

Mar 1 Census Act enacted.

Mar 22 Jefferson becomes Secretary of State.

Apr 10 Patent Act enacted.

May 25 Universalism formally organ- ized at convention in Philadelphia May 25–June 8.

May 26 Territorial government cre- ated for region south of the Ohio, called Southwest Territory (Tennessee).

May 29 Rhode Island ratifies Consti- tution, 34–32, last of the 13 to do so.

May 31 First copyright law enacted.

July 1 Samuel Hopkins of Vermont receives first patent under new Patent Act for improved method of "making Pot-ash and Pearl-ash."

July 16 Congress votes to establish permanent seat of government on Potomac River, site to selected by President. Philadelphia to be seat for 10 years.

Aug 4 Funding Act, establishing pub- lic credit, authorizes U. S. Treasury to accept war bonds at par in payment for new bonds. This act includes assumption of state debts.

Aug 4 Revenue Marine Service set up by act of Congress, beginning of Coast Guard.

Aug 7 Treaty of New York signed at Federal Hall with Alexander McGillivray, Creek, to keep Indians of Southwest at peace.

Aug 9 The *Columbia,* **Robert Gray** captain, lands in Boston, first American ship to circumnavigate the world.

Aug 15 Father John Carroll consecrated Bishop of Baltimore, providing separate status for Catholic Church in America.

Oct 18 General Josiah Harmar, in first of long series of expeditions to overawe Ohio Indians, defeated by them near Fort Wayne. Begins 5-year Indian war in Northwest.

Oct 28 Nootka Sound Convention between Great Britain and Spain strengthens British claim upon Oregon region.

Dec 13 Hamilton submits second report on public credit and report on national bank to Congress.

1791

American Protestant Sunday School Society begins in Philadelphia under Bishop William White and Dr. Benjamin Rush.

Discourses of Davila by John Adams published. Supports aristocratic government.

"Publicola" papers by John Quincy Adams published in *Columbian Centinel,* Boston. Attack on democratic principles of Thomas Paine.

Travels through North and South Carolina, Georgia, East and West Florida by William Bartram, naturalist, published.

Massachusetts Historical Society founded by Jeremy Belknap.

Massachusetts Humane Society incorporated.

Society for Establishing Useful Manufactures, founded by Alexander Hamilton, incorporated by New Jersey Legislature. Town laid out at Falls of the Passaic and factories built, by 1796 a failure.

Feb 15 Jefferson presents written opin-ion of constitutionality of a national bank to President Washington as requested.

Feb 23 Hamilton presents written opinion of constitutionality of a national bank to President Washington as requested.

Feb 25 National Bank Act.

Mar 3 Excise tax on distilled liquors, to be collected at stills, becomes law.

Mar 4 Vermont enters Union as four-teenth state.

Mar 30 President Washington proclaims boundary of future seat of government on the Potomac.

Apr 7 Washington begins 2-month tour of southern states.

July 4 Subscription books of new Bank of the United States opened, within 2 hours fully subscribed.

Oct George Hammond, first British minister to U. S., arrives.

Oct 31 *The National Gazette,* **Jeffer-**sonian organ, first appears, Philip Freneau editor.

Nov 4 General Arthur St. Clair defeated on Wabash River by Ohio Indians in expedition against them.

Dec Thomas Pinckney appointed minister to England.

Dec 5 Hamilton submits report on manufactures to Congress, strong case for protection.

Dec 12 Bank of the United States opens in Philadelphia.

Dec 15 First 10 amendments to Con-stitution, the Bill of Rights, go into effect when Virginia ratifies.

1792

Political parties emerge, largely from division over Hamilton's policies: Washington, Adams and Hamilton lead Federalists; Jefferson leads Republicans.

John Trumbull paints full-length portrait of Washington.

Benjamin West, American-born artist, becomes president of Royal Academy in England.

First important wooden truss bridge built, over Connecticut at Bellows Falls, Vt., by Colonel Ewel Hale.

The Farmer's Almanac founded by Robert B. Thomas, still appearing in original format 1951.

Advice to the Privileged Orders in the Several States of Europe by Joel Barlow published.

Historical Collections, State Papers and other Authentic Documents, Vol. I, by Ebenezer Hazard published.

Mar 1 Congress enacts that Presidential electors shall be chosen in each state within 34 days preceding first Wednesday in December, in every fourth year, on which day they shall cast their votes which shall be counted on the second Wednesday in February, following.

Apr David Rice, Presbyterian minister, in Kentucky constitutional convention, attempts without success to exclude slavery from that state. Similar attempt, 1799, fails.

Apr General Anthony Wayne commissioned commander-in-chief of Army by Washington, to act against Ohio Indians.

Apr 2 Mint Act provides for (1) decimal system of coinage with dollar as unit, (2) bimetallism with silver and gold full legal tender at ratio of 15 to 1, and (3) U. S. mint.

Apr 9 Philadelphia and Lancaster Turnpike chartered, providing for toll road of 62 miles between Philadelphia and Lancaster. Begins turnpike era which extends to 1820.

May New York Stock Exchange organized when 24 brokers gather beneath buttonwood tree before 68 Wall Street.

May 11 Columbia River entered by Captain Robert Gray of Boston and named for his ship *Columbia*.

June 1 Kentucky enters Union. The fifteenth, and a slave state.

Dec 5 Electors cast vote for President and Vice-President. Washington unanimously re-elected President, 132 votes; Adams re-elected Vice-President, 77 votes.

1793

1793–1815, Revolutionary and Napoleonic wars in Europe involve neutral rights of U. S.

Eli Whitney invents cotton gin.

Thomas Jefferson invents plow mould board.

Eli Terry at Plymouth, Conn., sets up clock shop using hand tools. Water power introduced 1800.

Mrs. Samuel Slater invents cotton sewing thread.

Massachusetts law of 1750, prohibiting the theatre, repealed.

Yellow fever epidemic in Philadelphia. Described in *A Short Account of the Malignant Fever lately prevalent in Philadelphia and a List of the Dead from August 1 to the middle of December 1793* by Mathew Carey, published 1794.

System of Doctrine Contained in Divine Revelation by Samuel Hopkins published.

Samuel Slater establishes a Sunday School to teach writing and arithmetic to poor children who work in his factory at Pawtucket, R. I.

Williams College founded at Williamstown, Mass. Accepts French in lieu of classics for entrance.

Jan 9 First balloon ascension in U. S. made by Frenchman, Jean Pierre Blanchard, in presence of President Washington in Philadelphia.

Feb 1 France declares war on Great Britain.

Feb 12 First Fugitive Slave Act.

Feb 18 In *Chisholm v. Georgia,* Supreme Court declares that a state may be sued by a citizen of another state in Federal courts. Leads to 11th amendment 1798.

Feb 25 Washington meets department heads at his house, earliest President's "Cabinet." Officially recognized 1907.

Mar 4 George Washington begins second term as President.
[President Washington's Cabinet: Thomas Jefferson, Secretary of State; Alexander Hamilton, Secretary of Treasury; Henry Knox, Secretary of War; Timothy Pickering, Postmaster General; Edmund J. Randolph, Attorney General.]

Apr 3 News of French declaration of war on Great Britain reaches New York by British packet.

Apr 8 "Citizen" Edmond Genêt arrives at Charleston from France as minister from French Republic to U. S.

Apr 18 Washington asks of his advisers opinions on our obligations under treaty with France of 1778.

Apr 22 Washington learns of Genêt's arrival at Charleston.

Apr 22 Washington issues proclamation of neutrality "toward the belligerents."

May 9 French government orders seizure of neutral vessels laden with provisions and bound for enemy ports.

May 18 Genêt received by Washington at Philadelphia.

June 8 Great Britain orders seizure of neutral vessels laden with provisions and bound for France, in accord with her Rule of 1756.

Summer Genêt fits out privateers in American ports to prey upon British ships and plans overland expedition against Spanish at New Orleans.

Summer France places embargo on foreign ships at Bordeaux.

Aug 23 Washington asks for recall of Genêt.

Sept 18 Cornerstone of Capitol in Washington laid by President Washington.

Nov 6 British Order in Council orders seizure of vessels carrying French West Indies produce.

Nov 9 *Centinel of the North-Western Territory,* first newspaper in Northwest, published at Cincinnati by William Maxwell.

Dec 31 Jefferson resigns as Secretary of State. Turns to organization of political party of opposition.

1794

Bellevue Hospital, New York City, has origin in pest house built on Belle Vue site to cope with plague.

Pennsylvania abolishes capital punishment for all offenses except murder, and revises criminal code.

Federal Society of Cordwainers organized in Philadelphia, America's first trade union.

Artist Charles Willson Peale starts museum in Philadelphia for popularization of science.

Duncan Phyfe begins furniture-making in New York. Americanizes Georgian styles.

A Vindication of the Rights of Women by Mary Wollstonecraft, England, published, Philadelphia.

The Age of Reason, first part, by Thomas Paine, published, Paris.

An Inquiry into the Principles and Tendencies of Certain Public Measures by John Taylor of Caroline published.

Jan 3 James Madison presents 7 commercial resolutions in House, reply to British navigation acts.

Feb Lord Dorchester, Sir Guy Carleton, governor of Canada, tells delegation of Indians at Quebec that lands in Northwest Territory belong to them, to be returned after coming war if Indians assist Great Britain.

Mar 22 Slave trade with foreign countries prohibited by act of Congress.

Mar 26 Embargo on foreign trade for a month adopted. Later extended one month.

Mar 27 Construction of 6 frigates authorized by Congress.

Apr 16 John Jay nominated by Washington as envoy extraordinary to England to seek commercial treaty.

May 8 Post Office Department permanently organized by Congress.

May 27 James Monroe appointed minister to France, John Q. Adams to Holland.

June 5 Neutrality Act of Congress.

July "Whiskey Rebellion" breaks out in western Pennsylvania in opposition to excise tax.

Aug 7 Washington calls out state militia of Virginia, Maryland and Pennsylvania, which suppresses Whiskey Rebellion by November.

Aug 20 Battle of Fallen Timbers. General Anthony Wayne defeats Indians in Ohio region, later builds Fort Wayne at source of the Maumee.

Sept 10 Blount College incorporated by assembly of Southwest Territory, predecessor of University of Tennessee.

Nov 19 Jay's Treaty with Great Britain signed. British agree to withdraw from military posts in U. S. territory. Trade conditions improved, but with restrictions in West Indies (Article XII). Provides for commissions to settle Pre-Revolutionary-War debts and Canada-Maine boundary.

1795

First primitive railroad in U. S. built, an inclined tramway with wooden rails running from brick kiln down slope of Beacon Hill, Boston.

Gilbert Stuart paints Vaughn portrait of Washington in Philadelphia.

"E Pluribus Unum" first appears on U. S. coinage, on half eagle.

John Rutledge appointed Chief Justice of Supreme Court.

Nathaniel Chipman, Vermont judge, argues value of a history emphasizing social forces instead of battles.

Boston Prices Current and Marine Intelligence, Commercial and Mercantile published. First commercial paper.

English Grammar by Lindley Murray published.

Jan 5 France officially announces knowledge of Jay's Treaty with Great Britain.

Jan 7 Yazoo Land companies, revived, fraudulently sold 30,000,000 acres of land (most of Alabama and Mississippi) at one and a half cents per acre by act of Georgia legislature.

Jan 29 Naturalization Act requires 5 years' residence.

Jan 31 Hamilton retires as Secretary of Treasury.

Apr Thomas Pinckney appointed envoy extraordinary to Spain.

May 1 U. S. flag is to have 15 stars and 15 stripes from this date, new states Vermont and Kentucky, by recognizing act of Congress.

June 8 President convenes Senate in extra session to consider Jay's Treaty.

June 24 Jay's Treaty, without Article XII, recommended for ratification by Senate.

Aug 3 Treaty of Greenville, ceding large areas to whites, concluded with Ohio Indians by General Wayne.

Aug 14   Washington signs Jay's Treaty.

Sept 5   Treaty of peace and amity concluded with Algiers, containing annual tribute to Algiers. Senate consents Mar. 2, 1796.

Oct 27   Thomas Pinckney's Treaty with Spain signed at San Lorenzo, establishing U. S. southern boundary at 31st parallel, right to navigate the Mississippi to its mouth, and right of deposit at New Orleans for 3 years.

1796

Committee of Ways and Means created in House by efforts of Albert Gallatin, representative from Pennsylvania.

Cleveland founded in Western Reserve by Connecticut settlers.

Syndicate for speculation in Washington city lots organized by Robert Morris and James Greenleaf, resulting in failure.

American Cookery . . . Adapted to this Country and all Grades of Life by Amelia Simmons published. First cookbook of American authorship.

Feb 15   French foreign minister announces to Monroe that Jay's Treaty annuls French treaties with U. S.

Feb 18   Yazoo Land Act of Jan. 7, 1795, rescinded by Georgia legislature as unconstitutional.

Feb 29   Jay's Treaty, after England has accepted Senate amendment, is promulgated by President Washington.

Mar 4   Oliver Ellsworth commissioned Chief Justice of Supreme Court.

Mar 8   In *Hylton v. United States*, Supreme Court declares tax on carriages is not direct tax to be apportioned among states, first internal revenue decision.

Apr 28   Fisher Ames gives famous speech in support of Jay's Treaty in House. Apr. 29, House votes appropriation to put Jay's Treaty into effect.

May 18   Public Land Act authorizes sale in minimum lots of 640 acres at 2 dollars per acre. Credit system inaugurated.

June 1   Tennessee enters Union as slave state.

June 29   Treaty with Creek Indians concluded at Colerain, Ga. Senate consents Mar. 2, 1797.

Aug 22   James Monroe, minister to France, recalled. Succeeded by Charles C. Pinckney, who is not received when he arrives in December.

Sept 17   Washington's Farewell Address published in *American Daily Advertiser*. Warns against "permanent alliances with any portion of the foreign world."

Oct 2   Last frontier post, Michilimackinac, evacuated by British in accord with Jay's Treaty.

Oct 29   Ebenezer Dorr, Yankee skipper, sails his ship *Otter* into Monterey Bay, first U. S. ship in California waters.

Nov   Andrew Jackson elected first Congressman from Tennessee.

Nov 4   Treaty with Tripoli signed. Senate consents June 7, 1797.

Nov 15   French minister Adet announces suspension of diplomatic relations with U. S.

Dec 7   Electors cast vote for President and Vice-President. John Adams with 71 votes elected President, Thomas Jefferson with 68, Vice-President.

1797

Charles Newbold of Burlington County, N. J., receives patent for first cast-iron plow.

A View of the Causes and Consequences of the American Revolution, 13 loyalist sermons by Jonathan Boucher as preached to his congregations in Maryland and Virginia, 1763–1775, published in England.

The Medical Repository founded, first American medical journal, Dr. Samuel L. Mitchill editor.

Mar 4 John Adams inaugurated President, and Thomas Jefferson Vice-President.
> [President Adams' Cabinet: Timothy Pickering, Secretary of State; Oliver Wolcott, Secretary of Treasurer; James McHenry, Secretary of War; Joseph Habersham, Postmaster General; Charles Lee, Attorney General.]

May 10 The *United States*, first vessel of new Navy, launched at Philadelphia, John Barry commander.

May 15 Congress meets in special session to consider relations with France. President Adams reports expulsion of Charles C. Pinckney, minister to France, assures Congress of further efforts to negotiate, and recommends defense measures.

May 31 President Adams submits to Senate nominations for commission to France, C. C. Pinckney, John Marshall, Elbridge Gerry.

June 24 Congress enacts that 80,000 state militia be held ready to march at moment's notice.

Aug 28 Treaty with Tunis signed at Tunis. Finally ratified by President Adams Jan. 10, 1800.

Sept 7 Frigate *Constellation* of new U. S. Navy launched at Baltimore, Md.

Oct 4 U. S. commissioners John Marshall, C. C. Pinckney and Elbridge Gerry arrive in Paris to re-establish friendly relations.

Oct 18 XYZ affair with France opens. Agents of Talleyrand, designated later as X, Y, and Z, demand loan and gift of $240,000 from U. S.

Oct 21 The *Constitution*, "Old Ironsides," launched at Boston Navy Yard.

Nov 1 U. S. commissioners decide to end negotiations with X, Y, and Z.

1798

Eli Whitney introduces principle of interchangeable parts in manufacture of firearms.

"Hail Columbia" written by Joseph Hopkinson, with imminence of war with France.

Massachusetts Mutual Insurance Company founded.

Georgia abolishes slave trade, last state to do so.

Jan 8 Eleventh amendment to Constitution declared in effect: one state is not suable by citizens of another state.

Jan 18 French Directory decree declares neutral vessels with cargo from Great Britain or her possessions are fair prize.

Mar 19 President Adams reports to Congress failure of negotiations with France.

Apr 3 Papers of XYZ affair transmitted to Congress by President Adams. Are ordered printed.

Apr 7 Mississippi territory formed by act of Congress.

Apr 30 U. S. Navy Department created, independent of War Department, by act of Congress.

Mar 28 President authorized by Congress to direct commanders of warships to seize any French armed vessels attacking American merchant ships.

May 28 President authorized by Congress to raise army of 10,000 volunteers for 3 years.

June 13 Commerce with France and her dependencies suspended by act of Congress.

June 18 Naturalization Act extends required time of residence for citizenship to 14 years. Repealed 1802.

June 21 President Adams in message to Congress declares: "I will never send another minister to France without assurances that he will be received, respected, and honored as the representative of a great, free, powerful, and independent nation."

June 25 Alien Act, concerns aliens in time of peace.

July 2 Washington nominated lieu-tenant general and Commander-in-Chief of the Army by President Adams. Confirmed by Senate July 3.

July 6 Alien Enemies Act.

July 7 All treaties with France re-pealed and alliance with France of 1778 thus terminated, by act of Congress.

July 11 Marine Corps established by act of Congress.

July 14 Sedition Act suppresses criti-cism of government.

July 16 Marine Hospital Service insti-tuted by act of Congress, forerunner of U. S. Public Health Service.

July 18 Alexander Hamilton commis-sioned major-general and placed second to Washington in command.

Oct   President Adams receives assur-ance that Talleyrand is willing to resume diplomatic relations.

Nov 16 The *Baltimore*, 20-gun Amer-ican ship, boarded by British who impress 5 or 6 of her men.

Nov 16 Kentucky Resolutions, drafted by Jefferson in reaction against Alien and Sedition acts, approved by governor: When Congress "assumes undelegated powers, its acts are . . . void and of no force."

Nov 20 Schooner *Retaliation*, Lieuten-ant William Bainbridge commander, captured by French off Guadeloupe. Bainbridge and crew of 250 held prisoners until February 1799.

Dec 24 Virginia Resolutions, drafted by Madison in reaction against Alien and Sedition acts, approved by the governor.

1799

Russian-American company founded, with headquarters at Sitka, Alaska. Seeks monopoly of trade in northeastern Pacific.

Medical department added to Transylvania University, Lexington, Ky. First beyond Alleghenies.

Federal Society of Cordwainers in Philadelphia launch first organized strike in America. Win wage increase after 9 weeks.

Feb 9 The *Constellation*, Captain Thomas Truxtun commander, captures French frigate *L'Insurgente* after hour's battle.

Feb 18 President Adams sends to Sen-ate nomination of William Vans Murray, minister to France. Refused by Senate.

Feb 25 President Adams nominates William Vans Murray, Patrick Henry and Oliver Ellsworth, ministers plenipotentiary to France. [Confirmed by Senate. W. R. Davie appointed in place of Patrick Henry who refuses because of age.]

Mar 4 Patrick Henry's words "United we stand, divided we fall," grace his campaign speech at Charlotte for Virginia assembly.

Mar 29 New York passes gradual emancipation law.

Nov 22 Kentucky Resolutions of 1799 reaffirms her Resolutions of 1798 and assert doctrine of nullification by states as remedy for infractions of Constitution.

Dec 14 George Washington dies at Mount Vernon.

Dec 26 Henry Lee pronounces oration before Congress, eulogizing Washington as "first in war, first in peace and first in the hearts of his countrymen."

1800

"The half century [1800–1850] . . . has been, on many accounts, the most remarkable the world has ever known." Emerson Davis, DD. *The Half Century,* Boston, 1851.

Population of U. S. 5,308,483.

Cotton crop, 73,000 bales for year.

Eli Terry's factory in Connecticut is first clock factory in America to use water power.

John Chapman, "Johnny Appleseed," begins scattering tracts and apple seeds among pioneer settlements in Ohio Valley, continuing for 50 years.

Massachusetts State House in Boston, designed by Charles Bulfinch, completed.

Life of Washington by Parson Weems published.

Feb 1 Frigate *Constellation* fights drawn battle with French frigate *La Vengeance.*

Mar 8 Commissioners to France respectfully received by Napoleon. Negotiations begin in April.

Spring Congressional party caucuses nominate candidates for President and Vice-President: Federalist, John Adams and C. C. Pinckney; Republican, Thomas Jefferson and Aaron Burr.

Apr 3 All mail sent or received by Martha Washington will go postage free, as authorized by act of Congress.

Apr 4 Congress passes Federal bank- ruptcy law, by virtue of which Robert Morris gains release from prison.

Apr 24 Library of Congress founded by act of Congress.

Apr 29 In case of the *Polly,* a British court accepts principle of the "broken voyage." American ships may carry goods to France from French West Indies, provided goods are first landed at an American port and duty paid.

May 7 Northwest Territory divided, western portion becoming Indiana Territory.

May 10 Public Land Act authorizes land sales of 320 acres at $2 an acre, on installments over 4 years. Sponsored by

William Henry Harrison, governor of Indiana Territory, it is known as Harrison Land Law.

Summer Seat of Federal government moved to permanent site on the Potomac.

Sept 30 Convention with France signed in Paris, ending navel war. Senate consents, with amendments, Dec. 19, 1801.

Oct 1 France acquires Louisiana from Spain by secret Treaty of San Ildefonso, not known to U. S. until May 1801.

Oct 19 Captain William Bainbridge compelled by Dey of Algiers to take the Dey's ambassador to Constantinople in the *George Washington.*

Oct 31 *The National Intelligencer,* Samuel Harrison Smith editor, begins publication in Washington. "For over fifty years, the most quoted paper in the Country."—Carl Russell Fish.

Nov 17 Congress convenes in Washing- ton for first time.

Dec 3 Electoral vote for President brings Republicans into power. Jefferson and Burr tied in count of electoral votes, Feb. 11, 1801, and election left to House.

1801

Philadelphia's new water system, forcing water from Schuylkill River by steam pumps to city, completed.

First American building in Greek temple form completed, designed by Benjamin Henry Latrobe for Bank of Pennsylvania, Philadelphia.

Paul Revere first in America to produce cold rolled copper.

Plan of Union entered into by Presbyterian and Congregational churches for cooperation in the West.

Jan 20 John Marshall nominated Chief Justice of Supreme Court by President Adams. Approved by Senate Jan. 27.

Feb 13 Judiciary Act of Congress approved, organizing new set of Federal courts between Supreme Court and district courts. Final Federalist effort to strengthen national government.

Feb 17 Election of Thomas Jefferson, for President and Aaron Burr for Vice-President decided by the House on 36th ballot, following tie vote of electors: 10 votes for Jefferson, 4 for Burr.

Feb 27 District of Columbia placed under jurisdiction of Congress.

Mar 3 President Adams makes last of his "midnight appointments" at 9 o'clock in evening, naming Hugh Barclay marshal of western district of Pennsylvania.

Mar 4 Thomas Jefferson inaugurated President and Aaron Burr Vice-President. In inaugural address, President Jefferson declares for "peace, commerce, and honest friendship with all nations, entangling alliances with none."
[President Jefferson's Cabinet: James Madison, Secretary of State; Samuel Dexter, Secretary of Treasury, succeeded by Albert Gallatin; Henry Dearborn, Secretary of War; Benjamin Stoddert, Secretary of Navy; Joseph Habersham, Postmaster General; Levi Lincoln, Attorney General.]

May 14 Pasha of Tripoli declares war against U. S., not having received sufficient tribute.

Aug 1 U. S. *Enterprize,* Captain Sterret, captures corsair *Tripoli.*

Aug 6 Cane Ridge, Ky., camp meeting begins Great Revival of the West, opened by Presbyterians.

Nov 16 New York *Evening Post,* William Coleman editor, first published.

Dec 8 President Jefferson's first annual message to Congress submitted in writing, a precedent unbroken until Woodrow Wilson.

1802

Library of Congress' first catalog issued: "964 volumes, 9 maps."

Merino sheep imported from Spain by Colonel David Humphreys, U. S. minister. By 1809 there are 5,000 merinos in the country.

Benjamin Silliman appointed to newly organized professorship of chemistry and natural history at Yale.

Principles of Nature by Elihu Palmer published, popular handbook for deists.

New American Practical Navigator by Nathaniel Bowditch published.

Jan 8 Revolutionary War claims of Great Britain against U. S. settled at $2,664,000 by commission, as provided by Jay's Treaty.

Feb 6 Congress recognizes war with Tripoli which lasts until 1805.

Feb 13 Federal aid for building of roads first proposed by Secretary Gallatin: that a tenth of proceeds from public lands within state of Ohio be used for roads from the East to Ohio River.

Mar 8 Judiciary Act of Feb. 13, 1801, repealed.

Mar 16 West Point Military Academy established by act of Congress.

Apr 6 Excise duties abolished by Congress.

Apr 14 Naturalization Act, requiring 5 years' residence, substitutes Act of 1795 for that of 1798.

Apr 24 Georgia cedes her western lands to U. S., last of original states to do so. Lands added to Mississippi Territory.

Apr 30 Congress passes act enabling district of Ohio to become a state and prescribing its boundaries.

May 3 Washington, D. C. incorporated as a city by act of Congress, its mayor to be appointed by President.

Oct 16 Spanish authorities at New Orleans withdraw U. S. right of deposit.

Nov 29 Ohio constitution for state government approved by a convention.

1803

Fort Dearborn (Chicago) built at head of Lake Michigan by U. S. government.

Peter Cartwright begins 50 years of circuit riding and preaching on frontier.

Jan 11 James Monroe nominated minister extraordinary to France, empowered to act with Robert Livingston to buy New Orleans and the Floridas.

Feb 24 *Marbury v. Madison*. Chief Justice Marshall declares an act of Congress null and void when in conflict with Constitution, establishing principle of judicial review.

Mar 1 Ohio enters Union as a free state.

May 2 Louisiana Purchase Treaty, dated Apr. 30, signed. France sells Louisiana to U. S. for 80,000,000 francs. Senate consents Oct. 20.

June 20 Meriwether Lewis and William Clark given instructions by President Jefferson for exploring expedition to the West.

Oct 31 The *Philadelphia* captured by enemy in Tripoli Harbor.

Nov 30 Louisiana formally transferred to Laussat, Napoleon's agent, by Count of Casa Calvo, Spanish governor.

Dec 20 Louisiana formally transferred by France to U. S. at New Orleans.

Dec 31 Middlesex Canal, connecting Merrimac River with Boston Harbor, opened.

1804

"Coonskin Library" formed in Marietta, Ohio, when group of settlers sends coonskins to Boston in exchange for books.

New York Historical Society founded.

First agricultural fair in U. S. held in Washington, D. C.

James Kent becomes New York's Chief Justice.

Ohio University founded at Athens.

Oliver Evans builds the "Oruktor Amphibolos," a steam-driven dredge.

Three hundred Rappites arrive at Baltimore from Würtemberg and establish communist settlement, Harmonie, Pa.

A northern confederacy proposed by Federalists of New England and New York.

Life of Washington, Vol. I, by John Marshall, published.

Feb 15 New Jersey passes act for gradual emancipation of slaves.

Feb 16 Stephen Decatur recaptures and destroys the *Philadelphia* in harbor of Tripoli without loss of a man.

Feb 25 Republican Congressional caucus unanimously nominates Jefferson for President and George Clinton of New York for Vice-President.

Mar 12 John Pickering, Federal district judge in New Hampshire, impeached as unfit, found guilty by U. S. Senate.

Mar 26 Public Land Act allows purchase of tracts of 160 acres at $2 an acre, on installments over 4 years.

Mar 26 District of Louisiana and Territory of Orleans formed by act of Congress.

May 14 Lewis and Clark begin ascent of Missouri River on their 2-year exploring expedition into Oregon country. Nov. 7, 1805, they come within sight of Pacific; Sept. 23, 1806, returning, they arrive at St. Louis.

July 11 Alexander Hamilton shot and killed by Vice-President Aaron Burr in duel at Weehawken, N. J., outcome of Hamilton's exposure of Burr's complicity in Federalist secession plot.

Sept 25 Twelfth amendment to Constitution declared in force. Requires separate electoral ballots for President and Vice-President.

Nov 3 Sauk and Fox Indian tribes in treaty at St. Louis cede 50,000,000 acres of land to U. S. with right to remain while tract is public land.

Dec 5 Thomas Jefferson re-elected President by electoral vote of 162, to 14 for Charles C. Pinckney, Federalist; George Clinton, Vice-President, 162 to 14 for Rufus King. First election with separate ballots for President and Vice-President.

1805

Pennsylvania Academy of Fine Arts organized by 71 gentlemen of Philadelphia.

Henry Ware (Unitarian) appointed Hollis professor of divinity at Harvard.

Frederic Tudor of Boston makes first experiment in shipping ice to hot countries in cargo to Martinique.

Democracy Unveiled by Thomas Green Fessenden published. Warns against ideas of French Revolution.

Jan 11 Michigan Territory formed by division of Indiana Territory.

Mar 1 Justice Samuel Chase, impeached by House for criticism of government and misconduct, acquitted by Senate, establishing precedent that a man cannot be impeached for what he cannot be indicted.

Mar 3 District of Louisiana becomes Louisiana Territory, with government at St. Louis, by act of Congress.

Mar 4 Thomas Jefferson begins second term as President, George Clinton Vice-President.
[President Jefferson's Cabinet: James Madison, Secretary of State; Albert Gallatin, Secretary of Treasury; Henry Dearborn, Secretary of War; Jacob Crowninshield, Secretary of Navy; Gideon Granger, Postmaster General; Robert Smith, Attorney General.]

May In the *Essex* case, British court reverses the *Polly* decision of 1800 and declares that U. S. re-export trade violates Rule of 1756.

June 4 Treaty with Tripoli signed, ends war. Senate consents Apr. 12, 1806.

Aug 9 Lieutenant Zebulon Montgom- ery Pike starts from St. Louis to explore headwaters of Mississippi River.

1806

Coal gas first used for lighting by David Melville in house and grounds at Newport, R. I.

President Jefferson orders U. S. mint to stop coinage of silver dollar. Not coined again until 1836.

Aaron Burr's Conspiracy (1806–1807) plots creation of an independent state at expense of either U. S. or Spain or both.

Congress authorizes construction of the Natchez Trace, following Indian trail, 500 miles from Nashville, Tenn., to Natchez, Miss.

The Compendious Dictionary of the English Language by Noah Webster published.

Mar 29 Cumberland Road from Cum- berland, Md., to Ohio River authorized by Congress.

Apr 18 Nicholson Non-Importation Act, to bring England to terms on commercial matters.

May 16 Charles James Fox, British secretary of state, declares European coast from Brest to Elbe River in state of blockade.

May 19 First Lancastrian school opened in New York City, under Free School Society.

Aug Haystack Prayer Meeting. Five Williams College students dedicate themselves to foreign missionary service. As "The Brethren," they form earliest foreign missionary society in America.

Nov 15 Zebulon Pike, in his exploration of the West, sees a distant mountain, "like a small blue cloud," later named Pike's Peak.

Nov 21 Berlin Decree of Napoleon, in reply to Fox's order of May 16, lays paper blockade about British Isles.

Nov 27 President Jefferson issues warning to citizens against persons [Burr] conspiring against Spain, and orders arrest of conspirators.

Dec 31 William Pinkney and James Monroe sign trade treaty with Great Britain. Suppressed by Jefferson and his advisers Mar. 1807.

1807

Jan *Salmagundi*, serial by Washington Irving and James Kirke Paulding, begins publication.

Jan 7 British Order in Council prohibits coasting trade of France and her allies to neutrals.

Jan 22 Congress officially informed of Burr Conspiracy by Jefferson.

Mar 2 Importation of slaves prohibited after Jan. 1, 1808, by act of Congress.

May 22 Aaron Burr, arrested in Alabama Feb. 19, brought to trial in circuit court at Richmond, Va., before Chief Justice Marshall.

June 22 U. S. frigate *Chesapeake* fired upon by British man-of-war *Leopard* and 4 alleged British deserters removed from it.

July 2 U. S. ports closed to all armed British ships, by proclamation of President Jefferson.

Aug 17 Robert Fulton's steamboat *Clermont* begins first trip up the Hudson, from New York to Albany, a trip of 32 hours.

Sept 1 Aaron Burr, tried for treason in circuit court at Richmond, Va., acquitted on ground that he was not present when overt act was committed.

Nov 11 British Order in Council prohibits neutral trade with Europe between Trieste and Copenhagen, a paper blockade.

Dec 17 Milan Decree, Napoleon's reply to British Order in Council of Nov. 11, further restricts neutral trade.

Dec 22 Embargo Act signed by Jefferson, prohibiting all ships from leaving U. S. for foreign ports, to force French and British withdrawal of restrictions on U. S. trade.

1808

American Academy of Fine Arts incorporated in New York.

Andover Theological Seminary established to carry on Calvinist tradition.

Vincennes, Ind., founds historical society, perhaps first beyond Alleghenies.

Daniel Pettibone invents stove for heating.

American Ornithology, first volume of 9, by Alexander Wilson, published. Earliest American ornithologist.

Plan and Method of Education by Francis Joseph Nicholas Neef published. Introduces Pestalozzi system of education in U. S.

Jan 1 Importation of slaves prohibited after this date, by act of Congress Mar. 2, 1807.

Apr 6 American Fur Company incorporated, John Jacob Astor sole stockholder.

Apr 6 Albert Gallatin, Secretary of Treasury, submits to Senate his *Report on the Subject of Public Roads and Canals*.

Apr 17 Bayonne Decree of Napoleon orders seizure of all U. S. ships found in French ports.

July 12 *The Missouri Gazette* published in St. Louis, first newspaper west of the Mississippi.

Oct Great Britain sends George Rose to U. S. as special envoy to settle *Chesapeake* affair.

Dec 7 James Madison elected President by electoral vote, 122, to 47 for

Charles C. Pinckney, Federalist; George Clinton, Vice-President, 113, to 47 for Rufus King.

1809

Jan 9 Enforcement Act passed to enforce Embargo Act of 1807.

Feb 3 Territory of Illinois established, cut from Indiana Territory.

Feb 20 In *United States v. Judge Peters* (Olmstead Case), Supreme Court upholds authority of Federal courts over state laws.

Mar 1 Embargo Act of Dec. 22, 1807, repealed, in effect Mar. 15.

Mar 1 Non-Intercourse Act substituted for Embargo Act, denying trade with Great Britain and France, but permitting it to all others.

Mar 4 James Madison inaugurated President and George Clinton, Vice-President. First Inaugural ball.
[President Madison's Cabinet: Robert Smith, Secretary of State; Albert Gallatin, Secretary of Treasury; William Eustis, Secretary of War; Paul Hamilton, Secretary of Navy; Gideon Granger, Postmaster General; C. A. Rodney, Attorney General.]

Apr 18–19 Erskine Agreement. David Erskine, British minister, unauthorized, informs Secretary of State Robert Smith that Orders in Council will be withdrawn on June 10 in so far as they apply to U. S.

Apr 19 President Madison issues proclamation renewing trade with Great Britain, based upon Erskine Agreement.

June John Stevens' *Phoenix,* first steamboat with American-made engine, makes ocean voyage from New York to Delaware River.

June 27 John Quincy Adams appointed minister to Russia.

Aug 9 Non-Intercourse with Great Britain again proclaimed by President Madison after repudiation of Erskine Agreement by Great Britain.

Sept 30 In Treaty of Fort Wayne, General William Henry Harrison obtains cession to U. S. of 3,000,000 acres of Indian land on Wabash River, in Indiana Territory.

1810

Population, 7,239,881.

Cotton crop, 178,000 bales for year.

American Board of Commissioners for Foreign Missions founded.

Balloon flight by A. R. Hawley and Augustus Post begins at St. Louis, ends in Canada, distance of 1,173 miles.

Cornelius Vanderbilt establishes ferry between Staten Island and New York City.

Joel R. Poinsett appointed commercial agent to southern South America. Arrives Buenos Aires Feb. 13, 1811.

Elkanah Watson stages cattle show at Pittsfield, Mass., forerunner of county fairs.

The Agricultural Museum established, first agricultural periodical in U. S.

Mar 16 In *Fletcher v. Peck,* interpreting contract clause of Constitution, Supreme Court holds void Georgia law of 1796 which declared contract rights of Yazoo land grants fraudulent.

Mar 23 Rambouillet Decree. Napoleon orders seizure and sale of all U. S. ships in French ports.

May 1 Macon's Bill Number Two repeals Non-Intercourse Act and promises restoration of non-intercourse with either France or Britain if the other removes offensive decrees before Mar. 3, 1811.

Aug 5 Cadore Letter. Napoleon's foreign minister writes to General John Armstrong, minister to France, revoking Milan and Berlin decrees to become effective Nov. 1, with understanding that U. S. will enforce her rights against England.

Aug 5 Trianon Decree of Napoleon condemns all U. S. vessels in French ports.

Oct 27 West Florida proclaimed by President Madison annexed to Territory of Orleans.

Nov 2 President Madison proclaims non-intercourse with Great Britain effective Feb. 2, 1811, relying on Cadore Letter Aug. 5.

1811

John Jacob Astor, New York Merchant, establishes fur trading post at Astoria, at mouth of Columbia River.

John Hall invents breech-loading carbine.

Jan 15 Congress adopts resolution that U. S. "cannot, without serious inquietude, see any part of . . . [the Floridas] pass into the hands of any foreign power." President authorized to take temporary possession of East Florida.

Feb 2 Russians land at Bodega Bay above San Francisco, there to establish Fort Ross, center of agricultural colony and sea otter trade. Sold to John A. Sutter 1841.

Feb 20 Bank of United States refused recharter by casting vote of Vice-President Clinton in Senate. Leads to establishment of many local banks.

Mar 2 Non-Intercourse Act revives Act of Mar. 1, 1809, against Great Britain who has not revoked her Orders in Council.

Apr 2 James Monroe appointed Sec- retary of State.

May   William Pinkney, minister to Great Britain, sails for home leaving diplomatic impasse.

May 16 U. S. frigate *President* defeats British sloop-of-war *Little Belt* off Sandy Hook, mistaking it for the *Guerriere*.

Sept 7 *Niles Weekly Register* begins publication in Baltimore.

Sept 11 The *New Orleans*, first steam- boat launched in Mississippi Valley, starts down the Ohio at Pittsburg for New Orleans, with Mr. and Mrs. Nicholas Roosevelt as passengers.

Nov 1 A. J. Foster, new British min- ister to U. S., presents offer of settlement in *Chesapeake* affair. Nov. 12, Secretary Monroe accepts offer.

Nov 4 Twelfth Congress convenes with new generation bringing into power the "War Hawks," including John Sevier and Felix Grundy of Tennessee, John C. Calhoun of South Carolina, and Henry Clay of Kentucky. Henry Clay chosen Speaker of the House.

Nov 7 Battle of Tippecanoe. General William Henry Harrison wins victory over Tecumseh's Indian settlement at Tippecanoe on the Wabash. Indian troubles are being laid to British.

Nov 29 Peter B. Porter, for committee on foreign affairs, reports 6 resolutions in support of defense. "It is a sacred duty of Congress to call forth the patriotism and resources of the country."

1812

Academy of Natural Sciences founded in Philadelphia.

American Antiquarian Society founded in Worcester, Mass.

Tomatoes quoted as a vegetable in New Orleans market.

Samuel J. Mills and John Schermerhorn, young missionaries, tour the West, find widespread lawlessness and scepticism. Their *Report of a Missionary Tour* published 1815.

Five Andover Seminary students, Adoniram Judson, Gordon Hall, Luther Rice, Samuel Newell and Samuel Mott, Jr., ordained missionaries to India at Salem, Mass.

Feb 11 Word "gerrymandering" first used, when under governorship of Elbridge Gerry, Massachusetts passes bill to so manipulate state election districts as to affect vote for senators.

Mar 14 Congress authorizes loan of $11,000,000, first of 6 war loans by 1815.

Apr 4 Ninety-day embargo placed on all vessels in U. S. harbors.

Apr 30 Territory of Orleans enters Union as Louisiana, a slave state.

May 14 West Florida, between Pearl and Perdido rivers, added to Territory of Mississippi by Congress.

May 18 Congressional caucus of Republicans nominates James Madison for President and John Langdon for Vice-President. Langdon refusing, Elbridge Gerry nominated June 8.

May 29 Caucus of Republican members of New York Legislature meets at Albany, nominates De Witt Clinton for President.

June 1 President Madison sends war message to Congress.

June 4 Territory of Missouri established.

June 4 The House votes, 79–49, for war with Great Britain.

June 17 The Senate votes, 19–13, for war with Great Britain.

June 18 Declaration of war approved by President. Proclaimed June 19.

June 22 Mob attacks office of *Federal Republican,* Baltimore, for denouncing declaration of war on Great Britain. Attack repeated July 27.

June 23 Great Britain revokes Orders in Council, unaware that war has been declared by U. S.

June 26 President Madison in letter to Jonathan Russell, chargé d'affaires in London, authorizes him to negotiate armistice on 2 conditions: revocation of Orders in Council, and abandonment of impressment.

June 30 Issue of $5,000,000 in Treasury notes authorized by Congress. First of 5 war issues.

July 1 Import duties doubled by Congress.

July 17 Michilimackinac, U. S. outpost on upper Lake Huron, surrenders to British. Result, Americans lose Indian respect.

July 23 William Ellery Channing preaches in Boston outspoken sermon against the war.

Aug 13 The *Essex,* David Porter captain, captures British sloop-of-war *Alert.*

Aug 15 Fort Dearborn (Chicago) surrenders to British. Americans massacred by Indians.

Aug 16 Detroit surrendered to British by General William Hull.

Aug 17 Federalists hold convention at New York of leading men, representing 11 states, and decide to support De Witt Clinton for President against Madison.

Aug 18 Friends of Liberty, Peace and Commerce hold mass meeting in New York City in opposition to the war.

Aug 19 U. S. frigate *Constitution,* Isaac Hull captain, captures British frigate *Guerriere.*

Aug 29 Lord Castlereagh, British Secretary for Foreign Affairs, refuses Russell's offer of armistice on matter of impressment.

Sept 13 Czar Alexander I of Russia offers mediation in war between U. S. and Great Britain.

Sept 30 Sir John Borlase Warren, from Halifax, proposes immediate cessation of warfare. Oct. 27, Secretary of State Monroe replies, insisting upon abandonment of impressment as condition for armistice.

Oct 4 Americans defeat British at Ogdensburg, N. Y.

Oct 13 U. S. severely defeated in attack upon Canada at Queenstown, 1,000 men lost.

Oct 18 U. S. sloop-of-war *Wasp* captures British sloop *Frolic.*

Oct 25 U. S. frigate *United States,* Stephen Decatur captain, captures British frigate *Macedonian* off Madeira Islands.

Nov 20 General Henry Dearborn's campaign against Montreal ends. At Canadian boundary, militia refuse to leave U. S.

Nov 27 British Admiralty orders blockade of Delaware and Chesapeake bays.

Dec 2 James Madison re-elected President by electoral vote 128, to 89 for De Witt Clinton, Federalist; Elbridge Gerry, Vice-President, 131, to 86 for Jared Ingersoll.

Dec 29 The *Constitution,* William Bainbridge captain, takes British frigate *Java* off coast of Brazil.

1813

Massachusetts Society for Suppression of Intemperance formed.

Adoniram Judson goes to Burma as missionary. Is to translate Bible into Burmese language.

Jan 22 Battle of Raisin River [Michigan] disaster for Americans.

Feb 24 Sloop-of-war *Hornet,* James Lawrence captain, sinks British sloop *Peacock* off British Guiana.

Mar 4 James Madison begins second term as President. Elbridge Gerry inaugurated Vice-President.
    [President Madison's Cabinet: James Monroe, Secretary of State; Albert Gallatin, Secretary of Treasury; John Armstrong, Secretary of War; William Jones, Secretary of Navy; Gideon Granger, Postmaster General; William Pinkney, Attorney General.]

Mar 11 President Madison accepts Russian Czar's formal offer of mediation in war with Great Britain, and appoints commissioners. Great Britain rejects offer.

Mar 30 British Order in Council extends blockade from New York to New Orleans.

Apr 27 York (Toronto), capital of Upper Canada, raided by Americans who set fire to government buildings.

May 1–9 Fort Meigs on Maumee River besieged by British and Indians but successfully held by General Harrison.

May 24 Daniel Webster enters Congress from New Hampshire.

May 27 Americans take Fort George, on lower Niagara River, Canadian side.

June 1 British ship *Shannon* takes American *Chesapeake,* whose captain, James Lawrence, is killed. "Don't give up the ship," supposedly dying words of Lawrence.

June 24 Americans forced to surrender at Beaver Dams, Ontario.

Aug 14 British brig *Pelican* captures American brig *Argus,* W. H. Allen captain.

Aug 30 Fort Mims, Ala., massacre by Creek Indians, killing over 500 whites.

Sept 1 Czar of Russia renews offer of mediation, to be again rejected by Great Britain, although she is willing to treat with U. S.

Sept 10 Captain Oliver Hazard Perry and squadron win battle with British squadron on Lake Erie. "We have met the enemy and they are ours: two ships, two brigs, one schooner, and one sloop." Supremacy on Lake Erie goes to U. S.

Sept 30 U. S. troops reoccupy Detroit.

Oct 5 General Harrison defeats British and Indians under Colonel Henry Proctor in battle of Thames River. Ends menace of northwestern Indians. Tecumseh killed.

Nov 9 General Andrew Jackson defeats Creeks at Talladega, Ala.

Dec 19 Fort Niagara taken by British under General Gordon Drummond.

Dec 30 Buffalo and Black Rock burned by British and Indians under General Drummond.

Dec 30 British schooner *Bramble* arrives at Annapolis under flag of truce, bearing dispatches concerning peace.

1814

First circular saw in U. S. hammered out by Benjamin Cummings.

First textile mill in U. S., combining all processes in one plant and using power loom, established at Waltham, Mass., by Francis Cabot Lowell.

William Rush, first native sculptor, carves in wood full length statue of George Washington.

An Inquiry into Principles and Policy of the Government of the United States by John Taylor of Caroline published.

Records of the Lewis and Clark Expedition published.

Mar 27   General Andrew Jackson defeats Creeks at Horseshoe Bend, Ala., and breaks their power.

Mar 28   The U. S. *Essex* captured by British ships *Phoebe* and *Cherub* in harbor of Valparaiso, Chile.

Apr 29   U. S. sloop-of-war *Peacock* captures British brig *Epervier* with $120,000 in specie off coast of Florida.

May 6   Fort Oswego, N. Y., destroyed by British.

May 31   British blockade extended to New England coast. Raids on Massachusetts and Connecticut follow.

June 28   U. S. sloop-of-war *Wasp* destroys British sloop-of-war *Reindeer* near British Channel.

July 11   U. S. brig *Rattlesnake* captured by British frigate *Leander* off Cape Sable Island.

July 25   Battle of Lundy's Lane. Indecisive when Americans outfight British but fall back as British are reinforced.

Aug   Suspension of specie payment by banks outside New England.

Aug 8   U. S. peace commissioners, Albert Gallatin, John Quincy Adams, James A. Bayard, Henry Clay and Jonathan Russell, meet British commissioners at Ghent in the Netherlands.

Aug 9   Creeks sign treaty at Fort Jackson, Ala., turning over to U. S. most of their vast lands.

Aug 9   Nantucket Island promises to remain neutral if allowed by British Fleet to bring provisions from mainland.

Aug 15   British assault on Fort Erie repulsed by Americans.

Aug 24   British defeat Americans at Bladensburg, then enter Washington and burn Capitol, White House and other public buildings.

Sept 1   U. S. sloop-of-war *Wasp* sinks British sloop *Avon*.

Sept 11   Battle of Plattsburg on Lake Champlain. U. S. fleet under Commodore Thomas Macdonough wins decisive victory over British.

Sept 12–14   British make unsuccessful land and naval attack upon Baltimore.

Sept 14   Words of "Star Spangled Ban-ner" written by Francis Scott Key during bombardment of Fort McHenry before Baltimore.

Sept 14   General Society of the War of 1812 organized.

Oct 21   Congress authorizes purchase of library of Thomas Jefferson to replace Library of Congress, burned by British.

Nov 5   Fort Erie abandoned and blown up by American troops who now retire from Canada.

Nov 7   General Jackson takes Pensacola, clearing East Florida of British.

Dec 1   General Jackson reaches New Orleans to take command.

Dec 15   Hartford Convention of New England delegates meets at Hartford, Conn. Voices New England opposition to the war and the Union, and proposes amendments to Constitution. Adjourns Jan. 5, 1815.

Dec 23   General Jackson checks British about 7 miles below city of New Orleans.

Dec 24   Treaty of Ghent signed with Great Britain, brings to close War of 1812. Simply an end to hostilities on basis of *status quo ante bellum*.

Dec 25 Rev. Noah Worcester of Brighton, Mass., publishes anonymous pamphlet *Solemn Review of the Customs of War*. Early movement for peace.

1815

U. S. Coast and Geodetic Survey established.

Massachusetts Peace Society organized by Rev. Noah Worcester.

The North American Review founded in Boston, William Tudor editor.

Jan 8 Battle of New Orleans. General Jackson defeats British under General Edward Pakenham, most notable victory of the war. Casualties: American, 8 killed, 13 wounded; British, 700 killed, 1,400 wounded.

Jan 15 Frigate *President* under Commodore Decatur taken by British squadron 50 miles off Sandy Hook.

Feb 16 Senate unanimously consents to Treaty of Ghent.

Feb 17 Treaty of Ghent ratified.

Feb 20 U. S. frigate *Constitution* takes British sloops-of-war *Cyane* and *Levant* off Lisbon.

Mar 3 Policy of reciprocity of trade with all nations first approved by act of Congress.

Mar 3 Congress authorizes use of force against Dey of Algiers for protection of U. S. commerce.

Mar 3 Congress reduces Army to peace-time number of 10,000 men, 2 major generals, 4 brigadier generals.

Mar 23 Sloop-of-war *Hornet* captures British sloop-of-war *Penguin* off Cape of Good Hope.

May *Enterprise* steams from New Orleans to Louisville in 25 days.

May 20 Commodore Decatur sails from New York for Mediterranean with 10 vessels.

June 30 Commodore Decatur signs treaty with Dey of Algiers. No further ransom or tribute to be paid by U. S. Followed by concessions from Tunis and Tripoli.

July–Sept Treaties of Portage des Sioux signed by 3 peace commissioners with 2,000 tribesmen to free prairies below Lake Michigan for settlement.

July 3 Commercial treaty signed in London with Great Britain.

1816

"The year in which there was no summer" in New England. On June 6 snow 10 inches deep in Berkshires, Vermont and New Hampshire. In July and August, ice half an inch thick. "Very little corn ripened."

American Colonization Society founded in Washington to deport freed Negroes to Africa.

American Bible Society formed in New York.

Ontario, first steamboat on Great Lakes, launched at Sackett's Harbor on Lake Ontario.

Baltimore, Md., first American city to be lighted by gas.

George E. Clymer introduces iron hand-printing press, "The Columbian."

The *Boston Recorder* published, first religious newspaper in America.

Vocabulary of Words and Phrases . . . Peculiar to the United States by John Pickering published.

Mar 16 Congressional Republican caucus nominates James Monroe for President with 65 votes over William H. Crawford with 54.

Mar 20 In *Martin v. Hunter's Lessee*, Supreme Court's jurisdiction over Virginia state court maintained.

Apr 10 Second Bank of United States incorporated by act of Congress, with charter for 20 years.

Apr 27 Tariff of 1816 maintains most of duties of War of 1812, in interest of American industries. Duty on foreign books included.

Oct 22 William H. Crawford, Georgia, appointed Secretary of Treasury.

Dec Boston Provident Institution for Savings incorporated, first savings bank in U. S.

Dec 4 James Monroe, Republican, elected President by electoral vote, 183, to 34 for Rufus King, Federalist; Daniel D. Tompkins elected Vice-President.

Dec 11 Indiana enters the Union without slavery.

1817

American asylum opened at Hartford, Conn., first institute for deaf mutes.

University of Michigan founded at Detroit, first of western state universities, as the Catholepistemiad or University of Michigania. Opened 1841.

Law school established at Harvard.

Medical faculty at Transylvania University, Lexington, Ky., organized by Dr. Benjamin Winslow Dudley.

New York Stock and Exchange Board organized. Name changed to New York Stock Exchange 1863.

Observations on the Geology of the United States by William Maclure published.

Life of Patrick Henry by William Wirt published.

Jan 7 Second Bank of United States opens in Philadelphia.

Jan 31 Massachusetts Peace Society presents memorial to Congress for congress of nations for settlement of controversies.

Feb 6 John Trumbull commissioned by Congress to paint 4 pictures of the Revolution for rotunda of Capitol.

Mar 3 Alabama Territory formed out of Mississippi Territory.

Mar 3 President Madison vetoes Calhoun's Bonus Bill of Dec. 1816 to set aside the Bank bonus for internal improvements.

Mar 3 The *Washington*, steamboat with stern paddle wheels, Henry Shreve captain, leaves Louisville for New Orleans on round trip. Steam navigation on Mississippi definitely begun.

Mar 4 James Monroe inaugurated President and Daniel D. Tompkins Vice-President. "The Era of Good Feeling" (1817–1825) ascribed to administration of President Monroe. Term originated by Boston *Columbian Centinel,* June 1817.

[President Monroe's Cabinet: John Quincy Adams, Secretary of State; W. H. Crawford, Secretary of Treasury; Isaac Shelby, Secretary of War; B. W. Crowninshield, Secretary of Navy; R. J. Meigs, Postmaster General; Richard Rush, Attorney General.]

Apr 15 Erie Canal authorized by New York Legislature to be built at expense of state. Ground broken July 4.

Apr 28–29 Rush-Bagot Agreement between Great Britain and U. S. limits naval forces on Great Lakes to police force only.

Sept 27 Ohio Indians in treaty cede their remaining lands, about 4,000,000 acres, to U. S.

Oct 8 John C. Calhoun of South Carolina appointed Secretary of War.

Nov 20 Seminole war, 1817–1818, begins with attack by whites upon Indians just above Florida border, followed by Indian depredations among Georgia backwoodsmen.

Dec 2 James Monroe, in first annual message to Congress, takes stand that Constitution does not empower Congress to establish system of internal improvements.

Dec 10 Mississippi enters Union, a slave state.

Dec 26 **Action against Seminoles as-signed to General Jackson by Secretary of War Calhoun.** "Adopt the necessary measures to terminate the conflict."

1818

Architect Charles Bulfinch placed in charge of work on national Capitol.

Cumberland Road opened from Cumberland on the Potomac to Wheeling on the Ohio.

Baltimore branch of second Bank of United States fails, precipitating financial crisis.

The tin can introduced in America by Peter Durand.

The American Journal of Science, earliest scientific periodical, founded by Benjamin Silliman.

Jan 8 **First of series of petitions for admission of Missouri as a state presented in Congress.**

Mar 18 **First U. S. Pension Act, grants pensions to needy Revolutionary War veterans.**

Mar 25 **Henry Clay in 3-hour speech** before Congress pleads for recognition of revolutionary republics in South America.

Apr 4 **Present U. S. flag, with 13** alternate red and white stripes and white star for each state in blue ground, adopted by Congress.

Apr 7 **Spanish fort at St. Marks, Fla.,** taken by General Jackson.

Apr 29 **General Jackson approves** court martial verdict and execution of Alexander Arbuthnot and Robert C. Ambrister, British citizens, for inciting Indians against U. S. Results in long debate in Congress on question of censure of Jackson.

May 10 **Henry Clay before Congress** advocates sending ministers to independent governments of South America.

May 24 **Pensacola, Fla., seized from** Spanish by General Jackson.

Aug 23 **The *Walk-in-the-Water,* first** steamboat on Lake Erie, leaves Buffalo for Detroit on first trip.

Oct 5 **Connecticut state constitution** adopted by popular vote.

Oct 19 **Chickasaw Indians in treaty** cede to U. S. all their lands between Mississippi River and northern course of the Tennessee.

Oct 20 **Convention between Great** Britain and U. S. establishes 49th parallel as their common boundary from Lake of the Woods to Rocky Mountains. Oregon boundary question left unsettled for 10 years. American citizens gain right to fish in coastal waters of Newfoundland and Labrador.

Dec 3 **Illinois enters Union as free** state.

1819

1819–1822. Financial panic, product of business readjustment, banking expansion, and land speculation, following return of peace.

Secretary of Treasury W. H. Crawford instructs U. S. consuls in foreign countries to collect seeds and plants as well as agricultural inventions.

Secretary of War J. C. Calhoun in report to Congress recommends comprehensive system of internal improvements requisite to defense.

Jethro Wood patents iron plow with interchangeable parts.

John Conant of Vermont invents stove for cooking.

Ezra Daggett and Thomas Kensett start canning of fish in New York.

Joseph Smith, founder of Mormonism, comes with his parents from Vermont to Palmyra, N. Y.

University of Virginia established by Jefferson. Opens 1825.

Major S. H. Long begins 2-year scientific exploration of Far West, from which he reports Great Plains to be "almost wholly unfit for cultivation." Discovers Long's Peak.

The American Farmer, first real farmer's magazine, started in Baltimore.

The Sketch Book by Washington Irving, first installment, published.

Jan 20 Henry Clay leads attack in House upon Andrew Jackson's conduct during Seminole War.

Feb 2 In *Dartmouth College v. Woodward,* Chief Justice Marshall of Supreme Court hands down decision that charter of a benevolent institution is a contract, therefore inviolate.

Feb 13 Missouri Bill introduced in House, to enable Missouri to draft constitution and prepare for statehood.

Feb 13 James Tallmadge of New York proposes amendment to Missouri Bill (1) prohibiting further introduction of slavery, (2) children born after admission to be free at twenty-five. Passed in House Feb. 17, lost in Senate Feb. 27, it precipitates slavery struggle.

Feb 17 In *Sturges v. Crowninshield,* Supreme Court decides that a state bankruptcy law enacted after a contract has been made violates contract clause of the Constitution.

Feb 22 Treaty with Spain signed. Spain cedes East and West Florida to U. S., also defines western boundary of Louisiana purchase to the 42nd parallel and designates that parallel as northern limit of Spanish territorial claims; U. S. renounces claim to Texas. Senate consents Feb. 24; ratified by King of Spain Oct. 20, 1820; re-ratification advised by Senate Feb. 19, 1821; ratified by President Monroe Feb. 22, 1821.

Mar 2 First act of Congress regulating immigration passed, requiring of ship captains descriptive statements of passengers brought on each voyage.

Mar 2 Arkansas organized as a territory.

Mar 2 Missouri Bill without Tall-madge amendment passed by Senate. House fails to concur.

Mar 6 In *McCulloch v. Maryland,* involving taxation by Maryland of Baltimore branch of Bank of United States, Supreme Court denies right of states to tax instrumentalities of national government.

Apr 7 New York Board of Agriculture established by the Legislature.

May 5 William Ellery Channing preaches sermon, "Unitarian Christianity" at ordination of Jared Sparks in Baltimore. Marks break between Unitarians and Trinitarians.

May 26 The *Savannah* leaves Savannah, Ga., for Liverpool, crossing "mostly under steam." First trans-Atlantic passage of a steamship.

June 19 Massachusetts consents to separate statehood for District of Maine.

Dec 8 Maine asks for admission into Union as a state.

Dec 14 Alabama enters Union, with slavery.

1820

Population, 9,638,453.

Cotton crop, 335,000 bales for year.

1820–1830, merchant marine: 90 per cent of our imports and exports by sea carried in American ships, a figure unequalled before or since.

Annual immigration during the 1820's less than 10,000.

New England missionaries settle in Hawaiian Islands.

Thomas Blanchard invents copying lathe.

A steamboat line established between New York and New Orleans.

The *Emancipator* published by Elihu Embree, Quaker, at Jonesboro, Tenn., begins abolitionist press in the South.

Construction Construed, first in series of pamphlets in defense of state courts, by John Taylor of Caroline, published.

Jan 3 Bill for admission of Maine as a state passed by House.

Jan 26 Taylor amendment. J. W. Taylor of New York proposes amendment to House Bill for admission of Maine, prohibiting slavery in Missouri.

Feb 3 Missouri Compromise. Senator J. B. Thomas of Illinois submits in Senate amendment to bill for admission of Maine, prohibiting slavery in territory of Louisiana Purchase north of 36°30', except Missouri, during territorial period.

Feb 17 Thomas amendment adopted by Senate, 34–10.

Feb 18 Bill for admission of Maine, with Thomas amendment, passed by Senate.

Mar 1 Bill for admission of Maine, with Taylor amendment prohibiting slavery in Missouri, passed by House, 91–82. Rejected by Senate.

Mar 2 Conference committee of the 2 houses votes to strike out Taylor amendment and add Thomas amendment to Maine Bill. The House accepts, 90–87.

Mar 3 Bill for admission of Maine approved by President.

Mar 6 Missouri Enabling Bill, with Thomas compromise provision, approved by President.

Mar 15 Maine enters Union.

Apr 24 Public Land Act authorizes purchase in 80-acre lots at $1.25 an acre, for cash. Abolishes credit system.

May 4 Tariff bill, passed by House, 91–78, fails in Senate by one vote.

May 15 Foreign slave trade declared to be piracy and punishable by death, by act of Congress.

May 15 Tenure of Office Act limits term of certain appointments to 4 years. Contributes to principle of rotation.

Dec 6 James Monroe re-elected President with 231 electoral votes, all but one which was given by New Hampshire to John Quincy Adams. Daniel D. Tompkins re-elected Vice-President.

Nov 14 Missouri Constitution, adopted by convention July 19, containing clause forbidding free Negroes to enter state, submitted to Senate, reviving whole controversy.

Dec 26 Moses Austin seeks permission of Spanish authorities at San Antonio to settle 300 American families in Texas.

1821

English Classical School, first high school in U. S., established in Boston. Later known as English High School.

Roman Catholics in Massachusetts allowed for first time to hold office.

Benjamin Lundy begins publication of *The Genius of Universal Emancipation,* anti-slavery periodical, at Mount Pleasant, Ohio.

The *Journal* (1771–1815) of Bishop Francis Asbury published.

Jan 17 Grant of land in Texas to Moses Austin for settlement certified by Spanish authorities.

Feb 23 Joint committee of the 2 houses appointed, on Clay's proposal, to report on advisability of admitting Missouri as a state.

Feb 24 Mexico proclaims independence of Spain.

Mar 2 Joint resolution of Congress approved to admit Missouri as a state on condition that nothing in her constitution will ever be construed to deny to citizen of any state [free Negro] privileges he is entitled to under Constitution. Second Missouri Compromise.

Mar 2 Relief Act of Congress allows adjustments in unpaid-for claims to western lands.

Mar 3 In *Cohens v. Virginia,* Chief Justice Marshall declares power of Supreme Court superior to that of state courts whenever Federal rights are involved.

Mar 5   James   Monroe   inaugurated President and Daniel Tompkins Vice-President for second terms.
[President Monroe maintains cabinet of first term.]

Mar 10   Andrew Jackson commissioned governor of newly acquired Florida and empowered to receive the territory from Spain.

June 26   Missouri   legislature   accepts joint resolution of Congress of Mar. 2.

Aug 10   Missouri   admitted   to   Union by proclamation of President Monroe.

Aug 10   Thomas   Hart   Benton   begins term of service as Senator from Missouri, continuing until Mar. 3, 1851.

Sept 1   William   Becknell,   with   wagon train of goods, leaves Independence, Mo., for Santa Fe, beginning of Santa Fe trade and Santa Fe Trail.

Sept 16   Russian   ukase   claims   Pacific coast of America north of 51st parallel and exclusive rights within 100 Italian miles of coast.

Dec 24   Statue of Washington, executed by Canova, unveiled in rotunda of North Carolina State House at Raleigh. Roman in style and costume, it sets style for American political sculpture. Destroyed by fire in 1831.

1822

Rocky Mountain Fur Company organized by William Henry Ashley of Virginia.

Boston capitalists found town of Lowell, Mass., on the Merrimac and set up new cotton factory.

William   Church   invents   mechanical typesetter.

William Beaumont begins 22-year series of observations of digestion in open wound of injured French Canadian.

Slave insurrection at Charleston, S. C., led by Denmark Vesey, free Negro. Results in strict system of slave control throughout lower South.

Liberia on west coast of Africa founded by freed Negroes, under Colonization Society.

Travels in New England and New York, 1796–1815 by Timothy Dwight published.

Essays on Political Economy by Mathew Carey, in support of protective tariff and internal improvements at government expense, published.

Mar 8   Recognition of Latin American republics advised by President Monroe in message to Congress.

Mar 30   Florida   Territory   organized, combining East and West Florida.

May 4   Appropriation   of $100,000   for diplomatic missions to Latin American republics approved by President.

May 4   Cumberland   Road   Tolls   Bill for jurisdiction and upkeep of Cumberland Road vetoed by President Monroe.

June 19   U. S. recognizes Republic of Colombia as independent state.

July 20   Tennessee   legislature   nomi- nates Andrew Jackson for President.

July 24   U. S. protests, in strong note, Russia's ukase of Sept. 16, 1821, and points out possibility of war if it is put into effect.

Nov 18   Kentucky   legislature   proposes Henry Clay for President.

Dec 12   U. S.   recognizes   Mexico   as independent state.

1823

George Bancroft and Joseph G. Cogswell, returned from study in German universities, combine classical studies with gymnastics in their school at Round Hill, Northampton, Mass.

The Pioneers, first Leather-Stocking tale, by James Fenimore Cooper, published.

Jan   Nicholas Biddle of Philadelphia becomes president of Bank of the United States.

Feb 18 Stephen F. Austin receives from Emperor Iturbide of Mexico official confirmation of grant of land on the Rio Brazos, in Texas, made to his father by Spanish viceroy, for colonization.

Mar 3 Building of lighthouses and beacons authorized by Congress, first national act for improvement of harbors.

July 17 Russia is told that U. S. would contest her right to any territorial establishment on American continent.

Aug 20 George Canning, British Minister of Foreign Affairs, proposes to Richard Rush, U. S. minister, joint declaration by U. S. and Great Britain of disapproval of transfer of Spain's American colonies to any other power.

Oct 18 Charles J. Ingersoll delivers his "Discourse Concerning the Influence of America on the Mind" before American Philosophical Society, Philadelphia, a reply to British indictments of American culture.

Dec 1 Daniel Webster from Massa-chusetts takes seat in Congress.

Dec 2 Monroe Doctrine announced by President in annual message to Congress, declaring that American continents are no longer subject to colonization by European powers, that U. S. will not meddle in European affairs nor countenance interference in destinies of independent American governments by any European power.

1824

American Sunday School Union formed.

Auburn system of prison management adopted at Auburn, N. Y. Silent but not solitary confinement.

Rensselaer Polytechnic Institute founded at Troy, N. Y., earliest engineering and technical school.

Frances Wright arrives in America from Scotland to champion free thought, labor, public education, anti-slavery and woman's rights.

Charles G. Finney in western New York begins long career as evangelist, extends evangelism throughout East.

John Quincy Adams nominated for President by legislatures of most of New England states, early in year.

Feb   South Pass, gateway of Rocky Mountains, discovered by Jedediah Strong Smith of Rocky Mountain Fur Company.

Feb 14 William H. Crawford nomi-nated for President in last Congressional caucus.

Mar 2 In *Gibbons v. Ogden,* steamboat case, Supreme Court declares fundamental principles of Federal control of interstate commerce.

Mar 4 Andrew Jackson nominated for President and John C. Calhoun for Vice-President at state nominating convention, Harrisburg, Pa.

Mar 19 In *Osborn v. Bank of the United States,* Supreme Court settles question of constitutionality of Bank of the United States and declares that U. S. has power to protect the Bank against acts of state officials.

Mar 30–31 Henry Clay in tariff debate in House advocates his American System, the development of home industries by protective tariff and internal improvements.

Apr 1–2 Daniel Webster delivers in House speech in favor of free trade.

Apr 17 Russia and U. S. conclude a treaty. Russia recognizes 54°40′ parallel as southern limit of expansion and abandons extreme claims in northern Pacific of ukase of Sept. 16, 1821. Senate consents 41 to 1, Jan. 5, 1825.

Apr 30 Road Survey Act authorizes survey of possible roads and canals of national importance.

May 22 **Tariff Act increases protec-**tion of American products.

Aug 14 **Lafayette arrives in New York** with his son for American tour, remaining until Sept. 8, 1825.

Dec 1 **Electors cast votes for President:** John Quincy Adams, 84; Andrew Jackson, 99; William H. Crawford, 41; Henry Clay, 37. John C. Calhoun elected Vice-President. With no electoral majority for President, John Quincy Adams chosen by House, Feb. 9, 1825, when votes are counted.

1825

American Tract Society founded.

House of Refuge founded in New York, a reformatory for juvenile delinquents.

Hudson River School of landscape painting in America develops from this date, Asher Brown Durand and Thomas Cole, co-founders.

Sandwich Manufacturing Company established on Cape Cod by Deming Jarves for making pressed table glass.

Ohio begins building state system of canals connecting Ohio River with Lake Erie.

Pennsylvania system of canals authorized by legislature to unite various sections of the state.

John Stevens invents steam engine for railways. Operates this first steam locomotive built in America on small circular track in Hoboken, N. J.

Thomas Blanchard builds a steam carriage, but finds neither interest nor backing.

Robert Owen establishes community at New Harmony, Ind., taking over German Rappite settlement.

Homeopathy introduced in America by Dr. Hans Burch Gram from Germany.

Jan 31 **Chesapeake and Ohio Canal** Company chartered in Maryland.

Feb 9 **John Quincy Adams elected** President in House on first ballot, with votes of 13 states; 7 for Andrew Jackson, 4 for W. H. Crawford.

Feb 12 **Treaty at Indian Springs** in which Creek leaders cede all their Georgia lands to U. S. and promise to leave for the West by Sept. 1, 1826. Treaty promptly repudiated by great body of Creeks.

Mar 3 **Congress authorizes survey and** marking of Santa Fe Trail between Missouri River and New Mexico.

Mar 4 **John Quincy Adams and John** C. Calhoun inaugurated President and Vice-President.
[President Adams' Cabinet: Henry Clay, Secretary of State; Richard Rush, Secretary of Treasury, James Barbour, Secretary of War; S. L. Southard, Secretary of Navy; John McLean, Postmaster General; William Wirt, Attorney General.]

Mar 7 **Joel R. Poinsett nominated first** minister of U. S. to Mexico. Confirmed by Senate Mar. 8.

Mar 24 **Mexican state, Texas-Coa-**huila, enacts general colonization law, opening door of Texas to American settlers.

June 17 **Bunker Hill Monument cor-**nerstone laid by Lafayette with Daniel Webster delivering oration.

July 4 **Ground broken for extension** of Cumberland Road westward from Wheeling [West Virginia], called National Road west of Wheeling.

Oct **Andrew Jackson again nom-**inated for President by Tennessee legislature.

Oct 26 **Erie Canal completed,** connecting New York City with Great Lakes.

Dec 5 **Treaty of amity and commerce** concluded with Central American Confederation. Dec. 29, Senate consents unanimously.

Dec 6 **President Adams urges internal** improvements, including establishment of national university and erection of national astronomical observatory at Washington, in first annual message to Congress.

1826

American Home Missionary Society formed, uniting efforts of several denominations.

American Seamen's Friend Society founded.

American Temperance Society formed.

High school for girls is opened in Boston. Proving too popular, it closes 2 years later.

Josiah Holbrook organizes first lyceum at Millbury, Mass.

National Academy of Design established at New York City, Samuel F. B. Morse president, 1826–1842.

Duff Green buys *United States Telegraph*, Washington, to establish anti-administration paper in support of Jackson.

Pennsylvania law makes kidnapping a felony, nullifying in effect Fugitive Slave Act of 1793. Declared unconstitutional by Supreme Court 1842, in *Prigg v. Pennsylvania*.

William Morgan, Free Mason, accused of revealing secrets of the order, is abducted and killed. His supporters organize Anti-Masonic party.

Thomas Cooper, president of South Carolina College, publishes his first pro-slavery pamphlet, *On the Constitution of the United States and the Questions that have Arisen under it.*

American Journal of Education first published in Boston, earliest education periodical. Continues as *American Annals of Education*, 1831–1839.

Atlantic Souvenir, first of American annuals, published.

Recollections of the Last Ten Years, Passed in Occasional Residences and Journeyings in the Valley of the Mississippi by Timothy Flint published.

Commentaries on American Law by James Kent published, 1826–1830.

Jan 24 Treaty of Washington, con-cluded with Creeks, abrogates Treaty of Indian Springs, 1825, cedes smaller area to U. S. and allows Indians to remain on lands until Jan. 1, 1827.

Apr 8 Henry Clay and John Randolph fight duel over Randolph's "corrupt bargain" charge of deal by Clay with John Quincy Adams over election in House.

June Panama Congress, inter-American, called by Simon Bolivar, is held. U. S. not represented; one delegate dies en route, the other arrives too late.

July 4 Deaths of ex-Presidents John Adams and Thomas Jefferson on 50th anniversary of Declaration of Independence.

Aug 22 Jedediah Strong Smith, fur trader, leaves Great Salt Lake on first overland expedition to California, reaching San Diego Nov. 27.

Oct 7 The Quincy tramway completed, first railroad in U. S., extends 3 miles from granite quarries at Quincy, Mass., to tidewater on Neponset River, for horse-drawn wagons.

Nov Mid-term elections result in anti-administration majority in House.

1827

American labor movement has its real beginning this year, says John R. Commons.

Philadelphia journeymen carpenters go on strike for 10-hour day. Joined by painters, glaziers and bricklayers.

Mechanics' Union of Trade Associations formed in Philadelphia.

Alexander Campbell from Ireland organizes Church of the Disciples, or Campbellites, later called Christians.

Book of Mormon revealed to Joseph Smith.

First state high school law enacted in Massachusetts, requiring tax-supported high school in every town of 500 families or over. Study of U. S. history made a requirement in the curriculum.

Joseph Dixon sets up factory in Salem, Mass., for manufacture of lead pencils, which he invented.

Francis Wayland becomes president of Brown, serving until 1855.

Fort Leavenworth built as protective post for Santa Fe trade.

Gila Route begun by traders from Santa Fe, along the Rio Grande and west to Gila River and San Diego.

Outline of American Political Economy by Friedrich List published.

The Youth's Companion, Nathaniel Willis editor, first published, continuing until 1929.

Feb 2 In *Martin v. Mott,* Supreme Court declares the President final judge as to exigency under which he is authorized to call out militia.

Feb 28 Woolens Bill, providing for increased duties on raw and manufactured wool, passing House, is tabled in Senate by casting vote of Vice-President Calhoun.

Mar 8 Baltimore and Ohio Railroad Company incorporated in Maryland.

Mar 13 In *Ogden v. Saunders,* Supreme Court declares that a contract made after passage of a bankruptcy law is limited by provisions of such a law.

May Mauch Chunk gravity railroad completed, extending 9 miles from coal mines at Carbondale, Pa., to Lehigh River.

July 30 Protectionists, with delegates from 13 states, hold convention at Harrisburg, Pa., demanding higher tariff.

Aug 6 U. S. and Great Britain conclude treaty to renew commercial agreements of 1818 and to continue the quasi-joint occupation of Oregon. Senate consents Feb. 5, 1828.

Nov 15 Creeks in treaty make final cession of their lands in Georgia to U. S.

1828

American Peace Society founded in New York by William Ladd.

Joseph Henry invents insulation of electric wire.

William Woodworth invents woodworking machine for planing and cutting tongue and groove.

Workingmen's party formed in Philadelphia to strive for social and political equality.

First recorded strike of factory operators takes place at Paterson, N. J.

The Mechanics' Free Press, first labor paper, started at Philadelphia.

Birds of America, first volume, by John James Audubon, published.

An American Dictionary of the English Language by Noah Webster published.

Jan 12 Treaty with Mexico fixes boundary line at Sabine River, as designated in Treaty of 1819 with Spain, after failure of Poinsett to gain more for U. S. Senate consents Apr. 28.

May 19 Tariff of Abominations passes Congress, is signed by President Adams to confusion of Jackson men who framed it for defeat.

May 24 Reciprocity Act offers abolition of all discriminative trade duties in favor of reciprocating nations.

July 4 Baltimore and Ohio Railroad construction begins when ground is broken by Charles Carroll, last surviving signer of Declaration of Independence.

July 4 Chesapeake and Ohio Canal begun when President Adams breaks ground for it at Washington.

Dec 3 Andrew Jackson, Democrat, elected President, electoral vote, 178, to 83 for John Quincy Adams, National Republican; John C. Calhoun elected Vice-President.

Dec 12 Treaty of peace and navigation with Brazil signed. Senate consents Mar. 10, 1829.

Dec 19 South Carolina Exposition and Protest, drafted by Calhoun, reported by special committee to South Carolina legislature, protesting against Tariff Act of 1828 and setting forth doctrine of nullification. Legislature orders it printed.

Dec 30 Protest of Georgia legislature against Tariff Act of 1828 transmitted to Senate.

1829

Workingmen's party organized in New York, following similar organization in Philadelphia in 1828.

American Society for Encouraging Settlement of Oregon Territory founded in Boston.

Governor Stephen D. Miller, in message to South Carolina legislature, says, "Slavery is not a national evil; on the contrary, it is a national benefit."

Sarah and Angelina Grimke leave Charleston for the North. Become Quakers and are active in causes of anti-slavery and women's rights.

G. A. Shrycock invents process of making paper from straw.

Francis Lieber, German immigrant, begins publication of *Encyclopedia Americana,* 1829–1832, 13 volumes.

Feb 5 Mississippi Legislature declares tariff of 1828 "contrary to the spirit of the Constitution."

Feb 24 Virginia General Assembly declares tariff of 1828 unconstitutional.

Mar 4 Andrew Jackson inaugurated President and John C. Calhoun Vice-President.
   [President Jackson's Cabinet: Martin Van Buren, Secretary of State; Samuel D. Ingham, Secretary of Treasury; John H. Eaton, Secretary of War; John Branch, Secretary of Navy; John M. Berrien, Attorney General; William T. Barry, Postmaster General.]
Spoils system of appointments, based on party service, now extended on national scale by President Jackson.

Aug 8 The "Stourbridge Lion," imported from Stephenson Engine Works in England, is first steam locomotive to be used in America, on railroad from Carbondale to Honesdale, Pa.

Aug 25 President Jackson offers to buy Texas from Mexico. Offer refused.

Dec 2 Texas declared exempt from Mexican anti-slavery decree of Sept. 15 by President Gauerreo.

Dec 8 President Jackson in first annual message to Congress raises question of continuance of Bank of the United States.

Dec 29 Senator Samuel A. Foot of Connecticut offers resolution proposing restriction of land sales in West. Point of departure for Webster-Hayne debate of Jan. 19–27, 1830.

1830

Population, 12,866,020.

Cotton crop, 732,000 bales for year.

Failure of Revolution of 1830 in German states revives German migration to U. S.

Constitution revision in several states provides for broader representation and suffrage.

Robert L. Stevens invents the T-rail.

Woolen manufacture by Waltham factory system begun at Lowell, Mass.

Town of Chicago laid out at Fort Dearborn, Federal post since 1803.

First covered wagons from Missouri River to the Rockies led by Jedediah Strong Smith and William Sublette of Rocky Mountain Fur Company.

Sylvester Graham begins lectures on diet, advocating whole wheat and vegetables.

Francis Preston Blair becomes editor of *Washington Globe,* Democratic administration paper.

Illinois Monthly, James Hall editor, first published at Vandalia.

Godey's Lady's Book founded at Philadelphia by Louis A. Godey. Mrs. Sarah J. Hale becomes editor in 1837.

Jan 18 Thomas Hart Benton, in support of the West, replies in Senate to Foot Resolution of Dec. 29, 1829.

Jan 19–27 Webster-Hayne debate in Senate on nature of the Union. Debate opens when Robert Young Hayne, in defense of the West, replies to Foot Resolution.

Jan 20 Daniel Webster defends New England against charge of hostility to the West.

Jan 21 and 25 Hayne, in first reply to Webster, declares for state's rights and nullification.

Jan 26–27 Webster's reply to Hayne asserts national view of constitution. Said to be greatest recorded American oration. "Liberty and union, now and forever, one and inseparable."

Jan 27 Hayne's second reply gives def-inite statement of principle of nullification. Webster, in second reply to Hayne, concludes debate.

Feb Kentucky legislature passes reso-lutions in favor of protective tariff.

Feb 4 Camden-Amboy Railroad char-tered, first in New Jersey.

Mar 12 In *Craig v. Missouri,* Supreme Court declares state loan certificates intended for circulation are bills of credit and therefore unconstitutional.

Mar 15 Louisiana Legislature in joint resolution approves of protective tariff.

Mar 31 Andrew Jackson nominated for President by Democratic-Republican members of Pennsylvania legislature. Endorsed in several states.

Apr 6 Church of Latter-Day Saints (Mormon) organized by Joseph Smith at Fayette, N. Y. *Book of Mormon* published this year.

Apr 6 Colonization law of Mexico for-bids further colonization in Texas by U. S. citizens and prohibits importation of Negro slaves.

Apr 13 Jefferson birthday dinner in Washington. President Jackson's toast, "Our Federal Union—it must be preserved," answered by Senator Calhoun's, "The Union—next to our liberty, the most dear."

May Rupture between Jackson and Calhoun, outgrowth of Calhoun's advocacy of censure of Jackson's action in Florida in 1818, when Calhoun was Secretary of War under Monroe.

May 7 Treaty of commerce and navi-gation signed with Ottoman Empire. Senate consents Feb. 1, 1831.

May 20 and 29 Duties on tea, coffee, salt and molasses reduced by Congress.

May 21 Foot Resolution tabled.

May 24 Baltimore and Ohio Railroad, first division of 13 miles from Baltimore to Ellicott's Mills completed.

May 27 Maysville Road Bill, author-izing Federal aid to Kentucky turnpike from Maysville to Lexington, vetoed by President Jackson as unconstitutional, a Federal expenditure for a local project.

May 28 Indian Removal Act, for gen-eral removal of Indians to lands west of the Mississippi, signed by President Jackson.

May 31 President Jackson vetoes bill authorizing subscription to stock of Washington Turnpike Company, calls it a local project.

May 31 President Jackson approves act appropriating $30,000 for surveys of, and $100,000 for extension of, Cumberland Road, calls it a national project.

Aug 28 Peter Cooper's "Tom Thumb," first American-built locomotive, used on Baltimore and Ohio Railroad from Baltimore to Ellicott's Mills.

Sept Henry Clay nominated for President by Republican convention at Hartford, Conn. Endorsed in several states.

Sept 15 Choctaws in treaty at Danc-ing Rabbit Creek cede their lands east

21926

of the Mississippi to U. S. Senate consents Feb. 21, 1831.

Oct 5   Re-establishment of trade with British West Indies proclaimed by President Jackson.

Dec   Schooner *Comet* sails from Alex- andria, Va., for New Orleans. Wrecked on Bahamas, slaves aboard are declared free by British authorities, source of long contention between U. S. and Britain.

Dec 6   President Jackson in annual message returns to attack on the Bank, confirms his support of principle of protection and argues proposed distribution of surplus revenue among states for internal improvements.

1831

Isaac Dripps invents cow-catcher for locomotive.

The *Yellowstone* of American Fur Company makes first steamboat trip on upper Missouri River.

A Guide to Emigrants by John M. Peck published.

Jan   Mormon Church takes up tem- porary residence at Kirtland, Ohio.

Jan 1   The *Liberator*, William Lloyd Garrison editor, begins publication in Boston.

Jan 15   "Best Friend," First American- built locomotive in actual service, makes passenger run on South Carolina Railroad, from Charleston to Hamburg.

Feb 3   Copyright Act is more generous to authors than law of 1790.

Mar 5   "West Point," first locomotive with four-wheeled truck, makes trial trip on South Carolina Railroad.

Mar 18   In *Cherokee Nation v. Geor-* *gia,* Supreme Court denies right of an Indian tribe, not being a foreign nation, to sue in Federal courts.

Apr 5   Commercial treaty concluded with Mexico. Senate consents Apr. 4, 1832.

Apr 7   Secretary Eaton resigns from Jackson's Cabinet. This, plus opposition to Calhoun, results in Cabinet break-up. By summer, Jackson's new cabinet: Edward Livingston, Secretary of State; Louis McLane, Secretary of Treasury; Lewis Cass, Secretary of War; Levi Woodbury, Secretary of Navy; Roger B. Taney, Attorney General; William T. Berry, from previous Cabinet, Postmaster General.

Apr 26   New York Legislature abol- ishes imprisonment for debt.

June 30   Black Hawk, leader of Sauk and Fox Indians, agrees to withdraw to lands west of the Mississippi.

July 4   "America" by Samuel Francis Smith first sung at Worcester, Mass.

July 4   Treaty concluded with France by which she agrees to pay 25,000,000 francs to U. S. in satisfaction of spoliation claims, dating from Napoleonic wars; U. S. agrees to pay 1,500,000 francs to satisfy French claims. Ratifications exchanged at Washington Feb. 2, 1832

Aug   Independence, Mo., chosen by Joseph Smith as site for Holy City of Zion (Mormon).

Aug 9   John C. Calhoun nominated for President by public meeting in New York.

Aug 21   Nat Turner leads slave insur- rection in Southampton, Va., killing 55 whites and arousing public opinion on danger from slaves.

Sept 26   Anti-Masonic party holds con- vention at Baltimore. Nominates William Wirt of Maryland for President and Amos Ellmaker of Pennsylvania for Vice-President. With a party platform and delegates from 13 states with fixed representation, it is considered the first national political convention.

Sept 30–Oct 7   Free trade convention meets in Philadelphia. Adopts memorial to Congress, drafted by Albert Gallatin.

Oct 26   Protective   tariff   convention opens in New York.

Dec 5   Ex-President   John   Quincy Adams takes seat in House, serving until Feb. 23, 1848.

Dec 12 National Republican party meets in convention at Baltimore. Henry Clay nominated for President and John Sergeant of Pennsylvania for Vice-President.

Dec 12 John Quincy Adams presents in House 15 petitions from Pennsylvania calling for abolition of slavery in District of Columbia.

1832

New England Anti-Slavery Society founded.

Lyman Beecher goes to Lane Seminary, Cincinnati, as professor of theology.

Perkins Institute for the Blind opened in Boston, Samuel Gridley Howe superintendent.

Horatio Greenough commissioned to make statue of Washington for rotunda of the Capitol, where it is placed in 1842.

Egbert Egberts invents power knitting machine.

First horse-drawn streetcar appears in New York.

Canal from Cleveland to the Ohio at Portsmouth completed.

Wabash Canal in Indiana begun, will be 459 miles long, to connect Ohio River with Lake Erie at Toledo. Finished in 1853.

Oregon Trail, from Independence on the Missouri by way of the Platte and Snake river valleys to mouth of the Columbia, comes into use as main route for settlers of Oregon country.

Nathaniel Jarvis Wyeth leads party of New Englanders by way of Oregon Trail to establish trading and fishing post on the Columbia.

Thomas O. Larkin opens a store at Monterey, Cal.

Thomas R. Dew's *Review of the Debate in the Virginia Legislature of 1831 and 1832* published, his formulation of proslavery argument.

Domestic Manners of the Americans by Mrs. Frances Trollope published in London following her residence in U. S., 1827–1831.

Legends of the West by James Hall published.

Fruits of Philosophy published, first American publication on birth control, by Dr. Charles Knowlton.

Jan 9 Bank of the United States presents application for renewal of charter to Congress.

Jan 9 Henry Clay introduces in Senate resolution to abolish duties on foreign goods not in competition with American, in line with his "American system."

Jan 21 Thomas Jefferson Randolph, grandson of Thomas Jefferson, revives Jefferson's plan of gradual emancipation during debate on abolition of slavery in Virginia assembly.

Mar 3 In *Worcester v. Georgia,* Supreme Court declares that Federal government has exclusive authority over tribal Indians and their lands within a state.

Mar 24 Creek Indians cede to U. S. by treaty all their lands east of the Mississippi. Senate consents Apr. 2.

Apr 6 Black Hawk War begins in northern Illinois and southern Wisconsin when the Sauks under Black Hawk recross the Mississippi and retake a village. Abraham Lincoln and Jefferson Davis both serve in the war.

May 1 Captain Benjamin Louis Eulalie de Bonneville with wagon-train leaves Fort Osage on the Missouri for the Columbia. Begins 3-year exploration of the West.

May 9 Fifteen Seminole chiefs cede their lands in Florida to U. S. by treaty, and agree to move across the Mississippi. Senate consents Apr. 8, 1834.

May 16 Treaty of peace and commerce with Chile signed at Santiago. Senate consents Dec. 19.

May 21 **Jackson men, now organized as Democratic party, hold first Democratic National Convention in Baltimore.** Convention concurs in "repeated nominations" of Jackson for President, nominates Martin Van Buren for Vice-President. Requires two-thirds majority for nomination of Vice-President, origin of the two-thirds rule governing subsequent Democratic conventions.

June **Cholera appears in New York City,** causing 4,000 deaths by October. Spreads south and west, continues into 1834.

July 10 **Bill to recharter Bank of the United States vetoed by President Jackson.** Passed by Senate June 11; by House with amendments, Senate concurring, July 3. Senate fails to pass bill over veto, 22 to 19, July 13.

July 13 **Henry R. Schoolcraft with exploring party discovers source of Mississippi River to be Lake Itasca** [Minnesota].

July 14 **Tariff Act,** though reducing revenue by some millions, maintains protective system. High duties remain on textiles and iron.

Aug 2 **Black Hawk War ends when warriors are massacred by Illinois militia.** Black Hawk seeks refuge with Winnebagoes, is surrendered Aug. 27.

Aug 28 **Calhoun's "Fort Hill" letter,** addressed to Governor Hamilton of South Carolina, gives classical exposition of theory of state sovereignty, his Doctrine of Concurrent Majority.

Sept 21 **Sauk and Fox Indians in treaty agree to remain west of the Mississippi.** Senate consents Feb. 9, 1833.

Oct 14 **Chickasaws cede to U. S. all their remaining lands east of Mississippi River.**

Oct 26 **Mississippi adopts new state constitution,** moving many offices into elective class.

Nov 19 **South Carolina Convention,** called by legislature, meets at Columbia to protest tariff acts of 1828 and 1832.

Nov 24 **Ordinance of Nullification** passed by South Carolina Convention, declaring tariff acts of 1828 and 1832 "null, void, and no law."

Nov 27 **South Carolina legislature** adopts measures to give effect to her Ordinance of Nullification.

Dec 5 **Andrew Jackson, Democrat, re-elected President** by electoral vote, 219, to 49 for Henry Clay, National Republican. Martin Van Buren elected Vice-President.

Dec 10 **President Jackson issues proclamation against nullification** to people of South Carolina.

Dec 12 **Henry Clay introduces bill** providing for distribution of surplus revenue from public lands among the states. [Passed by both houses of Congress, given pocket veto by Jackson in 1833.]

Dec 13 **Robert Young Hayne inaugurated governor** of South Carolina.

Dec 18 **Treaty of commerce with Russia** signed at St. Petersburg. Senate consents Feb. 27, 1833.

Dec 27 **Gulian C. Verplanck of New York introduces bill** in Congress to reduce tariff duties.

Dec 28 **Calhoun resigns from Vice-Presidency** to take Hayne's seat in Senate.

1833

1833–1837, wildest speculation in U. S. up to this time, in public lands, roads, canals, banks, buildings and cotton.

Oberlin, first coeducational college, founded in Ohio. Admits Negroes.

Elijah P. Lovejoy establishes anti-slavery *Observer* in St. Louis.

Peterboro, N. H., establishes first tax-supported library under state law.

Prudence Crandall, admitting Negro girls to her school at Canterbury, Conn., imprisoned for violating special act of legislature directed against her.

William Lloyd Garrison visits England to confer with English abolitionists.

Disestablishment of Congregational Church in Massachusetts, last state to separate state and church.

United States Temperance Union organized by national convention of temperance workers at Philadelphia. Becomes American Temperance Union 1836.

General Trades Union organized, linking all trade unions of New York. Ely Moore, its first president, elected to Congress.

Obed Hussey patents first successful horse-drawn grain reaper.

Samuel Preston invents shoe-pegging machine.

Commentaries on the Constitution by Joseph Story published.

Justice and Expediency published, abolition tract by John Greenleaf Whittier.

Jan 1 *Knickerbocker Magazine* first published at New York.

Jan 16 President Jackson asks power from Congress to enforce tariff law in South Carolina.

Jan 21 "Force Bill" introduced in Senate to empower President to enforce tariff law.

Feb 12 Henry Clay introduces Compromise Tariff in Senate, while Verplanck tariff bill is being considered in House.

Feb 15–16 Calhoun denounces "Force Bill" in speech in Senate, bringing nullification again into debate.

Feb 16 In *Barron v. Baltimore*, Supreme Court declares that Bill of Rights in Constitution does not protect against actions of state governments.

Feb 20 "Force Bill" passed by Senate, 32–1.

Feb 26 Compromise Tariff Bill passed by House, 119–85.

Mar 1 "Force Bill" passed by House, 149–47.

Mar 1 Compromise Tariff Bill passed by Senate, 29–16.

Mar 2 "Force Bill" signed by President Jackson.

Mar 2 Compromise Tariff Bill signed by President Jackson. This act with "Force Bill" effects compromise on nullification.

Mar 4 Andrew Jackson inaugurated President for second term; Martin Van Buren inaugurated Vice-President.
[President Jackson's Cabinet: Louis McLane, Secretary of State; W. J. Duane, Secretary of Treasury; Lewis Cass, Secretary of War; Levi Woodbury, Secretary of Navy; William T. Barry, Postmaster General; Roger B. Taney, Attorney General.]

Mar 11 South Carolina Convention meets.

Mar 15 Ordinance rescinding Ordinance of Nullification of Nov. 24, 1832, adopted by South Carolina Convention.

Mar 18 Ordinance to nullify "Force Bill" adopted by South Carolina Convention. Convention adjourns.

Mar 20 Commercial treaty with Siam signed at Bangkok. Senate consents June 30, 1834.

June 6 President Jackson begins tour of Atlantic states from Virginia to New Hampshire.

Aug 1 Strike of journeymen shoemakers at Geneva, N. Y., for wage increase is successful. Leads to *The People v. Fisher*, 1835.

Aug 28 Great Britain abolishes slavery in her colonies.

Sept 3 The New York *Sun* appears, Benjamin H. Day editor. First successful penny newspaper.

Sept 18 President Jackson presents to Cabinet reasons, drafted by Roger B. Taney, Attorney General, for removal of public deposits from Bank of United States.

Sept 21 Commercial treaty with Sultan of Muscat signed. Senate consents June 30, 1834.

Sept 23   William J. Duane, Secretary of Treasury, removed from office when he refuses to order removal of deposits from Bank of United States. Roger B. Taney appointed in his place.

Sept 26   Secretary of Treasury Taney issues first orders for removal of deposits from Bank of United States.

Oct 1   Removal of public deposits from Bank of United States to certain state banks, called "pet banks," begins.

Nov 13   Extraordinary   shower   of shooting stars seen in nearly every part of North America. "They fell like snow."

Dec   Female Anti-Slavery Society or- ganized at Philadelphia, Lucretia C. Mott president.

Dec 4   American Anti-Slavery Society founded at Philadelphia.

Dec 26   Henry Clay introduces in Sen- ate 2 resolutions, one of censure of President for removal of deposits from Bank of United States, one declaring Taney's explanation for removal "unsatisfactory and insufficient."

1834

Fourierism introduced in America by Albert Brisbane, returning from France where he studied under Fourier.

Methodist mission to Indians established on the Willamette in Oregon by Rev. Jason Lee from Boston.

Ursuline convent burned at Somerville, near Boston, a protest against Roman Catholics.

Cyrus Hall McCormick patents horse-drawn grain reaper.

Thomas Davenport invents electric motor.

National Trades Union, of all crafts, organized by General Trades Union of New York.

Delaware and Raritan Canal across New Jersey from New Brunswick to Trenton completed.

Portage Railroad opened, uses canal and railroad from Philadelphia to Pittsburgh.

Weekly steamboat service between Buffalo and Chicago begins.

Whig party organized by anti-Jackson forces. The name "Whig" appears in *Niles' Register* in April.

The Life and Writings of George Washington, first of 12 vols., by Jared Sparks, published.

History of the United States from the Discovery of the American Continent, Vol. I., by George Bancroft, published. Vol. X published 1874.

Southern Literary Messenger founded at Richmond, Va.

Jan 29   President Jackson orders Sec- retary of War Cass to send troops to quell riots of workmen along Chesapeake and Ohio Canal. First use of Federal troops in a labor conflict.

Feb 17   Van Ness Convention signed at Madrid, settling claims between Spain and U. S. Senate consents May 13.

Mar 28   Senate adopts Clay's resolu- tion of Dec. 26, 1833, censuring President Jackson for removal of deposits from Bank of United States.

Apr 15   President Jackson enters for- mal protest against Senate's resolution of censure, which was finally removed from Senate Journal Jan. 16, 1837.

June 15   N. J. Wyeth begins Fort Hall on Snake River, first settlement in Idaho.

June 28   Second Coinage Act author- izes ratio of 16 to 1 between silver and gold. Undervalues silver and drives it from circulation.

June 30   Department of Indian Af- fairs, and Indian Territory west of Mississippi River, established by Congress.

July 4   Independence Day meeting of anti-slavery society at Chatham Street Chapel in New York broken up by rioters because of Negroes in audience. Anti-abolition rioting continues until July 12, with destruction of churches and houses.

Oct   Pro-Slavery riot in Philadelphia. About 40 houses of Negroes destroyed.

Oct 28   Seminole Indians called upon by U. S. government to move from Florida, according to treaty of May 9, 1832.

1835

Benjamin Silliman, in series of lectures on geology before Boston Society of Natural History, expresses doubts of Biblical theory of the Creation.

Telegraph invented by Samuel F. B. Morse.

New York *Herald,* penny newspaper, founded by James Gordon Bennett.

Theodore D. Weld, abolitionist, refused permission to speak in Episcopal and Presbyterian churches in Circleville, Ohio.

In *The People v. Fisher,* New York court declares strikes are illegal. Resulting from Geneva strike, Aug. 1, 1833.

The Records of a School of A. Bronson Alcott, edited by Elizabeth Peabody, published.

Democracy in America by Alexis de Tocqueville published at Brussels.

A Plea for the West by Lyman Beecher published.

Slavery, first of 3 anti-slavery pamphlets by William Ellery Channing published.

Jan   Final payment of national debt. Problem of surplus revenue arises.

Jan 30   Attempt to assassinate President Jackson by insane man in Washington.

Mar 3   Branch United States mints established at New Orleans, Charlotte, N. C., and Dahlohega, Ga., by act of Congress.

May 20   Democratic National Convention meets at Baltimore. Nominates Martin Van Buren of New York for President and Colonel Richard M. Johnson of Kentucky for Vice-President.

July   President Jackson authorizes purchase of Texas. [Refused by Mexico.]

July 29   Anti-slavery literature taken from Charleston, S. C., post office and burned.

Aug 10   Academy in Canaan, N. H., dragged from its foundations because 14 of its pupils are Negroes.

Sept 13   James G. Birney writes to Gerrit Smith, "The antagonist principles of liberty and slavery have been roused into action and one or the other must be victorious. There will be no cessation of strife until slavery shall be exterminated or liberty destroyed."

Oct 21   Mob prevents English abolitionist George Thompson from speaking before Female Anti-Slavery Society in Boston. Mob seizes William Lloyd Garrison, drags him through streets.

Oct 29   Name "loco-focos" first given to radical section of New York Democracy, meeting in Tammany Hall. When lights are put out by their opponents, they resort to candles and loco-foco matches.

Nov   Second Seminole War in Flor- ida begins, lasting until Aug. 14, 1843.

Dec 7   President Jackson in annual message endorses Charleston's request for Federal aid to close mails to abolitionist literature.

Dec 16   Anti-Masons in Pennsylvania state convention meet at Harrisburg and nominate William Henry Harrison for President.

Dec 28   General Wiley Thompson and his soldiers massacred by Seminoles at Fort King, Fla.

Dec 28   Major Dade and 100 men massacred at Fort Brooke, Fla.

Dec 29   Cherokee Indians of Georgia cede all their lands east of the Mississippi to U. S. for $5,000,000 plus land in Indian Territory.

1836

More than 500 abolition societies active in northern states.

Illinois and Michigan Canal begun, connecting Chicago with Illinois River and Mississippi system.

First cargo of grain from Chicago arrives at Buffalo for shipment by Erie Canal.

Meeting of Ohio Anti-Slavery convention at Granville, Ohio, leads to violence by ruffians brought in by respectable elements of town.

Supreme Court of Massachusetts decides that a slave brought within its boundaries by his master is thereby set free.

Mark Hopkins becomes president of Williams College.

David Bruce invents type-casting machine.

Samuel Colt patents revolver. Important weapon in Mexican War, the "six-shooter."

Transcendental Club organized in Boston by Ralph Waldo Emerson, A. Bronson Alcott and George Ripley.

Partisan Leader by Nathaniel Beverley Tucker of Virginia published. Prophesies disunion.

Nature by Ralph Waldo Emerson published.

William Holmes McGuffey begins publication of his *Eclectic Readers* with *First Reader* and *Second Reader*.

Jan The *Philanthropist,* organ of Ohio State Anti-Slavery Society, James G. Birney editor, first published at Cincinnati.

Jan 11 Abolitionists petition Congress to abolish slavery in District of Columbia. Calhoun moves petitions be laid upon the table, "being foul slander" of South.

Jan 27 Great Britain offers mediation in settling spoliation claims issue of U. S. against France, resulting from treaty July 4, 1831. May 10, President Jackson announces 4 installments paid.

Feb 18 Bank of United States receives new charter in Pennsylvania as Bank of United States of Pennsylvania.

Mar 2 Texas declares her independence of Mexico.

Mar 6 Santa Anna, leading the Mexicans, captures the Alamo at San Antonio and massacres its garrison. David Crockett one of the dead.

Mar 15 Appointment of Roger B. Taney as Chief Justice of Supreme Court confirmed by Senate.

Mar 17 Republic of Texas adopts constitution, legalizes slavery.

Mar 25 The *Public Ledger* first published in Philadelphia.

Apr 20 Territory of Wisconsin established by Congress.

Apr 21 Battle of San Jacinto. General Samuel Houston wins decisive victory over Mexicans under Santa Anna.

May 11 The *Dubuque Visitor,* first newspaper in Wisconsin Territory, begins publication.

May 25 John Quincy Adams in great speech in House opposes annexation of Texas if at cost of war with Mexico.

May 26 Gag Rule passed by House, 117–68, laying all abolition petitions on the table.

June 15 Arkansas enters the Union.

June 23 Deposit Act requires Secretary of Treasury to designate at least one bank in each state as place of public deposit. Also provides for distribution among the states of Treasury surplus above $5,000,000, Jan. 1, 1837.

July 1 Calhoun's resolution of June 18 recognizing independence of Texas adopted by Senate, 30–0. House follows July 4. Question of annexation of Texas becomes 9-year controversy, prolonged in U. S. because of its bearing upon slavery and by British and French ambitions.

July 11 Specie Circular issued by President Jackson, directing that payment for government lands be made only in gold or silver.

July 12 Type of press of *Philanthropist,* James G. Birney's anti-slavery paper in Cincinnati, destroyed by mob.

Sept   Republic of Texas by popular vote declares in favor of annexation by U. S.

Sept 1   Marcus Whitman, having come through South Pass by wagon train with company of missionaries and their wives, arrives at Walla Walla on Columbia and Snake rivers.

Oct 22   Samuel Houston takes oath of office as President of Republic of Texas.

Oct 24   Friction match patented by Alonzo Dwight Phillips.

Dec 7   Martin Van Buren, Democrat, elected President by electoral vote of 170. Whigs distribute their vote among favorite sons, hoping to throw election into House. Richard M. Johnson chosen Vice-President by Senate Feb. 8, 1837, no candidate having received electoral majority.

1837

American Peace Society condemns all war, defensive as well as offensive.

Ohio establishes free common school system, based upon Prussian plan reported to state legislature by Calvin E. Stowe.

Horace Mann appointed Secretary of newly created State Board of Education of Massachusetts. Introduces Prussian system of education.

Music introduced in Boston public schools through efforts of Lowell Mason and Horace Mann.

Ole Rynning arrives in Illinois from Norway. His *True Account of America for the Information and Help of Peasant and Commoner,* Christiana, 1838, leads to great increase of Scandinavian migration after 1840.

Mount Holyoke Female Seminary founded by Mary Lyon, pioneer institution for higher education for women. Chartered as Mount Holyoke College 1893.

John Deere of Vermont begins manufacture of steel-faced plows.

United States Democratic Review first published, Washington.

Society in America by Harriet Martineau published, London.

American Archives . . . Documentary History of . . . North American colonies by Peter Force, first of 9 vols., published.

Jan 26   Michigan enters the Union.

Feb   In *New York v. Miln,* Supreme Court upholds state law requiring a ship captain to present report of each immigrant brought in.

Feb   Congress receives memorial from 56 British authors asking U. S. for copyright protection.

Feb 11   In *Briscoe v. The Bank of Commonwealth of Kentucky,* Supreme Court holds that a state-owned bank may issue bills of credit.

Feb 14   In *Charles River Bridge v. Warren Bridge,* Supreme Court declares against monopoly of transportation by one bridge company.

Mar   Failure of big cotton house of Herman Briggs & Co., New Orleans.

Mar 3   Republic of Texas recognized by President Jackson after approval by Congress.

Mar 3   Supreme Court membership increased from 7 to 9 by act of Congress.

Mar 4   Martin Van Buren inaugurated President, Richard M. Johnson Vice-President.
[President Van Buren's Cabinet: John Forsyth, Secretary of State; Levi Woodbury, Secretary of Treasury; Joel A. Poinsett, Secretary of War; Mahlon Dickerson, Secretary of Navy; Amos Kendall, Postmaster General; B. F. Butler, Attorney General.]

May 10   Panic begins with suspension of specie payment by New York banks; 618 banks fail during 1837. Depression of 7 years sets in.

June 10   Connecticut passes first general incorporation law in U. S.

Aug 31 Ralph Waldo Emerson delivers Phi Beta Kappa oration, "The American Scholar," at Harvard.

Sept 4 President Van Buren, in message to special session of Congress, advocates independent treasury system and temporary issue of treasury notes.

Sept 14 Independent Treasury Bill introduced in Senate. Passed by Senate Oct. 4, tabled in House Oct. 14.

Oct 2 Fourth installment of distribution of surplus revenue among states suspended because of bank failures.

Oct 12 Congress authorizes issue of treasury notes not exceeding $10,000,000, to ease financial situation.

Nov 7 Elijah P. Lovejoy killed and his anti-slavery printing press destroyed by pro-slavery mob at Alton, Ill.

Dec 8 Wendell Phillips in Faneuil Hall, Boston, gives his first abolition speech, in protest against murder of Elijah P. Lovejoy.

Dec 25 General Zachary Taylor defeats Seminoles at Okeechobee Swamp, Fla.

Dec 29 The *Caroline* affair. U. S. steamboat *Caroline,* leased to Canadian insurrectionists, seized by Canadian militia on U. S. side of Niagara River, and an American killed by a Canadian. Subsequent acquittal of Canadian averts trouble.

1838

Specie payment resumed by most banks by end of year.

Underground Railroad organized.

Improved Edition of the Rules for the Playing of Fashionable Games by Edward Hoyle published.

Self-Culture by William Ellery Channing published. Expresses American "doctrine of self-improvement."

Jan 5 Following the *Caroline* affair, President Van Buren issues neutrality proclamation in Canadian civil war, warning Americans not to aid Canadian revolt.

Feb 14 John Quincy Adams presents before House 350 petitions against slavery and annexation of Texas, all laid on the table.

Feb 16 School suffrage granted widows with children of school age by Kentucky legislature.

Mar 26 Independent Treasury Bill passed second time in Senate but lost in House.

Apr 19 Massachusetts law prohibits retail sale of spirituous liquors except in 15-gallon quantities.

May 17 Pennsylvania Hall in Philadelphia burned by pro-slavery mob because of anti-slavery meetings held there.

June 12 Iowa Territory carved out of Wisconsin Territory.

June 16 John Quincy Adams begins 3-week speech in House (June 16–July 7) against annexation of Texas.

July 7 All railroads within U. S. designated by Congress as postal routes.

Aug 18 U. S. Exploring Expedition, commanded by Lt. Charles Wilkes, sets out for 4 years' exploration of Pacific and Antarctic oceans.

Oct 12 Texas formally withdraws her request for annexation to U. S.

Autumn   Van Buren administration loses control of both houses of Congress in mid-term elections.

Nov 7 William H. Seward, a young Whig, elected governor of New York.

Dec   Last of the Cherokees forcibly removed from Georgia by Federal troops.

Dec 3 Joshua R. Giddings of Ohio takes seat in House as a Whig, first abolitionist Congressman.

Dec 11 The "Atherton gag," a resolution of Charles G. Atherton of New Hampshire, to prohibit discussion of

slavery in House adopted as a House rule.

1839

Free distribution of seeds inaugurated by Congress with appropriation of $1,000.

Double-row, horse-drawn corn planter invented by D. S. Rockwell.

Erastus B. Bigelow invents power loom to weave 2-ply ingrain carpets.

Samuel F. B. Morse brings from Paris process of photography learned from Daguerre. He, with Dr. John W. Draper, makes first daguerreotype portraits in America.

Charles Goodyear discovers method for vulcanizing rubber.

First state-supported normal school in America founded at Lexington, Mass., by efforts of Horace Mann.

William F. Harnden undertakes express service on railroad between Boston and New York, carrying packages in carpet-bag.

Lowell Institute in Boston for public lectures inaugurated by Benjamin Silliman. Institute provided for by will of John Lowell.

Vincennes [Indiana] Historical and Antiquarian Society founded.

Mississippi emancipates women from guardianship in matter of property, first state to do so.

Abner Doubleday, Cooperstown, N. Y., lays down first rules for baseball.

Nauvoo, Ill., established as Mormon town by Joseph Smith.

L'Amistad incident. Negroes being transported as slaves from Africa in Spanish ship mutiny and are captured by U. S. warship. Declared free men by U. S. Supreme Court in 1841.

John Augustus Sutter begins a Swiss settlement at Sutter's Fort on present site of Sacramento, Cal., strategic point in route across the Sierras from Utah and Nevada.

Hunts' Merchants' Magazine established, first general business periodical in U. S.

Feb–Mar Aroostook War in boundary dispute with British trespassers in Aroostook County, Maine.

Feb 20 Dueling in District of Columbia forbidden by act of Congress.

Apr 11 Treaty with Mexico signed, providing for arbitration of claims of U. S. citizens. Senate consents Mar. 17, 1840.

Sept 25 Commercial treaty between France and Texas signed. France is first European country to recognize independence of Texas.

Nov 13 Abolitionists meet in convention at Warsaw, N. Y., from which develops Liberty party. James G. Birney of New York nominated for President and Francis J. Lemoyne of Pennsylvania for Vice-President.

Dec 4–7 Whig National Convention, Harrisburg, Pa., nominates William Henry Harrison of Ohio for President and John Tyler of Virginia for Vice-President.

1840

Population, 17,069,453.

Cotton crop, 1,348,000 bales for year.

World's Anti-Slavery Convention held in London. American women delegates not admitted. A spur to woman's rights movement in U. S.

Brigham Young visits England in interest of Mormon Church. 4,000 English converts come to Nauvoo, Ill., 1840–1846.

Washingtonian Temperance Society, organization of reformed drunkards, founded in Baltimore.

James Madison's *Reports of Debates . . . in the Federal Convention 1787,* first published.

An Essay on a Congress of Nations by William Ladd published. Advocates congress to formulate principles of international law and international court to settle disputes by judicial decision.

The Dial, transcendentalist organ, founded at Boston, Margaret Fuller editor.

Jan 19 Wilkes expedition discovers Antarctic continent.

Mar 31 Ten-hour day established for Federal employees on public works, by executive order of President Van Buren.

Apr 1 Liberty party (abolitionist) meets in convention at Albany, N. Y. Renominates James G. Birney of New York for President and nominates Thomas Earle of Pennsylvania for Vice-President.

May 5 Democratic National Conven-tion meets at Baltimore. Nominates Van Buren for President, leaving nomination of Vice-President to states.

June 20 Samuel F. B. Morse receives patent for telegraph.

July 4 Independent Treasury Act at last becomes law.

July 7 Daniel Webster addresses 15,000 people on Stratton Mountain, Vt., in Whig campaign for Harrison and Tyler.

Nov 13 Commercial treaty made be-tween Republic of Texas and Great Britain. Great Britain recognizes independence of Texas. Ratifications exchanged July 28, 1842.

Dec 2 William H. Harrison and John Tyler, "Tippecanoe and Tyler, too," Whig, elected President and Vice-President after 6-month "hard cider and log cabin" campaign, by electoral vote of 234, to 60 for Van Buren. J. G. Birney, Liberty party, receives popular vote, 7,069.

1841

Brook Farm Institute of Agriculture and Education established by George Ripley and Brook Farm Association at West Roxbury, Mass.

Marlboro Association, first Fourierist community, formed in Ohio.

First emigrant train to California, caravan of 48 wagons, via Oregon Trail, Humbolt River and the Sierras, reaches Sacramento.

Sir Charles Lyall, British geologist, travels in U. S. His *Travels in North America* published 1845.

Graham's Magazine, Edgar Allan Poe associate editor, founded in Philadelphia.

Essays, First Series, by Ralph Waldo Emerson, published.

Mar 4 William Henry Harrison and John Tyler inaugurated President and Vice-President.
[President Harrison's Cabinet: Daniel Webster, Secretary of State; Thomas Ewing, Secretary of Treasury; John Bell, Secretary of War; George E. Badger, Secretary of Navy; Francis Granger, Postmaster General; J. J. Crittenden, Attorney General.]

Mar 9 Supreme Court sustains decision of lower courts in *L'Amistad* case: the Negroes to be freed and returned to Africa.

Apr 4 President Harrison dies of pneumonia and Vice-President John Tyler succeeds to Presidency.

Apr 10 New York *Tribune,* Horace Greeley editor, begins publication.

May 19 Theodore Parker preaches famous Unitarian sermon "On the Transient and Permanent in Christianity" in South Boston.

May 31 Twenty-seventh Congress con-venes in special session to consider revenue and finance.

June 7 Henry Clay introduces Whig program in Senate: repeal of Independent Treasury Act, incorporation of new bank, adoption of new tariff, and distribution among states of proceeds from sale of public lands.

July 28 Fiscal Bank Bill passes Senate, 26–23. Passes House Aug. 6. Vetoed by President Aug. 16.

Aug 13 Independent Treasury Act repealed.

Aug 19 Uniform bankruptcy system throughout U. S. becomes law. Repealed 1843.

Aug 23 Second Fiscal Bank Bill passes House 125–94. Passes Senate Sept. 3. Vetoed by President Sept. 9.

Sept 4 Pre-emption-Distribution Act. Combines Thomas Hart Benton's preemption plan and Clay's plan for distribution of receipts from public land sales.

Sept 11 President Tyler's Cabinet re-signs, except Secretary of State Daniel Webster, because of Tyler's veto of Bank bills.

Nov 7 Slaves being transported from Virginia to New Orleans on U. S. ship *Creole* mutiny and take over ship, sailing it into British port of Nassau. There by British law they are freed, excepting those held for murder. Causes great excitement in U. S.

1842

Croton River aqueduct bringing water to New York City completed.

First grain elevator in U. S. constructed, Buffalo, N. Y.

First Christmas tree in America reputed to have been set up in Williamsburg, Va., by Dr. Charles Frederick Ernest Minnegerode, political exile from Hesse.

Members of German League of the Nobility arrive as settlers in Texas.

Colonel John C. Frémont begins 4 years of exploration of the Far West.

Dr. Elijah White, newly appointed Indian Agent for U. S. in Oregon, leads party of 130 persons with 18 wagons from Independence, Mo., to Whitman's mission at Walla Walla.

Cincinnati-Toledo canal completed.

George Latimer, fugitive slave from Virginia, seized in Boston. Abolitionists force his purchase from owner.

In *Commonwealth v. Hunt,* Chief Justice Lemuel Shaw of Massachusetts rules that a trade union is a lawful organization, and not responsible for illegal acts of individuals, and that a strike for a closed shop is legal.

War and Peace, the Evils of the First and a Plan for Preserving the Last by William Jay published.

Thoughts on the Present Collegiate System in the United States by Francis Wayland, president of Brown, published. Advocates free election of studies.

Jan 24 Citizens of Haverhill, Mass., through John Quincy Adams, petition Congress for a peaceful dissolution of the Union.

Mar 1 In *Prigg v. Pennsylvania,* Su-preme Court rules that the owner of a fugitive slave may recover him under Fugitive Slave Act of 1793, in spite of conflicting state laws, though state authorities are not obligated to assist.

Mar 3 Massachusetts act requires min-imum of education for every child, and no more than 10-hour day in factory labor for children under 12.

Mar 4 In *Dobbins v. Commissioners,* Supreme Court rules that a state cannot tax salary of a Federal officer.

Mar 22 Joshua R. Giddings, censured by House for introducing antislavery resolutions, resigns his seat. Re-elected by his Ohio district, is back in House May 8.

Mar 30 Dr. Crawford Long of Geor-gia is first to use ether as anaesthetic in surgical operation. Not reported until 1849.

Mar 31 Henry Clay resigns from Sen-ate after 40 years' public service. Returns to Senate, 1849.

Spring Dorr Rebellion in Rhode Island against restricted suffrage sweeps away charter of 1663, state constitution since 1776, and broadens suffrage in new constitution.

June 10 Lt. Charles Wilkes returns to New York after 4-year expedition of over 90,000 miles in Pacific and Antarctic oceans.

June 25 Reapportionment Act. Congressmen, from Mar. 3, shall be elected by districts, equal in number to each state's quota of representatives, each district to elect one representative.

Aug 9 Webster-Ashburton Treaty between U. S. and Great Britain signed, defining boundary between Maine and Canada and settling minor boundary disputes between Atlantic Ocean and Rocky Mountains. Senate consents Aug. 20.

Aug 26 Fiscal year defined by Congress as beginning July 1.

Aug 30 Tariff Act, highly protective, restores duties to general level of 1832. Effective upon expiration of Compromise Tariff of 1833.

Oct 3 Marcus Whitman begins winter journey on horseback from Oregon to Boston and Washington, in interest of his mission.

Oct 20 Commodore Thomas Ap Catesby Jones of U. S. Navy, hearing that British are about to seize California and believing that U. S. must be at war with Mexico, lands at Monterey, seizes fort and raises American flag. Shown his error by Thomas O. Larkin, he hauls down flag and apologizes to Mexico.

Dec 30 President Tyler, upon advice of Webster, in message to Congress declares that U. S. would look with disfavor upon any attempt of another power to take possession of Hawaiian Islands.

1843

Dr. Oliver Wendell Holmes in lecture, "The Contagiousness of Puerperal Fever" before Boston Society for Med-

ical Improvement, reports that puerperal fever can be prevented by cleanliness.

B'nai B'rith organized in New York by newly arrived German Jews.

Harvard Astronomical Observatory founded.

Astronomical Observatory established at Cincinnati by Professor Ormsby M. Mitchell.

Hiram Powers, sculptor, completes his "Greek Slave."

Settlers arrive in Dane County, Wis., from "British Temperance Emigration Society," Liverpool.

Joseph Smith at Nauvoo, Ill., declares revelation sanctioning polygamy.

U. S. sends George Brown, its first diplomatic agent, to Hawaiian Islands as commissioner. U. S. refuses to join an Anglo-French declaration to observe the complete independence of Hawaii.

Great comet appears, tail visible even at noon. Great conversion to Millerism, whose founder has prophesied since 1836 end of world in 1843.

North American Phalanx, most important Fourierist community, established at Red Bank, N. J.

Vermont Assembly passes act to prevent execution of Fugitive Slave Act of 1793.

De Wette's *Critical and Historical Introduction to the Old Testament,* translated by Theodore Parker, published.

Jan   Dorothea Lynde Dix presents "Memorial to the Legislature of Massachusetts" on treatment of the insane.

Feb 3 Oregon Bill to encourage immigration passes Senate, introduced by Senator Lewis F. Linn of Missouri Dec. 16, 1841. Lost in House.

May 2 Oregon settlers meet at Champoeg and decide to form a local government.

May 8 Daniel Webster retires from President Tyler's Cabinet.

May 22 A thousand emigrants from

the East leave Independence, Mo., for Oregon, beginning of large migration of homeseekers to Oregon.

June   World Peace Congress meets in London. U. S. delegates attend.

June 17   Bunker Hill Monument dedicated. Daniel Webster delivers oration.

July 5   Oregon settlers at Champoeg adopt constitution for provisional government based upon laws of Iowa, as far as applicable.

Aug 14   Second Seminole Indian War in Florida ends, with Seminoles nearly exterminated.

Aug 23   President Santa Anna gives notice to U. S. that passage of an act to annex Texas will be considered "equivalent to a declaration of war against the Mexican government."

Aug 31   Liberty party (abolitionist) meets in convention at Buffalo. Nominates James G. Birney of Michigan for President and Thomas Morris of Ohio for Vice-President. Platform denounces extension of slave territory.

1844

Amos Bronson Alcott establishes short-lived community of Fruitlands, near Harvard, Mass.

Dr. Horace Wells, dentist at Hartford, Conn., proves that nitrous oxide, "laughing gas," can be used as anaesthetic.

Mesaba iron range discovered at head of Lake Superior.

Thomas O. Larkin made U. S. consul at Monterey, Cal.

Baptist Church splits on question of slavery, into Northern and Southern conventions.

Essays, Second Series, by Ralph Waldo Emerson, published.

Feb 28   Abel P. Upshur, Secretary of State, killed by gun explosion on warship *Princeton.*

Mar   Frémont expedition reaches Sutter's Fort in Sacramento Valley via Sierra Nevada Mountains.

Mar 6   John C. Calhoun nominated and confirmed Secretary of State.

Mar 27   Springfield *Republican,* coun-try daily newspaper, first published, Samuel Bowles, Jr., editor.

Apr 4   Fourierists hold convention in Clinton Hall, New York, at peak of Fourierism. Elect George Ripley president, Horace Greeley, Charles A. Dana and Parke Godwin vice-presidents.

Apr 12   Texas Annexation Treaty signed by U. S. and Texas, providing for admission of Texas as territory.

Apr 22   Texas Annexation Treaty sub-mitted to Senate by President Tyler, urging ratification.

Apr 27   Martin Van Buren and Henry Clay, Presidential aspirants, publish letters opposing annexation of Texas without Mexico's consent. Van Buren's costs him Democratic nomination. Clay's costs him support of South in Whig campaign.

May 1   Whig National Convention, Baltimore. Henry Clay nominated unanimously for President and Theodore Frelinghuysen of New Jersey Vice-President.

May 24   Samuel F. B. Morse sends first telegraphic message, "What hath God wrought," from Washington to Baltimore.

May 25   Gasoline engine patented by Stuart Perry.

May 27–29   Democratic National Con-vention meets at Baltimore. James K. Polk of Tennessee, first "dark horse," nominated unanimously on eighth ballot for President and George M. Dallas of Pennsylvania for Vice-President. First nominating convention to use telegraph. Platform: reannexation of Texas and reoccupation of Oregon.

May 27   Tyler Democrats meet at Bal-timore, nominating John Tyler for President. Tyler resigns from campaign Aug. 20.

June 8   Texas Annexation Treaty rejected by Senate, 35–16.

June 27   Joseph Smith, head of Mormon Church, killed in riot at Nauvoo, Ill. Brigham Young succeeds as head.

July 1 and July 27   Henry Clay in 2 "Alabama letters" declares he has no objection to annexation of Texas if it can be accomplished "without dishonor, without war." Loses northern support.

July 3   Treaty of Wanghia signed, first treaty between China and U. S. Negotiated by Caleb Cushing, it provides for full trading pivileges to Americans in treaty ports. Senate consents Jan. 18, 1845.

Aug 13   New Jersey's revised constitution ratified by people. Restricts ballot to white male citizens.

Dec 3   Resolution submitted by John Quincy Adams for repeal of Gag Rule of 1836 adopted by House.

Dec 3   President Tyler in fourth annual message recommends adoption of terms of annexation of Texas by joint resolution of Congress.

Dec 4   James K. Polk and George M. Dallas, Democrats, elected President and Vice-President by electoral vote of 170, to 105 for Henry Clay and Theodore Frelinghuysen, Whig. J. G. Birney, Liberty party, receives 62,300 popular votes. Slavery and foreign affairs determining factors in election.

1845

1845–1847. Potato famines in Ireland lead to great increase in Irish migration to America.

Clipper ship era launched with the *Rainbow,* built by John W. Griffiths in New York shipyard.

Lawrence, Mass., on Merrimac River, founded for manufacture of woolens.

Methodist Episcopal Church splits over slavery question into Northern and Southern conferences when Bishop James O. Andrew of Georgia is ordered by General Conference to give up his slaves or give up bishopric.

The Report of the Exploring Expedition to the Rocky Mountains in the Year 1842 and to Oregon and Northern California in the Years 1843–1844 by John C. Frémont published.

Woman in the Nineteenth Century by Margaret Fuller published.

Jan 23   National election day for electors of President and Vice-President established by Congress as first Tuesday following first Monday in November of election year.

Feb 3   Bill to organize territorial government for Oregon with northern limit at 54°40′ passes House. Not considered by Senate because it prohibits slavery.

Mar 1   Joint resolution of Congress for annexation of Texas as a state approved by President Tyler.

Mar 3   Florida enters the Union.

Mar 3   Postal Act. Postal rates reduced to 5 cents for a half ounce for 300 miles, and subsidies granted to steamships for carrying of mail.

Mar 4   James Knox Polk and George M. Dallas inaugurated President and Vice-President.
> [President Polk's Cabinet: James Buchanan, Secretary of State; Robert J. Walker, Secretary of Treasury; William L. Marcy, Secretary of War; George Bancroft, Secretary of Navy; Cave Johnson, Postmaster General; John Y. Mason, Attorney General.]

Mar 6   General Almonte, Mexican minister at Washington, protests annexation of Texas and demands his passports.

Mar 28   Wilson Shannon, minister to Mexico, notified by Mexican government of end of diplomatic relations between U. S. and Mexico.

June 15   Secretary of State Buchanan assures Texas of U. S. protection if Texas consents to annexation terms.

June 15 General Zachary Taylor ordered to occupy a point "on or near the Rio Grande" for defense of territory of Texas.

June 23 Texas congress assents to annexation to U. S.

July Phrase "Manifest Destiny" first appears in *Democratic Review,* John L. O'Sullivan editor. First used in Congress Jan. 3, 1846.

July 4 Texans in convention at San Felipe de Austin accept terms of annexation offered by U. S. Ratified by popular vote Oct. 13.

July 12 Secretary of State Buchanan offers Great Britain extension of 49th parallel as boundary line for Oregon. July 29, Pakenham, British minister, refuses offer, but Dec. 27, asks its renewal.

Aug General Taylor establishes camp on west bank of Nueces River, near Corpus Christi.

Aug 27 Texans in convention at San Felipe de Austin frame state constitution. Ratified by popular vote Oct 13.

Oct 10 U. S. Naval Academy at Annapolis founded.

Oct 17 Thomas O. Larkin, U. S. consul at Monterey, appointed confidential agent by President Polk and instructed to induce Californians to seek annexation to U. S. and to watch for European interference in California affairs. Dispatch received by Larkin Apr. 17, 1846.

Nov 10 John Slidell commissioned by President Polk minister plenipotentiary to Mexico, primarily to counteract foreign influence against U. S. and to restore peaceful relations between the 2 countries.

Dec 20 Slidell officially informed by Mexican foreign minister that he will not be received by Herrera government as minister plenipotentiary.

Dec 29 Texas enters the Union.

1846

Some 500 Americans are in California by this date.

Richard March Hoe invents rotary printing press.

John A. Roebling completes first suspension bridge ever built, across Monongahela River.

Beloit College in Wisconsin Territory founded by New England Congregationalists.

Louis Agassiz arrives from Switzerland to lecture before Lowell Institute in Boston. Becomes professor of zoology and geology at Harvard.

DeBow's Review first published at New Orleans.

Jan 13 General Zachary Taylor ordered to advance from Nueces River to the Rio Grande.

Mar 12 John Slidell informed by Mexican foreign minister that he will not be received by the Paredes government. Slidell returns to U. S. shortly.

Mar 27 First free homestead bill introduced in Congress by Andrew Johnson of Tennessee. It is defeated.

Mar 28 General Taylor reaches left bank of the Rio Grande and begins building fort opposite Matamoras.

Spring and Summer Twelve thousand Mormons leave Nauvoo, Ill., for Council Bluffs on Missouri River.

Apr 12 Ampudia, Mexican commander, orders General Taylor to retire beyond the Nueces.

Apr 13 Pennsylvania Railroad chartered.

Apr 25 Mexican troops of General Arista cross the Rio Grande and engage in cavalry skirmish with reconnoitering party under Captain Thornton, killing or capturing all.

Apr 25 President Polk begins preparation of war message to Congress on basis of unpaid claims against Mexico and her rejection of Slidell.

Apr 27 Congress in joint resolution authorizes President to terminate Oregon Treaty of Aug. 6, 1827, with Great Britain.

May 8   General Taylor wins battle of Palo Alto.

May 8   John Slidell, returned from Mexico, urges President Polk to act promptly in Mexican affair.

May 9   Saturday morning. President Polk informs Cabinet he believes he should send war message to Congress the following Tuesday. Secretaries Bancroft and Buchanan feel that act of Mexican hostility should precede such a message.

2 P.M. Cabinet adjourns.

6 P.M. Dispatches arrive at White House from General Taylor with news of cavalry skirmish of Apr. 25.

7:30 P.M. In second Cabinet meeting called by the President, members agree unanimously that war message should be sent to Congress, Monday the 11th.

May 9   General Taylor wins battle at Resaca de la Palma, driving Mexicans across the Rio Grande.

May 11   President Polk sends war message to Congress. Mexico "has invaded our territory and shed American blood upon American soil."

May 13   Congress declares that a state of war exists between Mexico and U. S. by act of Mexico. Congress authorizes enlistment of 50,000 soldiers and appropriates $10,000,000 to prosecute the war.

May 18   General Taylor crosses the Rio Grande and occupies Matamoras.

June 3   Colonel Stephen W. Kearney ordered to occupy New Mexico and California.

June 14   Bear Flag Revolt. Republic of California proclaimed at Sonoma by band of U. S. settlers from Sacramento Valley. Flag bearing black bear and star is raised.

June 15   Oregon Treaty with Great Britain signed, extending boundary between U. S. and Canada along the 49th parallel to Puget Sound, thence through Strait of Juan de Fuca to the Pacific. Senate consents June 18.

June 17   James Russell Lowell's first

"Bigelow Paper" appears in *Boston Courier,* against Mexican war. *Bigelow Papers,* First Series, published 1848.

June 19   Knickerbockers vs. New Yorks plays first match game of baseball in U. S., in Hoboken, N. J., score 23–1 for New Yorks.

June 26   Corn Laws repealed in Great Britain, greatly increasing export of agriculture products from U. S.

July 7   Commodore John Drake Sloat takes possession of Monterey, hoists U. S. flag and proclaims possession of California for U. S.

July 9   Captain John Berrien Montgomery, under orders of Commodore Sloat, takes San Francisco.

July 29   Commodore Robert F. Stockton succeeds Commodore Sloat in command of Pacific fleet.

July 30   Walker Tariff Act enlarges free list, lowers import tariffs, taxes luxuries highly.

Aug 6   Independent Treasury re-established by Congress.

Aug 6   State government for Wisconsin Territory authorized by act of Congress.

Aug 8   President Polk sends special message to Congress asking for $2,000,000 for adjustment of boundary with Mexico.

Aug 8   Appropriation Bill introduced in House by James I. McKay to make appropriation requested by the President.

Aug 8   Wilmot Proviso. David Wilmot moves amendment to McKay Appropriation Bill, excluding slavery from any territory acquired from Mexico.

Aug 10   Appropriation Bill with Wilmot proviso fails in Senate.

Aug 10   Smithsonian Institution chartered, with Joseph Henry first director.

Aug 13   Commodore Stockton and Captain Frémont take Los Angeles.

Aug 15   The *Californian,* first newspa-

per in California, published in Monterey.

Aug 16 General Santa Anna, exiled in Cuba, with fall of Paredes government is allowed to pass U. S. blockading squadron at Vera Cruz.

Aug 18 Colonel Kearney occupies Santa Fe. Organizes temporary government for New Mexico in month following.

Aug 31 News of U. S. occupation of California by naval forces reaches Washington.

Sept 10 Elias Howe patents sewing machine.

Sept 14 General Santa Anna enters Mexico City to become commander-in-chief of Mexican army.

Sept 24 General Taylor occupies Monterey, Mexico, after 3 days' battle.

Sept 25 Colonel Kearney leaves Santa Fe for California.

Oct 16 Dr. William Thomas Green Morton performs first public surgical operation with use of ether, in Massachusetts General Hospital, Boston.

Nov 5 Commodore Stockton ordered by Navy to recognize Colonel Kearney as governor and commander-in-chief of California.

Nov 15 Commodore David Conner takes Tampico, Mexico.

Nov 16 General Taylor takes Saltillo, capital of Coahuilla.

Nov 23 General Winfield Scott or- dered by War Department to command Gulf expedition in Mexico.

Dec 7 Colonel Kearney, after drawn engagement with Spanish Californians at San Pascual, retreats toward San Diego.

Dec 12 Treaty signed with New Granada (Colombia) grants to U. S. right of transit over Isthmus of Panama and guarantees to New Granada neutrality of the Isthmus and her rights of sovereignty over it. Senate consents June 3, 1848.

Dec 28 Iowa enters the Union.

Dec 29 General Taylor occupies Victoria, capital of Tamaulipas.

1847

Great migration from the Netherlands to Middle Western states begins.

Cyrus H. McCormick, moving from Cincinnati, opens reaper factory in Chicago.

S. Page patents revolving disc harrow.

American Medical Association founded at Philadelphia.

New Hampshire establishes first state 10-hour law for workers.

Evangeline by Henry Wadsworth Longfellow published.

Jan 15 Robert Barnwell Rhett of South Carolina, in House, declares for the South that the states are joint owners of the territories and the Federal government is agent of the states.

Jan 16 Oregon Bill, for territorial or- ganization of Oregon, excluding slavery by restrictions of Northwest Ordinance, passes House, 133–35. Is tabled in Senate, 26–18, Mar. 3.

Feb 19 John C. Calhoun introduces in Senate resolutions of Virginia legislature embodying his doctrine of obligation of Federal government to protect property interests of slave owners in territories.

Feb 22–23 Battle of Buena Vista. Gen- eral Taylor defeats General Santa Anna.

Mar 3 Three million dollars appropri- ated by Congress to enable the President to conclude treaty of "peace, limits, and boundaries" with Mexico.

Mar 3 Adhesive postage stamps pro- vided by act of Congress. Placed on sale in New York July 1, 1847.

Mar 3 Gas lighting for the Capitol and grounds adopted by Congress.

Mar 6 In the *License Cases*, Supreme Court, in decision on commerce power, rules that state license to sell liquor covers that imported from outside the state.

Mar 9 General Winfield Scott lands at Vera Cruz.

Mar 29 General Scott takes Vera Cruz from the Mexicans.

Apr 8 General Scott begins advance upon Mexico City.

Apr 15 Nicholas P. Trist appointed commissioner by President Polk to negotiate peace with Mexico.

Apr 16 Brigham Young with small company of Mormons leaves Council Bluffs "to spy out the land" toward the west.

Apr 18 General Scott defeats Mexicans at Cerro Gordo.

May 15 General Scott defeats Mexicans at Puebla.

June 6 Nicholas P. Trist opens negotiations with Mexico through British minister Charles Bankhead.

July 24 Mormons with **Brigham Young** arrive on shore of Great Salt Lake [Utah].

Aug 20 General Scott wins battle of Churubusco.

Sept Native American party meets at Philadelphia. Recommends General Zachary Taylor of Louisiana for President and nominates Henry A. S. Dearborn of Massachusetts for Vice-President.

Sept 8 Battle of Molino del Rey victory for General Scott. Over 700 Americans killed and wounded.

Sept 13 General Scott captures fortified hill of Chapultepec, last obstacle before Mexico City.

Sept 14 General Scott takes possession of Mexico City.

Nov Liberty party (abolitionist) meets in convention at New York. Nominates John P. Hale of New Hampshire for President and Leicester King of Ohio for Vice-President. Hale later withdraws in favor of Martin Van Buren.

Nov 29 Marcus Whitman, his wife and party massacred by Oregon Indians.

Dec 6 Abraham Lincoln of Illinois takes seat in 30th Congress.

Dec 14 Doctrine of popular sovereignty, leaving slavery in territories to respective legislatures, affirmed in resolutions introduced in Senate by D. S. Dickinson of New York.

Dec 22 Abraham Lincoln makes debut in House, introducing his "spot" resolutions in sharp issue with President Polk on Mexican War. Makes speech in support of resolutions Jan. 12, 1848.

Dec 29 Lewis Cass approves doctrine of popular sovereignty, or "squatter sovereignty," in letter to A. O. P. Nicholson, senator from Tennessee.

1848

German migration to U. S. given great impetus by failure of Revolution of 1848.

Swedish migration into Mississippi Valley begins.

Oneida, N. Y., socialist community, founded by Perfectionists under John Humphrey Noyes.

American Association for the Advancement of Science founded.

Alexander T. Stewart erects first department store, on Broadway, New York.

Telegraph communication between New York and Chicago established.

Elihu Burritt, leader of American peace movement, organizes international congress, meeting in Brussels, and persuades it to ratify proposal to establish a court of arbitration.

Andrew Carnegie arrives in U. S. from Scotland.

John Jacob Astor, richest man in America, dies, leaving fortune of $20,000,000.

Evening Schools started in New York City by Public School Society.

U. S. sends Jacob L. Martin, chargé d'affaires, as her first representative to the Vatican.

President Polk proposes purchase of Cuba from Spain, ready to pay $100,-000,000.

University of Wisconsin founded.

Associated Press organized by group of New York newspapers.

Alabama Platform introduced by William L. Yancey, emphasizing duty of Congress to protect all persons and all their property in the territories, adopted by Alabama Legislature.

Vermont legislature resolves that slavery should be prohibited in territories and abolished in District of Columbia.

Jan 24 Gold discovered in California by James W. Marshall in mill race above Sutter's Fort.

Jan 31 Captain John C. Frémont, upon charges of Colonel Kearney, found guilty by court martial of mutiny and disobedience.

Feb 2 Treaty of Guadalupe Hidalgo signed by Nicholas P. Trist with Mexico. Mexico accepts Rio Grande boundary and cedes New Mexico and California to U. S. upon payment of $15,-000,000. Senate consents, 38–14, Mar. 10.

Feb 23 John Quincy Adams dies in his 81st year, while speaking on floor of House.

Apr   Pacific Mail Steamship Com-pany incorporated to make use of route across Isthmus of Panama.

Apr 3 Chicago Board of Trade estab-lished.

May   Swarm of locusts, descending upon new Mormon settlement at Salt Lake, destroyed by sea gulls flocking in from the lake.

May 22–26 Democratic National Con-vention meets at Baltimore. Nominates Lewis Cass of Michigan for President and William O. Butler of Kentucky for Vice-President.

May 29 Wisconsin enters the Union.

June 2 Liberty League, an abolition group, in convention in Rochester, N. Y., nominates Gerrit Smith of New York for President and Charles E. Foote of Michigan for Vice-President.

June 7–9 Whig National Convention meets at Philadelphia. Nominates General Zachary Taylor of Louisiana for President and Millard Fillmore of New York for Vice-President.

June 13 Industrial congress with rep-resentatives of labor organizations meets at Philadelphia. Nominates Gerrit Smith of New York for President and William S. Waitt of Illinois for Vice-President.

June 22 Barnburners, withdrawn from Democratic convention at Baltimore, meet at Utica, N. Y. Nominate Martin Van Buren for President and Henry Dodge of Wisconsin for Vice-President.

July 4 Cornerstone of Washington monument laid in Washington.

July 19 First Woman's Rights Conven-tion launched at Seneca Falls, N. Y., by Lucretia Mott and Elizabeth Cady Stanton.

July 27 Clayton Compromise. Bill to organize Oregon, New Mexico and California, validating abolition of slavery in Oregon and prohibiting passage of laws relative to slavery by territorial legislatures of New Mexico and California, passed in Senate. Tabled in House July 28.

Aug 9 Free Soil party, anti-slavery, emerges in national convention at Buffalo, N. Y. Nominates Martin Van Buren for President and Charles Francis Adams of Massachusetts for Vice-President. "Free soil, free speech, free labor and free men."

Aug 14 Bill organizing Oregon as a territory without slavery, by applying restrictions of Northwest Ordinance, finally becomes law.

Aug 19 Discovery of gold in Califor-nia first reported in New York press, in the *Herald.*

Sept 16 Lt. Edward F. Beale arrives in Washington with specimens of gold from California.

Nov 7 Presidential election. Zachary Taylor and **Millard Fillmore,** Whig, elected President and Vice-President, 163 electoral votes to 127 for Lewis Cass and William O. Butler, Democrats. Van Buren, Free Soiler, receives popular vote of 291,263.

Dec 5 President Polk in annual message officially confirms reports of discovery of gold in California.

Dec 15 Postal treaty between U. S. and Great Britain signed at London. Senate consents Jan. 5, 1849.

Dec 22 Southerners in Congress hold caucus on slavery question. Jan. 22, 1849, adopt "An Address to the People of the Southern States," prepared by Calhoun.

1849

Charles Sumner in annual address before American Peace Society makes strong plea for a congress of nations with high court of judicature.

Elizabeth Blackwell receives medical degree from Geneva College, Geneva, N. Y., first American woman physician.

Wisconsin State Historical Society founded.

Holyoke dam built, first successful dam across Connecticut River.

Safety pin patented by Walter Hunt of New York. Had invented eye-pointed needle for sewing machine.

Mail stagecoach line opened between Independence, Mo., and Santa Fe.

Spiritualism founded by Fox sisters, Margaret and Kate, in Rochester, N. Y.

Cholera scourge begins in the South, spreads through the Middle West in 1850, to the Pacific in 1851.

History of the United States, first 3 of 6 vols., by Richard Hildreth, published.

Civil Disobedience, essay by Henry D. Thoreau, published. The State, a malevolent institution, is a threat to liberty of the individual.

Disquisition on Government by John C. Calhoun published.

Feb 7 In the *Passenger Cases,* Supreme Court disallows laws of New York and Massachusetts laying a tax on each alien arriving, as regulation of foreign commerce.

Feb 12 Mass meeting in San Francisco establishes temporary government for that area.

Feb 28 The *California* of Pacific Mail Steamship Company arrives at San Francisco with first load of gold seekers from the East.

Mar 3 Territorial government for Minnesota established, slavery prohibited.

Mar 3 Department of the Interior created. Patent office transferred from State Department to it.

Mar 3 Coinage of gold dollar and double eagle authorized by Congress.

Mar 5 General Zachary Taylor inaugurated President and **Millard Fillmore** Vice-President.
> [President Taylor's Cabinet: John M. Clayton, Secretary of State; William M. Meredith, Secretary of Treasury; G. W. Crawford, Secretary of War; William B. Preston, Secretary of Navy; Thomas Ewing, Secretary of Interior; Jacob Collamer, Postmaster General; Reverdy Johnson, Attorney General].

Mar 10 Missouri legislature declares that "the right to prohibit slavery in any territory belongs exclusively to the people thereof."

Apr 7 Panama Railroad Company incorporated by New York Legislature. Begins regular operation Jan. 28, 1855.

Aug 11 President Taylor enjoins Americans against making filibustering expeditions into Cuba.

Sept 1–Oct 13 California convention meets at Monterey. Drafts a constitution, prohibiting slavery. Petitions Congress for admission to the Union as a free state. Constitution ratified by popular vote Nov. 13.

Dec 4 President Taylor in annual message informs Congress of situation in California and of his wish that California may be admitted immediately as a state.

Dec 20 Treaty of amity, commerce and navigation with the Hawaiian Islands signed. Senate consents Jan. 14, 1850.

Dec 22 Howell Cobb of Georgia elected Speaker of House after 3 weeks' contest in wild disorder and 63 ballots.

1850

Population, 23,191,876.

Cotton crop, 2,136,000 bales for year.

University of Utah, Salt Lake City, founded.

A hundred and twenty colleges in U. S. listed by *American Almanac* for this year.

English sparrows, 8 pairs, imported under auspices of Brooklyn Institute to protect shade trees from caterpillars. In 1890, 100 starlings are brought from Europe to Central Park, New York, to prey upon sparrows.

Jenny Lind, "Swedish Nightingale," brought to U. S. by P. T. Barnum.

Harper's Monthly Magazine begins publication.

Deseret News, Mormon Church organ, begins publication, Salt Lake City.

Jan 29 Compromise of 1850. Henry Clay introduces in Senate a series of 8 resolutions "to settle and adjust amicably all existing questions of controversy . . . arising out of the institution of slavery." Between Sept. 9 and 20, resolutions incorporated in 5 acts of Congress.

Feb 5–6 Henry Clay gives last great speech, in support of his Compromise.

Mar 4 John C. Calhoun's speech against the Compromise presented by Senator Mason of Virginia. Calhoun's last effort for the South. Dies Mar. 31.

Mar 7 Daniel Webster's "Seventh of March" speech for the Compromise. His last great speech.

Mar 11 William Henry Seward speaks in Senate against the Compromise.

Mar 26–27 Salmon P. Chase speaks in Senate against the Compromise.

Apr 18 Compromise resolutions referred to committee of 13, Henry Clay, chairman.

Apr 19 Clayton-Bulwer Treaty signed. Great Britain and U. S. declare "that neither one nor the other will ever obtain . . . for itself any exclusive control" over any ship canal across Nicaragua, nor "exercise any dominion over . . . any part of Central America." Ratified by both countries July 4.

Apr 27 The *Atlantic*, first of 4 steamships of Collins Line, begins competition with British Cunard Line in transatlantic passenger service.

May 8 Clay and committee of 13 report Compromise bills in Senate.

June 3 Nashville Convention, called by radical Southern leaders to consider Compromise of 1850, convenes with 9 slave states represented. Moderates maintain control. Adjourned convention of smaller number meets Nov. 11, denounces Compromise and asserts right of secession.

July 9 President Zachary Taylor dies at White House.

July 10 Vice-President Millard Fillmore takes oath of office and succeeds to Presidency.
[President Fillmore's Cabinet: Daniel Webster, Secretary of State; Thomas Corwin, Secretary of Treasury; C. M. Conrad, Secretary of War; William A. Graham, Secretary of Navy; A. H. H. Stuart, Secretary of Interior; Nathan K. Hall, Postmaster General; J. J. Crittenden, Attorney General.]

Sept 9 California enters the Union as free state.

Sept 9 Territories of New Mexico and Utah organized without provision regarding slavery, by act of Congress.

Sept 9   Texas boundaries defined and Texas compensated for land surrendered to New Mexico with payment of $10,-000,000, by act of Congress.

Sept 18   Fugitive Slave Act of 1850, to strengthen Act of 1793, provides Federal in place of state jurisdiction.

Sept 20   Slave trade in District of Co- lumbia forbidden after Jan. 1, 1851, by act of Congress.

Sept 20   First Federal land grant for railroad construction made to Illinois, Mississippi and Alabama for railroad between Chicago and Mobile, through activity of Senator Stephen A. Douglas.

Sept 28   Flogging in the Navy abol- ished by act of Congress.

Oct 21   Chicago City Council refuses to enforce Fugitive Slave Act.

Oct 30   Mass meeting in New York re- solves to sustain Fugitive Slave Act.

Dec   Georgia Platform, drafted by state convention, accepts Compromise of 1850, asserts Union sentiment of the state, but warns of secession if Compromise is violated by the North.

1851

Donald McKay in his *Flying Cloud* establishes record, never beaten, for clipper ships: New York to San Francisco in 89 days, 8 hours.

Sixty delegates from U. S. attend Peace Conference, London.

Amelia Jenks Bloomer in her magazine, the *Lily,* launches campaign for women's dress reform.

Emanuel Leutze paints "Washington Crossing the Delaware" in Düsseldorf, Germany.

Young Men's Christian Association established in Boston.

John Gorrie patents mechanical refrigeration.

William Kelly begins "air-boiling" proc-

ess in steel making, anticipating Bessemer process.

Lt. William Lewis Herndon explores Amazon River. Reports published 1853–1854.

General Lopez, Cuban, with company of Americans, makes filibustering expedition to free Cuba from Spanish rule. Captured, he is shot in Havana, and his followers either shot or taken prisoners to Spain.

In *Strader v. Graham,* Supreme Court decides slaves returning to Kentucky from Ohio are subject to Kentucky law.

"Old Folks at Home" by Stephen C. Foster published. One of his 175 songs.

Moby Dick by Herman Melville published.

Karl Marx' *Revolution and Counter Revolution* published serially in Greeley's New York *Tribune,* 1851–1852.

Feb 15   Shadrach, fugitive slave, res- cued from jail in Boston by mob of Negroes in resistance to new Fugitive Slave Law. President Fillmore, Feb. 18, calls upon citizens and officials of Massachusetts to execute the law.

Mar 3   Cheaper postage rates, 3 cents for a half ounce up to 3,000 miles, adopted by Congress.

Mar 3   Coinage of 3-cent pieces author- ized by Congress.

May 15   First train on Erie Railroad reaches Dunkirk on Lake Erie. The Erie is first railroad to connect New York City with Great Lakes.

June 2   Maine Prohibition Law passed, sponsored by Neal Dow. Prohibits manufacture and sale of intoxicating liquors in Maine.

June 9   Vigilantes organized by lead- ing citizens of San Francisco to deal with lawlessness.

July 23   Sioux chieftains in treaty cede to U. S. all their lands in Iowa and most of their lands in Minnesota. Senate consents June 23, 1852.

Aug 22   U. S. yacht *America,* compet-

ing with British *Aurora* in international yacht race at Cowes, wins cup offered by Royal Yacht Society of England. Cup has remained in America ever since. Final race, 1937, won by U. S. yacht *Ranger.*

Sept 18 New York *Times* **first published,** Henry J. Raymond editor.

Oct 1 "Jerry," fugitive slave, rescued from jail in Syracuse, N. Y., by abolitionists.

Oct 8 Hudson River Railroad between New York City and Albany opened.

Oct 22 President Fillmore by proclamation warns against participation in military expeditions into Mexico.

Dec 1 Charles Sumner of Massachusetts and Benjamin Wade of Ohio enter U. S. Senate.

Dec 5 Louis Kossuth, Hungarian patriot, guest of U. S., given great welcome in New York.

Dec 24 Fire destroys two-thirds of Library of Congress collection.

1852

First effective compulsory school attendance law enacted by Massachusetts.

Yale and Harvard hold first intercollegiate rowing match in U. S. on Lake Winnipesaukee.

E. G. Otis invents elevator with safety appliances.

Christopher Dorflinger invents a lamp chimney.

Journeymen printers form National Typographical Union in convention at Cincinnati.

Prohibition laws adopted by Massachusetts, Louisiana and Vermont.

Spiritualists conventions held in Cleveland, Boston and Worcester.

Pennsylvania adopts railroad gauge different from that of New York lest Erie Railroad pass through the state to Ohio.

Pennsylvania Railroad between Philadelphia and Pittsburgh completed.

Uncle Tom's Cabin by Harriet Beecher Stowe published.

The Pro-Slavery Argument, essays by leading pro-slavery Southerners, published.

Jan 5 Southern Commercial Convention meets at New Orleans with 600 delegates from 11 states, first of series of Southern economic conventions.

Feb 6 In *Pennsylvania v. Wheeling Bridge Company,* Supreme Court decides against right of Virginia to authorize bridging of a navigable stream wholly within her limits, Justice Taney dissenting.

Feb 20 First through train from the East reaches Chicago by way of Michigan Southern Railway.

Mar 13 First newspaper cartoon of Uncle Sam appears in New York comic weekly, *Diogenes, Hys Lantern.*

June 1–6 Democratic National Convention meets at Baltimore. Nominates Franklin Pierce of New Hampshire for President on 49th ballot, and William R. King of Alabama for Vice-President. Convention proclaims Compromise of 1850 as solution of slavery question.

June 16–21 Whig National Convention meets at Baltimore. Nominates Winfield Scott of New Jersey for President on 53rd ballot, and William A. Graham of North Carolina for Vice-President. Convention "acquiesces" in Compromise of 1850 and commits party to its strict enforcement.

July 3 Branch of U. S. mint at San Francisco established by act of Congress.

Aug 11 Free Soil National Convention meets at Pittsburgh. Nominates John P. Hale of New Hampshire for President and George W. Julian of Indiana for Vice-President. Convention declares "Slavery is a sin against God and a crime against man."

Aug 24 "Uncle Tom's Cabin," dramatization of Harriet Beecher Stowe's novel, first appears on stage.

Aug 26 Senator Charles Sumner in 4-hour speech attacks Fugitive Slave Law in support of his resolution against it.

Nov 2 Presidential election. Franklin Pierce and **William R. King**, Democrats, elected President and Vice-President, 254 electoral votes to 42 for Winfield Scott and William A. Graham, Whig. John P. Hale, Free Soiler, receives popular vote of 155,825.

1853

Mrs. Amos Bronson Alcott heads petition of 74 women for woman suffrage at Massachusetts Constitution Convention.

New York City policemen required to wear official uniforms and caps. Similar attire soon required of police of Boston and Philadelphia.

Norwegian Evangelical Church of America organized by Norwegians in Wisconsin.

Baltimore and Ohio Railroad reaches Wheeling on the Ohio.

New York Central Railroad formed by merger of 10 short lines between Albany and Buffalo.

Flush Times of Alabama and Mississippi by Joseph Glover Baldwin published.

Feb 21 Coinage Act of 1853 reduces amount of silver in all silver coins except the dollar, to keep smaller coins in circulation, and authorizes coinage of 3-dollar gold pieces.

Mar 2 Territory of Washington formed, set off from Oregon Territory.

Mar 3 Army Appropriation Act. Congress authorizes $150,000 to make survey of most practicable transcontinental railroad routes, under direction of War Department.

Mar 4 Franklin Pierce inaugurated President. Vice-President William R. King takes oath of office in Cuba. In inaugural address President Pierce urges annexation of Cuba.

[President Pierce's Cabinet: William L. Marcy, Secretary of State; James Guthrie, Secretary of Treasury; Jefferson Davis, Secretary of War; James C. Dobbin, Secretary of Navy; Robert McClelland, Secretary of Interior; James Campbell, Postmaster General; Caleb Cushing, Attorney General.] [Diplomatic appointments of President Pierce: James Buchanan to Great Britain, John Y. Mason of Virginia to France, Pierre Soulé to Spain. All expansionists.]

Apr 18 Vice-President William R. King dies.

May 31 Dr. Elisha K. Kane sets out from New York in brig *Advance,* in command of second Grinnell Arctic expedition. [Expedition reaches Cape Constitution, farthest north for a sailing vessel.]

June Secretary of State Marcy directs diplomatic agents abroad to appear at court "in simple dress of an American citizen."

July 8 Commodore Matthew Calbraith Perry arrives in Yedo Bay, Japan. Leaves letter for Emperor from President Pierce with message that he will return in the spring for favorable reply.

July 14 Crystal Palace exhibition opens in New York City.

Dec 30 Gadsden Purchase. James Gadsden signs treaty with Mexico for purchase of tract south of Gila River, containing best railroad route from Texas to California, for $10,000,000, and for grant to U. S. of right of transit across Isthmus of Tehuantepec with right to protect it.

1854

1854–1858. War for Bleeding Kansas.

Astor Library opens in New York City.

Boston Public Library opens its doors.

A Systematic Treatise . . . on the Principal Diseases of the Interior Valley of North America by Dr. Daniel Drake published.

The Hireling and the Slave by William J. Grayson published.

Jan 4 Nebraska Bill for organization of Nebraska as a territory "with or without slavery" introduced in Senate by Stephen A. Douglas.

Jan 16 Senator Archibald Dixon of Kentucky proposes amendment to Nebraska Bill, repealing Missouri Compromise.

Jan 17 Senator Charles Sumner of Massachusetts proposes amendment to Nebraska Bill, reaffirming Missouri Compromise.

Jan 18 William Walker, filibuster, proclaims new republic of Sonora, containing Mexican states of Sonora and Lower California, with himself president. Subsequently tried by U. S. for violation of neutrality.

Jan 19 "The Appeal of the Independent Democrats in Congress, to the People of the United States," written by Salmon P. Chase, signed by 6 abolitionists of Congress, protesting Kansas-Nebraska Bill. Appears in *New York Daily Times* Jan. 24.

Jan 23 Kansas-Nebraska Bill offered by Senator Douglas, creating 2 territories from Nebraska section and repealing Missouri Compromise.

Feb 28 *Black Warrior*, packet ship plying between New York and Mobile and stopping at Havana, seized and fined by Spanish authorities for error in manifest.

Mar 4 Kansas-Nebraska Bill passes Senate, 37–14, after all-night session.

Mar 31 Treaty of Kanagawa, treaty of friendship and trade, is signed by Commodore Perry with Japan. Senate consents July 15. Ratifications exchanged Feb. 21, 1855.

Apr 26 Massachusetts Emigrant Aid Society chartered, organized by Eli Thayer to encourage immigration to Kansas. Soon rechartered in Connecticut as New England Emigrant Aid Society.

May 22 Kansas-Nebraska Bill passes House, 113–100.

May 26 Kansas-Nebraska Bill, amended, passes Senate, 35–13, at 1:10 A.M.

May 26 Boston mob attacks a Federal court house in vain effort to rescue Anthony Burns, arrested fugitive slave.

May 30 Kansas-Nebraska Bill signed by President Pierce.

May 31 President Pierce issues proclamation against filibustering invasions of Cuba.

June 5 Reciprocity with Canada obtained by treaty with Great Britain. Trade, fishing and navigation covered. Senate consents Aug. 2.

July Land office opened in Kansas Territory by Federal government.

July 6 Republican party's formal beginning made in a state mass convention at Jackson, Mich., which nominates mixed slate of Free-Soilers, Whigs and Democrats and adopts name Republican, after Jefferson's old party.

July 13 "People's" conventions meet in Wisconsin, Ohio and Indiana, bringing about union of anti-slavery forces and planning for fall elections.

July 19 Wisconsin Supreme Court releases Mr. Booth, convicted by a Federal court for rescuing runaway slave, and declares Fugitive Slave Act unconstitutional and void.

Summer Lawrence, Kan., settled by 2 parties of immigrants sent out from New England by Massachusetts Emigrant Aid Society. Town named for Amos Lawrence, patron of the Society.

Leavenworth, Kan., settled by slaveholders from western Missouri.

Oct 4 Abraham Lincoln replies to speech of Stephen A. Douglas at Springfield, Ill., on Kansas-Nebraska question. At Peoria, Oct. 16, Lincoln essentially repeats this speech, making him famous throughout the Northwest.

Oct 7 Andrew H. Reeder, Pennsylvania Democrat, arrives at Fort Leavenworth, first territorial governor of Kansas.

Oct 18 Ostend Manifesto, drafted by U. S. ministers Buchanan, Mason and Soulé at Ostend, Belgium, declares that if Spain will not sell Cuba, U. S. is justified in forcibly taking it.

Nov Know-Nothing party, "native-born Protestants," holds national council at Cincinnati. Throughout year alarming disturbances between Roman Catholics and Know-Nothings have occurred.

Nov 29 J. W. Whitfield elected Con-gressional representative from Kansas by 1,600 armed ruffians from across the border in Missouri, organized to extend slavery in Kansas.

1855

Elmira (N. Y.) Female College founded, first institution for women to grant academic degrees.

Salmon P. Chase elected governor of Ohio.

Castle Garden, at foot of Manhattan Island, leased by New York State Immigration Commission for reception of immigrants. 400,000 arrived in 1854.

Inspirationists arrive from Germany to make communistic settlement in Amana, Iowa.

Mrs. Carl Schurz, pupil of Friedrich Froebel, establishes first kindergarten in America, a German school at Watertown, Wis.

Prohibition laws are adopted by 6 states—Iowa, Michigan, Indiana, Delaware, New York, New Hampshire—and Nebraska Territory.

Niagara Falls suspension bridge opened, built over gorge by John Augustus Roebling.

The Sault Ste Marie, "The Soo," canal, connecting Lake Superior and Lake Huron, completed.

Railroad across Isthmus of Panama completed, built with U. S. capital.

American Journal of Education (1855–1882), Henry Barnard editor, begins publication.

William Bradford's *History of Plymouth Plantation,* long lost, discovered in library of Bishop of London in manuscript. Published 1856 by Massachusetts Historical Society.

Leaves of Grass by Walt Whitman published.

My Bondage and My Freedom by Frederick Douglass published.

Jan 9 *Creole* case of 1841 finally decided by umpire Joshua Bates, American-born English banker, who awards damages of $110,330 to U. S.

Jan 16 Nebraska's first territorial leg-islature meets at Omaha City.

Feb 10 Citizenship rights of children born abroad to U. S. citizens made secure by act of Congress. Alien women married to U. S. citizens are deemed citizens.

Feb 17 Construction of telegraph line from Mississippi River to the Pacific, by James Eddy and Hiram O. Alden, authorized by Congress.

Mar 3 Introduction of camels into arid Southwest authorized by appropriation of $30,000 by Congress, by recommendation of Secretary of War Jefferson Davis. [33 camels are brought from Egypt and prove satisfactory.]

Mar 30 Kansas' first territorial legis-lature elected by border ruffians from Missouri. Legislature first meets at Pawnee, July 2. Moves to Shawnee Mission, July 16.

June 5 National Council of Know-Nothing party meets at Philadelphia, as American party. Control seized by Southerners.

July 28 Andrew Reeder removed from governorship of Kansas Territory by President Pierce.

Aug 15 Free-state convention meeting at Lawrence, Kansas Territory, repudiates fraudulently elected legislature, calls for constitutional convention.

Sept 3 Wilson Shannon, new governor, arrives in Kansas Territory.

Sept 3 William Walker lands in Nicaragua with 160 men on filibustering expedition. Sets himself up as dictator for 2 years.

Oct 1 J. W. Whitfield again elected Congressional delegate from Kansas Territory by Missourians from across the border.

Oct 9 Andrew Reeder elected Congressional delegate from Kansas Territory by free-state men.

Oct 23 Free-state constitutional convention meets at Topeka, Kansas Territory, and drafts Topeka Constitution prohibiting slavery. Ratified Dec. 15, by vote of 1,731 to 46, only free-state men voting.

Dec 7 "Wakarusa War," threatened by Missouri men camped on Wakarusa River near Lawrence in Kansas Territory, ended by Governor Shannon without bloodshed.

Dec 8 President Pierce issues proclamation against filibustering in Nicaragua.

1856

Governor James H. Adams of South Carolina, in public message, argues for repeal of law of 1807 outlawing slave trade.

Whaling ship *E. L. B. Jenney,* after four and a half years out, returns to New Bedford, Mass., with 2,500 barrels of sperm oil.

Gail Borden patents process for condensing milk.

Western Union Telegraph Company organized.

The Backwoods Preacher by Peter Cartwright published.

Narrative of the Expedition of an American Squadron to the China Seas and Japan Performed in the Years 1852, 1853, and 1854. Compiled from the Original Notes and Journals of Commodore Perry and his Officers . . . , published.

Jan 1 Use of adhesive postage stamps becomes obligatory by act of Congress. Available since 1847.

Jan 15 Free-state party in Kansas, under Topeka Constitution, elects governor and legislature.

Jan 24 Senator Robert A. Toombs of Georgia gives address at Tremont Temple, Boston, in defense of slavery.

Jan 24 President Pierce in special message to Congress recognizes pro-slavery legislature in Territory of Kansas and condemns Topeka movement as revolutionary.

Feb 2 Anti-Nebraska members of Congress elect Nathaniel Banks of Massachusetts Speaker of the House after contest of 2 months.

Feb 11 President Pierce issues proclamation against both "border ruffians" and free-state men seeking unlawful control in Kansas Territory.

Feb 22 National Convention of Know-Nothing party, from now on calling itself American party, meets at Philadelphia. Nominates ex-President Millard Fillmore for President and Andrew J. Donelson of Tennessee for Vice-President.

Mar 4 Topeka legislature memorializes Congress for admission to Union.

Apr 21 First railroad bridge across Mississippi River opened, between Rock Island, Ill., and Davenport, Iowa.

May 19–20 Senator Charles Sumner gives "Crime against Kansas" speech in Senate.

May 21 Lawrence, Kansas Territory, taken and sacked by pro-slavery armed force.

May 22 Preston S. Brooks, Congressman from South Carolina, attacks Senator Charles Sumner as he sits at his desk in Senate chamber.

May 24 John Brown of Osawatomie and his followers massacre 5 pro-slavery men along Pottawatomie Creek in Kansas.

June 2–5 Democratic National Convention meets at Cincinnati. Nominates James Buchanan of Pennsylvania for President and John C. Breckinridge of Kentucky for Vice-President.

June 2 Anti-Slavery Know-Nothing se-ceders meet in convention at New York. Nominate John C. Frémont of California and W. F. Johnston of Pennsylvania for President and Vice-President. "Free territory and Free Kansas."

June 17–19 Republican party meets in first national convention at Philadelphia, nominates John C. Frémont of California for President and William L. Dayton of New Jersey for Vice-President. Denounces polygamy and slavery.

July 3 Bill to admit Kansas under free-state constitution passed in House, 100–97. Rejected in Senate July 8.

July 4 Free-state legislature at To-peka, Kansas Territory, dispersed by U. S. troops from Fort Leavenworth.

July 20 Handcart Migration of Mor-mons to Salt Lake begins with first company leaving Florence, Neb.

Aug 18 Annexation by U. S. of any guano island unclaimed by another government authorized by act of Congress. Jarvis and Baker's islands in mid-Pacific accordingly annexed 1857, Howland's Island 1858.

Sept 15 John W. Geary, newly appointed governor of Kansas Territory, with Federal troops disperses armed Missourians marching upon Lawrence. Brings temporary peace to Territory.

Sept 17 Whig National Convention meets at Baltimore. Endorses Know-Nothing candidates Fillmore and Donelson.

Sept 21 Illinois Central Railroad be-tween Chicago and Cairo completed.

Nov 4 Presidential election. James Buchanan and John C. Breckinridge, Democrats, elected President and Vice-President with 174 electoral votes to 114 for Frémont and Dayton, Republican, and 8 for Fillmore and Donelson, American.

1857

Railroad celebration, country-wide, commemorates railroad connection of St. Louis with New York.

Pennsylvania Railroad buys up main canal system of Pennsylvania to eliminate competition.

Michigan State College of Agriculture opens as first state institution in U. S. to offer courses in scientific and practical agriculture.

Cooper Institute founded in New York by Peter Cooper.

The Atlantic Monthly founded, James Russell Lowell editor.

Harper's Weekly founded, George William Curtis editor.

The Impending Crisis of the South by Hinton Rowan Helper published.

Jan 15 State Disunion Convention held at Worcester, Mass. William Lloyd Garrison comes out for "No union with slave holders."

Feb 21 Legal tender quality of for-eign coins removed by act of Congress.

Mar 3 Tariff Act lowers duties to gen-eral level of 20 per cent.

Mar 4 James Buchanan and John C. Breckinridge inaugurated President and Vice-President.

[President Buchanan's Cabinet: Lewis Cass, Secretary of State; Howell Cobb, Secretary of Treasury; John B. Floyd, Secretary of War; Isaac Toucey, Secretary of Navy; Jacob Thompson, Secretary of Interior; Aaron V. Brown, Postmaster General; J. S. Black, Attorney General.]

Mar 6 Dred Scott decision announced by Chief Justice Taney: Scott, a Negro, cannot bring suit in a Federal court. Moreover, the Missouri Compromise, under which he claims freedom because of residence in Territory of Minnesota, is unconstitutional.

Aug 24 Panic of 1857 precipitated by failure of Ohio Life Insurance and Trust Company. In 1857, 4,932 business failures; in 1858, 4,225 failures; in 1859, 3,913 failures.

Sept 11 Mountain Meadows Massacre Utah: 120 emigrants, bound for California, killed by band of Indians aroused by Mormon fanatic John D. Lee. Massacre follows President Buchanan's order of removal of Brigham Young as governor of Utah.

Oct 5 Free-state legislature chosen in in Kansas election, under supervision of Governor Robert J. Walker.

Oct 19–Nov 3 Lecompton Constitu-tional Convention. Managed by proslavery forces, it frames constitution legalizing property in slaves then in Kansas and leaving to popular vote the constitution with slavery or the constitution without slavery.

Dec William Walker, on second fili-bustering expedition to Nicaragua, arrested by U. S. Navy and returned to New York as prisoner.

Dec 8 President Buchanan in annual message asks Congress for troops to reassert Federal authority in Utah, and affirms legality of Lecompton Constitution.

Dec 9 Stephen A. Douglas comes out in Senate against Lecompton Constitution in Kansas.

Dec 21 Lecompton Constitution, with slavery, adopted in Kansas Territory, free-state men not voting.

1858

Defiance of Federal government by Brigham Young and Mormon followers finally put down by Federal troops.

Ship subsidy policy of U. S. abandoned by Congress.

Religious Revival of 1858, intensified by Panic, spreads over country.

YWCA organized in New York as "Ladies' Christian Association."

St. Patrick's Cathedral in New York begun, first great edifice of Catholic Church in America.

Frederick Law Olmsted appointed architect-in-chief of Central Park, New York.

Photographer Matthew B. Brady establishes studios in New York and Washington.

George M. Pullman invents sleeping car, first used on Chicago and Alton Railroad.

Harvester which gathers grain into bundles patented by Charles Wesley Marsh.

Modern mowing machine patented by Lewis Miller.

History of New England, first of 4 vols., by John Graham Palfrey, published.

Jan 4 Lecompton Constitution reject-ed, on second vote, in Kansas Territory, free-state men voting.

Feb 2 President Buchanan recom-mends to Congress admission of Kansas as slave state, under Lecompton Constitution.

Mar 23 Senate votes to admit Kansas as state under Lecompton Constitution.

Apr 1 The House substitutes bill to resubmit Lecompton Constitution to popular vote.

May 4 English Bill, a compromise measure submitted by W. H. English of Indiana, becomes law. Offers immediate admission of Kansas to Union, plus large grant of public land, if she accepts Lecompton Constitution, resubmitted for vote.

May 11 Minnesota enters the Union.

June 16 Abraham Lincoln, in accept-ing nomination for Senator from Illinois, says, " 'A house divided against itself cannot stand.' I believe this government cannot endure permanently half slave and half free."

June 18 Treaty of peace, amity and commerce concluded with China. Senate consents Dec. 15.

July 29 Treaty with Japan, which becomes basis for Japan's trade relations with foreign powers for rest of century, completed by Townsend Harris, first U. S. consul to Japan. Senate consents Dec. 15.

Aug 2 Lecompton Constitution submitted for third time in accordance with English Act, rejected by Kansas voters. Kansas not admitted to the Union until 1861.

Aug 5 First transatlantic cable completed, promoted by Cyrus W. Field.

Aug 16 Queen Victoria and President Buchanan exchange greetings over new Atlantic Cable.

Aug 21–Oct 15 Lincoln-Douglas debates, 7 in number, during campaign in Illinois for seat in U. S. Senate.

Aug 27 Freeport Doctrine of Stephen A. Douglas announced in second debate with Abraham Lincoln: The people of a territory can introduce or exclude slavery as they please, "for the reason that slavery cannot exist a day unless it is supported by local police regulations." Probably wins his re-election to Senate.

Sept   Oberlin-Wellington   rescue. John, fugitive Negro, rescued by crowd of Oberlin students and one of their professors, and sent off to Canada.

Oct 9 Overland Mail stage, on first trip from San Francisco, reaches St. Louis after 23 days and 4 hours; Westbound stage, leaving at same time, reaches San Francisco Oct. 10 after 24 days, 20 hours, and 35 minutes.

Oct 13 Abraham Lincoln in Quincy debate says the Republican party thinks slavery is "a moral, a social, and a political wrong."

Autumn   Gold discovered on Cherry Creek in Kansas Territory, 90 miles from Pike's Peak [Colorado].

Autumn   Republican party wins plurality of seats in House.

Dec 6   President Buchanan in annual message asks authority to set up a "temporary protectorate" over northern Chihuahua and Sonora in Mexico, and also an appropriation to purchase Cuba.

1859

"Pike's Peak or Bust." Gold rush develops from discovery of 1858.

Great Atlantic and Pacific Tea Company founded, with one general store on Vesey Street, New York.

John F. Appleby invents self-knotting grain binder.

John Rogers models sculpture group, "Slave Auction."

First intercollegiate baseball game played between Williams and Amherst at Pittsfield, Mass.

Feb 14   Oregon enters the Union.

Mar 7   In *Ableman v. Booth,* **Supreme** Court declares Fugitive Slave Act of 1850 constitutional, reversing decision of Wisconsin Supreme Court of July 19, 1854.

Spring   Comstock Lode discovered in present-day Nevada. First large deposit of silver found in history of the country.

Apr 4   "Dixie," written by Dan D. Emmett for Bryant's Minstrels, first sung in Mechanics' Hall, New York.

May 12   Vicksburg Commercial Convention adopts resolution that all laws, state or Federal, prohibiting African slave trade ought to be repealed.

July 5   Kansas constitutional convention opens at Wyandotte. Constitution prohibiting slavery completed July 29.

Aug 27   Edwin L. Drake, drilling near Titusville, Pa., strikes oil, beginning of modern oil industry.

Sept   Merchants'   Grain   Forwarding Association organized in Chicago.

Oct 4 Wyandotte Constitution ratified in Kansas Territory by popular vote, 10,421 to 5,530.

Oct 16–18 John Brown's raid on Harpers Ferry. With 13 whites and 5 Negroes, he seizes U. S. arsenal. Is captured by Colonel Robert E. Lee and marines.

Nov 28 Great Britain by treaty cedes the Bay Islands to Honduras. This, with cession of Mosquito coast to Nicaragua by treaty of Jan. 28, 1860, clears up Anglo-American friction in Isthmian area.

Dec 2 John Brown hanged in public square of Charlestown, Va.

Dec 5 Two-months contest over Speakership of House precipitated by resolution that anyone who has endorsed Hinton Helper's *Impending Crisis* is unfit for position. William Pennington, conservative Republican of New Jersey, finally elected.

Dec 14 Georgia enacts law prohibiting post mortem manumission of slaves by deed or will.

Dec 17 Georgia legislature passes act permitting sale into slavery of free Negroes indicted as vagrants.

1860

Population, 31,443,321. Foreign born, 4,000,000.

Cotton crop, 3,841,000 bales for year.

First English-speaking kindergarten in America opened in Boston by Elizabeth Palmer Peabody.

Edward, Prince of Wales, visits U. S.

Beadle's dime novels first published.

Asa Gray publishes essays in support of Darwinism in *Atlantic Monthly*.

Feb 2 Jefferson Davis introduces in Senate resolutions calling for Federal slave code for protection of property in slaves in territories.

Feb 22 Wide-spread strike in Massachusetts shoe factories begins at Lynn. Result, higher wages.

Feb 27 Abraham Lincoln at Cooper Union, New York, addresses Young Men's Central Republican Union. Discusses power of Constitution to control slavery in territories.

Mar 19 Elizabeth Cady Stanton addresses joint session of New York Legislature on woman suffrage.

Apr 3 Pony Express inaugurated. Riders start from each terminus, Sacramento, Cal., and St. Joseph, Mo., covering route in 10 days.

Apr 11 Bill to admit Kansas with Wyandotte Constitution passed by House. No action by Senate.

Apr 23 Democratic National Convention meets at Charleston. Delegates from cotton South walk out after dispute over platform, Apr. 30. Convention adjourns May 3 without making nominations.

May 9 Constitutional Union party meets in convention at Baltimore. Nominates John Bell of Tennessee for President and Edward Everett of Massachusetts for Vice-President.

May 10 Morrill Tariff Bill, increasing duties moderately, passed by House. Becomes law Mar. 2, 1861.

May 14 Japan's first diplomat to a foreign state received in Washington.

May 16–18 Republican National Convention meets at Chicago. Nominates Abraham Lincoln for President on third ballot, and Hannibal Hamlin of Maine for Vice-President.

May 28 American Peace Society meets without quorum, first time in its history.

June 18–23 Democratic National Convention (adjourned session) meets at Baltimore. Nominates Stephen A. Douglas of Illinois for President and Herschel V. Johnson of Georgia for Vice-President.

June 22 Homestead Bill, passed by both houses of Congress, vetoed by of Congress to give land to individuals President Buchanan, who doubts power and objects to resulting discrimination.

June 28 Democratic party seceders from Charleston convention meet at Baltimore. Nominate John C. Breckinridge of Kentucky and Joseph Lane of Oregon for President and Vice-President.

Sept 12 William Walker, filibuster, meets his end before firing squad in Honduras.

Nov 6 Presidential election. Electoral vote: Abraham Lincoln, Republican, 180; John C. Breckinridge, Democrat, 72; Stephen A. Douglas, Democrat, 12; John Bell, Constitutional Union, 39. Hannibal Hamlin elected Vice-President.

Nov 14 Alexander H. Stephens in anti-secession speech before Georgia legislature appeals for support of the Constitution.

Dec 3 President Buchanan in annual message to Congress says that Southern states have no legal right to secede, nor has the Government any power to prevent it, and recommends an explanatory amendment of the Constitution on subject of slavery.

Dec 6 House Committee of Thirty-three appointed by Speaker to consider state of the Union.

Dec 17 Congress authorizes $10,000,000 issue of Treasury notes.

Dec 18 Crittenden Compromise. Sena-tor John Jordan Crittenden of Kentucky introduces compromise resolutions for preservation of Union, in form of amendments to Constitution.

Dec 20 Senate Committee of Thirteen, headed by Crittenden, appointed to consider his proposals of Dec. 18.

Dec 20 South Carolina, in convention meeting at Charleston, secedes from Union by vote of 169–0, unanimously declaring that "the union now subsisting between South Carolina and other States, under the name of the 'United States of America,' is hereby dissolved."

Dec 22 South Carolina appoints 3 commissioners to lay ordinance of secession before the President and Congress and to treat for delivery of forts and other public property within the state.

Dec 24 South Carolina issues an "Ad-dress to the People of the Slave-Holding States," and a "Declaration of the Causes of Secession," to the world.

Dec 26 Major Robert Anderson aban-dons Fort Moultrie and occupies Fort Sumter in Charleston Harbor.

Dec 27 Fort Moultrie and Castle Pinckney seized by South Carolina state forces.

Dec 28 President Buchanan holds in-terview with South Carolina commissioners as "private gentlemen."

Dec 29 South Carolina commissioners demand of the President immediate withdrawal of troops from Charleston Harbor.

Dec 30 South Carolina troops seize U. S. arsenal at Charleston.

Dec 31 President Buchanan replies to South Carolina commissioners that he cannot and will not remove troops from Charleston Harbor.

Dec 31 Senate Committee of Thirteen reports it has "not been able to agree upon any general plan of adjustment."

1861

American Miners' Association organized.

Anson Burlingame appointed first resident U. S. minister to China.

Telegraph connection from New York to San Francisco completed.

Jay Cooke establishes Jay Cooke and Company, a private bank, in Philadelphia.

Kansas grants school suffrage to women.

Freedmen's Relief associations formed in Boston, New York and Philadelphia.

Massachusetts Institute of Technology incorporated in Boston.

Sheffield Scientific School established at Yale.

Yale awards first American degree of doctor of philosophy.

Vassar Female College chartered.

Jan 3 Georgia state troops seize Fort Pulaski.

Jan 4 Alabama state troops seize U. S. arsenal at Mount Vernon, next day, Fort Morgan and Fort Gaines on Mobile Bay.

Jan 6 Fernando Wood, mayor of New York, proposes that in case of disunion, city of New York declare itself free and maintain neutrality.

Jan 6 Florida state troops seize U. S. arsenal at Apalachicola.

Jan 9 The *Star of the West*, unarmed merchant ship sent by government to reinforce Fort Sumter, fired upon by South Carolina guns and prevented from entering Charleston Harbor. Returns to New York.

Jan 9 Mississippi state convention adopts ordinance of secession, 84–15.

Jan 10 Louisiana state troops seize ar- senal and barracks at Baton Rouge.

Jan 10 Florida state convention adopts ordinance of secession, 62–7.

Jan 11 Alabama state convention adopts ordinance of secession, 61–39.

Jan 14 House Committee of Thirty- three recommends enforcement of Fugitive Slave Act and repeal of personal liberty laws in the North, and proposes amendment to the Constitution to protect South from future interference with slavery in the states. [Proposed amendment adopted by both houses of Congress, never ratified by the states.]

Jan 19 Georgia state convention adopts ordinance of secession, 208–89.

Jan 24 Georgia troops seize U. S. ar- senal at Augusta.

Jan 26 Louisiana state convention adopts ordinance of secession, 113–17.

Jan 29 Kansas enters Union, a free state under Wyandotte Constitution.

Feb 1 Louisiana seizes U. S. mint and customs house at New Orleans.

Feb 1 Texas state convention adopts ordinance of secession, 166–7.

Feb 4–27 Peace Convention called by Virginia, with representatives from 21 states, ex-President Tyler chairman, meets in Washington. Its proposed amendments to Constitution, rejected by Senate Mar. 2, not brought to vote in House.

Feb 4 Convention of delegates of 6 seceded states meets in Montgomery, Ala., to form provisional government.

Feb 8 Constitution for the Provisional Government of the Confederate States of America adopted by Montgomery convention.

Feb 8 Arkansas state troops seize U. S. arsenal at Little Rock.

Feb 9 Confederate Congress elects Jef- ferson Davis provisional President and Alexander H. Stephens provisional Vice-President.

Feb 9 People of Tennessee in public referendum reject proposal to call convention to consider secession, by vote of 68,282 to 59,449.

Feb 9 Confederate Congress declares in force all laws of U. S. which are not inconsistent with Constitution of Confederate States.

Feb 13 Official count of Presidential electoral votes made, election of Abraham Lincoln announced.

Feb 13 Virginia state convention as- sembles at Richmond to consider secession. Majority of delegates are unionist and prevent secession until after attack upon Fort Sumter.

Feb 16 Texas state troops seize U. S. arsenal at San Antonio.

Feb 18 General David E. Twiggs of U. S. Army surrenders U. S. military posts in Texas to the state.

Feb 18 Jefferson Davis and Alexander

H. Stephens inaugurated provisional President and Vice-President of Confederacy.

[Jefferson Davis' Cabinet: Robert Toombs of Georgia, Secretary of State; C. G. Memminger of South Carolina, Secretary of Treasury; L. P. Walker, of Alabama, Secretary of War; S. R. Mallory of Florida, Secretary of Navy; J. H. Reagan of Texas, Postmaster General; Judah P. Benjamin of Louisiana, Attorney General.]

Feb 23 Abraham Lincoln arrives se-cretly in Washington, having been warned of assassination plot in Baltimore.

Feb 27 President Davis appoints commissioners to U. S. to negotiate treaty of amity.

Feb 28 Colorado Territory formed.

Feb 28 Missouri state convention meets to consider secession. [Unionist sentiment prevents secession, 89–1.]

Feb 28 Confederate Congress authorizes domestic loan of $15,000,000.

Feb 28 and Mar 6 Confederate Congress authorizes call for 100,000 volunteers for 12 months.

Mar 2 Nevada Territory formed.

Mar 2 Dakota Territory formed.

Mar 2 Morrill Tariff Bill finally becomes law after secession has removed many Southern senators.

Mar 4 U. S. Army numbers 13,024 officers and men.

Mar 4 Abraham Lincoln inaugurated President and Hannibal Hamlin Vice-President.

[President Lincoln's Cabinet: William H. Seward, Secretary of State; Salmon P. Chase, Secretary of Treasury; Simon Cameron, Secretary of War; Gideon Welles, Secretary of Navy; Caleb B. Smith, Secretary of Interior; Montgomery Blair, Postmaster General; Edward Bates, Attorney General.]

Mar 4 Confederate flag of stars and bars adopted.

Mar 9 Confederate Congress authorizes issue of treasury notes up to $1,-000,000.

Mar 11 Constitution of Confederacy unanimously adopted by Congress at Montgomery. By end of April ratified by 7 seceded states.

Apr 1 Secretary of State Seward presents to President Lincoln "Some Thoughts for the President's Consideration," suggesting that he, Seward, take over administration of government, and that U. S. engage in a European war in order to unite North and South.

Apr 12 Fort Sumter in Charleston Harbor fired upon by General P. T. Beauregard.

Apr 14 Fort Sumter surrendered to Confederacy.

Apr 15 President Lincoln, declaring that "insurrection" exists, calls for 75,-000 volunteers for 3 months' service to put it down.

Apr 16 North Carolina state troops seize Fort Caswell and Fort Johnston.

Apr 17 Virginia state convention adopts ordinance of secession, 88–55. Popular referendum approves May 23.

Apr 17 President Davis invites application for letters of marque and reprisal for capture of ships flying U. S. flag.

Apr 18 Union commander abandons and burns U. S. arsenal at Harpers Ferry.

Apr 19 Blockade of ports of South Carolina, Georgia, Florida, Alabama, Mississippi, Louisiana and Texas declared by Lincoln. Apr. 27, extended to Virginia and North Carolina.

Apr 19 Baltimore riot. Massachusetts 6th Regiment, passing through Baltimore, attacked by secessionist mob. First bloodshed in Civil War.

Apr 20 Robert E. Lee resigns commission as colonel in U. S. Army. Apr. 23, accepts chief command of Virginia state forces.

May 3 President Lincoln appeals for 42,034 volunteers to serve for 3 years, or duration of the war.

May 6 Confederate Congress recognizes state of war between U. S. and Confederate States.

May 6 Arkansas convention adopts ordinance of secession, 69–1.

May 13 Queen Victoria issues proclamation of neutrality in American conflict.

May 13 Charles Francis Adams arrives in London as U. S. minister.

May 16 Confederate Congress authorizes loan of $50,000,000 to be raised by bonds or treasury notes.

May 20 North Carolina convention adopts ordinance of secession without dissenting vote.

May 21 Confederate Congress prohibits payment of debts to Northern creditors. Prohibits export of cotton except through Confederate seaports.

May 25 General Benjamin F. Butler, in command of Fortress Monroe, Va., declares Negroes escaped to within his lines are contraband of war.

May 27 American Peace Society meets at Park Street Church, Boston, and justifies the war being waged by the North.

June Great comet appears, considered prophetic of war by many.

June 3 Union forces under General George Brinton McClellan defeat Confederates at Philippi, in campaign in western Virginia.

June 8 Tennessee secedes from Union by popular vote of over 2 to 1.

June 9 U. S. Sanitary Commission organized by Secretary of War, forerunner of Red Cross.

June 10 France proclaims neutrality in American conflict.

June 11 Convention called by loyal element in Virginia, meets at Wheeling and organizes a Union government. Francis H. Pierpont elected governor June 19.

June 17 Spain proclaims neutrality in American conflict.

June 27 Central Pacific Railroad incorporated in California with Leland Stanford president and Collis P. Huntington vice-president.

July 2 President Lincoln empowers General Scott to suspend privilege of habeas corpus.

July 4 Thirty-seventh Congress meets in special session, called by President Lincoln to provide means for crushing rebellion.

July 13 Congress passes act recognizing that insurrection exists in certain states.

July 17 Loan not to exceed $250,000,-000 authorized by act of Congress.

July 20 Confederate Congress meets in Richmond, Va., capital of Confederacy from this date.

July 21 First battle of Bull Run, Northern Army under General Irvin McDowell routed by Confederates under Generals Joseph E. Johnston and P. T. Beauregard.

July 22–25 Crittenden resolutions that war is being waged to "defend and maintain the supremacy of the Constitution and to preserve the Union" and not to overthrow or interfere with "rights or established institutions" of Confederate states, adopted by House. Senate adopts similar resolutions July 25.

Aug 5 Direct tax law passed by Congress, calling for $20,000,000 to be raised by the states.

Aug 5 First income tax ever levied by U. S. government passed by Congress—tax of 3 per cent on incomes in excess of $800.

Aug 5 Tariff Act increases rates on some schedules.

Aug 7 Construction of 7 iron-clad gunboats by J. B. Eads of St. Louis ordered by U. S. government.

Aug 10 Union forces under General Nathaniel Lyon defeated at Wilson's Creek, Mo.

Aug 16 President Lincoln in proclamation forbids trading with seceded states.

Aug 19 Confederate Congress author- izes $100,000,000 loan, largely a pro- duce loan. Chiefly taken up by planters.

Aug 19 Confederate Congress levies direct tax upon real estate, slaves and other property.

Aug 28 President   Davis   appoints James M. Mason commissioner to Great Britain and John Slidell commissioner to France.

Aug 28–29 Forts Clark and Hatteras on N. C. coast captured by Union forces under General Butler.

Aug 30 General John C. Frémont, in command of Department of Missouri, institutes martial law and by proclama- tion declares that slaves of all Missouri- ans taking up arms against U. S. are free. Sept. 2, President Lincoln orders modi- fication to conform with existing law.

Sept 6 General Ulysses S. Grant occu- pies Paducah, Ky., countering Confed- erate occupation of Columbus.

Oct 21 Battle of Ball's Bluff on the Potomac. Union forces defeated.

Nov 1 General George B. McClellan appointed general-in-chief of U. S. Army, to succeed General Winfield Scott.

Nov 2 General John C. Frémont re- moved from command by the President for insubordination and incompetence.

Nov 6 Jefferson Davis elected Presi- dent of Confederacy under ratified con- stitution.

Nov 7 Battle of Belmont, Mo., lost to Confederates. General Grant retires to Cairo, Ill.

Nov 7 Port Royal on S. C. coast taken in important victory by Federal fleet.

Nov 8 "Trent Affair" opens when James M. Mason and John Slidell, Confederate commissioners to Great Britain and France, are taken from Brit- ish mail packet *Trent* by Federal war- ship *San Jacinto,* Charles Wilkes cap- tain, precipitating crisis with Great Britain.

Nov 15 U. S. Christian Commission

organized by YMCA for service to Union soldiers.

Dec   S. C. planters near the coast burn their year's crop of cotton to pre- vent seizure by Union troops.

Dec 9–10 Committee on the Conduct of the War established by Congress to consist of 3 senators and 4 representa- tives.

Dec 24 Tariff duties increased on tea, coffee and sugar, as a war measure.

Dec 30 New York City banks suspend specie payment. Banks in other cities quickly follow. Jan. 1, 1862, national government suspends specie payment.

1862

"John Brown's Body" being sung and whistled all over the North.

Winslow Homer follows General Mc- Clellan in Peninsular Campaign as spe- cial war artist for *Harper's Weekly.*

Gordon McKay patents sewing machine for sewing soles to uppers of boots and shoes.

Gatling machine gun patented by Rich- ard Jordan Gatling.

Jan   *Bigelow Papers,* second series, by James Russell Lowell, begins publi- cation in *Atlantic Monthly.*

Jan   Average gold price of green- back dollar on New York market is 98 cents.

Jan 11 Edwin M. Stanton appointed by President Lincoln Secretary of War in place of Simon Cameron.

Jan 19–20 Battle of Mill Springs, Ky., decisive Union victory under General George H. Thomas.

Jan 27 President Lincoln issues Gen- eral War Order, No. 1, commanding for- ward movement of all Union land and naval forces to begin Feb. 22.

Jan 30 Federal   ironclad   *Monitor* launched, built by John Ericsson.

Feb Julia Ward Howe's "Battle Hymn of the Republic" appears in February *Atlantic Monthly*.

Feb The war in the West begins with great flanking movement by Union forces.

Feb 6 Fort Henry on Tennessee River forced to surrender to General U. S. Grant and Commodore A. H. Foote.

Feb 8 Roanoke Island captured by Union Army under General A. E. Burnside in expedition to North Carolina.

Feb 16 Fort Donelson on Cumberland River after 4 days' siege surrenders with some 14,000 men to General Grant.

Feb 18 Convention at Wheeling adopts pro-Union constitution for proposed state of West Virginia. Apr. 3, ratified by popular vote, 18,862 to 514.

Feb 22 Jefferson Davis inaugurated President of Confederacy. Permanent Constitution goes into effect.

Feb 23 Andrew Johnson appointed military governor of Tennessee by President Lincoln.

Feb 25 Nashville, Tenn., evacuated by Confederates under General Albert Sidney Johnston.

Feb 25 Legal Tender Act provides for (1) issue of $150,000,000 of non-interest bearing treasury notes, "greenbacks," and (2) loan of $500,000,000 in 6 per cent 5–20 bonds.

Feb 27 Power to suspend privilege of writ of habeas corpus granted the President by Confederate Congress.

Mar-May Shenandoah Valley Campaign, General Thomas J. ("Stonewall") Jackson seeks to divert attention from Richmond.

Mar 3 Columbus, Ky., occupied by Union forces, beginning of opening of the Mississippi.

Mar 6–8 Battle of Pea Ridge, Ark. Confederates under General Earl Van Dorn defeated by Union force under General Samuel R. Curtis.

Mar 8 Confederate ironclad frigate *Virginia,* formerly the *Merrimac,* sinks the *Cumberland* and defeats the *Congress* in Hampton Roads.

Mar 9 The *Monitor,* Federal ironclad with revolving gun-turret, forces the *Virginia* (the *Merrimac*) to withdraw, first battle of ironclads.

Mar 11 General McClellan relieved of command of Union forces except the Army of the Potomac, by Presidential order. General Henry W. Halleck given command of armies in the West.

Mar 14 General John Pope defeats Confederates at New Madrid, Mo., and occupies town.

Mar 14 New Bern, N. C., captured by Union force under General Burnside, a base from which to threaten Richmond.

Mar 17 General McClellan's Army of the Potomac begins embarkation from Alexandria, Va., for Peninsular Campaign.

Apr 5 General McClellan begins siege of Yorktown, Va., occupies it, May 4.

Apr 6–7 Battle of Shiloh on Tennessee River, in which both sides claim victory. General A. S. Johnston killed. Confederates driven back by General Grant.

Apr 7 Treaty signed with Great Britain for efficient suppression of slave trade.

Apr 7 Island No. 10, Confederate fort in Mississippi River, taken by Commodore Foote and General Pope.

Apr 10 Joint resolution of Congress, adopting President Lincoln's plan of compensated emancipation in the states, signed by the President.

Apr 11 Fort Pulaski, Ga., commanding approaches to Savannah, surrenders to Union force.

Apr 16 Confederate Congress calls into military service every white man between 18 and 35 for 3 years' service in its first Conscription Act.

Apr 16 Slavery abolished in District of Columbia by act of Congress.

Apr 24 Forts St. Philip and Jackson on the Mississippi, guarding approach to New Orleans, passed by Flag-officer David Glasgow Farragut with 13 of his 17 ships.

Apr 25 Farragut occupies New Orleans.

Apr 28 Forts St. Philip and Jackson surrender to Commander David Porter.

May 1 New Orleans turned over to General Benjamin F. Butler.

May 2 Edward Stanly appointed military governor of North Carolina by President Lincoln.

May 5 Battle of Williamsburg, Va. Union loss, 456 killed, 1,410 wounded; Confederate, 1,570 killed and wounded. Confederates retire toward Richmond.

May 9 General David Hunter pro- claims emancipation of slaves in his Department, including Georgia, Florida and South Carolina. Disavowed by President Lincoln May 19.

May 11 Confederates blow up the *Virginia* (the *Merrimac*) to prevent capture.

May 15 Department of Agriculture established by act of Congress. No Cabinet status until 1889.

May 20 Homestead Act grants free farm of 160 acres to any person who will occupy and improve it for 5 years.

May 25 Battle of Winchester, Va. Union forces under General Banks forced across the Potomac by General Jackson.

May 30 Corinth, Miss., evacuated by Confederates under General Beauregard, is occupied by General Halleck.

May 31–June 1 Battle of Fair Oaks (Seven Pines), Va., victory for Union army. Confederate General Joseph E. Johnston severely wounded. Union loss, 790 killed, 3,594 wounded; Confederate, 980 killed, 4,749 wounded.

June 2 General Robert E. Lee takes command of Confederate Army of Eastern Virginia and North Carolina.

June 3 Colonel George F. Shepley ap- pointed military governor of Louisiana by President Lincoln.

June 5 Fort Pillow, Tenn., evacuated by Confederates after 2-months' land and river siege.

June 6 Memphis, Tenn., surrenders to Union gunboat fleet under Captain Charles H. Davis.

June 19 Slavery abolished in terri- tories of U. S. by act of Congress.

June 25 Union League of America formed in Pekin, Ill. [Union League clubs organized in many cities.]

June 25–July 1 The Seven Days Bat- tles, Va., in which General Lee forces General McClellan to withdraw from the Peninsula to protection of Union gunboats on James River. Casualties of Seven Days: Union loss, killed 1,734, wounded 8,062, missing 6,053; Confederate, killed 3,478, wounded 16,261, missing, 875.

June 26 Battle of Mechanicsville, Confederates repulsed.

June 27, Gaines' Mill, Union force retreats.

June 28, On the Chickahominy, Con- federates unsuccessful in holding General McClellan's Army.

June 29, Savage's Station. Confed- erate attempt to stop Union retreat unsuccessful.

June 29–30, In crossing White Oak Swamp, Confederate pursuit unsuccessful.

July 1, Malvern Hill taken by Union Army, within sight of James River, one of terrible conflicts of the war. End of Peninsular Campaign.

June 27 Major-General John Pope assumes command of a new Union-Army of Virginia.

July 1 Union Pacific-Central Pacific railroad project approved by Congress.

July 1 Polygamy in the territories penalized with fine and imprisonment, by act of Congress. Three convictions in next 20 years.

July 1 Internal Revenue Act. Moderate duties levied upon many things.

July 2 Oath of loyalty required by act of Congress of all persons elected to Federal office.

July 2 Morrill Act provides for land grants for agricultural colleges.

July 11 $150,000,000 in additional treasury notes, "greenbacks," authorized by Congress. $35,000,000 to be in denominations less than 5 dollars.

July 11 Major-General Halleck appointed general-in-chief of all land forces of U. S. Army, with headquarters at Washington. U. S. Grant left in command of Army of West Tennessee.

July 14 Tariff Act increases duties to offset new internal revenue taxes.

July 14 Pension Act establishes system of pensions for men disabled in service since Mar. 4, 1861, and for next of kin in cases of death.

July 16 John Slidell, Confederate commissioner to France, received by Napoleon III. Asks recognition of Confederacy and warships to break blockade in exchange for cotton.

July 17 President Lincoln authorized by Congress to call out militia between 18 and 45 for period not to exceed 9 months, the so-called "Draft of 1862."

July 17 Currency Act of Congress authorizes use of postage stamps as currency.

July 17 Confiscation of rebel property authorized by Congress. Freed Negroes may be used in the Army.

July 19 John S. Phelps of Missouri appointed military governor of Arkansas by President Lincoln. Commission revoked July 9, 1863.

July 22 President Lincoln submits first draft of Emancipation Proclamation to Cabinet, received with surprise and partial approval.

July 29 Confederate cruiser *Alabama* leaves Liverpool where it was built.

July 30 "Copperhead," term of op-probrium applied to Northern sympathizers with the South, first appears in Cincinnati *Gazette,* referring to Indiana state Democratic Convention.

Aug 2 Secretary of State Seward in-structs Charles Francis Adams, minister to Great Britain, to neither receive nor discuss any offer of mediation in the war from Great Britain.

Aug 9 At Cedar Mountain, Va., Gen-eral "Stonewall" Jackson defeats Union forces.

Aug 18 Sioux uprising begins in Min-nesota under Little Crow.

Aug 20 Horace Greeley's editorial, "The Prayer of Twenty Millions," appears in New York *Tribune,* demanding that President Lincoln commit himself to emancipation of slaves.

Aug 22 President Lincoln replies to Greeley's editorial. "My paramount object in this struggle is to save the Union, and it is not either to save or to destroy slavery."

Aug 30 Second Battle of Bull Run, or Manassas. Union Army under General Pope defeated.

Sept 1 Battle of Chantilly, Va. "Stonewall" Jackson defeated at great sacrifice. Casualties at Manassas and Chantilly: Union, killed and wounded, 10,096; Confederate, 9,108.

Sept 4–7 Lee's Confederate Army crosses Potomac for Maryland campaign, occupies Frederick, Md., Sept. 7.

Sept 14 Battle of South Mountain, Md. General McClellan defeats General Lee.

Sept 15 Harpers Ferry, Md., captured by "Stonewall" Jackson. 12,000 prisoners, 13,000 small arms and quantities of stores surrendered.

Sept 17 Munfordville, Ky., taken by Confederates under General Braxton Bragg. 4,076 Union troops captured.

Sept 17 Battle of Antietam, Md., in-decisive. General Lee checked, retreats across the Potomac Sept. 18. Casualties: Union, 2,108 killed, 9,549 wounded; Confederate, 2,700 killed, 9,029 wounded.

Sept 19 At Iuka, Miss., General William Starke Rosecrans defeats Confederate General Sterling Price.

Sept 22 President Lincoln's preliminary Emancipation Proclamation, presented to Cabinet, is approved.

Sept 23 Emancipation Proclamation broadcast by press.

Sept 27 Second Conscription Act passed by Confederate Congress authorizes President to call out men between 35 and 45.

Oct   Grant's Vicksburg campaign begins. Ends July 1863.

Oct 3–4 Battle of Corinth, Miss. General Rosecrans defeats Confederate forces of Generals Price and Van Dorn.

Oct 7 W. E. Gladstone, British chancellor of the exchequer, in a speech at Newcastle declares, "Jefferson Davis and other leaders of the South . . . have made a nation. We may anticipate with certainty the success of . . . their separation from the North."

Oct 8 Battle of Perryville, Ky. Confederates under General Bragg defeated by General Don Carlos Buell. Philip H. Sheridan, commanding a center brigade, gains recognition. Casualties: Union, 845 killed, 2,851 wounded; Confederate, 510 killed, 2,635 wounded.

Nov   First Regiment of South Carolina Volunteers organized, first slave regiment in U. S. service. Colonel Thomas Wentworth Higginson of Boston commander.

Nov 5 General McClellan relieved of command of Army of the Potomac and ordered to turn command to General Ambrose E. Burnside, by order of the President.

Nov 14 Brigadier-General Andrew J. Hamilton appointed military governor of Texas.

Nov 24 Confederate General Joseph E. Johnston appointed in command of Army in the West.

Dec 7 Battle of Prairie Grove, Ark., Union victory.

Dec 13 Battle of Fredericksburg, Va. General Burnside severely defeated by General Lee. Casualties: Union, 1,284 killed, 9,600 wounded; Confederate 595 killed, 4,061 wounded.

Dec 20 Holly Springs, General Grant's main depot in northern Mississippi, taken by Confederates. Stores of $1,-500,000 value carried off or destroyed. Checks Grant's advance on Vicksburg.

Dec 29 At Chickasaw Bayou, Miss., General Sherman repulsed with great loss by Confederates.

Dec 31–Jan 2, 1863 Battle of Murfreesboro, or Stone's River, Tenn. Neither side can claim victory. Union advance toward Chattanooga checked. Casualties: Union, 1,677 killed, 7,543 wounded; Confederate, 1,294 killed, 7,945 wounded.

1863

Cornelius Vanderbilt secures control of New York and Harlem Railroad.

Tweed Ring begins in New York City with appointment of William M. Tweed as Street Commissioner.

Free delivery of mail begun in largest cities.

Robert College founded in Turkey by Christian educators in America.

William Bullock patents continuous roll printing press.

Fincher's Trades' Review founded in Philadelphia. Most influential labor paper of Civil War years.

Instructions for the Government of Armies in the United States in the Field, General Order No. 100 by Francis Lieber published with approval of the President.

Man Without a Country by Edward Everett Hale published in December *Atlantic Monthly.*

Jan   Average gold price of green-back dollar on New York market, 69 cents.

Jan 1   Emancipation Proclamation is-sued by President Lincoln, proclaiming freedom for slaves in states or parts of states in rebellion.

Jan 6   Bill introduced in Congress of-fering $10,000,000 to Missouri for emancipation of her slaves. Defeated through efforts of Missouri Democrats in House.

Jan 17   Third issue of $100,000,000 of legal tender notes, "greenbacks," authorized by Congress. Mar. 3, increased to $150,000,000.

Jan 20   General Burnside renews ad-vance upon Fredericksburg, Va., which rain turns into a mud march, resulting in failure and demoralization.

Jan 25   General Joseph Hooker suc-ceeds General Burnside in command of Army of the Potomac.

Jan 29   Confederate Congress author-izes loan of $15,000,000 to be placed abroad through Emil Erlanger, French financier.

Jan 30   General Grant takes command of expedition against Vicksburg, grand objective being opening of Mississippi River.

Feb   Emperor Napoleon III offers mediation to governments of North and South. North refuses Feb. 6.

Feb 22   Ground broken for Central Pacific Railroad at Sacramento, Cal.

Feb 24   Arizona, cut from New Mex-ico, organized as a territory.

Feb 25   National banking system estab-lished by act of Congress. Reframed in National Bank Act of June 3, 1864, it is basis for banking system as it emerged from Civil War.

Mar 3   National Academy of Science authorized by act of Congress.

Mar 3   Power to suspend privilege of writ of habeas corpus during the war granted the President by Congress.

Mar 3   Territory of Idaho formed, cut

from territories of Washington, Utah, Dakota and Nebraska.

Mar 3   Conscription Act adopted in North by Congress. Exemption allowed by payment of $300.

Mar 3   Number of Supreme Court justices increased from 9 to 10 by act of Congress. [Stephen J. Field appointed 10th justice.]

Mar 3   Act of Congress authorizes loans of $300,000,000 for 1863, and of $60,000,000 for 1864, in 10-40's, at 6 per cent. Also $400,000,000 of treasury notes at 6 per cent to pass as legal tender and $50,000,000 in fractional currency to replace postage currency. [Jay Cooke as government agent directs campaign to popularize sale of U. S. bonds, reporting $400,000,000 by Dec.]

Mar 3   Congress adopts concurrent resolution opposing foreign intervention in the war.

Mar 14   At Port Hudson, La., Ad-miral Farragut carries the *Hartford* and the *Albatross* past Confederate batteries.

Apr 2   Bread riot in Richmond, Va., one of many.

Apr 7   Fleet of Union monitors under Admiral Samuel F. Dupont fails in attack upon Fort Sumter.

Apr 10   Confederacy urged by Pres-ident Davis to plant corn, peas and beans instead of cotton and tobacco.

Apr 16   Admiral David Dixon Porter, in downstream run, passes Confederate batteries at Vicksburg, Miss.

Apr 24   Confederate Congress levies comprehensive tax law, including a "tax in kind" of one-tenth of produce of the land for 1863. Re-enacted Feb. 17, 1864.

Apr 29–May 8   General George Stone-man's cavalry raid in Virginia cuts General Lee's communications and rips up Virginia Central Railroad.

Apr 30   General Grant begins transfer of troops across the Mississippi to left bank below Vicksburg.

May   Gold discovered in Alder

Gulch [Montana]. Virginia City grows up over night.

May 1–4 Battle of Chancellorsville, Va. Union forces under General Hooker defeated by General Lee. General "Stonewall" Jackson mortally wounded. Casualties: Union, 1,575 killed, 9,594 wounded; Confederate, 1,665 killed, 9,081 wounded.

May 1 Union victory at Port Gibson, Miss., first engagement in General Grant's campaign against Vicksburg.

May 5 Clement L. Vallandigham, Ohio, arrested in Dayton, for public condemnation of the war administration. May 16, convicted of treasonable utterance by court-martial in Cincinnati, sentenced to imprisonment. Sentence soon commuted to banishment by President Lincoln.

May 9 General Joseph E. Johnston ordered to the command of Confederate forces in Mississippi.

May 14 Jackson, Miss., captured by General Sherman and General James B. McPherson, defeating General J. E. Johnston.

May 16 Battle of Champion's Hill, Miss. General Grant with 2 corps under General McClernand and General McPherson defeats Confederates under General John C. Pemberton.

May 17 Union troops seize Big Black River Bridge, an outpost of Vicksburg, from General Pemberton, who retires within defenses of Vicksburg.

May 18–July 4 Siege of Vicksburg. Union assaults repeatedly repulsed in skillful but losing defense of General Pemberton, who surrenders July 4 to General Grant. Union casualties from Vicksburg campaign, Oct. 1862 to July 4, 1863, 9,362; Confederate losses, some 10,000, prisoners, 29,491.

June 1 Chicago *Times*, anti-Lincoln newspaper, ordered suppressed by General Burnside. Order rescinded by President Lincoln June 4.

June 3 Peace party meeting at Cooper Union in New York under direction of Fernando Wood, mayor.

June 11 C. L. Vallandigham nominated governor by peace party in Ohio.

June 13–15 Battle of Winchester, Va. Confederate General Richard S. Ewell defeats General R. H. Milroy.

June 15 President Lincoln calls for 100,000 volunteers for 6 months' service.

June 20 West Virginia enters the Union with constitution providing for gradual emancipation of slaves.

June 24–25 General Lee with about 80,000 men crosses the Potomac at Harpers Ferry for invasion of Pennsylvania.

June 25 Confederate General James E. B. Stuart makes useless sally eastward from Lee's army to neighborhood of Washington.

June 25–27 Union army under General Hooker crosses the Potomac in pursuit of General Lee.

June 28 Confederate General Jubal A. Early captures York, Pa.

June 28 Major-General George Gordon Meade replaces General Hooker in command of Army of the Potomac.

July   Confederate General John H. Morgan and his cavalry begin raids through Kentucky, Ohio and Indiana. July 26, Morgan captured.

July 1–3 Battle of Gettysburg. Turning point of the war.

July 1 *First day:* **General John** Buford with 2 brigades of Union cavalry driven back by Confederate advance guard under General Ambrose P. Hill. Reinforced by noon, Union force stems Confederate advance and establishes lines on Cemetery Ridge.

July 2 *Second day:* **Union Army on** Cemetery Ridge attacked by Confederates but General Lee makes no decisive gains. Great loss on both sides.

July 3 *Third day:* **Union counter-** attack regains Culp's Hill, lost on previous day. In afternoon, Confederate attack breaks General Meade's first line at the center, but, lacking support, gives way to retreat and end of battle.

Casualties: Union, 3,155 killed, 14,529 wounded, 5,365 missing; Confederate, 3,903 killed, 18,735 wounded, 5,425 missing.

July 4 General Lee begins retreat from Gettysburg to Virginia.
10 A.M. President Lincoln "announces to the country" victory at Gettysburg.

July 4 Vicksburg surrendered to General Grant by Confederate General Pemberton. Key to control of Mississippi River.
10:30 A.M. General Grant from Vicksburg to Major General Halleck: "The enemy surrendered this morning."

July 8 Port Hudson, La., 300 miles down the Mississippi from Vicksburg, falls to Union Army after 6-week siege. Entire river now open to the Union.

July 13–16 Anti-draft mob takes over New York City. Killed and wounded, 1,000.

July 18 Colonel Robert Gould Shaw, commander of the 54th Massachusetts, first Negro regiment from the North, killed in attack upon Fort Wagner in Charleston Harbor.

Sept–Oct Russian fleets in New York and San Francisco harbors on friendly visit.

Sept 7 Fort Wagner in Charleston Harbor taken by Union force.

Sept 9 Chattanooga, Tenn., taken by Union forces under General Rosecrans.

Sept 9 The "Laird rams," being built for Confederacy, placed under surveillance by British government, taken over by it in October.

Sept 19–20 At Chickamauga, Ga., General Rosecrans and Union forces defeated. Casualties: Union, 1,657 killed, 9,756 wounded, 4,757 missing; Confederate, 2,312 killed, 14,674 wounded, 1,468 missing.

Oct 16 General Grant given command of western armies.

Oct 17 President Lincoln calls for 300,000 volunteers to serve 3 years.

Nov 19 President Lincoln's Gettys-burg address delivered at dedication of national cemetery on Gettysburg battlefield.

Nov 23–25 Battle of Chattanooga, in which 4 Union generals, Grant, Sherman, Hooker and Thomas, defeat Confederates under General Bragg. On second day of battle, General Hooker drives Confederates from Lookout Mountain. Missionary Ridge on third day of battle carried by General George Henry Thomas and Army of the Cumberland. Confederates driven from Tennessee. Casualties: Union, 753 killed, 4,722 wounded, 349 missing; Confederates, 361 killed, 2,160 wounded, 4,146 missing.

Nov President Lincoln proclaims last Thursday of November as day of general thanksgiving. [Continued until 1939, when changed to next to last Thursday by President Roosevelt. 1941, Congress established fourth Thursday as legal holiday.]

Dec 2 Headpiece of the statue of Freedom, Thomas Crawford, sculptor, to crown Capitol dome in Washington, swung into place.

Dec 2 Ground broken for Union Pa-cific Railroad at Omaha, Neb.

Dec 3 Confederate General James Longstreet abandons siege of Knoxville, Tenn., and retreats.

Dec 8 Proclamation of Amnesty and Reconstruction issued by President Lincoln. Offers pardon to all Southerners who will take a prescribed oath and provides for restoration of loyal governments in seceded states when a number, equal to one-tenth of those qualified to vote in a state in 1860, "shall take a prescribed oath" and organize a government.

Dec 8 President Lincoln asks Congress to establish system for encouragement of immigration.

1864

"In God We Trust" first appears upon the 2-cent piece.

Bessemer steel first made in U. S., at Wyandotte, Mich. (Bessemer invented process in England, 1856.)

Cigar Makers' National Union, Brotherhood of Locomotive Engineers, and Iron Moulders' International, organized.

Cornelius Vanderbilt secures control of Hudson River Railroad.

Frederick A. Barnard becomes president of Columbia University.

Joseph Pulitzer arrives in U. S. from Hungary.

Massachusetts sets up state board of charities.

Paper money in Confederacy has reached $1,000,000,000 in issue. Gold value, first quarter, 1864, has dropped to $4.60 per $100 and by early 1865 to $1.70 per $100.

Winslow Homer paints "Prisoners from the Front."

Saratoga, N. Y., race track opened by John C. Morrissey.

The *Unabridged Dictionary* of Noah Webster, edited by C. A. Goodrich and Noah Porter, published, 5th edition of Webster's *Dictionary*.

Jan Average gold price of greenback dollar on New York market, 64 cents.

Jan 11 Joint resolution proposed in Senate by John B. Henderson of Missouri to abolish slavery throughout U. S. by amendment to Constitution. Passed in Senate Apr. 8; rejected in House June 15.

Jan 19 Arkansas in convention adopts anti-slavery constitution. Ratified by popular vote, Mar. 14.

Jan 28 Tariff convention with Japan signed at Yedo for reduction of import duties. Senate consents Feb. 21, 1866.

Feb Union prisoners begin to arrive at Andersonville Prison, Ga.

Feb 1 President Lincoln calls for 500,000 men to serve 3 years or for duration of the war.

Feb 6 Confederate Congress prohibits importation of luxuries.

Feb 14 General Sherman occupies Meridian, Miss., followed by destruction of railroads and supplies.

Mar 3 Secretary of Treasury authorized by Congress to issue $200,000,000 in bonds, due in 40 years, redeemable in 10, the "10-40's," at not over 6 per cent.

Mar 9 Ulysses S. Grant commissioned Lieutenant-General and, Mar. 10, assigned to command of all Union Armies.

Mar 12 General Nathaniel Prentiss Banks and his Union Army start up Red River in Louisiana with Admiral Porter's gunboats on their flank.

Mar 14 President Lincoln calls for another draft of 200,000 men for 3 years.

Apr 8 General Banks, in advance up Red River, turned back at Sabine Cross Roads, La., by Confederates.

May 3 Generals Grant and Meade, with Army of the Potomac, start across Rapidan River in their advance into the Wilderness.

May 5–6 First Battle of the Wilderness, near Chancellorsville, Va. Generals Grant and Meade come to grips with General Lee. Indecisive. Union losses, 17,666, of which over 2,000 killed. Confederate, over 10,000 killed and wounded.

May 6 General Sherman sets forth from Chattanooga with 100,000 troops to march through Georgia.

May 8–12 Battle around Spotsylvania Court House. General Grant unable to defeat General Lee, but on May 11 he sends word to General Halleck, "I propose to fight it out along this line if it takes all summer." Union losses, 10,120.

May 13–15 General Sherman defeats General Johnston at Resaca, Ga.

May 17 Money Orders Division of the Post Office established by Congress.

May 26 Montana Territory formed, cut from Idaho Territory.

May 28 Maximilian, tool of Napoleon III, lands at Vera Cruz to assume throne of Mexico.

May 31 Radicals in Republican party meet in convention at Cleveland, Ohio. Nominate General John C. Frémont for President and General John Cochrane for Vice-President. Both candidates withdraw Sept. 21.

June 1–3 Battle of Cold Harbor, Va. General Grant defeated by General Lee in one of severest engagements of the war. Union killed and wounded, about 12,000.

June 7 Republican, or Union, party meets at national convention at Baltimore. Nominates Abraham Lincoln for President and Andrew Johnson for Vice-President.

June 10 Confederate Congress author-izes use of men between 17 and 18 and between 45 and 50 for military service.

June 15–18 General Grant makes un-successful assault upon Petersburg, 20 miles below Richmond.

June 19 Siege of Petersburg begun by Union Army.

June 19 Confederate cruiser *Alabama* destroyed off Cherbourg, France, by the *Kearsarge*.

June 27 Battle of Kenesaw Mountain, Ga., defeat for General Sherman. Casualties: Union, 1,999 killed and wounded; Confederate, 270 killed and wounded.

June 28 Fugitive Slave Law of 1850 repealed by act of Congress.

June 29 Secretary of Treasury Chase resigns. Resignation speedily accepted by President Lincoln, who appoints William P. Fessenden of Maine to the post.

June 30 Tariff Act increases average rate of duty from 37 to 47 per cent, to compensate for wartime excise taxes.

June 30 Internal Revenue Act. Certain businesses taxed by means of li-censes, and a second income tax authorized of 5 per cent on incomes between $600 and $5,000 and up to 10 per cent on incomes above $10,000.

June 30 Congress authorizes bond is-sue of $400,000,000 in 6 per cent "5-30's."

July 2 Northern Pacific Railroad char-tered by Congress.

July 4 Immigration Act. Contract labor can be imported under regulations set up by a Commissioner of Immigration.

July 4 Wade-Davis Reconstruction Bill, having passed Congress, given pocket veto by President Lincoln. Bill maintains reconstruction is matter for Congress alone.

July 8 President Lincoln issues proc-lamation defending his pocket veto of Wade-Davis Bill, but offers to assist any state choosing Wade-Davis plan.

July 9 General Jubal A. Early's at-tempted raid upon Washington blocked at Monocacy River, Md., by General Lew Wallace who loses battle but wins time for approach of General Grant's troops, saving the Capital.

July 11 Greenback dollar at lowest point in war, worth 39 cents in terms of gold.

July 17 Jaquess-Gilmore unofficial peace mission confers with President Davis, with no result. Confederate leaders declare the South must be independent.

July 17 Horace Greeley at Niagara Falls, with President Lincoln's approval, confers with alleged Confederate peace commissioners.

July 22 Battle of Atlanta. Confederate General Hood defeated by General Sherman. Union General McPherson killed.

July 23 Louisiana in convention adopts anti-slavery constitution. Ratified by popular vote Sept. 5.

July 28 Second battle of Atlanta, or Ezra Church. General Hood again defeated. Union casualties in Atlanta battles, over 9,000; Confederate, over 10,000.

July 30 Union men explode a mine beneath Confederate fort at Petersburg, Va., but are repulsed. Union casualties, 2,864 killed and wounded, 929 missing.

Aug   Americans participate in puni-tive bombardment of Shimoneseki, Japan, in first step toward policy of cooperation with European powers in Far East.

Aug 5 Wade-Davis manifesto, reply to President Lincoln's proclamation of July 8, appears in New York *Tribune*. Severest attack upon Lincoln ever made by members of his own party.

Aug 18 General Grant again refuses exchange of prisoners as prolonging the war. First refusal, Apr. 1.

Aug 21 Weldon Railroad south of Richmond seized by General Grant after 3 days' battle.

Aug 23   Port of Mobile closed to block-ade runners with capture of Fort Morgan by Admiral Farragut.

Aug 29 Democratic National Conven-tion meets at Chicago. Nominates General McClellan for President and George H. Pendleton of Ohio for Vice-President. Controlled by Copperheads, convention declares the war a failure.

Sept 1 Atlanta evacuated by General Hood and occupied by General Sherman, Sept. 2.

Sept 19 General Sheridan and Union troops victorious over General Early's cavalry at Winchester, Va. Lt. Charles Russell Lowell killed. Casualties: Union, 697 killed, 3,983 wounded, 338 missing; Confederate, 276 killed, 1,827 wounded, 1,818 missing.

Sept 22 At Fisher's Hill, Va., General Sheridan victorious over General Early's cavalry.

Oct 13 Maryland adopts anti-slavery constitution by popular vote.

Oct 19 Battle of Cedar Creek, Va. Con-federates under General Early defeated by General Sheridan, forced to leave Shenandoah Valley and their threat to Washington. Casualties: Union, 644 killed, 3,430 wounded, 1,591 missing; Confederate, 320 killed, 1,540 wounded, 1,050 missing.

Oct 28 The *Albemarle,* last of Confed-erate rams, torpedoed on Roanoke River by Lt. W. B. Cushing.

Oct 31 Nevada enters the Union.

Nov 8 Presidential election. Abraham Lincoln re-elected President, Andrew Johnson elected Vice-President, with electoral vote, 212, to 21 for McClellan and Pendleton.

Nov 16 General Sherman with army of 60,000 starts from Atlanta on "march to the sea."

Nov 29 Sand Creek, Colo., massacre of Cheyennes, by U. S. troops under Colonel J. M. Chivington, ends year of Indian uprising.

Nov 30 Battle of Franklin, Tenn. Union General John M. Schofield wins victory over classmate, Confederate General Hood. Casualties: Union, 189 killed, 1,033 wounded; Confederate, 1,750 killed, 3,800 wounded.

Dec 6 Salmon P. Chase appointed Chief Justice of Supreme Court by President Lincoln. Chief Justice Roger Taney died Oct. 12.

Dec 10 General Sherman and Union Army arrive before Savannah after ravaging march across Georgia.

Dec 15–16 Battle of Nashville, Tenn. General Thomas defeats Confederates under General Hood, after which cavalry of General James H. Wilson sweeps all trace of Confederate power from Tennessee. Casualties: Union, 387 killed, 2,562 wounded, 112 missing; Confederate, 4,462 missing.

Dec 20 Savannah abandoned by Con-federate Army.

Dec 22 General Sherman occupies Sa-vannah, Ga., sends dispatch to President Lincoln, "I beg to present you as a Christmas gift the city of Savannah."

1865

1865–1873 Serious and recurring epidemics of smallpox, typhus and yellow fever in Philadelphia, New York, Boston, Baltimore, Washington, Memphis, New Orleans.

Oil refining company of John D. Rockefeller and Samuel Andrews formed at Cleveland, Ohio.

The "Pioneer," first real sleeping car, completed by George M. Pullman.

American Social Science Association founded at Boston.

The *Nation* founded, Edwin Lawrence Godkin editor.

Jan Average gold price of greenback dollar on New York market, 46 cents.

Jan 9 Tennessee, in convention, adopts anti-slavery amendments to its constitution. Ratified by popular vote Feb. 22.

Jan 12 Francis P. Blair, with permission of President Lincoln, meets President Davis in Richmond to explore possibilities of peace. President Davis writes a letter, to be shown to President Lincoln, saying that he is willing "to enter into negotiations . . . with a view to secure peace to the two countries."

Jan 15 Fort Fisher, N. C., captured by Union forces under General Alfred Howe Terry and Admiral Porter.

Jan 18 President Lincoln, upon seeing President Davis' letter of Jan. 12, writes to Francis P. Blair of his readiness to bring "peace to the people of our one common country." Leads to Hampton Roads Conference.

Jan 30 Congress in joint resolution prohibits grants of mineral lands under public land laws.

Jan 31 General Robert E. Lee appointed commander of all Confederate Armies by President Jefferson Davis.

Jan 31 The House resolves to submit to states an amendment to Constitution, prohibiting slavery in U. S. Resolution was adopted by the Senate Apr. 8, 1864.

Feb 1 General Sherman leaves Savannah for his march northward through the Carolinas.

Feb 3 Hampton Roads Conference on board Union transport *River Queen.* President Lincoln and Secretary Seward confer with Alexander H. Stephens and 2 other Confederate agents concerning peace. No result.

Feb 4 Congress in joint resolution excludes electoral vote of 11 rebel states, and sends resolution to President Lincoln, who approves it Feb. 8.

Feb 6 Congress by concurrent resolution adopts 23rd Rule, providing for joint sessions to count electoral votes.

Feb 17 Columbia, S. C., occupied by General Sherman. City burned, by whom is still a question.

Feb 18 Charleston falls to the Union.

Feb 22 Wilmington, N. C., captured by Union forces under General Schofield. Last open port of Confederacy.

Mar 2 General George A. Custer of Sheridan's cavalry defeats General Early and captures 1,600 prisoners near Waynesboro, Va.

Mar 3 Bond issue of $600,000,000, interest not exceeding 5 per cent and payable in coin, authorized by Congress.

Mar 3 Freedmen's Bureau established by Congress.

Mar 4 Abraham Lincoln inaugurated President for second term. "With malice toward none; with charity for all. . . ." Andrew Johnson inaugurated Vice-President.
[President Lincoln's Cabinet: W. H. Seward, Secretary of State; Hugh McCulloch, Secretary of Treasury; E. M. Stanton, Secretary of War; Gideon Welles, Secretary of Navy; John P. Usher, Secretary of Interior; William Dennison, Postmaster General; James Speed, Attorney General.]

Mar 13 Confederate Congress authorizes use of slaves in army. Slaves given their freedom by enlisting.

Mar 23 Armies of General Sherman

and General Schofield join at Golds-boro, N. C.

Mar 26 General Sheridan joins General Grant and Army of the Potomac before Petersburg, Va., with 10,000 cavalry, after winter's raid of Confederate communications.

Mar 27–28 President Lincoln meets General Grant and General Sherman (up from North Carolina by steamboat), in conference on *River Queen* in James River at City Point. President Lincoln deplores further bloodshed and urges offer of generous terms to the South.

Mar 29 General Grant moves south-west of Petersburg, Va., beginning Appomattox campaign.

Apr 1 Battle of Five Forks near Peters-burg won by General Sheridan. Last important battle of the war.

Apr 1 Louis Agassiz sails from New York on scientific expedition to South America.

Apr 2 General Grant takes fortified lines before Petersburg. Confederate General Ambrose P. Hill killed.

Apr 2 President Davis and all of his Cabinet, except Secretary of War Breckinridge, leave Richmond. Richmond and Petersburg abandoned by General Lee.

Apr 3 Union Army occupies Richmond and Petersburg. Fire breaks out in Richmond.

Apr 5 President Lincoln arrives in Richmond and walks to center of the city. Makes clear his wish for peaceable settlement.

Apr 7 General Grant requests surren-der of General Lee. General Lee asks General Grant for terms.

Apr 9 General Grant meets General Lee at Appomattox Courthouse. Terms are discussed and Lee surrenders with 28,000 men, who are allowed to retain private horses and side arms. By noon, word of surrender reaches Washington.

Casualties of Appomattox campaign, Mar. 29–Apr. 9: Union, 1,316 killed, 7,750 wounded, 1,714 missing; Confederate, indefinite.

Apr 11 President Lincoln makes last public address before a company at the White House, treats problem of reconstruction in spirit of generous conciliation.

Apr 13 General Sherman takes Ra-leigh, N. C., ending his "march."

Apr 14 President Lincoln holds Cabi-net meeting, expresses wish that there may be no persecution after the war.

Apr 14 President Lincoln shot by John Wilkes Booth at Ford's Theater, Washington. Secretary Seward, ill in bed, stabbed by fellow conspirator of Booth.

Apr 15 President Lincoln dies at 7:22 A.M.

Vice-President Andrew Johnson takes oath of office as President 3 hours later. President Johnson retains Cabinet of President Lincoln.

Apr 19 Funeral services held for Presi-dent Lincoln at Washington and at Springfield, Ill. Burial at Springfield May 4.

Apr 26 General Johnston surrenders to General Sherman at Hillsboro, N. C., with 37,000 men.

Apr 26 John Wilkes Booth, assassin of President Lincoln, discovered in barn near Bowling Green, Va., is shot.

Apr 29 President Johnson orders re-moval of restrictions upon domestic trade in all rebel territory east of the Mississippi, within Union military lines.

May   General Grant sends General Sheridan to Texas with orders to assemble large force on the Rio Grande with object of driving French power from Mexico.

May 2 President Johnson proclaims offer of reward of $100,000 for arrest of Jefferson Davis, charged with complicity in assassination of President Lincoln.

May 9 Francis H. Pierpont, as gover-nor of Virginia, formally recognized by President Johnson.

May 10 Jefferson Davis captured at Ir-winsville, Ga., and imprisoned in Fortress Monroe.

May 13 Confederate force under General Slaughter defeats Union force under Colonel Barrett at Palo Pinto, Tex., last military engagement of the war.

May 26 General Kirby Smith at New Orleans surrenders to General Canby remaining Confederate forces west of the Mississippi, ending Southern resistance.

May 29 President Johnson issues proc-lamation of amnesty to all ordinary persons who were in the rebellion and who will take oath of allegiance to U. S., exceptions being Confederate officers and persons worth over $20,000.

May 29 North Carolina's reorganiza-tion begun by Presidential proclamation, appointing W. W. Holden provisional governor.

June 2 Galveston, Tex., last seaport held by Confederates, surrenders, final act in naval war.

June 6 Missouri ratifies new constitu-tion, disfranchising Southern sympathizers.

June 6 Confederate prisoners of war who will take oath of allegiance declared released by President Johnson.

June 13–July 13 President Johnson names provisional governors and re-establishes Federal administration in remaining 6 states of Confederacy, Mississippi, Georgia, Texas, Alabama, South Carolina and Florida.

July 1 All Southern ports open to for-eign trade, by executive order.

July 7 Four of the eight alleged as-sassins of President Lincoln hanged.

July 21 James Russell Lowell reads his "Ode Recited at the Harvard Commemoration."

Sept 1 U. S. public debt reaches high-est point—$2,846,000,000, minus $88,-000,000 in Treasury. $433,160,000 of debt in greenbacks.

Sept 15 South Carolina Constitutional Convention, meeting at Charleston, repeals ordinance of secession.

Oct General Carl Schurz returns from 3 months' tour in the South, with report in support of radical reconstruction measures.

Nov 24 Mississippi passes a vagrant act, beginning "black codes" of the South.

Dec All seceded states except Texas have fulfilled the President's requirements, have elected Federal representatives and senators and are ready for recognition by this date.

Dec 1 President Johnson restores priv-ilege of writ of habeas corpus in Northern states.

Dec 4 Thirty-ninth Congress convenes. Members from reconstructed former Confederate states denied recognition and seats.

Dec 4 House votes to establish Joint Committee on Reconstruction, 9 from House and 6 from Senate. Senate concurs Dec. 12.

Dec 5 Secretary of Treasury Hugh McCulloch submits to House his annual report on finances, dated Dec. 4, recommending speedy retirement of greenbacks. On Dec. 18 House passes concurring resolution by large majority.

Dec 14 House appoints members of Joint Committee on Reconstruction, Thaddeus Stevens of Pennsylvania chairman. Senate appoints members Dec. 21, William P. Fessenden of Maine chairman.

Dec 16 Napoleon III informed by Sec-retary of State Seward that his designs in Mexico will imperil friendly relations between France and U. S.

Dec 18 Thirteenth Amendment of Constitution, abolishing slavery in U. S., ratified by 27 states, formally proclaimed in effect by Secretary of State Seward.

Dec 25 Union stockyards, incorporated by Illinois legislature, opened at Chicago.

1866

Postwar depression begins, with rapid decline in prices.

Rangers' frontier begins, lasting until late '80's. It is discovered, about this year, that cattle can withstand the cold of the great plains and thrive on wild grass.

American Society for Prevention of Cruelty to Animals chartered in New York by Henry Bergh.

Western Union Telegraph absorbs United States and American Telegraph companies giving it control of 75,000 miles of wire. First great industrial monopoly in U. S.

First oil pipe line in U. S. completed from Pithole, Pa., to railroad connection 5 miles distant.

New York City's board of health created, following epidemics of war years.

Jesse James forms his band of brigands in the West.

Ku Klux Klan organized at Pulaski, Tenn.

Jan 1 David A. Wells, special Commissioner of Revenue, presents to Congress his first report, proposing reduction of internal taxes.

Jan 17 Engineers and firemen on Michigan Southern and Northern Indiana railroads strike for higher wages.

Feb 12 Secretary of State Seward demands of Napoleon III that time limit be set for French evacuation of Mexico. Last French troops embark, spring, 1867.

Feb 19 President Johnson vetoes bill to extend life of Freedmen's Bureau. Widens breach between President and Congress.

Feb 22 President Johnson, speaking from steps of the White House, violently denounces Joint Committee on Reconstruction. Loses support for himself.

Mar 2 Concurrent resolution, reported from Joint Committee on Reconstruction, declares that no senator nor representative shall be admitted from any of late Confederate states until Congress shall have declared the state entitled to representation.

Mar 17 Reciprocity with Canada, by treaty with Great Britain, June 5, 1854, terminated.

Apr Fair held in Baltimore for relief of destitute in the South collects $165,000.

Apr 2 Proclamation by President Johnson declares the insurrection "which heretofore existed in the States of Georgia, South Carolina, Virginia, North Carolina, Tennessee, Alabama, Mississippi, Louisiana, Arkansas, and Florida is at an end."

Apr 3 In *Ex parte* Milligan, Supreme Court sets limits to authority of martial law and to suspension of writ of habeas corpus in time of war: "Martial law can never exist where the courts are open and in the proper and unobstructed exercise of their jurisdiction." Opinion of Court not handed down until Dec. 17.

Apr 6 Texas, last of Confederate states to do so, completes her reconstruction in conformity with President Johnson's plan.

Apr 9 Civil Rights Bill passed by Congress over President Johnson's veto.

Apr 12 Funding Act provides for (1) conversion of short-term securities into long-term bonds, result being the 6 per cent 5–20's, and (2) retirement of legal tender notes, "greenbacks," at a limited rate.

May 10 American Equal Rights Association formed in New York City. Changes name from Woman's Rights Society.

June Fenian raids upon Canada made by a brotherhood of Irish-Americans in interest of Irish freedom.

June 13 Fourteenth Amendment to Constitution, presented to Congress Apr. 4, passed and, June 16, sent to the states for ratification.

June 23 Rivers and Harbors Appropriations Act authorizes appropriation of over $3,000,000 for public works.

July   Tariff Bill, continuing high war schedules, passed in House. Fails in Senate.

July 1   Tax of 10 per cent upon state banknotes, to tax them out of existence, goes into effect by act of Congress, Mar. 3, 1865.

July 2   Admission of Canada into the Union proposed in House bill introduced by Representative Nathaniel P. Banks of Massachusetts.

July 13   Reduction of wartime internal revenue to extent of $45,000,000 enacted by Congress.

July 16   New Freedmen's Bureau Bill passed over President's veto of same day.

July 19   Tennessee ratifies 14th Amendment.

July 23   Gradual reduction of Supreme Court justices to 7 to lessen Presidential power of appointment, enacted by Congress.

July 24   Tennessee restored as a state of the Union by joint resolution of Congress.

July 25   Time and manner of election of senators regulated by act of Congress.

July 27   Atlantic cable completed between U. S. and Great Britain by Cyrus W. Field and Peter Cooper.

July 28   Metric system of weights and measures authorized by act of Congress.

July 30   Race riot in New Orleans results from effort to introduce Negro suffrage into Louisiana constitution. Some 200 casualties.

Aug 14   National Union Convention meets in Philadelphia, upholding President Johnson's reconstruction policy.

Aug 20   President Johnson proclaims insurrection in Texas at an end and that peace, order, tranquility and civil authority exist throughout the U. S.

Aug 20   National Labor Congress convenes at Baltimore. National Labor Union formed, W. H. Sylvis, prime mover.

Sept 3   Southern Republicans meet in convention at Philadelphia, in support of reconstruction policy of Congress as against that of the President.

Sept 6   President Johnson lays cornerstone of monument to Stephen A. Douglas in Chicago. Part of a "swing around the circle" in which he gives many vote-losing speeches.

Sept 17   Soldiers' and Sailors' Convention meets in Cleveland and supports President Johnson's reconstruction policy.

Sept 25   Republican war veterans meet in convention in Pittsburgh and support reconstruction policy of Congress.

Autumn   Congressional elections return anti-Johnson majorities to both houses, large enough to override any veto of the President.

Nov 20   Grand Army of the Republic holds first national encampment at Indianapolis. First post organized at Decatur, Ill., Apr. 6.

Dec 21   Massacre of U. S. troops under Colonel William Judd Fetterman at Fort Philip Kearney, Wyo., by Sioux Indians.

1 8 6 7

First elevated railroad in U. S. begins operation on Ninth Ave. in New York City.

Howard University for Negroes incorporated in Washington.

George Peabody Fund of $3,500,000 for Southern education established.

Knights of St. Crispin, shoemakers' labor organization, formed in Milwaukee, Wis.

Windmill manufacture begins in Beloit, Wis. Windmill patented by L. H. Wheeler, Sr., Sept. 10, 1867.

Cornelius Vanderbilt secures control of New York Central Railroad from Albany to Buffalo.

Steel rail manufacture in U. S. begun.

Credit Mobilier scandal. Company formed by Union Pacific directors, to build the railroad with fat profits for themselves, sells shares at par to Congressmen to ward off investigation.

Pacific Mail Steamship Company opens regular line between San Francisco and Hong Kong.

Geological survey of 40th parallel, Clarence King director, authorized by Congress.

Patrons of Husbandry, the Grange, farmers' organization, formed in Washington by Oliver H. Kelley and William Saunders.

New England Conservatory of Music founded in Boston.

Steinway and Chickering, American-made pianos, receive first prizes at Paris Exposition.

Henry Timrod writes "Ode Sung on the Occasion of Decorating the Graves of the Confederate Dead at Magnolia Cemetery, Charleston, South Carolina, 1867."

Ragged Dick by Horatio Alger published. Begins long series of boys' success stories. "There's always room at the top."

Jan 8 Negro suffrage in District of Columbia established by act of Congress over President's veto of Jan. 7.

Jan 14 In *Cummings v. Missouri*, Supreme Court declares that a state test oath excluding Confederate sympathizers from the professions is unconstitutional as *ex post facto* law.

Jan 31 Negro suffrage in the territories established by act of Congress.

Mar   Fourteenth Amendment by this date rejected by 12 of the 37 states, including all Confederate states except Tenn., and is defeated for time being.

Mar 1 Nebraska enters the Union. Admitted as a state over President's veto Feb. 9.

Mar 2 Department of Education created by act of Congress.

Mar 2 Tenure of Office Bill becomes law over President's veto. Prohibits President from removing any civil officer without consent of Senate.

Mar 2 Reconstruction Bill passed over President's veto of same day. The 10 states not restored to the Union to be governed in 5 military districts. Restoration to the Union to be upon reorganization on basis of Negro suffrage, rebel disfranchisement, and ratification of 14th Amendment.

Mar 2 Command of the Army Act provides that all military orders of the President shall be issued through General of the Army, whose headquarters shall be in Washington.

Mar 2 Wool and Woolens Act increases tariff protection for both interests.

Mar 2 Internal Revenue Act removes more excise tax and exempts incomes under $1,000. Anticipated tax reduction, $40,000,000.

Mar 4 Fortieth Congress meets, instead of in December, by provision of preceding Congress, to keep watch over the President.

Mar 11 President Johnson assigns commanders to the 5 military districts created by Reconstruction Act.

Mar 23 Second Reconstruction Bill, supplementing act of Mar. 2, becomes law over President's veto of same day.

Mar 30 Treaty signed by which U. S. purchases Alaska from Russia for $7,-200,000. Senate consents Apr. 9. Russia transfers territory Oct. 18.

Apr 16 Free public school system in state of New York established by act of Legislature.

May 13 Jefferson Davis released from prison on bail. Among his bondsmen are Horace Greeley, Gerrit Smith and Cornelius Vanderbilt.

May 14 New York enacts first tenement house law.

July 19 Third Reconstruction Bill, to interpret and make effective preceding acts, passed by Congress over President's veto.

July 20   Commission created by Congress to conclude peace treaties with Indians.

Aug 5   President Johnson requests res-ignation of Secretary of War Stanton. Stanton refuses.

Aug 12   The President orders suspen-sion of Secretary Stanton and names General Grant Secretary of War *ad interim.*

Aug 28   Midway Islands in the Pacific formally occupied in name of U. S. by Capt. William Reynolds of the *Lackawanna.*

Oct 24   Treaty for purchase of Virgin Islands except Santa Cruz from Denmark for $7,500,000, concluded by Secretary of State Seward. Ignored by Senate.

Nov 25   Judiciary Committee of House brings in recommendation of impeachment of President Johnson for "high crimes and misdemeanors."

Dec 7   House, 108–57, rejects resolu-tion that President Johnson be impeached, because of lack of specific act of high misdemeanor.

Dec 12   The President sends to Senate his reasons for suspending Secretary of War Stanton.

1868

Cornelius Vanderbilt fights Daniel Drew, Jay Gould and Jim Fisk for possession of Erie Railroad, at loss of over $1,000,000.

George Westinghouse perfects air brake, marking beginning of modern railroad.

Typewriter patented by Christopher L. Sholes. Patent rights sold to Eliphalet Remington 1873.

Refrigerator car invented by William Davis of Detroit. First shipment of fresh meat from Chicago to Boston Sept. 1869.

Philip D. Armour begins meat packing in Chicago.

New England Women's Club organized in Boston by Julia Ward Howe.

Sorosis, women's club, founded in New York by Mrs. Jane C. Croly.

James McCosh becomes president of Princeton University.

Walter L. Newberry dies, leaving $4,-000,000 for free public reference library in Chicago.

University of California founded.

Overland Monthly, Bret Harte editor, begins publication in California.

Jan 13   The Senate, 35–6, refuses to concur in suspension of Secretary of War Stanton. Jan. 14, Grant surrenders War office to Stanton.

Feb 4   Congress suspends further re-tirement of greenbacks, leaving $356,-000,000 in circulation.

Feb 21   President Johnson again dis-misses Secretary of War Stanton and appoints General Lorenzo Thomas in his place. The President reports action to Senate, as does Stanton.

Feb 24   House adopts resolution that President Johnson "be impeached of high crimes and misdemeanors in office."

Mar 5   Senate organized as Court of Impeachment for trial of President Johnson, Chief Justice Chase in the chair. Trial formally opens Mar. 13.

Mar 11   Fourth Reconstruction Act de-signed to "facilitate the restoration of the late rebel states."

Mar 31   Internal Revenue Act removes most of remaining war excise taxes.

May 16   Vote taken on 11th article of impeachment, in trial of President Johnson, stands 35–19, one less than enough for conviction.

May 20–21   Republican National Con-vention meets at Chicago. Adopts name of "National Republican Party" and nominates General U. S. Grant for President and Schuyler Colfax of Indiana for Vice-President.

May 26   Votes on impeachment articles 2 and 3 stand one short of conviction.

Senate orders that President Johnson be acquitted of charges for which he has been impeached. Court adjourns *sine die*.

May 26   Secretary of War Stanton resigns in letter to President Johnson.

May 29   Senate ratifies appointment of General John M. Schofield as Secretary of War.

May 30   Decoration or Memorial Day first observed, as designated by Grand Army of the Republic.

June 22   Arkansas re-admitted to representation in Congress by act of Congress over President's veto of June 20.

June 25   North Carolina, South Carolina, Georgia, Florida, Alabama and Louisiana readmitted to representation in Congress by act of Congress over President's veto of same day, the "Omnibus Act."

June 25   Eight-Hour Act for government laborers passed by Congress.

July 4–9   Democratic National Convention meets at New York. Nominates Horatio Seymour of New York for President and Francis P. Blair, Jr. of Missouri for Vice-President. Its platform demands expansion of greenbacks, the "Ohio idea."

July 25   Territory of Wyoming created from parts of Dakota, Idaho and Utah, by act of Congress.

July 27   Rights of U. S. citizens in foreign countries defined by act of Congress.

July 28   Burlingame Treaty with China signed at Washington, defining mutual rights of immigration and emigration. Senate consents July 24.

July 28   Fourteenth Amendment declared ratified by Secretary of State Seward.

Sept   Georgia legislature expels Negro members. Result, postponement of readmission to statehood until adoption of 15th Amendment.

Oct   Cuba begins 10-year war against Spain.

Oct 7   Cornell University opens, free from all sectarian control. Andrew D. White president.

Nov 3   Presidential election. Ulysses S. Grant and Schuyler Colfax, Republicans, elected President and Vice-President, 214 electoral votes to 80 for Horatio Seymour and Francis P. Blair, Jr., Democrat. Grant's popular majority only 309,594.

Dec 3   Trial of Jefferson Davis, charged with treason against U. S., under statute of Apr. 13, 1790, opens before U. S. Circuit Court of Virginia.

Dec 25   President Johnson proclaims unconditional pardon and amnesty for all concerned in the Rebellion. Trial of Jefferson Davis dropped in consequence, Feb. 19, 1869.

1869

Jay Cooke and Company appointed financial agent for Northern Pacific Railroad.

Cornelius Vanderbilt consolidates Hudson River and New York Central railroads, New York to Buffalo.

Knights of Labor organized by Uriah S. Stephens, a tailor.

Massachusetts establishes first state board of health in U. S.

Massachusetts establishes bureau of labor statistics.

Yale opens first university school of fine arts.

Charles W. Eliot inaugurated president of Harvard. Serves until 1909.

Charles Kendall Adams introduces first historical seminar in U. S. at University of Michigan.

John Fiske lectures on evolution at Harvard, 1869–1871. Lectures published in 1874 as *Outline of Cosmic Philosophy*.

Cincinnati Museum of Art founded.

Corcoran Art Gallery given to Washington by William W. Corcoran.

American Museum of Natural History, New York, founded.

Jan 12 National convention of Negroes meets in Washington, first attempt to organize on national scale.

Jan 19 American Equal Rights Association (woman suffrage) meets in Washington.

Feb 2 James Oliver patents chilled iron plow.

Feb 24 Increased tariff on copper enacted by Congress over President's veto of Feb. 23. Protects Lake Superior copper interests.

Feb 26 Fifteenth Amendment to the Constitution passed by both houses and duly sent to states for ratification.

Mar 4 Ulysses S. Grant inaugurated President and Schuyler Colfax Vice-President.

[President Grant's Cabinet: E. B. Washburne, Secretary of State; A. T. Stewart, Secretary of Treasury; J. A. Rawlins, Secretary of War; Adolph E. Borie, Secretary of Navy; Jacob D. Cox; Secretary of Interior; J. A. J. Creswell, Postmaster General; E. R. Hoar, Attorney General.]

Mar 9 A. T. Stewart, nominated Secretary of Treasury, found ineligible because engaged in commerce (law of Sept. 2, 1789). George S. Boutwell appointed in his place, Mar. 11.

Mar 11 Hamilton Fish appointed Secretary of State succeeding E. B. Washburne, resigned to become minister to France.

Mar 15 Woman suffrage amendment to the Constitution proposed in joint resolution in Congress.

Mar 18 Public Credit Act. From fear of greenback movement, it provides for payment of bonds in coin or its equivalent.

Apr 5 Tenure of Office Act of Mar. 2, 1867, amended by Congress, but still restricts the President.

Apr 10 Virginia, Mississippi and Texas authorized by Congress to submit their constitutions to popular vote for ratification but required to ratify 15th Amendment before admission to representation in Congress.

Apr 10 Judiciary Act amended by Congress to restore number of Supreme Court justices from 7 to 9 and to authorize appointment of circuit judges.

Apr 10 Board of Indian Commissioners created by act of Congress.

Apr 13 Johnson-Clarendon Convention on *Alabama* claims, signed with Great Britain Jan. 14, rejected by Senate. [Senator Sumner, in speech against it, demands that Britain pay damages up to half the cost of Civil War, and in lieu of cash turn Canada over to U. S.]

May 10 Central Pacific and Union Pacific railroads meet at Promontory Point, Utah, where a golden spike completes rail connection between Atlantic and Pacific. Country-wide celebration.

May 15 National Woman Suffrage Association formed at New York, Elizabeth Cady Stanton president. Objective, suffrage by Federal amendment, a break from American Equal Rights Association.

June 15–19 National Peace Jubilee in Boston.

July 13 Street riots against Chinese la- borers occur in San Francisco, Cal.

July 27 Cable connection with France completed at Duxbury, Mass.

Sept National Prohibition party or- ganized by National Temperance Convention in Chicago.

Sept 24 "Black Friday." Panic on Wall Street, New York, because of collapse of attempted gold corner by Jay Gould and James Fisk. Gold drops from 162 to 135.

Oct 13 Commercial convention opens at Louisville, Ky., with delegates from 29 states, presiding officer, ex-President Fillmore. Other commercial conventions at Memphis and New Orleans during year.

Oct 17   James Gordon Bennett, owner of New York *Herald,* directs Henry Stanley: "Find Livingstone." [Stanley finds David Livingstone, English explorer lost in Africa, on Lake Tanganyika, Nov. 10, 1871.]

Nov 6   First intercollegiate game of football in U. S. played by Rutgers and Princeton at Rutgers, Rutgers winning.

Nov 24   American Woman Suffrage Association organized at Cleveland, Henry Ward Beecher president. For suffrage by state action.

Nov 29   Treaty for annexation of Santo Domingo to U. S. signed in Santo Domingo. Senate refuses consent June 30, 1870.

Dec 6   National Negro labor convention meets in Washington. Creates a national Negro labor union.

Dec 10   Wyoming Territory grants full suffrage to women.

Dec 22   Georgia, by act of Congress, must ratify 15th Amendment and restore expelled Negro members of her legislature to be restored to statehood.

1870

Population, 38,558,371.

Cotton crop, 4,025,000 bales for year.

Museum of Fine Arts, Boston, incorporated. Opened to public July 4, 1876.

Metropolitan Museum of Art, New York, incorporated.

Hampton Normal and Agricultural Institute, Virginia, chartered.

Hiram R. Revels from Mississippi, first Negro senator, and J. H. Rainey from South Carolina, first Negro member of House, enter Congress.

Foot-and-mouth disease among cattle first reported in U. S.

Virginia sends agents to Great Britain and Germany to encourage immigration.

Scribner's Monthly (Century Magazine, 1881) founded, J. G. Holland editor.

Old Sleuth published by Harlan P. Halsey, first of his 650 dime novels.

Jan   National Woman Suffrage Association holds convention in Washington. Mrs. Elizabeth Cady Stanton, before joint committee of Congress, makes plea for woman suffrage

Jan 4   Telegraph operators' strike spreads throughout the country.

Jan 10   Standard Oil Company incorporated in Cleveland, Ohio, with million-dollar capital, John D. Rockefeller a principal incorporator.

Jan 26   Virginia readmitted to representation in Congress.

Feb 7   In *Hepburn v Griswold,* Supreme Court decides Legal Tender Act of 1862 unconstitutional so far as concerns debts contracted prior to passage of Act.

Feb 7   William Strong of Pennsylvania and J. P. Bradley of New Jersey nominated justices of Supreme Court by President Grant.

Feb 9   U. S. Weather Bureau established by act of Congress.

Feb 12   Territory of Utah grants full suffrage to women.

Feb 23   Mississippi readmitted to representation in Congress.

Mar 30   Fifteenth Amendment to Constitution proclaimed ratified by Secretary of State Hamilton Fish.

Mar 30   Texas readmitted to representation in Congress.

May 31   Enforcement Act. Purpose, to enforce 15th Amendment.

June 3   Convention for suppression of African slave trade concluded with Great Britain. Senate consents July 8.

June 13   President Grant announces in special message to Congress that U. S. will maintain strict non-intervention in Cuban rebellion.

June 15 President Grant requests resignation of Ebenezer Rockwood Hoar, Attorney General, in effort to get votes for annexation of Santo Domingo. A Southerner, Amos T. Akerman of Georgia, replaces Hoar.

June 22 Department of Justice with Attorney General at its head, created by act of Congress.

June 30 David A. Wells, special Commissioner of Revenue, advocate of tariff reform, dismissed from office at close of his term.

July 14 Internal Revenue and Tariff Act eliminates most of excise taxes, and makes only slight changes in tariff duties, in compliance with demands of protectionists. Provides for expiration of income tax in 1872.

July 14 Funding Act authorizes refunding national debt in 10-, 15-, and 30-year bonds, to amount of $1,500,000,000, with interest rates from 5 to 4 per cent, and exemption from national and local taxation.

July 15 Georgia readmitted to representation in Congress the second time, last state to be so readmitted.

July 24 First through railroad car from Pacific coast reaches New York City.

Aug 4 Democrats in North Carolina election gain control of legislature, ending rule of carpetbag Republicans.

Aug 22 Neutrality in Franco-Prussian War proclaimed by President Grant.

Sept 20 First editorial attacking Tweed rule in New York City appears in *New York Times.*

Oct 3 Jacob D. Cox, Secretary of Interior, under pressure of spoilsmen and unsupported by Grant, resigns. [Grant's Cabinet greatly weakened. Columbus Delano succeeds Cox.]

Nov 8 Benjamin Gratz Brown elected governor of Missouri by coalition of Liberal Republicans and Democrats, opposing Radical Republican reconstruction program.

Dec 5 Forty-first Congress, third session, convenes. Every state represented, first time since 1860.

Dec 5 President Grant in annual message to Congress calls for civil service reform, and recommends that all individual claims against Great Britain for losses due to the *Alabama* and other cruisers be assumed by U. S. government.

1871

James Burrill Angell elected president of Michigan University. Serves until 1909.

Noah Porter becomes president of Yale University.

Thomas Nast's cartoons in New York *Times* and *Harper's Weekly* show up Tweed Ring in New York City.

Ten Great Religions by James Freeman Clarke published.

Jan 20 Second Funding Act increases amount of 5 per cent 10-year bonds, authorized by Act of July 14, 1870, from $200,000,000 to $500,000,000, without increasing total issue.

Feb 21 Territorial government provided for District of Columbia by act of Congress.

Feb 28 Supplementary Enforcement Act to enforce 15th Amendment. Puts Congressional elections under Federal supervision.

Mar 3 Civil Service Commission authorized by Congress. [George William Curtis appointed first commissioner by President Grant.]

Mar 3 Centennial Exposition authorized by Congress to be held in Philadelphia in 1876.

Mar 3 Indian Appropriation Act makes Indians national wards and ends Indian treaties.

Mar 9 Charles Sumner deposed from chairmanship of Foreign Relations Committee in Senate. Had helped to defeat

President Grant's plan to annex Santo Domingo.

Apr 3   In *Collector v. Day*, Supreme Court holds salaries of state officers are not taxable by U. S.

Apr 7   First "Granger" legislation, Il-linois Railroad Act, creates railroad and warehouse commission with power to fix maximum rates and prohibit discriminations.

Apr 20   Ku Klux Act, to enforce 14th Amendment, authorizes President to suspend writ of habeas corpus and use military force to suppress disturbances in Southern states.

May   U. S. naval vessels destroy 5 Korean forts in effort to secure treaty relations with Korea. Retire without a treaty.

May 1   In *Knox v. Lee*, the Supreme Court, increased to 9 members, reversing decision in *Hepburn v. Griswold*, Feb. 7, 1870, declares Legal Tender Act constitutional and greenbacks legal tender in payment of debts made before Act of 1862.

May 8   Treaty of Washington with Great Britain signed, providing for arbitration of the *Alabama* claims by a tribunal to sit at Geneva, for renewal of Canadian-American fishing agreement, and for arbitration of San Juan Island maritime boundary dispute by German emperor. Senate consents May 24.

Oct 2   Brigham Young, Mormon lead-er, arrested at Salt Lake City, Utah, on charge of polygamy.

Oct 8   Chicago fire breaks out, rages for 24 hours, with property loss of $200,-000,000.

Oct 24   Race riot in Los Angeles, Cal., 15 Chinese lynched.

Oct 27   William Tweed arrested after looting New York City of between 30 and 200 millions. Jay Gould most generous signer of his million-dollar bail bond.

Nov 7   Election of reform candidates in New York City marks overthrow of Tweed Ring.

Nov 19   Grand Duke Alexis, third son of Czar of Russia, with fleet of war vessels, arrives at New York to pay U. S. a visit.

1872

American Public Health Association founded.

William Graham Sumner becomes professor of political and social science at Yale.

Henry Hobson Richardson introduces Romanesque architecture in his design for Trinity Church, Boston.

Samuel Ward McAllister organizes the Patriarchs, 25 gentlemen, socially impeccable, to censor guest lists for New York society gatherings. In 1892 he chooses "the 400" for Mrs. William Astor's ball.

Montgomery Ward and Company, first mail order house, opens in Chicago; its first catalog a single sheet.

Popular Science Monthly founded by Edward Livingston Youmans.

Feb 2   Date of Congressional elections fixed by act of Congress as first Tuesday after first Monday in November, effective 1876.

Feb 17   Treaty signed with Samoan chief, giving U. S. exclusive coaling station at Pago Pago on Tutuila and role of protector of natives. Senate takes no action.

Feb 21–22   National Labor Convention meets at Columbus, Ohio. Nominates David Davis of Illinois for President and Joel Parker of New Jersey for Vice-President.

Feb 22   Prohibition party meets in na-tional convention at Columbus, Ohio. Nominates James Black of Pennsylvania for President and John Russell of Michigan for Vice-President.

Mar 1   Yellowstone National Park es-tablished by act of Congress.

May 1   Liberal Republicans meet in national convention at Cincinnati, Ohio.

Nominate Horace Greeley for President and B. Gratz Brown for Vice-President.

May 22 Amnesty Act removes political disabilities from practically all those excluded from office by 14th Amendment, a concession to Liberal Republicans.

May 23 Workingmen's National con- vention meets at New York, nominates Ulysses S. Grant for President and Henry Wilson of Massachusetts for Vice-President.

June 5–6 Republican National Con- vention meets at Philadelphia. Nominates Ulysses S. Grant and Henry Wilson for President and Vice-President.

June 6 Tariff Act makes 10 per cent horizontal reduction in duties on major protected items.

June 10 Freedmen's Bureau discon- tinued by act of Congress, effective June 30.

July 9 Democratic National Conven- tion meets at Baltimore. Nominates Horace Greeley for President and B. Gratz Brown for Vice-President.

Sept 3 "Straight" Democratic National Convention meets at Louisville, Ky. Nominates Charles O'Conor of New York for President and John Quincy Adams II of Massachusetts for Vice-President.

Sept 4 New York *Sun* begins exposure of the Credit Mobilier.

Sept 14 Geneva Tribunal, meeting un- der Treaty of Washington, awards U. S. $15,500,000 damages in *Alabama* claims against Great Britain.

Sept 25 Liberal Colored Republicans meet in national convention at Louisville, Ky. Nominate Horace Greeley and B. Gratz Brown for President and Vice-President.

Oct 21 Islands of San Juan awarded to U. S. by German emperor, arbitrator in settlement of boundary claims of Great Britain and U. S. in Puget Sound, as provided by Treaty of Washington.

Nov 5 Presidential election. U. S. Grant re-elected President and Henry

Wilson Vice-President by 286 electoral votes. 66 electors chosen for Horace Greeley, who died Nov. 29 before electoral vote was cast in Feb. In electoral balloting 42 of his votes go to Thomas A. Hendricks, 18 to B. Gratz Brown, 2 to Charles J. Jenkins, 1 to David Davis. Popular vote: Grant, 3,597,132; Greeley, 2,834,125; O'Conor, 29,489; Black, 5,608.

Nov 9 Great fire breaks out in Boston Property loss $73,000,000.

Nov 29 Horace Greeley dies at Pleas- antville, N. Y.

Dec 2 Poland committee appointed by House to investigate the Credit Mobilier.

1873

Carpetbag government at its worst in South Carolina and Louisiana, yet with support of President Grant.

Silver discovered in Nevada. The Great Bonanza mine.

Cable car adopted for use over hilly streets of San Francisco.

Remington Fire Arms Company begins manufacture of typewriter. Sholes, the inventor, sold his rights for $12,000.

Bethlehem Steel Works established in Pennsylvania.

Mount Whitney in Sierra Nevadas, highest peak in U. S., climbed successfully by members of California Geological Survey, first time on record.

Grasshopper plagues become serious in the West.

Joseph G. Cannon enters Congress from Illinois.

Nightingale System of nurses' training established at Bellevue Hospital, New York.

Cornelius Vanderbilt, leasing Lake Shore and Michigan Southern Railroad, completes his railroad control from New York to Chicago.

William Tweed found guilty and sentenced to 12 years in prison with fine of $12,000. Released after a year.

Feb 12   Fourth Coinage Act, the "crime of 1873." Silver dollar, except heavier trade dollar for use in Orient, dropped from list of coins, gold dollar made unit of value.

Feb 18   In Credit Mobilier affair, Po-land committee of House reports Oakes Ames and James Brooks guilty and recommends expulsion, but House merely censures, Feb. 27.

Mar 3   Passing of obscene literature through the mails prohibited by act of Congress. Sponsored by Anthony Comstock, secretary of Society for Supression of Vice.

Mar 3   Timber Culture Act provides for grants of a quarter section of land to anyone who will set out trees on 40 acres of it.

Mar 3   "Salary Grab" Act. Salary of the President doubled, that of Senators and Representatives increased 50 per cent and made retroactive to beginning of term.

Mar 4   President Grant inaugurated for second term, and Henry Wilson Vice-President.
[President Grant's Cabinet: Hamilton Fish, Secretary of State; W. A. Richardson, Secretary of Treasury; W. W. Belknap, Secretary of War; George M. Robeson, Secretary of Navy; Columbus Delano, Secretary of Interior; J. A. J. Creswell, Postmaster General; George H. Williams, Attorney General.]

Apr 14   In *Slaughter-House* cases, Su-preme Court declares that 14th Amendment does not give Federal jurisdiction over "entire domain of civil rights heretofore belonging exclusively to the States." First Supreme Court interpretation of 14th Amendment.

May 1   One-cent postal cards issued by U. S. government.

July 4   Farmers' Fourth of July. Farm-ers' Declaration of Independence read

before hundreds of Granger audiences in Northwest.

Sept 8   New York Warehouse and Se-curity Company fails, casting gloom over business world.

Sept 18   Banking house of Jay Cooke and Company, overinvolved in finance of the Northern Pacific, fails. Precipitates panic of 1873 and great depression which follows. 5,000 business failures by end of year. 10,478 failures, 1878.

Sept 20   New York Stock Exchange closes its doors.

Sept 20–Jan 15, 1874   Secretary of Treasury Richardson reissues $26,000,-000 of legal tenders, increasing their circulation to $382,000,000.

Sept 30   New York Stock Exchange re-opens.

Oct 18   First football conference, held by colleges of Yale, Princeton and Rutgers, drafts code of laws.

Oct 31   Filibustering ship *Virginius*, fraudulently flying U. S. flag and carrying men and arms to insurgents in Cuba, seized on high seas by Spain, 53 passengers and crew, some American, executed.

Nov 29   Settlement of *Virginius* affair reached. Spanish government will pay indemnity of $80,000 to families of Americans executed.

1874

Chautauqua Assembly established by Lewis Miller and Bishop John H. Vincent.

Woman's Christian Temperance Union organized in Cleveland, Ohio, Frances E. Willard corresponding secretary.

Young Men's Hebrew Association organized in New York, Lewis May president.

Social Democratic Workingmen's Party organized in New York.

Tennis introduced in America from England.

Washburn and Pillsbury flour mills in Minneapolis adopt Hungarian system of grinding wheat between chilled iron rollers.

Potato bug reaches Atlantic coast states, having spread from eastern slopes of Rocky Mountains.

Outlines of Cosmic Philosophy by John Fiske published.

Jan 20 "Salary Grab" Act of 1873 repealed with exception of increase of salaries for the President and Supreme Court justices.

Jan 21 Morrison R. Waite becomes Chief Justice of Supreme Court to succeed Salmon P. Chase.

Mar 4 In *Bartemeyer v. Iowa,* Supreme Court declares that denial of right to sell liquor does not deprive one of any privilege or immunity protected by 14th Amendment.

Mar 11 Granger legislation in Wisconsin, the Potter Law, regulates intrastate railroad freight rates.

Mar 23 Granger legislation regulates intrastate railroad freight rates in Iowa.

Apr 14 Inflation Bill passed in House, validates the $26,000,000 of greenbacks issued in 1873 and adds $18,000,000 more, to bring total in circulation to $400,000,000. Vetoed by President Grant Apr. 22.

May 4 Scandal of Sanborn contracts with U. S. Treasury to collect delinquent excise taxes established by report of House Committee on Ways and Means. Leads to resignation of Secretary of Treasury Richardson, succeeded by Benjamin H. Bristow June 1.

May 8 Massachusetts enacts first effective 10-hour day law for women.

June 20 Currency Act fixes maximum of greenbacks at amount now in circulation, $382,000,000.

June 20 Territorial government of District of Columbia abolished. Government by Congress through 3 commissioners, appointed by the President, set up.

July 4 First steel arch bridge opened, built across Mississippi River at St. Louis by James Buchanan Eads.

Sept 17 White League of New Orleans, in revolt against the state government, suppressed by Federal troops.

Nov Samuel J. Tilden elected governor of New York in Democratic "tidal wave."

Nov Congressional elections return Democratic majority to House.

Nov 24 Patent for barbed wire granted to Joseph F. Glidden. Manufacture of the wire increases to 80,500,000 pounds in next 6 years.

Dec 7 Race riots at Vicksburg, Miss., 75 Negroes killed.

1875

Gold discovered in Deadwood Gulch [South Dakota].

First state agricultural experiment station established at Wesleyan University, Middletown, Conn.

Luther Burbank in his California nursery begins development of new forms of plant life by selection and cross-fertilization.

American Bankers' Association organized at Saratoga Springs, N. Y.

Northwestern Interstate Collegiate Association organized for oratorical contests.

First Christmas cards in America engraved by Louis Prang.

Dr. Andrew T. Still begins practice of osteopathy at Kirksville, Mo.

Theosophical Society founded by Madame Helena P. Blavatsky.

School suffrage granted to women by Michigan and Minnesota.

Society for Prevention of Cruelty to Children incorporated, Henry Bergh president.

John McCloskey first American appointed to College of Cardinals.

Dwight Lyman Moody begins evangelistic revivals in the East.

Territory in Oregon, occupied by Nez Percé Indians by treaty, 1855, thrown open to settlement by President Grant.

Science and Health by Mary Baker Eddy published.

Jan 14 Specie Resumption Act provides for exchange of gold for legal tenders at U. S. Treasury, effective Jan. 1, 1879, in meantime, their circulation to be reduced to $300,000,000.

Jan 30 Treaty of commercial reciprocity with Hawaii signed. Provides that no Hawaiian territory shall be disposed of to any third power. Senate consents Mar. 18.

Mar 1 Civil Rights Act guarantees equal rights to the Negro in public places and prohibits his exclusion from jury duty.

Mar 3 Tariff Act restores 10 per cent horizontal reduction of rates of Tariff Act of 1872.

Mar 3 Coinage of silver 20-cent piece authorized by act of Congress. Discontinued May 2, 1878.

Mar 30 In *Minor v. Happersett*, Supreme Court declares 14th Amendment does not deprive a state of its right to set up suffrage requirements. Women citizens not given right to vote by privileges-and-immunities clause.

May 1 Whiskey Ring of revenue officers and distillers who had defrauded government of millions in excise taxes uncovered in St. Louis.

May 3 U. S. accepts membership in Universal Postal Union.

May 29 President Grant reluctantly disclaims ambition for third term.

June 17 Centenary of Battle of Bunker Hill. General Fitzhugh Lee, ex-Confederate, and General W. T. Sherman voice same note of reconciliation and patriotism.

Oct 12 Rutherford B. Hayes elected governor of Ohio on anti-greenback platform.

Nov 22 Henry Wilson, Vice-President, dies at Washington.

Dec 6 Forty-fourth Congress convenes with Democratic majority in House for first time since 1859.

Dec 15 Anti-third-term resolution, against third term for President Grant, passes House, 233–18.

1876

Centennial year.

American Chemical Society organized.

American Library Association organized.

Melvil Dewey originates Dewey decimal system of library classification.

Society for Ethical Culture founded by Dr. Felix Adler.

Polo introduced in U. S. at Newport by James Gordon Bennett, Jr.

Johns Hopkins University established at Baltimore for advanced study, Daniel Coit Gilman president.

Josiah Willard Gibbs, physical chemist at Yale, advances his Rule of Phase.

Thomas A. Edison invents mimeograph.

Machine for cigarette manufacture patented.

On Being A Christian by Washington Gladden, published. Social Christianity.

Jan 10 James G. Blaine in House proposes motion to deny amnesty to Jefferson Davis.

Mar 2 Impeachment of Secretary of War William W. Belknap for malfeasance in office recommended by House committee. Acquitted Aug. 1 by Senate Court of Impeachment.

Mar 10 Alexander Graham Bell's telephone transmits to adjoining room first complete intelligible sentence: "Mr. Watson, come here. I want you."

Mar 27 In *United States v. Cruikshank*, Supreme Court declares that

14th Amendment protects a Negro only from state action, not from action of individuals, thus invalidates much of Enforcement and Ku Klux acts.

Mar 27 In *United States v. Reese,* Supreme Court holds that 15th Amendment, while forbidding certain restrictions on suffrage, confers no rights of suffrage.

Apr 24 In *Walker v. Sauvinet,* Supreme Court holds that trial by jury in suits at common law in state courts is neither a privilege nor an immunity of national citizenship.

May 10 Centennial Exposition opened officially by President Grant at Fairmont Park, Philadelphia. Closes Nov. 10. Typewriter and telephone introduced to public at Centennial Exposition.

May 15 Judiciary Committee of House begins investigation of James G. Blaine's acceptance of favors from Union Pacific and other railroads while Speaker of House.

May 17 Prohibition party meets in national convention at Cleveland, Ohio. Nominates General Green Clay Smith of Ky. for President and Gideon T. Stewart of Ohio for Vice-President.

May 18 Independent, or Greenback, party holds its first national convention at Indianapolis, Ind. Nominates Peter Cooper of New York for President and Samuel F. Cary of Ohio for Vice-President.

June 5 James G. Blaine makes speech of defense before House. Dramatically reads selected parts of incriminating Mulligan letters.

June 14–16 Republican National Convention meets at Cincinnati. Rutherford B. Hayes of Ohio nominated for President, although James G. Blaine is in lead until seventh ballot. William A. Wheeler of New York nominated for Vice-President.

June 25 General George Armstrong Custer and his entire force massacred at Little Big Horn River in Montana by Sioux Indians, led by Sitting Bull, angered by advance of the whites, slaughter of the buffalo, and Black Hill gold rush.

June 27–29 Democratic National Convention meets at St. Louis. Nominates Samuel J. Tilden of New York for President and Thomas A. Hendricks of Indiana for Vice-President.

July 25 Richard P. Bland of Missouri introduces in House a bill for free and unlimited coinage of silver.

Aug 1 Colorado enters the Union.

Nov 7 Presidential election. Popular vote: Tilden, Democratic count, 4,300,-590, Republican count, 4,285,992; Hayes, Democratic count, 4,036,298, Republican count, 4,033,768; Cooper, Greenback, 81,737; Smith, Prohibition, 9,522.
Returns from Florida, Louisiana, South Carolina and Oregon in dispute. Electoral vote gives 184 undisputed votes to Tilden, 163 to Hayes. 185 needed to elect.

Nov 10 President Grant dispatches group of "visiting statesmen" to New Orleans to witness canvass of the votes.

Dec 6 Electoral vote cast in states. (See Nov. 7.)

Dec 12 First prohibition amendment to Constitution proposed in House by Henry W. Blair of New Hampshire.

1877

Physical Education introduced in public schools in Milwaukee, Wis., result of German Turner influence.

New York State Reformatory opened at Elmira, putting prison reform into operation.

Thomas Alva Edison invents phonograph.

Anti-Chinese riots in California. In San Francisco, unemployed "Sand-Lotters" under Denis Kearney form Workingmen's party of California in protest against Chinese.

Silver rush to Leadville, Colo., begins.

Ancient Society by Lewis Henry Morgan published. Formulation of laws of social progress.

Jan 2 Carpetbag government ends in Florida with inauguration of George F. Drew, Democratic governor.

Jan 29 Electoral Count Act provides for commission of 15 to judge and decide "as to which is the true and lawful electoral vote" of states from which there is more than one return in the 1876 disputed presidential election.

Feb 1 Count of Presidential electoral vote begins before the 2 houses of Congress.

Mar 1 In *Peik v. Chicago and North-western Railroad Company,* Granger case, Supreme Court declares that a state has power to fix rates for intrastate traffic and for interstate traffic originating within it. If acts appear unjust, legislature and not courts must be appealed to.

Mar 1 In *Munn v. Illinois,* **important** Granger case, Supreme Court declares that a state legislature has power to regulate warehouse and intrastate railroad rates.

Mar 2, 4:10 A.M. President of the Senate announces to the 2 houses of Congress election of Rutherford B. Hayes and William A. Wheeler by vote of 185 to 184 for Samuel J. Tilden. Justice Bradley's vote decisive in Electoral Commission.

Mar 3 U. S. Entomological Commis- sion established for work on grasshopper control by act of Congress.

Mar 3 Desert Land Act, to encourage development of irrigation in arid lands, offers land at 25 cents an acre if irrigated and cultivated for 3 years.

Mar 5 Rutherford B. Hayes inaugu- rated President and William A. Wheeler Vice-President. Oath taken privately Mar. 3, Mar. 4 being a Sunday.
[President Hayes' Cabinet: W. M. Evarts, Secretary of State; John Sherman, Secretary of Treasury; G. W. McCrary, Secretary of War; R. W. Thompson, Secretary of Navy; Carl Schurz, Secretary of Interior; David M. Key, Postmaster General; Charles Devens, Attorney General.]

Apr Four Eastern railroads—New York Central, Erie, Pennsylvania, and Baltimore and Ohio—call off their long rate war and announce 10 per cent cut in wages.

Apr 10 South Carolina passes into hands of its Democratic majority when Federal troops by order of the President quit Columbia, and its carpetbag governor leaves for the North.

Apr 20 President Hayes orders with- drawal of Federal troops from vicinity of State House, New Orleans.

Apr 24 Federal troops withdrawn from barracks in New Orleans. Carpetbag rule in Louisiana ends with Democratic government taking control. Last Southern state has now returned to control of its citizens.

May 17 U. S. Grant sails from Phila- delphia for trip around the world.

June–Oct War with Nez Percé In- dians in Idaho. War ends with defeat of Chief Joseph by Colonel Nelson A. Miles, and removal of Indians to Indian Territory.

June 14 Flag Day first observed, com- memorating 100th anniversary of U. S. flag.

June 21 Ten "Molly Maguires" hanged, members of secret society of terrorists active for a decade in Pennsylvania mining towns.

July–Aug Strike of all anthracite miners in eastern Pennsylvania spreads to bituminous districts. Return with general 10 per cent advance in wages.

July 16 Strike begins on the Balti- more and Ohio at Martinsburg, W. Va., following notice of another 10 per cent wage cut. Beginning of widespread railroad strikes. Strike ends after 2 weeks, following employment of Federal troops, each side claiming victory.

Nov 23 Halifax Fisheries Commission, provided by Treaty of Washington, awards $5,500,000 to Great Britain for U. S. fishing privileges in North-Atlantic. Payment made Nov. 21, 1878.

Dec 26 Workingmen's party in con-

vention at Newark, N. J., reorganized as Socialist Labor party, for political action.

1878

1878–1879, yellow fever epidemic sweeps through Gulf states and Tennessee.

Albert A. Michelson invents interferometer to measure vast distances by light wave lengths.

Terence V. Powderly elected mayor of Scranton, Pa., on Greenback-Labor ticket.

Photographic dry plate, invented by George Eastman, first manufactured.

Joseph Pulitzer buys St. Louis *Post Dispatch*.

Report on the Lands of the Arid Region of the United States by John W. Powell published.

Jan   First telephone exchange opened at New Haven, Conn., for 21 subscribers.

Jan 10   Woman Suffrage Amendment in words of its final form introduced in Congress by Senator A. A. Sargent.

Jan 14   In *Hall v. De Cuir*, Supreme Court holds that a state law requiring a railroad to give equal accommodations to all passengers without respect to race or color is unconstitutional because of its bearing upon interstate travel.

Jan 17   Treaty of amity and commerce signed with Samoa. Pago Pago Harbor acquired for coaling station and use of naval vessels. Senate consents Jan. 30.

Feb 22   National or Greenback Labor party organized at Toledo, Ohio. Unites Greenback and Labor Reform parties.

Feb 28   Bland-Allison Bill passed over President Hayes' veto. Authorizes purchase of from 2 to 4 million dollars worth of silver each month for coinage into dollars at old ratio of 16 to 1.

Mar 25   In *Pensacola Telegraph Company v. Western Union Telegraph Company*, Supreme Court declares that power to regulate interstate commerce adapts itself to development of instrumentalities of commerce, including the telegraph.

May 31   Reduction of greenbacks in circulation halted at $346,681,016, as of this day, by act of Congress.

June 3   Timber and Stone Act provides for private purchase of non-agricultural land, valuable chiefly for lumber and stone.

June 11   Permanent constitution for District of Columbia provided by act of Congress.

July 11   President Hayes removes from office Chester A. Arthur, Collector of the Port of New York, and Alonzo B. Cornell, Naval Officer, in opposition to New York bosses.

Oct 27   Robbery of Manhattan Savings Institution in New York of $3,000,000 by "Western George" L. Leslie, his biggest burglary.

Nov 5   Mid-Term elections give Dem- ocrats control of both houses of Congress, first time since 1858.

Dec 17   Term "Solid South" introduced in American vocabulary in speech in Senate by Senator Morgan of Ala.

Dec 17   Greenbacks reach face value in gold, on Wall Street, for first time since 1862.

1879

1879–1933, Era of Finance Capitalism.

Morgan and Company sells in London some holdings of W. H. Vanderbilt in New York Central Railroad.

Crop failure in Europe raises wheat prices for American farmers, resulting in increased acreage, extension of railroad mileage, and return of prosperity.

Standard Oil Company organizes temporary trust agreement.

Bureau of American Ethnology, within Smithsonian Institution, established through efforts of Major J. W. Powell.

Archaeological Institute of America organized.

Art Institute, Chicago, founded.

First citrus fair of California held at Riverside.

F. W. Woolworth's first five-and-ten-cent store opens in Utica, N. Y.

Arc-lamp system of street-lighting of Charles F. Brush installed in Cleveland and San Francisco.

Thomas A. Edison invents incandescent lamp.

William Deering's twine grain binder appears.

Lincoln County [New Mexico] cattle war, with William Bonney, "Billy the Kid," chief desperado, ended by Federal troops. "Billy the Kid" shot and killed 2 years later.

Large Negro exodus from the South to Kansas.

Carlisle (Pa.) Training and Industrial School for Indians founded.

Professor C. H. Toy forced to resign from Southern Baptist Seminary, Louisville, Ky., because of his scientific interpretation of the Bible.

Progress and Poverty by Henry George published.

Darwinism by John Fiske published.

Jan 1   Resumption of specie payment by U. S. government goes into effect, having been "off" specie since end of 1861.

Jan 25   Arrears of Pensions Act provide back payment of pensions from date of death or discharge.

Feb 4   President Hayes, in open letter to E. A. Merritt, successor of Chester A. Arthur, Collector of the Port of New York, directs him to conduct office according to Civil Service Commission rules.

Feb 15   Women gain right to practice law before U. S. Supreme Court by act of Congress.

Mar 1   Bill to restrict Chinese immi- gration vetoed by President Hayes as violation of Burlingame Treaty of 1868.

Mar 3   U. S. Geological Survey, bureau of Department of the Interior, established by act of Congress. [Clarence King first director.]

May 7   California by popular vote adopts new constitution, adopted in convention Mar. 3. Project of Denis Kearney and followers, it forbids employment of Chinese in the state.

May 15   International Congress of Geographic Sciences meets in Paris with delegates from 25 nations, including U. S. Seven possible routes for ship canal across the Isthmus considered.

June 28   Mississippi River Commission of 7 men to be appointed by the President is authorized by act of Congress, to improve navigation.

Summer   Uprising of Ute Indians in Colorado. By treaty, they are removed to reservation in Utah in 1880.

Sept 20   General Grant arrives at San Francisco from world tour, is given enthusiastic reception.

Nov 15   U. S. end of French Atlantic cable landed at North Eastham, Mass.

1880

Population, 50,155,783.

1880–1890, decade of unprecedented railroad construction.

American Society of Mechanical Engineers founded.

Salvation Army begins its work in U. S.

William D. Bloxham, governor of Florida, enters upon campaign for drainage of swamp lands.

Captain David L. Payne leads first of 8 "boomers'" raids from Kansas into

Oklahoma country to seize lands in defiance of law.

Gold brick swindle introduced in New York City by Reed Waddell from Springfield, Ill.

Cleopatra's Needle, Egyptian obelisk, brought to New York to be placed in Central Park.

Mar 1 In *Strauder v. West Virginia,* Supreme Court holds unconstitutional a West Virginia law of Mar. 12, 1863, excluding Negroes from jury duty.

Mar 8 President Hayes declares policy of U. S. is for any Isthmian canal to be strictly under its jurisdiction.

Mar 18 Ferdinand De Lesseps testifies before a House committee that France has no official connection with the French Canal Company.

Apr National Farmers' Alliance, or Northern Alliance, organized in Chicago by Milton George. Forerunner of People's Party.

Apr Wabash, Ind., lighted throughout by electricity in great public demonstration of Brush system.

May 4 President Hayes, in support of principle of military intervention at elections, vetoes Appropriation Bill because of its rider in opposition.

May 6 Republican Anti-Third Term convention meets in St. Louis in opposition to nomination of U. S. Grant for Presidency.

May 26 Miners' strike at Leadville, Colo., for more pay, fewer hours. Managers accept 8-hour day.

June 2–8 Republican National Convention meets at Chicago, U. S. Grant, leading candidate. James A. Garfield of Ohio nominated for President on 36th ballot with 399 votes, Grant, 306. Chester A. Arthur nominated for Vice-President.

June 9–10 Greenback, or National, party meets in convention at Chicago. Nominates James B. Weaver of Iowa for President and B. J. Chambers of Texas for Vice-President.

June 17 Prohibition party meets in convention at Cleveland. Nominates Neal Dow of Maine for President and A. M. Thompson of Ohio for Vice-President.

June 22–24 Democratic National Convention meets at Cincinnati. Nominates General Winfield S. Hancock of Pennsylvania for President and William H. English of Indiana for Vice-President.

July 3 U. S. in Convention of Madrid joins European powers to restrict extraterritorial protection of Moroccans. Senate consents May 5, 1881.

Nov 2 Presidential election. Garfield and Arthur elected by electoral vote of 214, to 155 for Hancock and English. Popular vote: Garfield, Republican, 4,454,416; Hancock, Democrat, 4,444,952; Weaver, Greenback, 308,578; Dow, Prohibition, 10,305.

Nov 17 Chinese Exclusion Treaty signed with China at Peking, giving U. S. power to "regulate, limit or suspend" coming of Chinese laborers into the country. Senate consents May 5, 1881.

Dec 20 Broadway in New York illuminated by electricity for one mile by Brush system of arc lighting.

1881

1881–1900, 23,800 strikes and lockouts recorded in U. S.

Migration of Russian-Jews to U. S. begins, following persecution.

National Civil Service Reform League formed, George William Curtis president.

New England Divorce Reform League organized. Becomes National Divorce Reform League, 1885.

Young People's Society of Christian Endeavor organized in Portland, Maine, by Rev. Francis E. Clark.

Andrew Carnegie begins his benefactions to libraries in gift to Pittsburgh.

Wharton School of Finance and Commerce founded by Joseph Wharton as department of University of Pennsylvania.

Tuskegee Institute, Ala., founded by Booker T. Washington.

First pure-food laws passed by New York, New Jersey, Michigan and Illinois.

Anaconda copper mine opened near Helena [Montana].

Pullman, Ill., made-to-order industrial town, begun by Pullman Car Company.

Governor of Missouri places price upon heads of Frank and Jesse James, bandits. Jesse James shot and killed next year.

Grover Cleveland elected "veto" mayor of Buffalo.

Star Route frauds, involving Senator Stephen W. Dorsey of Arkansas and Post Office Department, exposed in prosecution by Postmaster General Thomas L. James. Accused are acquitted 1883.

Diplomatic and commercial treaties signed with Serbia and Rumania who this year have won independence from Turkey.

Lt. Adolphus W. Greely sent by U. S. government to establish station for scientific observation in northern Greenland. Expedition reaches 83° 24' in 1882, farthest northern point yet attained.

The New Testament, revised version, appears, combined work of American and English scholars. Over 200,000 copies sold in New York City in first week after publication. Revision of *Old Testament* published 1885.

The Common Law by Oliver Wendell Holmes published.

Jan 19   Western Union Telegraph Company formed by Jay Gould and William H. Vanderbilt, consolidating Western Union, American Union, and Atlantic and Pacific companies.

Jan 24   In *Springer v. United States,* Supreme Court declares Federal income tax law of 1862 constitutional.

Feb 19   Kansas adopts state wide pro-hibition.

Feb 22   President Hayes, in executive order to Secretary of War Alexander Ramsey, prohibits sale of liquor at military posts.

Mar   *The Story of a Great Monopoly* by Henry Demarest Lloyd, aimed at Standard Oil Company, published in *Atlantic Monthly.*

Mar 3   Registration and protection of trademarks authorized by act of Congress.

Mar 4   James A. Garfield and Chester A. Arthur inaugurated President and Vice-President.
[President Garfield's Cabinet: James G. Blaine, Secretary of State; William Windom, Secretary of Treasury; Robert T. Lincoln, Secretary of War; William H. Hunt, Secretary of Navy; Samuel J. Kirkwood, Secretary of Interior; Wayne MacVeagh, Attorney General; Thomas L. James, Postmaster General.]

Mar 10   Santa Fe Railroad joins South-ern Pacific at Deming [New Mexico].

Mar 23   Judge William H. Robertson, political enemy of Senator Roscoe Conkling of New York, nominated Collector of the Port of New York by President Garfield. Confirmed by Senate May 18.

May 16   Senators Roscoe Conkling and Thomas C. Platt from New York resign their seats in protest against President's appointment of Robertson, Collector, without consulting Conkling.

May 21   American Red Cross organ-ized, Clara Barton president.

June 24   Secretary of State Blaine sends identical letter to U. S. ministers in Europe, serving notice that any European agreement for a joint guarantee of the De Lesseps canal at Panama would be regarded in U. S. as unfriendly.

July 2   President Garfield shot in Pennsylvania Railroad station in Washington by Charles Guiteau, disappointed office seeker.

Sept 19 **President Garfield dies at El-beron, N. J.**

Sept 20 **Vice-President Arthur takes** oath of office as President at his home in New York.

Oct 5 **International Cotton Exposition** opens at Atlanta, Ga.

Oct 19 **Hundredth anniversary of sur-render of Lord Cornwallis celebrated at Yorktown, Va.**

Nov 8 **Theodore Roosevelt elected to** New York assembly.

Nov 14 **Trial of Charles Guiteau for** murder of President Garfield opens. Convicted, he is hanged at Washington June 30, 1882.

Nov 17 **Federation of Organized** Trades and Labor Unions of U. S. and Canada formed at Pittsburgh by Samuel Gompers. Forerunner of AFL.

Nov 19 **Secretary of State Blaine pro-poses** to Great Britain a modification of Clayton-Bulwer Treaty of 1850, to give U. S. greater authority over any Isthmian canal.

Nov 29 **Secretary of State Blaine issues** invitations to Latin-American states to a congress at Washington for 1882, launching Pan-American movement. Blaine's successor, F. T. Frelinghuysen, withdraws invitations.

Dec 1 **Secretary of State Blaine de-clares** Hawaiian Islands part of Amer-ican system and within bounds of Mon-roe Doctrine.

Dec 1 **Southern Pacific Railroad com-pleted** between New Orleans and the Pacific when last spike is driven near El Paso.

Dec 12 **Frederick T. Frelinghuysen ap-pointed** Secretary of State by President Arthur to succeed James G. Blaine, re-signed.

1882

A year of strikes for higher wages, fol-lowing a year of poor crops and result-ing increase in prices.

American Association of University Women organized. Name adopted in 1921.

Knights of Columbus founded.

American Forestry Association organ-ized.

Frederick W. Taylor, gang boss for Midvale Steel Company, introduces "scientific management," Taylorization.

Robert E. Pattison, reform leader, elect-ed Democratic governor of Pennsyl-vania.

Jan 2 **Standard Oil Trust organized by** John D. Rockefeller.

Mar 22 **Edmunds Act prohibits polyg-amists** from voting or holding office.

Apr 4 **Bill to restrict Chinese labor** immigration for 20 years, in violation of Burlingame Treaty, vetoed by Presi-dent Arthur.

May 6 **First Chinese Exclusion Act** bars Chinese laborers from entering U. S. for 10 years.

May 15 **Tariff commission of 9 men, to** be appointed by the President from "civil life," authorized by Congress. [John L. Hayes, secretary of National Association of Wool Manufacturers, acts as chairman of commission.]

May 22 **U. S. signs treaty of commerce** and friendship with Korea on basis of an independent state and, so doing, hits upon crux of Far Eastern diplomacy, Sino-Russo-Japanese conflict. Senate con-sents Feb. 13, 1883.

July 26 **Acceptance of Geneva Con-vention** of 1864 for the care of wounded in war proclaimed by U. S. Senate con-sented Mar. 16.

Aug 2 **Rivers and Harbors Bill, passed** by Congress over President's veto, au-thorizes over $18,000,000 for public works.

Aug 3 **First act restricting general im-migration** excludes paupers, convicts and defectives, and imposes a head tax.

Sept 4 **Edison's Pearl Street plant for** incandescent electric lighting opened in New York.

Sept 5 First Labor Day parade held in New York. Inaugurated by Knights of Labor.

Nov 7 Grover Cleveland elected governor of New York on Democratic ticket with plurality of over 190,000.

Dec 4 Tariff commission submits report to Congress, with recommendations of substantial reductions. President Arthur supports report in message to Congress.

Dec 19 In *San Mateo County v. Southern Pacific Railroad Company* before Supreme Court, Roscoe Conkling argues that one purpose of 14th Amendment is to protect rights of corporations as persons.

1 8 8 3

Northern Pacific Railroad sends agents to Europe and British Isles to encourage immigration to the Northwest.

Southern Immigration Association formed to encourage European immigration to the South.

Ferdinand De Lesseps begins construction of Panama Canal for French Canal Company.

Joseph Pulitzer purchases New York *World* from Jay Gould, marking rise of modern American journalism.

Ladies' Home Journal founded in Philadelphia, Mrs. Cyrus H. K. Curtis, editor.

History of the People of the United States from the Revolution to the Civil War, first of 8 vols., by J. B. McMaster, published.

Dynamic Sociology by Lester Frank Ward published. May be called beginning of American sociology.

Jan 16 Pendleton Civil Service Reform Act provides for competitive examinations for Federal positions.

Mar 3 Secretary of the Navy authorized by Congress to construct 3 steel cruisers and one dispatch boat. Beginning of steel navy.

Mar 3 Tariff Act, "The Mongrel Tariff," continues protective principle.

Mar 3 Letter postage reduced to 2 cents for a half ounce by act of Congress.

Mar 26 William K. Vanderbilt fancy-dress ball given. The most sumptuous entertainment yet given in U. S.

May 24 Brooklyn Bridge between New York and Brooklyn opened, John A. Roebling designer. Chartered 1867.

Sept 8 Northern Pacific Railroad completed with "last spike" ceremony at Gold Creek [Montana]. Henry Villard president.

Sept 21 Telegraph connection established between U. S. and Brazil.

Oct 15 In *Civil Rights Cases,* Supreme Court declares Civil Rights Act of 1875, granting equal rights in public places to Negroes, unconstitutional except as it relates to jury duty and interstate travel.

Nov 18 Standard time established for the whole country, with adoption of 4 zones by railroads. Interstate Commerce Commission given supervision of zone limits by Congress 1918.

1 8 8 4

Severe coal strikes in Pennsylvania and Ohio.

American Historical Association organized, Herbert Baxter Adams first president.

American Catholic Historical Society organized.

American Institute of Electrical Engineers founded.

Long distance telephone first established between New York and Boston with use of double wire of copper.

First skyscraper, Home Insurance Building, erected in Chicago, 10 stories high, with use of steel framework.

Dr. James Woodrow forced out of Presbyterian Theological Seminary, Columbia, S. C., for support of doctrine of evolution.

Political cartoon made a feature of the newspaper by Joseph Pulitzer in New York *World,* in support of Grover Cleveland.

Montcalm and Wolfe by Francis Parkman published.

Jan 2 Discriminating duties in trade with Cuba and Puerto Rico removed in executive agreement with Spain.

Mar 3 In *Juilliard v. Greenman,* Supreme Court declares Congress has power to make treasury notes legal tender in peace time as well as in war.

Mar 4 Iowa adopts state prohibition.

May 6 Failure of stock exchange firm of Grant and Ward, New York. Ulysses S. Grant loses fortune.

May 14 Financial crisis in New York City. Panic follows and bank failures rise to 10,968 in U. S.

May 14 National Anti-Monopoly con- vention meets at Chicago. Nominates General Benjamin F. Butler of Massachusetts for President.

May 28 National or Greenback party convention meets at Indianapolis. Nominates General Benjamin F. Butler for President and Alanson M. West of Mississippi for Vice-President.

May 29 Bureau of Animal Industry in Department of Agriculture established by act of Congress.

June 3–6 Republican National Con- vention meets at Chicago. Nominates James G. Blaine for President on fourth ballot June 6, and General John A. Logan of Illinois for Vice-President.

June 6 "Mugwumps," reform wing of Republican Party, bolt following Blaine's nomination.

June 16 "Mugwumps" hold conference at New York, George William Curtis presiding. With overtures to Democrats, they pledge support if Democrats will nominate a liberal.

June 27 Bureau of Labor in Depart- ment of Interior established by act of Congress.

July 5 Second Chinese Exclusion Act makes more rigid restrictions.

July 8–11 Democratic National Con- vention meets at Chicago. Nominates Grover Cleveland, governor of New York, for President and Thomas A. Hendricks of Indiana for Vice-President.

July 23 Prohibition party meets in convention at Pittsburgh. Nominates John P. St. John of Kansas for President and William Daniel of Maryland for Vice-President.

July 30 National Labor party meets at Chicago. Nominates Grover Cleveland for President and Thomas A. Hendricks for Vice-President.

Summer Mulligan letters incriminat- ing James G. Blaine reprinted in *Harper's Weekly* May-Sept.

Oct 13 International Prime Meridian Conference, meeting at Washington, decides upon Greenwich as common prime meridian for the world.

Oct 29 The inept "Rum, Romanism and Rebellion" speech of Rev. Samuel D. Burchard in eulogy of James G. Blaine, one cause of Blaine's defeat in election.

Nov 4 Presidential election. Cleveland and Hendricks elected by electoral vote of 219, to 182 for Blaine and Logan. Popular vote: Cleveland, Democrat, 4,874,986; Blaine, Republican, 4,851,-981; Butler, Greenback, 175,370; St. John, Prohibition, 150,369.

Dec 16 World's Industrial and Cotton Centennial Exposition opened at New Orleans.

1885

Year of strikes because of wage cuts following panic and industrial depression of 1884.

American Economic Association formed. Young German University-trained economists revolt against determinist economics.

American Telephone and Telegraph Company formed.

Dr. Edward Livingston Trudeau opens Adirondack Cottage Sanatorium for tuberculosis patients at Saranac Lake, N. Y., first in U. S.

Orange Growers' Protective Union of Southern California organized.

Kansas, Nebraska and Colorado pass strict quarantine laws against driving of cattle across their borders in annual drive from Texas to northern range.

Linotype machine invented by Ottmar Mergenthaler.

Henry Hobson Richardson designs Marshall Field Building, Chicago.

Congressional Government by Woodrow Wilson published.

Evolution and Religion by Henry Ward Beecher published. Evolution and Christian faith are in harmony.

Our Country by Josiah Strong published. Imperialism is duty of U. S.

Feb 21   Washington Monument, Washington, D. C., dedicated. Cornerstone was laid July 4, 1848, monument completed Dec. 6, 1884.

Feb 25   Illegal fencing of public lands in the West prohibited by act of Congress.

Feb 26   Contract Labor Act prohibits importation of unskilled laborers, result of Knights of Labor lobby. Number of excluded classes increased to 7.

Mar 4   Grover Cleveland inaugurated President and Thomas A. Hendricks Vice-President.
[President Cleveland's Cabinet: Thomas F. Bayard, Secretary of State; Daniel Manning, Secretary of Treasury; W. C. Endicott, Secretary of War; W. C. Whitney, Secretary of Navy; L. Q. C. Lamar, Secretary of Interior; William F. Vilas, Postmaster General; A. H. Garland, Attorney General.]

Mar 13   President Cleveland in proclamation warns persons against entering and settling Oklahoma lands in Indian Territory.

Apr 24   Five hundred U. S. marines land on Isthmus of Panama to protect U. S. property.

July 1   Fisheries reciprocity with Canada, under Treaty of Washington, terminated by U. S. in accordance with joint resolution of Congress Mar. 3, 1883.

July 1   Letter postage reduced to 2 cents for an ounce by act of Congress.

Aug 7   President Cleveland in proclamation orders removal of all unlawful enclosures of western public lands.

Nov 7   President Cleveland, following anti-Chinese riots in Washington Territory, orders dispersal of trouble makers.

Nov 25   Vice-President   Thomas   A. Hendricks dies at Indianapolis.

1886

Peak year of strikes in 19th century. Number of workers out, 610,000; monetary loss, $33,580,000.

Cattle industry of Great Plains suffers disaster from overgrazing, drought and blizzard.

Neighborhood Guild, first social settlement in U. S., founded in New York by Dr. Stanton Coit.

Archbishop James Gibbons of Baltimore made Cardinal by Pope Leo XIII.

Process of extracting aluminum from ore discovered by Charles M. Hall.

Alternating current system of electricity for commercial purposes introduced by George Westinghouse.

Forum begins publication. Its crusading paves the way for muckrakers of 20th century.

Jan 19   Presidential Succession Act. In event of death of both President and Vice-President, Cabinet members, in definite order, shall succeed.

Feb 7 Anti-Chinese riots in Seattle [Washington]. 400 Chinese driven from their homes, some sent to San Francisco, and Federal troops called to scene.

Feb 14 First trainload of oranges leaves Los Angeles for the East.

Feb 15 Morrison Tariff Bill, providing for lower duties, introduced in House. Defeated June 17.

Mar 6 Strike by Knights of Labor on Gould system of railroads in the Southwest begins. With 9,000 shopmen out, freight traffic on over 5,000 miles of railroad is at standstill. Strike ends May 4 with no gains for strikers.

Apr 8 Free Coinage of Silver Bill, brought into House by Richard P. Bland, defeated, 163–126.

Apr 22 President Cleveland sends first Presidential labor message to Congress. Proposes Federal Commission to adjust difficulties.

May 1 Strikes and labor demonstra- tions occur over the country in demand for 8-hour day with 10-hour pay.

May 4 Haymarket Square riot in Chi- cago. Police, dispelling an anarchists' meeting, killed and wounded by dynamite bomb hurled into their midst.

May 8 President Cleveland sends to Congress first of his many vetoes of personal pension bills.

May 10 In *Yick Wo v. Hopkins,* Su- preme Court declares an alien is a person and rules that a municipal ordinance discriminating against Chinese laundries violates 14th Amendment.

May 10 In *Santa Clara County v.* *Southern Pacific Railroad,* a corporation is declared to be a person by the Supreme Court and is protected according to 14th Amendment.

June 29 Incorporation of national trades unions provided by act of Congress.

Aug 2 Oleomargarine Act imposes tax and regulates manufacture and sale under pressure of dairy interests.

Aug 3 Building of two iron-clads, one cruiser, and one torpedo boat authorized by act of Congress.

Aug 20 Seven of Haymarket Square rioters (May 4), convicted of murder, are sentenced to death.

Sept 4 Geronimo, Apache chief, cap- tured by Colonel Miles after 4 years of warfare in Arizona, New Mexico and Mexico. Ends last important Indian war.

Sept 16 Anti-Saloon Republicans meet in national convention at Chicago.

Oct 25 In *Wabash, St. Louis and Pa-* *cific Railway Co. v. Illinois,* Supreme Court declares that a state cannot regulate even that portion of interstate commerce within its borders.

Oct 28 Statue of Liberty, gift of peo- ple of France, dedicated on Bedloe's Island, New York Harbor.

Nov 2 Three-cornered mayorality con- test, New York, waged by Theodore Roosevelt, Henry George and Abram S. Hewitt, won by Hewitt.

Nov 2 Henry Cabot Lodge elected to Congress from Massachusetts.

Dec 8 AFL emerges from Federation of Trades and Labor Unions during its annual convention.

Dec 21 President Cleveland nominates James C. Matthews, Negro, of New York, recorder of deeds in District of Columbia, to succeed Frederick Douglass.

1887

American Protective Association, the "A.P.A.," organized. Anti-Catholic in propaganda and program.

Boone and Crockett Club, for protection of big game, organized by Theodore Roosevelt.

Augustus St. Gaudens' statue of Lincoln unveiled in Lincoln Park, Chicago.

First successful electric trolley line built, in Richmond, Va., by Frank J. Sprague.

Marine Laboratory established at Wood's Hole, Mass.

Lick Observatory established at Mount Hamilton, Cal.

Whiskey, sugar, cordage and lead trusts organized.

Territory of Cimarron proclaimed by settlers in No Man's Land, Oklahoma, but never recognized by Congress.

Jan 20 Lease of Pearl Harbor as naval station secured with Senate consent to amended convention with Hawaii (signed Dec. 6, 1884).

Jan 29 Old age pension for Mexican War veterans established by act of Congress.

Feb 4 Interstate Commerce Act pro-vides for Interstate Commerce Commission.

Feb 8 Dawes Act provides for allot-ment of individual land holdings to Indians, a quarter-section to each family head. Act sponsored by Senator Henry L. Dawes.

Feb 11 Dependent Pension Bill ve-toed by President Cleveland.

Feb 23 Importation of opium from China prohibited by act of Congress.

Mar 2 Hatch Act authorizes establish-ment of agricultural experiment station in each state having land-grant college.

Mar 3 Tenure of Office Act, Mar. 2, 1867, as amended in 1869, repealed by act of Congress, a victory for the President.

Mar 22 Interstate Commerce Commis-sion appointed by President Cleveland, Judge Thomas M. Cooley chairman.

June 16 President Cleveland, after bitter protest against his approval, revokes order for return of captured Confederate battle flags on grounds that such action is a Congressional function. Return of flags authorized Feb. 28, 1905, without protest.

Sept 15–18 Hundredth anniversary of formation of the Constitution of the United States celebrated in Philadelphia.

Dec 5 In *Mugler v. Kansas,* **Supreme** Court decides a state prohibition act is a police regulation protecting health and morals and is not contrary to 14th Amendment.

Dec 6 President Cleveland devotes en-tire annual message to Congress to the tariff question, urging reduction of duties.

1888

National Geographic Society founded at Washington.

Geological Society of America organized.

Eastman Company puts the Kodak, film-roll camera, on the market.

Federal survey of arid regions in the West begun by Frederick Haynes Newell.

Looking Backward by Edward Bellamy published.

American Commonwealth by James Bryce published.

Critical Period of American History by John Fiske published.

Acres of Diamonds, an address delivered some 6,000 times, 1861–1913, by Russell Herman Conwell, published. Popularizes stewardship of riches.

Feb   Australian ballot (secret) intro-duced in U. S. at municipal election, Louisville, Ky.

Mar 11–14 "Great blizzard of '88" on Atlantic Coast.

Mar 19 In *Bowman v. Chicago and Northwestern Railway Company,* **Su-**preme Court declares a state law prohibiting importation of liquor is void, being interstate commerce regulation.

Apr 25 Convention of delegates from Southern states east of the Mississippi meets at Hot Springs, N. C., to direct immigration to the South.

Apr 30 Melville W. Fuller appointed Chief Justice of Supreme Court by President Cleveland.

May 15 **Labor party meets simultane-ously in 2 conventions at Cincinnati.** Union Labor nominates Alson J. Streeter of Illinois for President and Samuel Evans of Texas for Vice-President. United Labor nominates Robert H. Cowdrey of Illinois for President and W. H. T. Wakefield of Kansas for Vice-President.

May 30 **Prohibition party meets in convention at Indianapolis.** Nominates Clinton B. Fisk of New Jersey for President and John A. Brooks of Missouri for Vice-President.

June 5 **Democratic National Convention meets at St. Louis.** Renominates Grover Cleveland for President and nominates Allen G. Thurman of Ohio for Vice-President.

June 13 **Department of Labor, without Cabinet status,** created from Bureau of Labor by act of Congress.

June 19–25 **Republican National Convention meets at Chicago.** Nominates Benjamin Harrison of Indiana for President and Levi P. Morton of New York for Vice-President.

July 1 **Union and Confederate veterans meet at Gettysburg** in celebration of 25th anniversary of the battle.

July 21 **Mills Tariff Bill, reducing duties** in line with Cleveland's tariff message of December 1887, passed by Democratic House. Roger Q. Mills chairman of Ways and Means Committee.

Aug 14 **American party meets at Washington.** Nominates James L. Curtis of New York for President and James R. Greer of Tennessee for Vice-President. All voting delegates from California and New York.

Oct 1 **Chinese Exclusion Act prohibits return of laborers** who have left U. S.

Oct 3 **Allison Tariff Bill, as substitute for Mills Bill of House,** reported to Republican Senate by Committee on Finance, Senator William B. Allison chairman. When Congress adjourns Oct. 20, Senate has not accepted Mills Bill of House nor passed its own.

Oct 24 **Fictitious Murchison letter ad-dressed to Lord Sackville,** British minister, asking advice on voting, and the reply, suggesting that its writer vote Democratic ticket, published by Republicans.

Nov 6 **Presidential election. Harrison and Morton elected** by electoral vote of 233, to 168 for Cleveland and Thurman. Popular vote: Harrison, Republican, 5,-439,853; Cleveland, Democratic, 5,540,-309; Fisk, Prohibition, 249,506; Streeter, Union Labor, 146,935; Cowdrey, United Labor, 2,818; Curtis, American, 1,600.

1889

American Academy of Political and Social Science organized in Philadelphia.

General Federation of Women's Clubs organized.

Sons of American Revolution organized.

Southern Alliance formed, merging Southern agricultural organizations, vehicle of farmer discontent.

Catholic University of America established at Washington, D. C.

Hull House founded in Chicago by Jane Addams.

John Crerar Library established in Chicago by will of John Crerar, merchant prince.

Herbartian system of instruction introduced in public schools of U. S. by students returning from University of Jena.

French Panama Canal Company goes into bankruptcy.

Safety bicycle introduced, with low wheels of equal size. By 1893, 1,000,000 in use.

Australian lady bug imported to destroy the white scale, endangering citrus industry in California.

H. S. Pingree elected reform mayor of Detroit, Mich., is continued in office for 7 years.

James J. Hill organizes Great Northern Railroad to run from Great Lakes to the Pacific.

Winning of the West, first of 4 vols., by Theodore Roosevelt, published.

Feb 9 Department of Agriculture raised to Cabinet status by act of Congress.

Feb 20 Maritime Canal Company of Nicaragua incorporated by Congress for construction, management and operation of ship canal from the Atlantic to the Pacific, under U. S. control without financial responsibility. Oct. 22, work on the canal begun.

Feb 22 Omnibus Bill signed by Pres- ident Cleveland for admission of four new states—North Dakota, South Dakota, Montana and Washington.

Mar 2 Seizure of vessels encroaching upon U. S. seal-fishing rights in Bering Sea authorized by Congress.

Mar 2 Congress appropriates $100,000 to establish coaling station at Pago Pago, Tutuila, Samoa.

Mar 2 Kansas passes first anti-trust law. During year, Maine, Michigan and Tennessee follow.

Mar 4 Benjamin Harrison inaugu- rated President and Levi P. Morton Vice-President.

[President Harrison's Cabinet: James G. Blaine, Secretary of State; William Windom, Secretary of Treasury; Redfield Proctor, Secretary of War; Benjamin F. Tracy, Secretary of Navy; John W. Noble, Secretary of Interior; N. J. Colman, Secretary of Agriculture; John Wanamaker, Postmaster General; W. H. H. Miller, Attorney General.]

Mar 16 Seven American, German and British warships in Samoan harbor of Apia struck by tropical hurricane at moment of critical international impasse. All wrecked save British *Calliope.*

Apr 22 At high noon Oklahoma country, part of Indian Territory, thrown open to settlers by Presidential order. By sundown, 2 tent towns are booming, Guthrie and Oklahoma City.

Apr 29–May 1 Centennial of Wash- ington's inauguration celebrated in New York City.

May 9 New Jersey amends its corpora- tion law to permit chartering of holding companies in the state. Delaware follows.

May 13 Theodore Roosevelt becomes Civil Service Commissioner, appointed by President Harrison.

May 31 Johnstown, Pa., flood, when Conemaugh Dam breaks, takes several thousand lives.

June 14 Samoan Treaty signed by which U. S. with Great Britain and Germany set up tripartite protectorate over Samoa. Senate consents Feb. 4, 1890.

Aug 6 Sioux reservation of 11,000,000 acres in Dakota ceded to U. S.

Oct 2 First International American Conference convenes at Washington. Establishes Pan-American Union.

Nov 2 North Dakota enters the Union.

Nov 2 South Dakota enters the Union.

Nov 8 Montana enters the Union.

Nov 11 Washington enters the Union.

Nov 14 Elizabeth Cochrane, "Nellie Bly," reporter for New York *World,* leaves Hoboken, N. J., to outdo Jules Verne's hero in *Around the World in Eighty Days.* Her record, 72 days, 6 hours, 11 minutes, 14 seconds.

Dec 3 President Harrison in annual message to Congress proposes that trusts be made subject of prohibitory legislation.

Dec 6 Jefferson Davis, ex-President of the Confederacy, dies in New Orleans.

1890

Population, 62,947,714.

Daughters of the American Revolution founded.

North River Sugar Refining Company, member of sugar trust, sued by state of New York for evading state control, loses charter.

The Influence of Sea Power upon History, 1660–1783 by A. T. Mahan published.

Principles of Psychology by William James published.

Jan 25 **UMW, affiliate of AFL, organized at Columbus, Ohio.**

Feb 10 **Eleven million acres of Sioux lands in South Dakota, ceded to U. S., 1889, thrown open to settlement by Presidential proclamation.**

Feb 14 **Speaker Thomas B. Reed of House sets up rules for determining quorums by counting all those present regardless of roll call.**

Feb 18 **National American Woman Suffrage Association formed, uniting 2 organizations, the American and the National.**

Mar 24 **In** *Chicago, Milwaukee, St. Paul Railroad, v. Minnesota,* **the Minnesota rate case, Supreme Court practically overrules decision in** *Munn v. Illinois,* **1877. Step in development of judicial review.**

Apr 4 **New York state adopts law to prevent corrupt practices at elections.**

Apr 28 **In** *Leisy v. Hardin,* **Supreme Court declares unconstitutional state prohibition of sale of liquor in original package imported from another state.**

May 2 **Oklahoma Territory established, cut from Indian Territory, by act of Congress.**

June 27 **Dependent Pension Act for Civil War veterans and widows.**

June 30 **Construction of 3 sea-going armored battleships authorized by act of Congress.**

July 2 **Force Bill, designed to insure Negro suffrage in the South, sponsored by Henry Cabot Lodge, passed by House. [Fails in Senate.]**

July 2 **Sherman Anti-Trust Act.** "Every contract, combination in the form of trust or otherwise, or conspiracy, in restraint of trade or commerce among the several States, or with foreign nations, is hereby declared to be illegal."

July 2 **International Act for Repression of African Slave Trade signed by U. S. Senate consents Jan. 11, 1892.**

July 3 **Idaho enters the Union.**

July 10 **Wyoming enters the Union.**

July 14 **Sherman Silver Purchase Act** supersedes Bland-Allison Act of Feb. 28, 1878.

Aug 8 **New York Central Railroad strike called by Knights of Labor.**

Aug 8 **Original Package Act subjects liquors imported from another state to laws of state receiving them. Sets aside decision in** *Leisy v. Hardin,* **Apr. 28.**

Aug 30 **Inspection by Department of Agriculture of pork products to be exported provided by act of Congress.**

Aug 30 **Congressional act, supplementing Morrill Act of July 2, 1862, provides annual subsidies to land-grant colleges for instruction in agriculture and mechanic arts.**

Sept **Centennial of introduction of cotton-spinning celebrated at Providence, R. I.**

Sept 2 **Single tax convention meets at New York with delegates from 30 states. [Forms Single Tax League of U. S.]**

Sept 25 **Yosemite National Park created by act of Congress.**

Sept 26 **Coinage of 1- and 3-dollar gold pieces and 3-cent nickel pieces discontinued by act of Congress.**

Sept 29 **Forfeiture of unearned Federal land grants to railroads provided by act of Congress.**

Oct 1 **McKinley Tariff Act raises tariff on manufactured goods to highest levels to this date. Act includes provision for reciprocity agreements with other powers.**

Oct 1 **Weather Bureau transferred from War Department to Department of Agriculture by act of Congress.**

Oct 6 **Mormon Church in general** conference endorses pledge of its president, Wilford Woodruff, to enforce anti-polygamy laws.

Nov   **Baring Brothers, London** banking house, fails and English investors dump U. S. securities on Wall Street market, causing stock-market panic.

Nov 1 **Mississippi adopts new constitution,** first state to restrict Negro suffrage through the "understanding" clause, requiring ability to read and interpret Constitution.

Nov 4 **Democratic landslide in No**vember elections, in revolt against McKinley Tariff Act. Republicans retain 88 seats out of 332 in Congress.

Nov 4 **Benjamin R. Tillman elected** governor of South Carolina, Farmers' Alliance candidate, victor over Bourbon Democracy.

Dec   **Southern Alliance, Farmers'** Mutual Benefit Association, and Colored Farmers' Alliance meet at Ocala, Fla., and prepare political program.

Dec 15 **Sitting Bull, Sioux chief,** arrested and killed in South Dakota in skirmish with U. S. troops.

Dec 29 **Battle at Wounded Knee** Creek, S. D. Sioux uprising against government agencies put down by U. S. troops under General Nelson A. Miles.

1891

Many strikes throughout year for increased wages and shorter hours.

Whitcomb L. Judson patents the zipper.

Western farmers send carloads of corn through Red Cross to famine-threatened Russia.

Restrictions on imports of American pork products removed by Germany, Italy, France, Belgium and Spain, following Congressional authorization of inspection of meats Aug. 30, 1890.

Basketball invented by James Naismith, Y.M.C.A. instructor in Springfield, Mass.

Jan   **American Sugar Refining Com**pany, incorporated under laws of New Jersey, takes over entire sugar trust business.

Mar 2 **Congress authorizes return to** states of amount collected as direct tax during Civil War.

Mar 3 **Forest Reserves Act authorizes** withdrawal of public lands for national forest reserve. 13,000,000 acres set aside during President Harrison's administration, beginning policy of conservation.

Mar 3 **Ocean Mail Subsidy Act au**thorizes subsidizing of merchant marine.

Mar 3 **Nine circuit courts of appeal** created by act of Congress.

Mar 3 **Office of Superintendent of** Immigration created by act of Congress.

Mar 4 **International Copyright Act** offers reciprocal rights to other nations.

Mar 4 **Fifty-first Congress, first "bil**lion dollar Congress," adjourns.

Mar 14 **Mob in New Orleans lynches** 11 Italian immigrants, in jail for lawlessness. After year of tension, U. S. government presents $25,000 to Italian government for families of lynched men.

Apr 7 **Eight-hour labor day provided** by act of Nebraska legislature.

Apr 14 **President Harrison begins** month's tour of Southern states and the Far West.

May 19 **People's or Populist party** launched as national organization at convention of farmer and labor groups at Cincinnati, Ohio.

Sept 14 **Empire State Express makes** record-breaking run on New York Central, covering 436 miles between New York and East Buffalo in 7 hours and 6 minutes.

Sept 22 **Nine hundred thousand acres** of Sauk, Fox and Potawatomie lands in Oklahoma, ceded to U. S., opened to settlement by Presidential proclamation of Sept. 18.

Oct 16 "War in Chile." Sailors from the U.S.S. *Baltimore* attacked on shore leave in Valparaiso, 2 killed, several wounded. Results in strained relations, finally settled with payment of $75,000 by Chilean government to the injured and heirs of the dead sailors.

Nov 3 William McKinley elected governor of Ohio.

1892

Society of Colonial Wars organized.

National Society of Colonial Dames organized.

Telephone connection completed between New York and Chicago.

First elevated railroad in Chicago opened.

University of Chicago founded.

Jan 1 Immigration receiving station at New York transferred from Castle Garden to Ellis Island.

Feb 6 James G. Blaine announces in letter to chairman of Republican National Committee that he is not candidate for Presidency.

Feb 29 U. S. and Great Britain sign convention to submit Bering Sea seal matter to arbitration by representatives of Italy, France and Sweden. Senate consents Mar. 29.

Mar Standard Oil Company of Ohio ordered by Ohio Supreme Court to sever connection with Standard Oil Trust, thus dissolving Trust.

Apr 1 Strike declared in the Coeur d'Alene silver mines in Idaho; July 11, battle breaks out between miners and strikebreakers; July 14, martial law declared and Federal troops called out. Guerrilla warfare continues for many years.

Apr 19 Charles E. Duryea finishes his gasoline buggy in Springfield, Mass. First American-made automobile.

Apr 19 Three million acres of Cheyenne and Arapaho lands in Oklahoma opened for settlement by Presidential proclamation of Apr. 12.

May 5 Geary Chinese Exclusion Act continues in force all existing Chinese exclusion laws for another 10 years and requires all resident Chinese in U. S. to register within a year or be deported.

June 4 James G. Blaine brusquely resigns Secretaryship of State with hopes for Presidential nomination.

June 7–10 Republican National Convention meets at Minneapolis. Renominates Benjamin Harrison for President on first ballot with 535 1-6 votes. (Blaine has 182 5-6 votes, McKinley 182 votes.) Whitelaw Reid of New York nominated for Vice-President.

June 21–23 Democratic National Convention meets at Chicago. Again nominates Grover Cleveland for President and nominates Adlai E. Stevenson of Illinois for Vice-President.

June 29–30 Prohibition party in convention meets at Cincinnati. Nominates General John Bidwell of California for President and James B. Cranfill of Texas for Vice-President.

July 1–Nov 20 Homestead Strike. Called by Amalgamated Association of Iron and Steel Workers at Carnegie Steel Company, Homestead, Pa., against reduced wages. Pinkerton detectives hired by company as guards, several killed. State militia ordered by governor to restore order. Henry C. Frick, manager, shot and stabbed by Russian anarchist. Strikers resume work on company terms.

July 2 People's or Populist party meets in first national convention at Omaha, Neb. Nominates James B. Weaver of Iowa for President and James G. Field of Virginia for Vice-President.

July 14 Pensions of $50 a month for Civil War soldiers and sailors, incapacitated in service, authorized by act of Congress.

July 23 Introduction of liquor into Indian country prohibited by act of Congress.

July 27 Pensions of $8 a month granted to survivors of Indian wars, 1832–1842, by act of Congress.

Aug 5 Pensions of $12 a month granted to Civil War women nurses by act of Congress.

Aug 28 Socialist Labor party meets in convention at New York. Nominates Simon Wing of Massachusetts for President and Charles R. Matchett of New York for Vice-President.

Aug 30 Cholera first brought to U. S. by steerage passengers on Hamburg-American *Moravia*.

Nov 8 Presidential election. Cleveland and Stevenson elected by electoral vote of 277, to 145 for Harrison and Reid, and 22 for Weaver. Popular vote: Cleveland, Democrat, 5,556,918; Harrison, Republican, 5,176,108; Weaver, People's, 1,041,028; Bidwell, Prohibition, 264,133; Wing, Socialist Labor, 21,164.

Dec 27 Cornerstone of Cathedral of St. John the Divine, New York, laid.

1893

Year of financial panic.

Anti-Saloon League founded at Oberlin, Ohio.

Thomas A. Edison produces the kinetoscope, making motion pictures possible.

Johns Hopkins Medical School founded, begins organized medical research.

Charles Augustus Briggs, after heresy trial, 1892, suspended from ministry by General Assembly of Presbyterian Church.

Henry Street Settlement, New York, founded by Lillian D. Wald, social worker.

Apostolic delegate sent from Rome to Washington.

Mormon Temple dedicated at Salt Lake City, Utah. Took 40 years to build.

McClure's is first published by Samuel S. McClure at 15 cents a copy. [Soon Munsey's and Cosmopolitan drop price to 10 cents.]

History of United States from Compromise of 1850 to Restoration of Home Rule in the South by James Ford Rhodes, first of 7 vols., published.

Jan 17 Political revolution in Hawaii, Queen Liliuokalani deposed and provisional government set up with connivance of U. S. minister John L. Stevens.

Feb 1 U. S. minister John L. Stevens, at request of Hawaiian provisional government, proclaims Hawaii a protectorate and raises U. S. flag over government building in Honolulu.

Feb 15 Treaty of annexation, signed with Hawaii, submitted to Senate.

Feb 20 Philadelphia and Reading Railroad falls into receivers' hands, with debts of over $125,000,000. A preliminary of Panic of '93.

Mar 1 Diplomatic Appropriation Act. Rank of ministers of U. S. shall correspond to that of ministers from countries to which they are accredited. Thomas F. Bayard becomes first minister with rank of ambassador, to Court of St. James, Apr. 3.

Mar 4 Grover Cleveland becomes President for second time, Adlai Stevenson inaugurated Vice-President.

Democratic majorities in both houses of Congress.
[President Cleveland's Cabinet: W. Q. Gresham, Secretary of State; John G. Carlisle, Secretary of Treasury; D. S. Lamont, Secretary of War; Hilary A. Herbert, Secretary of Navy; Hoke Smith, Secretary of Interior; J. S. Morton, Secretary of Agriculture; W. S. Bissell, Postmaster General; Richard Olney, Attorney General.]

Mar 9 President Cleveland withdraws Hawaiian Annexation Treaty from Senate. It is never ratified.

Apr Henry Ford wheels first Ford automobile from workshop for initial road test.

Apr 15 Issue of gold certificates suspended by U. S. Treasury, gold reserve in Treasury having fallen below legal minimum of $100,000,000.

May 1–Oct 30 World's Columbian Exposition in Chicago opened by President Cleveland. Commemorates 400th anniversary of discovery of America.

May 4 Failure of National Cordage Company.

May 5 Securities fall suddenly on New York Stock Exchange.

June 20 American Railway Union formed in Chicago by Eugene V. Debs.

June 26 Governor John P. Altgeld of Illinois pardons 3 of convicted anarchists imprisoned after Haymarket Square riot, May 4, 1886.

June 27 Stock market crash. Extreme depression to end of year. During year, 600 banks close, over 15,000 commercial houses fail, 74 railroads go into receivers' hands, including Northern Pacific, Union Pacific, Erie, and Atchison, Topeka and Santa Fe. Four years of depression follow.

July Free-Silver conventions meet in Denver and Salt Lake City.

July 1 President Cleveland undergoes operation for sarcoma of upper jaw, upon yacht in New York harbor. Unknown to the public.

July 12 Frederick Jackson Turner reads paper, "The Significance of the Frontier in American History," before American Historical Association at Chicago.

July 17 J. H. Blount, sent by the President to investigate Hawaiian revolution, reports it was started by aliens, mainly American, with support of U. S. minister John L. Stevens.

Aug 1 National Bimetallic League meets in Chicago to fight for silver.

Aug 8 President Cleveland before special session of Congress requests repeal of Sherman Silver Purchase Act.

Aug 15 Bering Sea Arbitration Court gives decision forbidding killing of seals within 60 miles of Pribilof Islands and, at greater distance, from May 1 to Aug. 1.

Sept 11 World's Parliament of Religions opens in Chicago in conjunction with World's Fair.

Sept 16 Cherokee Strip, between Kansas and Oklahoma, opened to settlement. More than 100,000 "boomers" pour in. The Strip of 6,000,000 acres had been purchased from Cherokees for $8,500,000 in 1891.

Nov 1 Sherman Silver Purchase Act repealed by act of Congress.

Nov 7 Colorado adopts woman suffrage by popular vote.

Dec 19 Wilson Tariff Bill to revise tariff reported to House.

1894

Strikes and riots characterize year. Some 750,000 workers go out on strike.

National Municipal League organized.

United Daughters of the Confederacy organized at Nashville, Tenn.

Field Museum of Natural History dedicated in Chicago.

John Dewey called to University of Chicago as professor of philosophy and psychology.

Professor Henry Preserved Smith of Lane Theological Seminary, Cincinnati, convicted of heresy by Presbyterian General Assembly.

Hydro-electric power first developed on large scale at Niagara Falls.

Wealth against Commonwealth by Henry Demarest Lloyd published. Plea for government control of monopoly.

Jan 17 Bond issue of $50,000,000 offered by U. S. Treasury to replenish gold reserve, with scant results.

Jan 30 Lexow Committee appointed by New York Senate to investigate New

York City government scandals, particularly in Police Department.

Feb 8 Enforcement Act of Feb. 28, 1871, providing Federal supervision of Congressional elections, repealed by act of Congress. Elections now in control of the states.

Mar 17 Chinese Exclusion Treaty signed in which China again consents to exclusion of Chinese laborers. Senate consents Aug. 13.

Mar 25 Coxey's Army of unemployed starts from Massillon, Ohio, on march to Washington. Apr. 30, 400 arrive with demand for issue of $50,000,000 in paper money and public works for unemployed. They are "spurned as a nuisance" and their leader, Jacob Sechler Coxey, arrested for walking on the grass and forced to leave Capitol.

Mar 29 Bill providing for coinage of accumulated silver seigniorage in Treasury vetoed by President Cleveland.

May 11 Pullman strike against reduc- tion of wages called in Chicago.

May 26 In *Reagan v. Farmers' Loan and Trust Company,* Supreme Court upholds right of judicial review of reasonableness of rates fixed not only by a state commission but by a legislature.

May 31 Senate unanimously agrees that Hawaii should maintain its own government, and that interference by any other country would be regarded as unfriendly to U. S.

June 21 Democratic silver convention held at Omaha, Neb., with 1,000 delegates under leadership of William Jennings Bryan. Adopts free-coinage plank on basis of "16 to 1."

June 26 General railroad strike on western roads ordered by American Railway Union through boycott of Pullman Palace Car Company.

June 28 Labor Day, first Monday in September, made legal holiday by act of Congress.

July 2 Eugene V. Debs, president of American Railway Union, ordered by Federal injunction not to interfere with trains carrying U. S. mail.

July 3 U. S. troops enter Chicago to enforce Federal laws in Pullman strike. July 6, state troops appear.

July 4 Republic of Hawaii pro- claimed.

July 8 The President orders dispersal of all unlawful assemblages in Illinois.

July 10 Eugene V. Debs indicted by Federal grand jury for interference with mails and interstate commerce. Dec. 14, sentenced to 6 months' imprisonment.

July 20 U. S. troops withdrawn from Chicago. Aug. 3, with power of railroad strikers broken, strike officially declared closed by American Railway Union.

Aug 1 Sino-Japanese war over Korea begins; ended by Treaty of Shimonoseki Apr. 17, 1895.

Aug 8 President Cleveland recognizes republic of Hawaii.

Aug 18 Carey Act grants 1,000,000 acres of land to each of Far-Western arid states on condition that they inaugurate irrigation projects.

Aug 18 Bureau of Immigration cre- ated by act of Congress.

Aug 27 Wilson-Gorman Tariff Act be- comes law without signature of President Cleveland. Includes income tax provision, providing for 2 per cent tax on incomes over $4,000, which Joseph H. Choate calls "communistic, socialistic."

Nov 2 Classified civil service extended by the President. Extended further, 1895, 1896.

Nov 6 Mid-term elections give Repub- licans plurality in Senate and majority in House.

Nov 13 Second bond issue of year of $50,000,000, to restore gold reserve, offered by Treasury.

Nov 22 Commercial treaty signed with Japan at Washington. Senate consents Feb. 6, 1895.

1895

Anti-Saloon League of America organized at Washington, D. C.

First Church of Christ, Scientist, opens in Boston as Mother Church of Christian Scientists.

Boston Public Library on Copley Square opened.

New York Public Library founded, combining Astor, Lenox and Tilden libraries.

Tammany government in New York overthrown as result of campaign of Rev. Charles H. Parkhurst and findings of Lexow Committee. Theodore Roosevelt appointed Police Commissioner.

William Randolph Hearst purchases New York *Journal.*

Rise of "Yellow journalism." Term results from struggle over publishing rights of series of "Yellow Kid" cartoons running at same time in New York *Journal* (Hearst) and New York *World* (Pulitzer).

American Historical Review founded.

Jan 21 In *United States v. E. C. Knight Co.*, Supreme Court declares Sherman Anti-Trust Act applies to monopoly in interstate trade and not in manufacture, although Sugar Trust controls more than 95 per cent of production of sugar in U. S.

Feb 6 Boundary dispute between Brazil and Argentina decided by President Cleveland in favor of Brazil.

Feb 8 U. S. Treasury contracts with banking houses of Morgan and Belmont for $65,000,000 in gold, to be paid for in government bonds. Gold in Treasury had fallen to $41,393,000.

Feb 24 Insurrection against Spanish rule breaks out in Cuba.

May 15 Silver convention meets at Salt Lake City with delegates from 17 states and territories. Many conventions for free silver held during year in West and South.

May 20 In *Pollock v. Farmers' Loan and Trust Co.*, Supreme Court declares income tax provision of Wilson-Gorman Tariff Act, Aug. 27, 1894, unconstitutional.

May 27 *In re* Debs, Supreme Court declares that Federal injunction to prevent strikers from interference with interstate commerce and mails is legitimate.

June 12 President Cleveland in proc-lamation calls for cooperation of citizens against giving aid to Cuban insurgents. In annual message of Dec. 2 he again calls for observance of neutrality.

July 20 Secretary of State Richard Ol-ney demands of Great Britain if she will or will not arbitrate her boundary dispute with Venezuela, which concerns Monroe Doctrine, and says: "Today the United States is practically sovereign on this continent, and its fiat is law upon the subjects to which it confines its interposition."

Sept 18 Cotton States and Interna-tional Exposition opens at Atlanta, Ga. Closes Dec. 31.

Nov 26 Lord Salisbury replies for Great Britain to Secretary Olney's note of July 20 that Venezuelan boundary question is not matter of Monroe Doctrine and that demand of U. S. for arbitration is not accepted.

Nov 28 First automobile race in U. S. takes place from heart of Chicago to suburbs, 54 miles at 7½ miles per hour. Won by J. F. Duryea in a Duryea automobile.

Dec 17 President Cleveland makes public Olney and Salisbury notes and requests authorization by Congress to appoint commission to ascertain true Venezuelan boundary in dispute with Great Britain.

Dec 21 Congress authorizes the Presi-dent to appoint Venezuelan Boundary Commission and appropriates $100,000 for its expenses. President appoints Commission Jan. 1, 1896.

1896

Failure of wheat crop in India raises prices of agricultural staples in U. S.

Volunteers of America organized by Ballington Booth, breaking from Salvation Army.

William Ashley (Billy) Sunday begins career as evangelist.

Robert G. Ingersoll gives his lecture, "Why I Am an Agnostic."

Americans contribute over $100,000 for Armenian relief, following Armenian massacres by Turks.

Rural Free Delivery, R.F.D., inaugurated by Federal government.

Roentgen's X-ray tried at Yale University. Discovered by Conrad Roentgen (German), 1895.

John B. Connally, Harvard Freshman, wins championship in revived Olympic games at Athens, first to be crowned in 1504 years.

History of the Warfare of Science with Theology in Christendom by Andrew D. White published.

Jan 4   Utah enters the Union. Its constitution prohibits polygamy and provides for woman suffrage.

Jan 6   Federal bond issue of $100,-000,000 offered to public and quickly subscribed. [Gold reserve of Treasury rises to safety mark.]

Jan 22   Free silver advocates meet in conference at Washington. Organize American Bimetallic Union and issue call for silver convention at St. Louis July 22.

Feb 7   President Cleveland submits to Congress adverse report of board of engineers concerning cost of construction of Nicaragua Canal.

Feb 10   General Weyler arrives in Cuba from Spain with policy of ruthless suppression of insurrection.

Mar 19   Silver Republican Senators hold secret session with Philadelphia manufacturers in Washington to consider linking of bimetallism and protection.

Mar 20   U. S. marines land at Corinto, Nicaragua, to protect life and property at outbreak of a revolution. Repeated in May.

Mar 31   Amnesty act of Congress re-peals law holding former officials in Confederacy ineligible to Army or Navy positions in U. S.

Apr 4   Secretary of State Olney offers to cooperate with Spain in pacification of Cuba.

Apr 6   Both houses pass concurrent resolution favoring recognition of Cuban belligerency and urging the President to offer Spain good offices of U. S. to obtain peace, with Cuban independence. Cleveland limits himself to proposing cooperation with Spain in bringing peace to Cuba with home-rule.

Apr 23   Edison's vitascope gives first showing of moving picture at Koster and Bial's Music Hall, New York. Projecting machine invented by Thomas Armat.

May 6   Samuel P. Langley flies heavier-than-air model airplane 300 feet. First successful demonstration of principle of air flight.

May 6   President Cleveland publishes civil service rules to improve system, bringing 85,000 under Civil Service Commission.

May 18   In *Plessy v. Ferguson*, Su-preme Court declares so-called Jim Crow Car Law of Louisiana constitutional.

May 22   Spain declines U. S. offer of mediation in Cuba, saying Cuba enjoys "one of the most liberal political systems in the world."

May 27–28   Prohibition party meets in convention at Pittsburgh. Platform strictly concerned with prohibition of manufacture and sale of intoxicating liquors. Nominates Joshua Levering of Maryland for President and Hale Johnson of Illinois for Vice-President. A minority in favor of free silver secedes, nominating own candidates.

June 16–18 Republican National Convention meets at St. Louis. Platform calls for protective tariff, gold standard, independence of Cuba, and building of a Nicaragua Canal. Nominates William McKinley of Ohio for President and Garret A. Hobart of New Jersey for Vice-President. Silver Republicans withdraw under Senator Teller.

July 4–9 Socialist Labor party convention meets at New York. Nominates Charles H. Matchett of New York for President and Matthew Maguire of New Jersey for Vice-President.

July 7–11 Democratic National Convention meets at Chicago. Platform is for "free and unlimited coinage of both silver and gold at the present legal ratio of sixteen to one." Nominates William J. Bryan of Nebraska for President and Arthur Sewall of Maine for Vice-President.

July 8 William J. Bryan gives "Cross of Gold" speech, concluding debate on adoption of platform at Democratic National Convention.

July 22–25 Populist party convention meets at St. Louis. Nominates William J. Bryan for President and Thomas E. Watson of Georgia for Vice-President.

July 22–24 National Silver Republicans meet at St. Louis. Adopt Democratic party nominees.

July 27 President Cleveland issues proclamation against American filibusters in Cuba.

Aug 16 Gold discovered in Klondike, near Alaskan border in Canada. News reaches U. S. Jan. 1897.

Aug 28 Li Hung Chang, Chinese statesman, arrives in New York, received by President Cleveland the following day.

Sept 2–3 "Sound Money" Democrats meet at Indianapolis as National Democratic party, on gold standard. Nominate John M. Palmer of Illinois for

President and Simon P. Buckner of Kentucky for Vice-President.

Nov 3 Presidential election. McKinley and Hobart elected by electoral vote of 271, to 176 for Bryan and Sewall. Popular vote: McKinley, Republican, 7,104,779; Bryan, Democrat, 6,502,925; Palmer, National Democrat, 133,148; Levering, Prohibition, 132,007; Matchett, Socialist Labor, 38,274.

Nov 3 Idaho grants woman suffrage by constitutional amendment.

Nov 12 Agreement reached by U. S. and Great Britain by which Venezuelan boundary dispute is to be settled by arbitration.

Dec 10 Liliuokalani, "Queen Lil," former queen of Hawaii, arrives in San Francisco for visit to U. S.

1897

U. S. enters upon decade of prosperity.

Short European wheat crop raises agricultural prices in U. S. Wheat on Chicago market reaches $1.09 a bushel in Dec., highest since 1891.

Klondike gold rush.

Boston subway completed, first in U. S.

National Congress of Mothers organized at Washington. Name changed to National Congress of Parents and Teachers (P.T.A.) 1924.

Society of Mayflower Descendants founded.

Yerkes Observatory of University of Chicago dedicated at Williams Bay, Wis.

Thomas C. Chamberlin, professor of geology at University of Chicago, announces his "planetesimal hypothesis" of formation of the earth.

Samuel Milton (Golden Rule) Jones, elected mayor of Toledo, Ohio, enters upon reform administration.

Jan Monetary conference representing business interests held at Indianapolis in support of gold standard. Commission subsequently appointed reports to Congress plan for monetary system later in year.

Jan 11 Olney-Pauncefote Convention signed at Washington by U. S. and Great Britain, providing for settlement of territorial issues between the 2 nations by arbitration. Parliament promptly ratifies, Senate refuses consent May 5.

Feb 2 Venezuela and Great Britain sign treaty submitting boundary dispute to arbitration, Cleveland's Boundary Commission abandons its work. Arbiters make award Oct. 3, 1899.

Feb 11 Entry and patenting of lands containing mineral oils, under placer mining laws, authorized by Congress.

Feb 21 Marcus Hanna appointed to Senate by Governor Bushnell of Ohio to replace John Sherman, slated for State Department.

Feb 22 President Cleveland sets aside 20,000,000 acres of new forest reserves in the West. Suspended by Congress June 4.

Mar 2 Bill providing literacy test for immigrants vetoed by President Cleveland, calling it a "radical departure from our national policy."

Mar 4 William McKinley and Garret A. Hobart inaugurated President and Vice-President. Entire government returns to Republican control.
[President McKinley's Cabinet: John Sherman, Secretary of State; Lyman J. Gage, Secretary of Treasury; R. A. Alger, Secretary of War; John D. Long, Secretary of Navy; C. N. Bliss, Secretary of Interior; James Wilson, Secretary of Agriculture; James A. Gary, Postmaster General; Joseph McKenna, Attorney General.]

Mar 15 Fifty-fifth Congress, called by President McKinley, meets in special session to revise tariff. Thomas B. Reed again chosen Speaker of House and Nelson Dingley, Jr. again appointed chairman of Ways and Means Committee.

Mar 22 In *Trans-Missouri Freight* case, Supreme Court in 5–4 decision declares railroads subject to Anti-Trust Law.

Apr President McKinley appoints commission of 3 to sound out Europe on international bimetallism. Commission, finding no encouragement, returns in November.

Apr 21 John Hay arrives in England as ambassador, one objective being to bring the powers into some accord in their common world-wide interests.

Apr 27 Grant's Tomb dedicated on Riverside Drive, New York, by President McKinley.

May 20 Senate passes resolution recog- nizing Cuban belligerency, similar to concurrent resolution of Apr. 6, 1896. House takes no action.

May 24 Congress, upon recommenda- tion of President McKinley, votes $50,000 relief for Americans in Cuba.

June 7 Appropriation for sectarian education in Indian schools prohibited by act of Congress.

June 16 Treaty of annexation signed by Secretary Sherman with government of Hawaii. [Senate refuses consent.]

June 19 Japan makes formal protest against annexation of Hawaii by U. S. About 25,000 Japanese are in Hawaii.

June 27 Secretary of State John Sher- man sends note of protest to Spain against General Weyler's inhuman conduct in Cuba.

July 5 Soft coal miners go on strike, ordered by UMW. Miners win 8-hour day, semi-monthly pay, abolition of company stores, and biennial conferences, after 12 weeks' contest.

July 14 The *Excelsior* arrives at San Francisco from the Klondike with $750,-000 in gold, first large shipment. The *Portland* with $800,000 in gold arrives at Seattle July 17.

July 24 Nicaragua Canal Commission appointed by President McKinley to examine possible routes and costs of a canal, Rear Admiral John G. Walker chairman.

July 24 Dingley Tariff Act provides for highest duties of any previous tariff and authorizes negotiation of reciprocal treaties.

Sept 14 Hawaiian Republic ratifies annexation treaty, signed June 16. Queen Liliuokalani, now in Washington, issues statement of dissent.

Sept 23 U. S. again tenders her good offices to Spain to obtain peace in Cuba.

Oct 6 Liberal ministry of Premier Sagasta inaugurated in Spain. Decision made to recall General Weyler from Cuba.

Oct 23 Stewart L. Woodford, U. S. minister to Spain, assured by Spain of Cuban autonomy, and U. S. urged to use more vigor in enforcing neutrality laws.

Nov 8 In *Interstate Commerce Commission v. Alabama Midland Railway Company*, Supreme Court nullifies "long and short haul" clause of Interstate Commerce Act of 1887.

Nov 25 Decree offering large measure of self-government to Cuba proclaimed in Madrid.

Dec 6 President McKinley's annual message to Congress optimistic on Cuban problem.

1898

Spanish-American War.

1898–1904. Annual yield of gold in the Klondike never less than $10,000,000.

Competition between Joseph Pulitzer of New York *World* and William Randolph Hearst of New York *Journal,* in exploitation of Cuban crisis, hastens war with Spain.

Mr. Dooley in Peace and War by Finley Peter Dunne published. From his "Mr. Dooley" column in Chicago *Journal.*

Jan 1 City of Greater New York, cre-ated by law of May 11, 1896, consolidating Kings and Richmond counties, Long Island City, Newtown and New York City, inaugurated. Population just under 3,500,000.

Jan 25 Battleship *Maine* arrives at Havana on friendly visit from Key West, Fla.

Feb 3 Joseph Chamberlain, British Colonial Secretary, in secret memorandum to Arthur J. Balfour, proposes requesting U. S. to stand with Great Britain in open door policy in China.

Feb 9 Private letter of Señor Dupuy de Lôme, Spanish minister to U. S., stolen from mails at Havana, published in Hearst's New York *Journal.* Letter characterizes President McKinley as spineless politician. Señor de Lôme recalled by Spanish government.

Feb 15 9:40 P.M. Battleship *Maine* destroyed by explosion in Havana Harbor, 2 officers and 258 sailors killed.

Feb 25 Theodore Roosevelt, Assistant Secretary of Navy, in secret cable orders Commodore George Dewey, in command of Asiatic squadron, to proceed to Hong Kong, to keep bunkers filled with coal, and in case of war to attack Spanish squadron in Philippines without delay.

Feb 28 In *Holden v. Hardy*, Supreme Court upholds Utah statute for 8-hour day in mines and smelters, as health measure.

Mar 7 In *Smyth v. Ames*, Supreme Court declares that courts have right to decide reasonableness of railroad rates. Fully establishes doctrine of judicial review.

Mar 8 Lord Pauncefote, British am-bassador, in "very confidential" inquiry asks if U. S. would join Great Britain in open door policy in China. Answer is no.

Mar 9 Fifty million dollars "for na-tional defense and each and every purpose connected therewith" appropriated by Congress without a dissenting vote.

Mar 9 Mobilization of U. S. Army be-gins.

Mar 17 Senator Redfield Proctor, just returned from Cuba, delivers in Senate report of appalling state of affairs there. Stirs war sentiment.

Mar 19 U. S. battleship *Oregon* leaves San Francisco for Florida by way of the Horn.

Mar 21 Report of naval court of inquiry on destruction of the *Maine* sent to President McKinley. Destruction attributed to an external cause. Report made public Mar. 28.

Mar 22 Spanish board of inquiry reports its conclusion that the *Maine* was destroyed by an internal explosion.

Mar 27 Assistant Secretary of State William R. Day sends dispatch to Minister Woodford at Madrid to urge that Spain grant an armistice to Cuban rebels until October, revoke immediately the *reconcentrado* order, accept aid of U. S. in peace negotiations, and permit relief to be sent to Cuba. If peace is not reached by Oct. 1, the President of U. S. to be final arbiter between Spain and insurgents.

Mar 28 In *United States v. Wong Kim Ark,* Supreme Court declares that a child born of Chinese parents in U. S. is a citizen and cannot be prevented from re-entrance into the country by Chinese Exclusion Law.

Mar 29 Minister Woodford presents Secretary Day's dispatch of Mar. 27 to Spanish government, essentially an ultimatum.

Mar 30 Spain revokes the *reconcentrado* order.

Mar 31 Spain replies that the *reconcentrado* order has been revoked and proposes arbitration of *Maine* affair and pacification of Cuba by a Cuban parliament to convene May 4, and a grant of armistice to the insurgents if requested by them.

Apr 3 Minister Woodford cables President McKinley: "If you can still give me time . . . I will get you the peace you desire so much."

Apr 5 President McKinley by this date has decided to submit Cuban question to Congress.

Apr 5 Consul General Fitzhugh Lee recalled from Cuba by President McKinley to consult on return of American citizens from Cuba.

Apr 6 Ambassadors of 6 great powers present joint note to President McKinley appealing for peaceful solution of Cuban question.

Apr 9 Spanish queen orders Captain-General Blanco in Cuba to suspend hostilities to "facilitate peace negotiations," in line with advice of the Pope.

Apr 10 News of Spanish queen's order to suspend hostilities presented in Washington after McKinley's war message is prepared.

Apr 11 President McKinley sends war message to Congress, asking authority to use armed force as may be necessary to enforce pacification of Cuba. "The issue is now with the Congress."

Apr 19 Congress in joint resolution recognizes independence of Cuba, authorizes the President to demand that Spain shall withdraw from the island and to use armed force if she refuses, and disclaims any intention of annexation (the Teller Amendment).

Apr 20 President McKinley signs joint resolution of Congress. The same day, formal ultimatum and resolution of Congress cabled to Spanish government. Spanish minister in Washington asks for his passports.

Apr 21 Spanish government sends passports to Mr. Woodford, U. S. minister, before he can deliver joint resolution of Congress to the Spanish government.

Apr 22 First shot of Spanish-American War fired by guns of the *Nashville* when she captures the *Buena Ventura,* Spanish merchant ship with valuable cargo, off Key West, first prize of the war.

Apr 22 Volunteer Army Act. Under its provisions, the 1st Volunteer Cavalry, or "Rough Riders," is organized under

Colonel Leonard Wood and Lieutenant Colonel Theodore Roosevelt.

Apr 22 Admiral William T. Sampson leaves Key West, Fla., to establish blockade on north coast of Cuba.

Apr 23 President McKinley calls for 125,000 volunteers.

Apr 24 Spain declares state of war to exist with U. S.

Apr 24 Great Britain proclaims neu- trality in war between U. S. and Spain.

Apr 24 Commodore Dewey at Mirs Bay, China, ordered to proceed at once to Philippines and begin operation against Spanish fleet.

Apr 25 John Sherman, Secretary of State, resigns. William R. Day succeeds him Apr. 26.

Apr 25 War with Spain formally de- clared by Congress as having existed since and including Apr. 21.

Apr 25 In *Morgan v. Illinois Trust and Savings Bank,* Supreme Court declares valid Illinois inheritance tax law of June 15, 1895.

Apr 26 Congress authorizes increase of regular army to about 60,000.

Apr 27 Commodore Dewey's fleet leaves Mirs Bay, China, for Philippine Islands.

Apr 27 Fortifications at Matanzas, Cuba, bombarded by U. S. fleet, first engagement of the war.

Apr 28 France declares neutrality in U. S. war with Spain.

Apr 29 Admiral Pascual Cervera's fleet leaves Cape Verde Islands for Cuban waters.

May 1 Battle of Manila Bay.
Apr. 30, 11:30 P.M. Dewey enters South Channel of Manila Bay.
May 1, 5:40 A.M. Dewey gives order to fire.
12:30 P.M. Squadron ceases firing. Commodore Dewey in command of Manila Bay. U. S. casualties, 8 men slightly wounded. Spanish casualties, 10 ships destroyed, 381 men killed.

May 2 U. S. squadron takes up posi- tion at Cavité, in Manila Bay.

May 6 Assistant Secretary of the Navy Theodore Roosevelt resigns post and is sworn in as Lieutenant Colonel of 1st regiment of U. S. Volunteer Cavalry, the Rough Riders.

May 11 Commodore George Dewey made Rear Admiral in Navy.

May 12 San Juan, Puerto Rico, bom- barded by Admiral Sampson.

May 12 Louisiana adopts new consti- tution, disfranchising Negroes under literacy and property tests and "grandfather clause."

May 13 Joseph Chamberlain, British Colonial Secretary, in address at Birmingham advocates alliance with U. S.

May 19 Aguinaldo, exiled Philippine insurrectionist, arrives at Cavité from Hong Kong on revenue cutter *McCulloch.* Proceeds to organize native army under American protection.

May 19 Spanish fleet under Admiral Cervera enters Santiago Harbor, Cuba.

May 24 Battleship *Oregon* **arrives at** Key West from San Francisco and joins Admiral Sampson's fleet.

May 25 President McKinley calls for 75,000 more volunteers.

May 29 Commodore Winfield Scott Schley, with orders from Admiral Sampson, begins blockade of Cervera's fleet in Santiago Harbor.

June Social Democratic party of America founded by Eugene V. Debs at Chicago.

June 1 Admiral Sampson arrives at Santiago and takes command of blockading squadron.

June 1 Trans-Mississippi Exposition opens in Omaha, Neb. Closes Oct. 31.

June 1 Erdman Arbitration Act pro- vides for mediation between interstate carriers and their employees.

June 3 *Merrimac* **sunk in channel of** Santiago Harbor by Lt. Richard P. Hobson in attempt to block exit of Spanish fleet. Plan fails, Hobson and his men captured.

June 6 Disabilities placed upon Confederate leaders by section 3 of 14th Amendment removed by act of Congress.

June 6 Bombardment of Spanish installations at mouth of Santiago Harbor.

June 10 Six hundred and twenty-three marines with 24 officers land on shores of Guantanamo Bay, beginning invasion of Cuba by U. S. troops.

June 12 Vice-Admiral von Diederichs arrives in Manila Bay on the *Kaiserin Augusta*. Now stationed in the harbor: 3 German warships, 2 British, 1 French and 1 Japanese. Shortly, 2 more German warships arrive.

June 13 War Revenue Act provides for excise duties, taxes upon tea, tobacco, liquor and amusements and, for first time, tax upon legacies. Authorizes bond issue, resulting in sale of $200,000,000 of 3 per cent bonds, and coinage of silver seigniorage in the Treasury.

June 14 Sixteen thousand eight hundred and eighty-seven U. S. troops, under General William R. Shafter, sail from Tampa, Fla., for Santiago, Cuba. Troops leave for Spanish War singing "There'll be a Hot Time in the Old Town Tonight."

June 15 Anti-Imperialist League founded at Faneuil Hall, Boston, by leading intellectuals, in opposition to annexation of Philippines.

June 18 Non-partisan U. S. Industrial Commission authorized by act of Congress. Its 19-volume report, 1900–1902, a mine of information.

June 20 U. S. Army under Shafter arrives off Santiago. Disembarks June 22. "Rough Riders" under Colonel Leonard Wood and Lieutenant Colonel Theodore Roosevelt are in this expedition.

June 20 Spanish island of Guam in the Pacific seized by Captain Henry Glass of U.S.S. *Charleston*, by order of Navy Department.

June 24 Las Guásimas, first land battle of the war, on road to Santiago. Spanish defeated by General Joseph Wheeler, Colonels Leonard Wood and Theodore Roosevelt with 1,000 regulars and Rough Riders pushing ahead of other troops.

June 30 First U. S. troops, sailing from San Francisco, arrive in Manila Bay to support Admiral Dewey in occupation of Manila. General Wesley Merritt in command of expeditionary forces arrives July 25.

July 1 Uniform system of bankruptcy throughout U. S. authorized by act of Congress.

July 1 Battle of El Caney. General Henry W. Lawton captures Spanish blockhouse after 8-hour fight.

July 1–2 Battle of San Juan Hill. General Hamilton S. Hawkins with infantry takes San Juan Hill. Colonel Roosevelt and Rough Riders help take Kettle Hill and charge up San Juan Hill. U. S. casualties in battles of El Caney, Kettle Hill and San Juan Hill, 112 officers, 1,460 men killed, wounded and missing.

July 3 Naval battle of Santiago destroys Admiral Cervera's fleet. Long and bitter controversy between Sampson and Schley, as to which was in command at battle, follows. U. S. casualties, one killed, one wounded.

July 4 U. S. flag raised on vacant Wake Island by troops en route to Philippines.

July 7 Annexation of Hawaii, by joint resolution of Congress, introduced in House May 4, signed by President.

July 10 Bombardment of Santiago begun by General Shafter.

July 13 Anglo-American League organized in London.

July 17 Santiago surrenders to General Shafter. U. S. flag raised over House of Civil Government while band plays "Rally Round the Flag, Boys," "Stars and Stripes Forever" and "Star Spangled Banner." U. S. losses in siege and capture, 260 killed, 1,431 wounded.

July 20   Colonel Leonard Wood appointed military governor of Santiago.

July 25   Conquest of Puerto Rico begins with landing of General Miles. Ponce surrenders July 28.

July 26   Spain, through French ambassador, asks for peace terms.

July 30   Peace terms of U. S. stated by President McKinley: armistice will be granted upon relinquishment of title to Cuba, cession of Puerto Rico and an island in the Ladrones to U. S., and occupation by U. S. of city, bay and harbor of Manila, pending peace negotiations.

Aug 3   Round Robin, drafted by group of volunteer officers, sent to General Shafter, urging removal of troops from Cuba because of fevers and unsanitary conditions. War Department orders prompt removal. Some 23,000 leave Cuba for Montauk Point, Long Island, Aug. 8.

Aug 12   Hawaiian Islands officially transferred to U. S.

Aug 12   4:30 P.M.   Peace protocol with Spain signed at Washington, suspending hostilities. It is 5:30 A.M., Aug. 13, Philippine time, just as U. S. forces are forming to move upon Manila.

Aug 13   Manila occupied by General Wesley Merritt and Admiral Dewey.

Aug 16   General Merritt in Manila receives news of signing of peace protocol.

Aug 20   Nation-wide peace celebrations reach climax in New York when Admiral Sampson returns and parades his fleet up Hudson River.

Aug 25   General Shafter, leaving Cuba in command of General Henry W. Lawton, goes to Montauk Point, Long Island.

Sept 8   Secretary of War Russell A. Alger requests President McKinley to appoint commission to investigate conduct of the war by War Department.

Sept 20   John Hay appointed Secretary of State by President, replacing William R. Day. Sworn into office Sept. 30.

Oct 1   Peace negotiations with Spain formally entered upon in Paris. U. S. delegation: W. R. Day, Whitelaw Reid, and Senators C. K. Davis of Minnesota, W. P. Freye of Maine and George Gray of Delaware.

Oct 18   U. S. flag raised over Puerto Rico.

Oct 31   U. S. commissioners at peace conference in Paris demand all the Philippine Islands.

Nov 8   Theodore Roosevelt elected governor of New York.

Nov 8   South Dakota adopts system of initiative and referendum by constitutional amendment. First state to do so.

Dec 10   Treaty of Paris signed, concluding war with Spain. Spain gives up Cuba, cedes Guam and Puerto Rico to U. S. as indemnity, and cedes the Philippines, for which U. S. will pay her $20,000,000.

1899

United Fruit Company organized. Extends U. S. sphere of influence in Latin America.

Boll weevil crosses the Rio Grande, to spread north and east through cotton states.

General Corporation Law of New Jersey passed, further relaxing its law. Standard Oil Company of New Jersey absorbs the whole trust under easy laws of state.

The Theory of the Leisure Class by Thorstein Veblin published.

School and Society by John Dewey published.

Jan 17   Wake Island, unclaimed by any power, taken possession of by U.S.S. *Bennington*.

Jan 20   Philippine Commission appointed by President McKinley, headed by Jacob G. Schurman, president of Cornell University.

Feb   Rudyard Kipling's "The White Man's Burden," a song of imperialism, published in *McClure's*. Published in London *Times* Feb. 4, under title, "An Address to the United States."

Feb 4   Philippine revolt under Aguinaldo breaks out with attempt to capture Manila.

Feb 6   Peace with Spain approved by Senate, 57 to 27.

Mar 2   Congress authorizes increase of regular Army to 65,000 and recruiting of 35,000 volunteers to suppress rebellion in Philippines.

Mar 3   Congress authorizes appropri-ation for construction of 3 battleships, 3 armed cruisers and 6 protective cruisers.

Mar 3   Third Isthmian Canal Commis-sion created by Congress to study choice of routes. Rear Admiral John G. Walker chairman. First commission 1895; second 1897.

Apr 11   Treaty of peace with Spain proclaimed.

Apr 21   Juvenile court system estab-lished by Illinois legislature.

May   First long distance automobile trip made, from Cleveland to New York, by Alexander Winton, automobile manufacturer. Running time, 707.4 miles in 47 hours, 34 minutes.

May 29   President McKinley reduces number of offices affected by Civil Service rules by about 4,000.

July 19   Secretary of War Alger re-signs under public criticism of his administration. Succeeded by Elihu Root Aug. 1.

July 29   Convention for Peaceful Ad-justment of International Differences, providing for Hague Permanent Court of Arbitration, signed by U. S. delegates at first Hague Conference, May 18 to July 29. Senate consents Feb. 1900.

Aug 8   Terrific hurricane in Puerto Rico, necessitating aid from U. S. 2,000 killed.

Sept 6   Open Door notes of Secretary of State Hay addressed to Great Britain, Germany and Russia, and later to Italy, France and Japan, ask for maintenance of open door in China. U. S. objective exactly that of Great Britain.

Sept 29   Great celebration in New York in honor of Admiral Dewey upon his return from Philippines.

Nov 21   Vice-President Garret A. Ho-bart dies at Paterson, N. J.

Dec 2   Samoan treaty signed by Great Britain, Germany and U. S. by which islands are partitioned between Germany and U. S., the latter receiving Tutuila with its harbor of Pago Pago. Senate consents Jan. 16, 1900.

Dec 4   In *Addyston Pipe and Steel Company v. United States,* Supreme Court declares that agreement between corporations to remove competition constitutes a pool and is violation of Anti-Trust Law.

Dec 5   President McKinley in third an-nual message to Congress attacks problem of trusts and monopolies: "Combinations of capital organized into trusts . . . should early claim the attention of Congress."

1 9 0 0

Population,   75,994,575;   foreign-born, 10,341,276.

Majority of immigrants come from southern and eastern Europe from this date until Immigration Quota laws of 1921 and 1924.

Automobiles in U. S. approximate 8,000, one for every 9,500 persons. 144 miles hard-surface roads in the country.

Jan   Chicago drainage canal opened.

Jan 26   "Speak softly and carry a big stick, you'll go far," writes Theodore Roosevelt to a friend.

Feb 5   First Hay-Pauncefote Treaty signed at Washington. Permits U. S. to build and maintain an Isthmian canal but without right to fortify it, and provides for its neutrality in peace or war. Amended to death by Senate Dec. 20, not accepted by Great Britain.

Feb 6 William Howard Taft appointed head of second Philippine commission by President McKinley.

Feb 6 Theodore Roosevelt announces that "under no circumstances could I or would I accept the nomination for the Vice-Presidency."

Mar 6 Social Democratic party formed in convention at Indianapolis. Nominates Eugene V. Debs for President and Job Harriman of California for Vice-President. 1901, party adopts name of Socialist.

Mar 14 Gold Standard Act. Gold dollar of 25.8 grains, nine-tenths fine, "shall be the standard unit of value, and all forms of money isued or coined by United States shall be maintained at a parity" with it.

Mar 20 Secretary of State Hay announces that all the powers, in spite of hedgings, have assented to his Open Door notes and that he considers the assents "final and definitive."

Apr 4 Admiral Dewey announces his availability for Presidential nomination. Nowhere taken seriously.

Apr 7 General Arthur MacArthur appointed military governor of Philippines.

Apr 12 Foraker Act gives Puerto Rico status of unincorporated territory and levies tariff on imports from Puerto Rico equal to 15 per cent of Dingley rates.

Apr 30 Hawaii accorded full territorial status by act of Congress.

May Boxer rebellion, antiforeign, breaks out in China.

May "An Ode in Time of Hesitation" by William Vaughn Moody published in *Atlantic Monthly*. Assails imperialistic spirit following Spanish-American War.

May 9 Populist party meets in 2 conventions. Anti-Fusion group meets at Cincinnati. Nominates Wharton Barker of Pennsylvania for President and Ignatius Donnelly of Minnesota for Vice-President. Fusion group meets at Sioux Falls, S. D. Nominates W. J. Bryan for President and Charles A. Towne of Minnesota for Vice-President.

May 14 In *Knowlton v. Moore*, Supreme Court declares inheritance tax provisions in War Revenue Act, 1898, constitutional.

June 2–6 Socialist Labor party meets at New York. Nominates Joseph P. Malloney of Massachusetts for President and Valentine Remmel of Pennsylvania for Vice-President.

June 6 Civil code and government for Alaska authorized by act of Congress.

June 19–21 Republican National Convention meets at Philadelphia. Renominates William McKinley for President and nominates Theodore Roosevelt for Vice-President.

June 20–Aug 14 U. S. legation with other foreign legations besieged in British embassy in Peking, China, by Boxers.

June 27–28 Prohibition party meets in convention at Chicago. Nominates John G. Woolley of Illinois for President and Henry B. Metcalf of Rhode Island for Vice-President.

Summer Major Walter Reed of U. S. Army Medical Corps, seeking cause of yellow fever raging in Cuba, discovers it is transmitted by a mosquito, the *stegomyia fasciata*. By Nov. 1901, Havana, under sanitation control of General Leonard Wood and Major William C. Gorgas, practically rid of the disease.

July 3 Secretary of State Hay, in note to the great powers interested in China, states that the U. S. policy concerning China is China's permanent safety and peace and preservation of her "territorial and administrative entity" and, "the principle of equal and impartial trade with all parts of the Chinese Empire."

July 4–6 Democratic National Convention meets at Kansas City. Nominates William J. Bryan for President and Adlai Stevenson of Illinois for Vice-President. Silver Republicans in convention, July 4–6, and Liberty Congress of American League of Anti-Imperialists, August 16, endorse nomination of Bryan.

Aug 14 U. S. with 2,500 troops participates with Western powers and Japan in rescue of legations in Peking.

Sept 8 Galveston, Tex., swept by great tidal wave and storm. Commission form of municipal government hastily adopted in emergency, made permanent the following year.

Sept 17–Oct 25 Anthracite coal strike. Mark Hanna, fearing its effect upon McKinley's campaign, persuades operators to make concessions to miners.

Nov 3 First Automobile show opens in New York City.

Nov 6 Presidential election. McKinley and Roosevelt elected by electoral vote of 292, to 155 for Bryan and Stevenson. Popular vote: McKinley, Republican, 7,-207,923; Bryan, Democrat, 6,358,133; Woolley, Prohibition, 208,914; Debs, Social Democrat, 87,814; Barker, Populist, 50,373; Malloney, Socialist Labor, 39,-739.

Nov 6 Robert M. LaFollette elected governor of Wisconsin.

Dec 16 National Civic Federation formed, Mark Hanna president and Samuel Gompers vice-president.

1901

1901–1905, 13,964 strikes and 541 lockouts recorded.

Rockefeller Institute for Medical Research founded, Simon Flexner director.

Daniel H. Burnham appointed to formulate building plan for Washington, D. C. His committee's report, 1902, begins city planning movement.

Judge Ben B. Lindsey appointed judge of Juvenile Court of Denver, Colo. Serves until 1927.

Gospel of Wealth by Andrew Carnegie published.

Jan 21 Carrie Nation makes her first hatchet raid upon Kansas saloons in Wichita.

Feb 2 Army reorganization provided by act of Congress. Minimum numerical strength placed at 58,000.

Feb 21 Cuba adopts constitution, pat-terned after that of U. S.

Feb 25 U. S. Steel Corporation, launched by John Pierpont Morgan, incorporated in New Jersey. First billion-dollar corporation.

Mar 2 Army Appropriation Act. Includes Platt Amendment, in effect establishing protectorate over Cuba, and Spooner Amendment establishing temporary civil government in Philippines.

Mar 3 National Bureau of Standards established by act of Congress.

Mar 4 William McKinley inaugurated President for second term and Theodore Roosevelt inaugurated Vice-President.
[President McKinley's Cabinet: John Hay, Secretary of State; Lyman J. Gage, Secretary of Treasury; Elihu Root, Secretary of War; John D. Long, Secretary of Navy; E. A. Hitchcock, Secretary of Interior; James Wilson, Secretary of Agriculture; Charles E. Smith, Postmaster General; Philander C. Knox, Attorney General.]

Mar 23 Aguinaldo, Philippine guer-rilla leader, captured by General Frederick Funston. Insurrection not ended until April 1902.

Apr 1 Tom Loftin Johnson elected re-form mayor of Cleveland, Ohio.

May 1–Nov 2 Pan-American Exposi-tion at Buffalo, N. Y.

May 9 Panic in Wall Street brought on by conflict between J. J. Hill and E. H. Harriman over control of Northern Pacific Railroad. Stock at one point run up to 1,000.

May 27   Insular Cases, *Downes v. Bidwell, De Lima v. Bidwell* and *Dooley v. United States,* involving applicability of existing U. S. customs laws to Puerto Rico after its cession to U. S., decided by Supreme Court. Decisions, though contradictory, apply principle that the Constitution follows the flag, when and to extent that Congress orders.

May 30   Hall of Fame for Great Americans dedicated on campus of New York University.

June 12   Platt Amendment appended to constitution of Cuba by its constitutional convention.

July 4   William H. Taft installed civil governor of Philippines.

July 25   Free trade between Puerto Rico and U. S. proclaimed by President McKinley.

Sept 5   President McKinley at Pan-American Exposition, Buffalo, in his last public speech advocates liberalization of our tariff policy: "The period of exclusiveness is past. . . . Reciprocity treaties are in harmony with the spirit of the times."

Sept 6   President McKinley attending Pan-American Exposition, Buffalo, shot by anarchist Leon Czolgosz.

Sept 7   Boxer indemnity agreement between China and foreign powers signed. Indemnity assigned U. S., $25,000,000 of the $333,000,000.

Sept 14   President McKinley dies in Buffalo at 2:15 A.M. Vice-President Roosevelt takes oath of office as President in Buffalo at 3:00 P.M. President Roosevelt requests President McKinley's cabinet to remain in office.

Oct 16   President Roosevelt entertains Booker T. Washington at dinner at White House. Results in reprisals against Negroes in the South.

Oct 22   Second International American Conference opens at Mexico City.

Nov 2   Henry Adams writes John Hay: "I wish we were out of the Philippines. That is a false start in a wrong direction."

Nov 13   Northern Securities Company, a holding company organized by J. J. Hill, E. H. Harriman and J. P. Morgan, incorporated in New Jersey to bring Northern Pacific, Great Northern and Chicago, Burlington and Quincy railroads under common control.

Nov 16   Third Isthmian Canal Commission reports in favor of Nicaragua route, as had the 2 preceding commissions.

Nov 18   Second Hay-Pauncefote Treaty signed, giving U. S. free hand to build and fortify an isthmian canal and superseding Clayton-Bulwer Treaty of 1850. Senate consents Dec. 16.

Nov 27   Army War College opened in Washington, D. C., Tasker H. Bliss president.

Nov 28   Alabama adopts new constitution, disfranchising Negroes by literacy and property tests and "grandfather clause."

Dec 3   President   Roosevelt recommends regulation of trusts and corporations in first annual message.

Dec 13   Court of inquiry declares Rear Admiral Schley guilty of charges of delay before Santiago, but recommends no action.

Dec 31   Cuba holds first general elec- tion under constitution.

1 9 0 2

Carnegie Institution of Washington founded for research by Andrew Carnegie's gift of $10,000,000.

General Education Board established by John D. Rockefeller for "the promotion of education within the United States, without distinction of race, sex, or creed." By 1909 he has given $53,000,000 to the Board.

Rhodes scholarships for study at Oxford by men selected from U. S., Germany and British Empire established by will of Cecil Rhodes, South African empire builder.

Hookworm disease in the South discovered by Dr. Charles Wardell Stiles.

Danbury Hatters' nation-wide boycott of product of D. E. Loewe and Co. of Danbury, Conn., begins. Suit against United Hatters of North America promptly brought in Federal courts, charging violation of Sherman Anti-Trust Act. Charge maintained by Supreme Court 1908.

Maryland adopts first workmen's compensation law, soon declared unconstitutional.

Flatiron Building, steel skyscraper of 20 stories, designed by Daniel Burnham, completed in New York.

McClure's begins publication of Ida M. Tarbell's *History of the Standard Oil Company* and Lincoln Steffens' articles on municipal corruption, pioneer writing in muckraking school.

Jan 4   Panama Canal Company of France offers to sell its interests to U. S. for $40,000,000, coming down from first offer of $109,000,000.

Jan 18   Isthmian Canal Commission in supplementary report recommends to the President adoption of the Panama rather than the Nicaragua route.

Jan 24   Treaty with Denmark signed for purchase of Danish West Indies for $5,000,000. Senate consents but Danish parliament rejects it. 1917, finally purchased for $25,000,000.

Feb 1   Secretary Hay protests granting to Russia any exclusive privileges in China, as contrary to policy of equal treatment of all nations.

Feb 23   Prince Henry of Prussia, brother of the Kaiser, arrives in New York for visit in U. S.

Mar 6   Bureau of the Census created by act of Congress.

Mar 8   Tariff Act allows Philippine products to enter U. S. at 25 per cent reduction of Dingley tariff rates.

Mar 10   U. S. government initiates suit in equity against Northern Securities Company under Sherman Anti-Trust Act in Circuit Court at St. Paul. Decision Apr. 9, 1903, in favor of government followed by appeal to Supreme Court.

Apr   Philippine insurrection finally brought to an end.

Apr 12   Last of Spanish-American War taxes repealed.

Apr 29   Chinese Exclusion Act extend-ed to prohibit immigration of Chinese laborers from island territories to mainland of U. S.

May 12   Anthracite coal strike called by UMW with 140,000 miners idle. Offers of union president John Mitchell to submit demands to arbitration have been refused by mine operators.

May 20   U. S. surrenders authority in Cuba and first Cuban president is installed.

June 2   Oregon adopts constitutional amendment providing for initiative and referendum, introduced by William U'Ren.

June 17   Newlands Reclamation Act authorizes Federal government to build great irrigation dams throughout the West.

June 28   Isthmian Canal Act author-izes the President to acquire concession of Panama Canal Company, arrange terms with Colombia and construct a canal through Panama; if unable to obtain title and necessary control, to proceed to construct canal through Nicaragua.

July 1   Philippine Government Act provides for government of the islands by commission appointed by the President, with advice and consent of Senate.

July 4   General Amnesty to revolution-ists in Philippines offered by Presidential proclamation.

July 17 George F. Baer, president of Philadelphia and Reading Coal and Iron Company, spokesman for mine owners during anthracite coal strike, says, "The rights and interests of the laboring man will be protected and cared for—not by the labor agitators, but by the Christian men to whom God in His infinite wisdom has given the control of the property interests of this country. . . ."

Aug 11 Oliver Wendell Holmes appointed Associate Justice of the Supreme Court.

Aug 19 President Roosevelt leaves Washington for speaking tour of New England and Middle West.

Sept 15 U. S. is first government to resort to Permanent Court of Arbitration at the Hague in submitting to it dispute with Mexico over the Pious Fund.

Oct 3 President Roosevelt intervenes in coal strike, calling conference of operators and miners to meet with him in Washington. Operators reject proposal of John Mitchell, president of UMW, to submit miners' claims to arbitration.

Oct 11 Secretary of War Elihu Root, representing the President, confers with J. P. Morgan, financial backer of coal operators, on settling the coal strike.

Oct 13 Coal operators agree to appointment by the President of commission to investigate and mediate in coal dispute. President Roosevelt appoints commission Oct. 16.

Oct 21 President John Mitchell of UMW declares coal strike at an end.

Oct 25 Woodrow Wilson inaugurated president of Princeton University.

Nov 4 Congressional elections give Republicans fifth consecutive Congress, but with reduced majority.

Dec 11 Reciprocity convention with Cuba signed, allowing 20 per cent reduction of general tariff rates on Cuban products. Senate consents Mar. 19, 1903. Finally proclaimed Dec. 17, 1903.

Dec 12 U. S. submits to Germany, Great Britain and Italy, Venezuela's request for arbitration of their claims against her for payment of debt, after they have blockaded 5 of her ports, seized her warships and bombarded Puerto Cabello.

Dec 29 Drago Doctrine, sent to U. S. Department of State by Argentine Minister of Foreign Affairs, declares that the "public debt cannot occasion armed intervention nor even the actual occupation of the territory of American nations by a European power."

1903

American Political Science Association organized.

Chicago celebrates centennial of its founding.

National Women's Trade Union League organized.

Ford Motor Company formed.

"Shop Management" by Frederick W. Taylor published in *Transactions of American Society of Mechanical Engineers*, 1903. Scientific management applied to industry is called Taylorization.

John D. Rockefeller gives $7,000,000 to fight against tuberculosis.

"The Great Train Robbery," first complete story in motion pictures, produced by Edison studio.

Educational Psychology by Edward L. Thorndike, first of 3 vols., published.

Jan 1 Pacific cable opens, connecting San Francisco with Hawaii.

Jan 22 Hay-Herrán canal treaty signed with Colombia providing for lease to U. S. of 6-mile strip across Isthmus of Panama for $10,000,000 and annuity of $250,000. U. S. Senate consents Mar. 17. Rejected by Colombian Senate Aug. 12.

Jan 24 Alaskan boundary question referred to mixed commission for arbitration in treaty signed with Great Britain. Senate consents Feb. 11, 1903.

Feb 11 Expedition Act, to speed progress of anti-trust cases through the courts.

Feb 14 General Staff of the Army authorized by act of Congress, urged by Secretary of War Elihu Root.

Feb 14 Department of Commerce and Labor, Secretary to be of Cabinet status, created by act of Congress. Bureau of Corporations within the Department created by the Act. George B. Cortelyou first Secretary of Commerce and Labor.

Feb 19 Elkins Act provides curb of railroad rebates.

Feb 23 Cuba signs agreement to lease Guantanamo and Bahia Honda to U. S. for naval stations.

Mar 3 Immigration Act increases head tax from $1 to $2.

Mar 22 President Roosevelt's Anthracite Coal Commission report published. Awards shorter hours and 10 per cent wage increase to miners, but denies recognition of UMW.

Apr 1–June 5 President   Roosevelt makes tour across the country. Stops off in Colorado for game hunting.

Apr 27 In *Giles v. Harris,* **Supreme** Court sustains clause in Alabama constitution by which Negroes may be disfranchised.

May 22 Treaty with Cuba signed, embodying provisions of Platt Amendment. Senate consents Mar. 22, 1904.

May 23 Wisconsin adopts direct primary for party elections. First state to do so.

June 1 In *Hawaii v. Mankichi,* **Su**preme Court reaffirms principle of Insular Cases of May 27, 1901.

July   Slight recession, called "rich man's panic," in period of prosperity.

July 4 Pacific cable completed from San Francisco to Manila. First message to Philippines sent by President Roosevelt.

Aug 1 First successful transcontinental automobile trip completed from San Francisco to New York, begun May 23.

Oct 8 Chinese-American treaty of commerce signed, incorporating Open Door doctrine. Senate consents Dec. 18, 1903.

Oct 20 Alaskan Boundary Commission reports in favor of U. S. in every particular.

Nov 2 President Roosevelt orders warships to proceed to Panama to maintain "free and uninterrupted transit" across the isthmus, a guarantee of success of projected Panamanian Revolution. The *Nashville* reaches Colon at 5:30 P.M.

Nov 3 Revolt of Panama against Colombia takes place at Panama City at 6 P.M., while U. S. naval forces prevent transit of Colombian troops.

Nov 4 Independence of Republic of Panama proclaimed by the revolutionists.

Nov 6 11:35 A.M.   President Roosevelt notified by U. S. consul in Panama City that "freedom is definitely accomplished." 12:51 P.M. Secretary Hay sends instructions to consul to declare recognition of the *de facto* government of Panama.

Nov 6 Philippe Buneau-Varilla designated minister to U. S. by Panama.

Nov 9 Joseph Gurney Cannon elected Speaker of House at opening of 58th Congress.

Nov 18 Treaty with Panama Republic signed with Buneau-Varilla on same general terms as those of Hay-Herrán treaty rejected by Colombian Senate. U. S. guarantees independence of Panama Republic. Senate consents Feb. 23, 1904.

Dec 17 Commercial   reciprocity   with Cuba goes into operation.

Dec 17 Orville and Wilbur Wright make first successful airplane flights, near Kitty Hawk, N. C.: Orville, 120 feet in 12 seconds; Wilbur, 852 feet in 59 seconds.

Dec 22 Purchase of friars' lands in Philippines by U. S. agreed to by the Philippine Commission and the papacy, 410,000 acres for $7,239,000.

Dec 23 Colombia protests U. S. action in Panama.

Dec 30 Iroquois Theatre fire in Chicago during holiday matinee; 588, mostly women and children, lose their lives.

1904

National Child Labor Committee organized to promote child labor legislation.

National Tuberculosis Association founded.

Carnegie Hero Fund established by Andrew Carnegie's gift of $5,000,000.

William C. Gorgas sent to Panama to eliminate yellow fever by mosquito control. Makes building of canal possible.

Oregon adopts popular election of senators by morally binding its legislature to elect the winning candidate in the primary election.

Shame of the Cities by Lincoln Steffens published.

Jan 4 President Roosevelt's defense of his action in Panama affair, submitted in message to Congress, based on Treaty of 1846 with New Granada (Colombia).

Jan 4 In *Gonzales v. Williams,* Supreme Court declares that Puerto Ricans are not aliens and are not subject to laws restricting immigration.

Feb 1 William Howard Taft becomes Secretary of War following resignation of Elihu Root.

Feb 10 Russo-Japanese War begins with formal declaration by Japan.

Feb 10 U. S. appeals to Japan and Russia to so limit their military operations as to preserve "neutrality and administrative entity" of China during the war.

Mar 2 Treaty signed with Cuba recognizing Cuba's sovereignty over Isle of Pines. Senate consents Mar. 13, 1925.

Mar 14 In *Northern Securities Company v. United States,* Supreme Court decides, 5–4, that the Company, organized to control majority of stock of Great Northern and Northern Pacific Railroad companies, violated Anti-Trust Law, and orders its dissolution.

Mar 15 President Roosevelt by executive order establishes service pension for all Civil War veterans over 62.

Apr 30–Dec 1 Louisiana Purchase Exposition at St. Louis, Mo.

May 5 Socialist party in convention at Chicago nominates Eugene V. Debs for President.

May 9 President Roosevelt by executive order places government of Panama Canal Zone and construction of canal in control of Isthmian Canal Commission, Rear Admiral John G. Walker chairman and John F. Wallace chief engineer.

May 18 Ion H. Perdicaris, an American citizen, kidnapped by Raizuli, Moroccan brigand.

June 6 Oregon adopts direct primary for party nominations.

June 21–23 Republican National Convention meets at Chicago. Nominates Theodore Roosevelt for President by acclamation and Charles W. Fairbanks of Indiana for Vice-President.

June 22 Secretary Hay, second day of Republican Convention, sends cable to Morocco, "We want Perdicaris alive or Raizuli dead." Perdicaris promptly released.

June 24 Dingley Tariff rates extended by executive order to Panama Canal Zone.

June 29–30 Prohibition party meets in convention at Indianapolis. Nominates Silas C. Swallow of Pennsylvania for President and George W. Carroll of Texas for Vice-President.

July 2–8 Socialist Labor party meets at New York. Nominates Charles Hunter Corregon of New York for President and William Wesley Cox of Illinois for Vice-President.

July 4–5 Populist party meets at Springfield, Ill. Nominates Thomas E.

Watson of Georgia for President and Thomas H. Tibbles of Nebraska for Vice-President.

July 6–10 Democratic National Convention meets at St. Louis. Nominates Alton B. Parker of New York for President and Henry G. Davis of West Virginia for Vice-President.

July 25 Strike of 25,000 textile workers for higher wages in Fall River, Mass. Ends successfully Jan. 8, 1905.

Oct 19 American Tobacco Company formed, a merger of its subsidiaries, Consolidated, American and Continental.

Oct 21 President Roosevelt proposes second peace conference at The Hague. Delayed until June 15, 1907, because of Russo-Japanese War.

Oct 27 First New York City subway opened to public.

Nov 8 Presidential election. Theodore Roosevelt and Fairbanks elected by electoral vote of 336, to 140 for Parker and Davis. Popular vote: Roosevelt, Republican, 7,623,486; Parker, Democrat, 5,-077,911; Debs, Socialist, 402,283; Swallow, Prohibition, 258,536; Watson, Populist, 117,183; Corregon, Socialist Labor, 31,249.

On night of his election, Roosevelt issues statement, "Under no circumstances will I be a candidate for or accept another nomination."

Nov 8 Joseph W. Folk elected gover- nor of Missouri in fight for clean government.

Dec 6 Roosevelt Corollary of Monroe Doctrine announced in annual message to Congress. "Chronic wrong-doing" such as failure to meet public debt obligations "in Western Hemisphere may force the United States, because of its adherence to the Monroe Doctrine, to exercise an international police power."

Dec 10 Bethlehem Steel Corporation incorporated under laws of New Jersey.

Dec 21 James R. Garfield, Commis- sioner of Corporations, recommends Congressional legislation placing corporations engaged in interstate trade under Federal supervision.

1905

American Federation of Labor registers 1,500,000 members, increase from 500,-000 since 1900.

Asiatic Exclusion League formed, aimed at Japanese immigrants.

Bureau of Forestry established in Department of Agriculture.

American Sociological Society founded.

California Fruit Growers' Exchange formed.

Carnegie Foundation for the Advancement of Teaching established with Andrew Carnegie's gift of $10,000,000.

Brand Whitlock elected mayor of Toledo, Ohio, succeeding "Golden Rule" Jones.

McClure's begins publication of articles by Ray Stannard Baker, "The Railroads on Trial." Aid in fight for railroad regulation.

Everybody's publishes articles by Charles E. Russell on Beef Trust, and "Frenzied Finance" by Thomas W. Lawson.

Jan 5 American Red Cross (1881) re- incorporated in accordance with Treaty of Geneva, signed by U. S. 1882, and brought under government supervision. William H. Taft elected president Feb. 8.

Jan 13 Secretary Hay proclaims policy of U. S. is "to maintain the integrity of China and the Open Door in the Orient."

Jan 30 Beef Trust declared illegal by Supreme Court in *Swift v. United States.* Dissolution only changes its form.

Feb 7 Protocol signed with Santo Do- mingo by which U. S. will supervise her customs in interest of both Santo Domingo and her creditors. After Senate refuses consent, President Roosevelt makes informal arrangement with Santo Domingo Mar. 28 to the same end, the Roosevelt Corollary in action.

Feb 20 In *Jacobson v. Massachusetts,* Supreme Court decides that to enact a compulsory vaccination law is within police power of a state.

Feb 23 First Rotary Club founded at Chicago by Paul H. Harris.

Mar 4 Theodore Roosevelt inaugurated President and Charles W. Fairbanks Vice-President.
[President Roosevelt's Cabinet: John Hay, Secretary of State; Leslie M. Shaw, Secretary of Treasury; William H. Taft, Secretary of War; C. J. Bonaparte, Secretary of Navy; E. A. Hitchcock, Secretary of Interior; James Wilson, Secretary of Agriculture; Victor H. Metcalf, Secretary of Commerce and Labor; G. B. Cortelyou, Postmaster General; W. H. Moody, Attorney General.]

Apr 17 In *Lochner v. New York,* Supreme Court declares unconstitutional a New York law fixing hours in bakeshops at 10 per day, on ground that it violates right of contract.

June 1 Lewis and Clark Exposition at Portland, Ore., opens. Closes Oct. 14.

June Industrial Workers of the World (I.W.W.) organized under Eugene V. Debs and William D. Haywood.

June 8 President Roosevelt makes formal offer of good offices to both Russia and Japan, to end Russo-Japanese War.

July–Oct Severe yellow fever epidemic in New Orleans. Ends under government-waged anti-mosquito campaign.

July Niagara Falls Conference held by young intellectuals of Negro race to improve their rights.

July 19 Elihu Root succeeds John Hay, died July 1, as Secretary of State.

July 21 China boycotts U. S. goods in protest against U. S. laws barring educated Chinese.

July 29 Taft-Katsura Memorandum. Secretary of War Taft, with President

Roosevelt's approval, negotiates secret agreement with Japan at Tokyo, approving free hand for Japan in Korea in exchange for her disavowal of any aggressive designs upon the Philippines.

Aug 9 Peace conference between Russia and Japan opens at Portsmouth, N. H., following acceptance of offer of good offices by President Roosevelt.

Sept 5 Treaty of Portsmouth signed by representatives of Japan and Russia. Roosevelt's influence results in easier terms for Russia.

Sept 6 Armstrong Insurance Investigating Committee of New York legislature begins hearings in scandals in life-insurance companies, Charles Evans Hughes prosecutor.

1906

National Recreation Association organized.

Reverend Algernon Sidney Cropsey, Batavia, N. Y., tried and unfrocked for use of higher criticism in New Testament interpretation.

Rudolph Spreckels organizes and finances exposure of graft in San Francisco.

Lee DeForest invents vacuum tube amplifier, making radio possible.

Hearst's International News Service organized.

Monsignor John A. Ryan, in his book *A Living Wage,* condemns any wage system unable to provide workers with basic comfort, recreation and security. An influence in Roosevelt's administration.

The Education of Henry Adams privately printed. Published 1918.

Jan 4 Robert M. LaFollette from Wisconsin takes seat in Senate. Elected Jan. 1905.

Jan 16 Algeciras Conference to adjust international conflicts in Morocco convenes through instrumentality of President Roosevelt. U. S. represented by Henry White and Samuel Gummere who follow Roosevelt's instructions, "Keep friendly with all . . . and help France get what she ought to have." Act of Algeciras signed Apr. 7; Senate consents Dec. 12.

Feb 3 Colonel George Harvey proposes Woodrow Wilson for Presidency at dinner given in honor of Wilson by Lotos Club, New York.

Mar 17 President Roosevelt at Grid-iron Dinner in Washington condemns muckraking writers and magazines. Apr. 14, delivers his "Man with the Muckrake" speech in public address.

Apr 10 Maxim Gorky arrives in New York to interest America in freedom for the Russian people.

Apr 18–19 Earthquake and fire reduce two-thirds of San Francisco to ruins.

Apr 19 Robert M. LaFollette begins 3-day set speech in Senate on railroad rate bill, in revolt against Aldrich dictatorship.

Apr 27 Ground broken for the building of Gary, Ind., in sand dunes and marshes along Lake Michigan, by U. S. Steel Corporation.

May 7 Alaska permitted a delegate to House of Representatives by act of Congress.

May 8 Burke Act authorizes Secretary of Interior to grant full property title to any Indian allottee when convinced of his fitness to manage his affairs.

May 21 Convention signed with Mexico providing for equitable distribution of water of the Rio Grande for irrigation. Senate consents June 26.

June 4 Reynolds and Neill report, revealing loathsome conditions in meat packing houses, made public by President Roosevelt.

June 11 Employers' Liability Act extends liability to common carriers in interstate traffic.

June 25 President Roosevelt sends greetings to Emperor of Japan over newly completed cable from Guam to Japan.

June 29 Hepburn Act extends jurisdiction of Interstate Commerce Commission and grants it rate-making power.

June 29 Lock type of canal for Panama authorized by act of Congress.

June 30 Pure Food and Drug Act prohibits misbranding and adulteration.

June 30 Meat Inspection Act.

July 4 Elihu Root, Secretary of State, begins good will tour of South America. Returns Sept. 30.

July 23 Third International American Conference convenes at Rio de Janeiro. July 27, Secretary Elihu Root, addressing Conference, foreshadows "good neighbor" policy: "We wish for no victories but those of peace; for no territory except our own; for no sovereignty except the sovereignty over ourselves."

Aug 13 At Brownsville, Tex., a few Negro soldiers shoot up the town. Nov. 6, President Roosevelt orders dishonorable discharge of 3 companies of Negro troops.

Sept 29 Military control of Cuba assumed by U. S. in accord with Platt Amendment, following insurrection against President Palma. Secretary Taft proclaims provisional government, which assumes duties 2 weeks later.

Oct 11 San Francisco board of education orders segregation of Japanese, Chinese and Korean children in separate school for Orientals. Emphatically protested by Japanese ambassador Oct. 25. Order rescinded Mar. 13, 1907.

Nov 4 Charles Evans Hughes elected governor of New York over William Randolph Hearst. Serves 2 terms.

Nov 9 President Roosevelt sails on battleship *Louisiana* to visit Panama and Puerto Rico. First U. S. President to pass bounds of U. S. jurisdiction.

Dec 10 President Roosevelt awarded Nobel Peace Prize for mediation in Russo-Japanese War.

1907

1,285,349 immigrants arrive, highest number in any year of U. S. history.

Dreadnought era begins for U. S. Navy with the laying of keels of two 20,000-ton ships. British *Dreadnought* was launched Feb. 10, 1906.

Over 300 railroad acts passed this year in 39 states, stimulated by Hepburn Act of 1906.

Chautauqua enters peak years (1907–1915) under Dr. George E. Vincent, president.

Larkin Building erected in Buffalo, a new note in industrial architecture, designed by Frank Lloyd Wright.

President Roosevelt orders withdrawal from entry of 16,000,000 acres in forest areas in the Northwest, part of 148,000,-000 withdrawn during his administration.

Russell Sage Foundation founded and endowed with $10,000,000 by Mrs. Sage for investigation and improvement of social and living conditions in U. S.

Albert Abraham Michelson first American to receive Nobel Prize in Physics, for his study of light.

James Bryce comes to U. S. as British ambassador, remaining until 1913.

The Spirit of American Government by James Allen Smith published, one of first critical works on development of American government.

Christianity and the Social Crisis by Walter Rauschenbusch published.

Pragmatism by William James published.

Jan 26 Contributions by corporations to election campaigns prohibited by act of Congress.

Feb 6 Old age pension for Mexican and Civil War veterans of 62 and over authorized by act of Congress.

Feb 8 Treaty with Santo Domingo signed, modification of unratified treaty of 1905, providing for collection of customs and adjustment of claims of foreign creditors. Senate consents Feb. 25.

Feb 20 Immigration Act excludes undesirables and raises head tax of aliens to $4. Authorizes the President to exclude from mainland of U. S. holders of passports to any other country, insular possessions of U. S., or Canal Zone. Act creates commission to investigate immigration.

Feb 24 Foreign minister Hayashi of Japan sends a note which forms basis of Gentlemen's Agreement of 1908.

Feb 26 General Appropriations Act provides increase of salaries of Speaker of House, Vice-President and Cabinet members to $12,000, and of Senators and Representatives to $7,500.

Feb 26 General George W. Goethals appointed chief engineer in charge of construction of Panama Canal.

Mar 13 New York stock market crashes suddenly in the "silent panic."

Mar 14 President Roosevelt by executive order excludes from continental U. S. all Japanese laborers coming from Mexico, Canada or Hawaii.

Mar 14 Inland Waterways Commission appointed by the President, Theodore E. Burton chairman, to study interlocking problems of forest preservation and waterways.

Mar 21 Revolution in Honduras leads to landing of U. S. marines to protect property.

Apr 14 National Arbitration and Peace Congress, Andrew Carnegie president, meets in New York City to mobilize backing for forthcoming Hague Conference.

Apr 26 Jamestown Tercentenary Exposition at Hampton Roads, Va., opened by President Roosevelt. Closes Nov. 30.

May Taximeter cabs arrive in New York from Paris, first taxis in U. S.

May 22 Public Utilities Commission established by New York Legislature.

June 15–Oct 18 Second Hague Peace Conference, called upon suggestion of President Roosevelt. Efforts to secure limitation of armaments wrecked. All 10 conventions adopted concern technique of war.

July 4 Woodrow Wilson makes his first public pronouncement on trust problem, advises attack on illegal manipulations of financiers rather than on corporations.

July 30 First Philippine election held. Oct. 16, Philippine legislature meets for first time.

Aug 3 Standard Oil of Indiana, in- dicted for receiving rebates in violation of Elkins Law of 1903 and found guilty in U. S. District Court at Chicago by Judge Kenesaw Mountain Landis, fined $29,240,000. July 22, 1908, fine set aside by Federal Circuit Court of Appeals at Chicago. Nov. 10, 1909, case dismissed on retrial.

Aug 21 "The Philippine Islands form our heel of Achilles. They are all that makes the present situation with Japan dangerous," writes President Roosevelt to Secretary of War Taft.

Oct 18 Marconi system of wireless telegraphy opened between U. S. and Ireland. Invented by Guglielmo Marconi (Italian) 1895.

Oct 22 "Bankers' panic" begins with run on Knickerbocker Trust Company in New York.

Nov 4 President Roosevelt permits U. S. Steel Corporation to acquire Tennessee Coal and Iron Company.

Nov 16 Oklahoma enters the Union.

Dec 11 President Roosevelt again de- clares, "I will not . . . accept another nomination" for the Presidency.

Dec 16 U. S. fleet of 16 battleships steams out of Hampton Roads for the Pacific and trip around the world. Returns Feb. 22, 1909.

Dec 20 Treaties providing for Central American Court of Justice signed by Central American states at Central American Peace Conference, convened Nov. 14 in Washington, sponsored by U. S. and Mexico.

Dec 20 Secretary of War Taft returns from good-will trip around the world, by way of Japan, Philippines and Russia.

1908

Federal Bureau of Investigation (FBI) established as division of Department of Justice.

Federal Council of the Churches of Christ in America established.

Catholic Church in America given full ecclesiastical status by Rome.

Harvard Graduate School of Business Administration established.

University of Missouri establishes first professional school of journalism.

Henry Ford's four-cylindered model-T goes on the market at $850.50.

Two subway tunnels in New York opened to traffic, one under East River, the other under the Hudson to Hoboken.

Christian Science Monitor first published.

Constitutional Government in the United States by Woodrow Wilson published. Delivered as George Blumenthal Foundation lectures at Columbia University 1907.

Jan 6 In *Employers' Liability Cases,* Supreme Court declares unconstitutional Employers' Liability Act of June 11, 1906, in that it seems to apply to injuries received in intrastate transportation.

Jan 21 Sullivan Ordinance passed in New York City, making smoking by women in public places illegal.

Jan 27 In *Adair v. United States,* Supreme Court holds the section of Erdman Act (June 1, 1898) prohibiting discrimination against union labor in interstate commerce, contrary to 5th Amendment.

Feb 3 In *Loewe v. Lawlor,* Danbury Hatters' case, Supreme Court holds for first time that Anti-Trust Law applies to combinations of labor as well as of capital: the Hatters' boycott, being a combination in restraint of trade, violates Sherman Anti-Trust law.

Feb 10 General arbitration treaty signed with France, first of some 20 within next 2 years. Senate consents Feb. 19.

Feb 18 Gentlemen's Agreement concluded with Japan. Japanese government acquiesces in Roosevelt's order of Mar. 14, 1907, and also binds itself to issue no more passports to coolies emigrating directly to U. S.

Feb 24 In *Muller v. State of Oregon,* Supreme Court sustains Oregon's 10-hour-day law for women in industry.

Mar 23 In suit of Buck's Stove and Range Company of St. Louis against AFL, Supreme Court grants injunction against AFL because of its boycott.

Apr 2–3 Populist party convention meets at St. Louis. Nominates Thomas E. Watson of Georgia for President and Samuel W. Williams of Indiana for Vice-President.

Apr 22 New Employers' Liability Act, applying to interstate railroads, takes away employers' defense of "contributory negligence."

May 10–17 Socialist party convention meets at Chicago. Eugene V. Debs nominated for President and Benjamin Hanford of New York for Vice-President.

May 13–15 White House Conference on Conservation attended by 24 governors, large number of government officials and scientists.

May 25 Central American Court of Justice inaugurated at Cartago, Costa Rica, resulting from Washington Conference Nov. 14, 1907.

May 25 Chinese Boxer indemnity awarded to U. S. reduced by Congress to about half of original figure of $24,440,-700. China earmarks this Boxer Fund for education of Chinese students in U. S.

Unpaid balance of indemnity remitted to China 1924.

May 30 National Monetary Commission provided for by Aldrich-Vreeland Currency Act which also provides for emergency currency in times of financial stringency.

June 1 Oregon adopts recall of elective officials by constitutional amendment.

June 8 National Conservation Commission appointed by President Roosevelt, Gifford Pinchot chairman.

June 16–20 Republican National Convention meets at Chicago. William H. Taft nominated for President on first ballot. James S. Sherman of New York nominated for Vice-President.

July 2–5 Socialist Labor party convention meets at New York. August Gilhaus of New York nominated for President and Donald L. Munro of Virginia for Vice-President.

July 7–10 Democratic National Convention meets at Denver. William J. Bryan receives nomination for President on first ballot, John W. Kern of Indiana nominated for Vice-President.

July 15–16 Prohibition party Convention meets at Columbus, Ohio. Nominates Eugene W. Chafin of Illinois for President and Aaron S. Watkins of Ohio for Vice-President.

July 27 Independence party Convention meets at Chicago, William R. Hearst temporary chairman. Nominates Thomas L. Hisgen of Massachusetts for President and John Temple Graves of Georgia for Vice-President.

Aug 10 Country Life Commission appointed by President Roosevelt, L. H. Bailey chairman.

Oct 1 Letter postage rate of 2 cents between U. S. and Great Britain becomes effective.

Oct 18 U. S. fleet in round-the-world tour arrives at Yokohama, at invitation of Japanese government, for 3-day reception.

Nov 3 **Presidential election. Taft and** Sherman elected by electoral vote of 321, to 182 for Bryan and Kern. Popular vote: Taft, Republican, 7,678,908; Bryan, Democrat, 6,409,104; Debs, Socialist, 420,-793; Chafin, Prohibition, 253,840; Hisgen, Independence, 82,872; Watson, Populist, 29,100; Gilhaus, Socialist Labor, 14,021.

Nov 30 **Root-Takahira agreement concluded** by exchange of notes between Secretary of State Root and Japanese ambassador to U. S. The 2 countries assert common desire for free and peaceful development of commerce in the Pacific and agree to maintain the status quo, including the Open Door in China, in the Far East.

Dec **Christmas seals (anti-tuberculosis)** sold for first time by American Red Cross. After 1920, activity of National Tuberculosis Association.

Dec 4–Feb 26, 1909 **London Naval** Conference. U. S. one of 10 naval powers attending. Results in Declaration of London, agreed to Feb. 26 but never ratified.

Dec 23 **Supreme Court sentences Samuel** Gompers, John Mitchell and Frank Morrison, officers of AFL, to 12, 9 and 6 months in prison, respectively, for violation of injunction against boycott of the Buck's Stove and Range Company.

Dec 25 **First Pan-American Scientific** Congress opens at Santiago, Chile.

Dec 31 **Wilbur Wright wins Michelin** cup in France for long-distance airplane flight, over 77 miles in 2 hours and 20 minutes.

1909

National Association for the Advancement of Colored People organized under leadership of W. E. B. DuBois.

Junior high school system inaugurated at Berkeley, Cal.

Chicago, Milwaukee and St. Paul Railroad reaches Seattle, completing seventh transcontinental line.

Rockefeller Sanitary Commission established to eradicate hookworm in Southern states.

Theory of the gene formulated by Thomas H. Morgan, zoologist at Columbia University. Receives 1933 Nobel Prize in Medicine.

Documentary History of American Industrial Society, 10 vols., John R. Commons and associates, editors, published 1909–10.

Harvard Classics, Charles W. Eliot editor, published 1909–10.

The Promise of American Life by Herbert D. Croly published. Provides essentials for Theodore Roosevelt's "New Nationalism."

Jan 11 **Treaty for regulation of** boundary waters between Canada and U. S. signed with Great Britain. Senate consents Mar. 3.

Jan 27 **North Atlantic Coast Fisheries** Treaty signed with Great Britain, submitting to the Hague Tribunal long standing dispute over U. S. claims under Treaty of 1818. Senate consents Feb. 18.

Jan 28 **Second military occupation of** Cuba by U. S. troops comes to an end, administration again turned over to Cuban authorities.

Feb 9 **Opium importation and use for** other than medical purposes prohibited by act of Congress.

Feb 19 **Homestead Act allows entry on** double the number of acres of grazing lands where irrigation would not be successful.

Mar **Los Angeles invokes recall of** elective officials against its mayor.

Mar 4 **The President's salary raised to** $75,000 by act of Congress.

Mar 4 **Amendment to Sundry Civil** Bill, signed this day, cuts off support of Conservation Commission.

Mar 4 **Inauguration of William Howard** Taft, President, and James S. Sherman, Vice-President.

[President Taft's Cabinet: Philander C. Knox, Secretary of State; Franklin

MacVeagh, Secretary of Treasury; Jacob M. Dickinson, Secretary of War; George von L. Meyer, Secretary of Navy; R. A. Ballinger, Secretary of Interior; James Wilson, Secretary of Agriculture; Charles Nagel, Secretary of Commerce and Labor; Frank H. Hitchcock, Postmaster General; George W. Wickersham, Attorney General.]

Mar 15 Sixty-first Congress meets in special session to consider tariff revision. Joseph G. Cannon re-elected Speaker of House, although 12 insurgent Republicans refuse to vote for him.

Mar 17 Sereno E. Payne, chairman of House Ways and Means Committee, introduces tariff bill with duties generally lower than in Dingley Tariff. Passed by House Apr. 9.

Mar 23 Theodore Roosevelt and party sail from Hoboken on African hunting expedition. Expedition disbands at Khartum Mar. 14, 1910.

Apr 6 Robert E. Peary places U. S. flag at North Pole. News received Sept. 6. Peary's records accepted by National Geographic Society as evidence of his success.

Apr 12 Aldrich Tariff Bill submitted in Senate by Finance Committee as substitute for Payne Bill. Increases many rates.

May 3 In *United States v. Delaware and Hudson Company*, Supreme Court upholds but emasculates commodities clause of Hepburn Act of June 29, 1906.

June 1 Alaska-Yukon-Pacific Exposi- tion at Seattle opens. Closes Oct. 16.

July 8 Aldrich Tariff Bill, after 11 weeks' discussion and hundreds of amendments to Payne Bill, passes Senate.

July 12 Sixteenth Amendment, per- mitting an unapportioned income tax, submitted to states for ratification.

July 27 and 30 Orville Wright demon- strates success of his airplane and assures its acceptance by the government.

July 31 Payne-Aldrich Bill, after con- ference committee compromise, passes House.

Aug 2 Lincoln penny issued by Phila- delphia mint, replacing the Indian head of 50 years' coinage.

Aug 5 Payne-Aldrich Tariff Bill passes Senate, is signed by President Taft.

Aug 26 National Conservation Associ- ation, Charles W. Eliot president, opens first convention at Seattle.

Aug 28 Glenn H. Curtiss wins James Gordon Bennet cup in first international air races at Rheims, France.

Sept 1 Dr. Frederick Cook announces that he reached North Pole Apr. 21, 1908. [University of Copenhagen examines records, enters verdict of no proof.]

Sept 15 Secretary of the Interior Rich- ard A. Ballinger upheld by President Taft in Ballinger-Pinchot controversy, 1909–1911, over conservation policy of Department of Interior.

Sept 17 President Taft in speech at Winona, Minn., insists that Payne-Aldrich Tariff is "the best tariff law the Republican party ever made and therefore the best the country ever had."

Sept 25–Oct 2 Hudson-Fulton celebra- tion in New York, tercentenary of Henry Hudson's arrival and centennial of Fulton's steamboat.

Sept 27 President Taft withdraws 3,000,000 acres of public oil lands in the West from entry, continuing conservation policy of President Roosevelt.

Oct Short Ballot Association organ- ized, Woodrow Wilson president.

Nov 6 Secretary of State Philander C. Knox announces to Great Britain plan for neutralization of railroads in Manchuria, China, to purchase them by means of international loan. Russia and Japan opposed. Plan dropped.

Nov 22 Ladies' Waist Makers' Union, Local 25, under International Ladies' Garment Workers, begins 3-month strike, 20,000 women in walkout, resulting in winning most of demands.

Dec 18 U. S. troops check hostilities in Nicaragua, supporting revolutionists against Dictator Zelaya.

1910

Population, 91,972,266; foreign-born, 13,515,886.

1910–1930, over a million Negroes migrate from the South to the North.

World Peace Foundation founded and endowed with $1,000,000 by Edwin Ginn.

Carnegie Endowment for International Peace established with gift of $10,000,000.

Pan-American Building at Washington dedicated, gift of Andrew Carnegie, to house Bureau of Pan-American Union.

Eight states by this date have adopted statewide prohibition: Maine (1858), Kansas (1880), North Dakota (1889), Georgia (1907), Oklahoma (1907), Mississippi (1908), North Carolina (1908), Tennessee (1909).

St. Patrick's Cathedral, New York, dedicated.

Shoshone Dam in Wyoming completed.

Arch Hoxsey of Los Angeles sets new airplane record for altitude, 11,474 feet.

Glenn H. Curtiss, flying from Albany to New York in 2½ hours, breaks long distance speed record and wins New York *World* $10,000 prize.

Barney Oldfield at Daytona Beach, Fla., breaks automobile speed record, one mile in 27⅓ seconds.

History of Great American Fortunes by Gustavus Myers published.

Jan 7 Chief Forester Gifford Pinchot removed by President Taft, result of Pinchot-Ballinger controversy over conservation program.

Jan 23 Gifford Pinchot elected president of National Conservation Association.

Feb "The Moral Equivalent of War," essay by William James, published in *International Concilium*.

Feb 8 Boy Scouts of America, started by William D. Boyce, chartered in District of Columbia.

Mar 19 Resolution to make Rules Committee of House of Representatives elective by House and excluding Speaker from the Committee introduced by Norris of Nebraska. Adoption curtails power of Speaker Joseph G. Cannon.

May 11 Glacier National Park, Mont., created by act of Congress.

May 23 U. S. financiers, at President Taft's intercession, admitted to 4-power consortium with Germany, Britain and France, to finance building of Hukuang railroad in China.

June 18 Mann-Elkins Act extends In-terstate Commerce jurisdiction to include telephone, telegraph, cable and wireless companies; increases power of Interstate Commerce Commission and provides Commerce Court, organized in December.

June 24 Radio equipment required on ocean steamers leaving U. S. ports and carrying U. S. passengers, by act of Congress.

June 25 Publicity of Campaign Con-tributions Act applies to election campaigns of Representatives.

June 25 Mann White Slave Traffic Act prohibits interstate transportation of women for immoral purposes.

June 25 Postal Savings Bank system established by act of Congress. Inaugurated Jan. 3, 1911.

June 25 The President authorized by Congress to withdraw from entry public lands valuable for irrigation and power sites.

July 7 Cloak-makers' strike in New York begins, under International Ladies' Garment Workers. After 9 weeks, settled favorably for strikers.

July 12 Fourth International Amer-ican Conference convenes at Buenos

Aires. Secretary of State Knox an honorary president. [Conventions relating to copyrights and inventions signed by delegates.]

Aug 31 New Nationalism outlined in notable speech by Theodore Roosevelt at Ossawatomie, Kan. "I stand for the square deal. . . . property shall be the servant and not the master of the commonwealth."

Sept 7 North Atlantic Fisheries case settled favorably for U. S. by Hague Tribunal.

Sept 30 All assistant postmasters and clerks in first and second class post offices placed under civil service by President Taft.

Oct 1 Los Angeles *Times* building de-stroyed by dynamite, 20 killed, 17 injured. Dec. 1, 1911, McNamara brothers plead guilty of dynamiting, sentenced to prison terms Dec. 5.

Nov 8 Democrats win decisive victory in mid-term elections, gaining control of House, first time since 1894. Democratic governors elected in 8 states, including Woodrow Wilson in New Jersey.

Nov 8 Hiram Johnson elected reform governor of California.

Nov 8 Emil Seidel, Socialist, elected mayor of Milwaukee, and Victor Berger, Representative from Wisconsin, first socialist in Congress.

Nov 8 Franklin D. Roosevelt elected to New York Senate from Dutchess County.

Nov 8 Oregon adopts presidential preferential primary by popular vote.

Nov 8 Washington (state) adopts woman suffrage by constitutional amendment.

Nov 10 President Taft sails for Pan-ama on inspection tour.

Dec 5 Immigration Commission, after nearly 4 years' effort, presents 41-volume report recommending especially restriction of unskilled labor.

Dec 9 Woodrow Wilson releases to the press manifesto in support of James

Martine, victor in New Jersey preferential primary for Senate, and in condemnation of announced candidacy of Democratic boss James Smith, Jr. Resulting fight with Smith makes Wilson national figure.

Dec 12 Edward Douglass White of Louisiana becomes Chief Justice of Supreme Court.

1911

Carnegie Corporation of New York for promotion of education and philanthropy established by Andrew Carnegie's gift of $125,000,000.

Glenn H. Curtiss invents hydroplane.

Jan 10 Loan convention signed with Honduras by which U. S. by collection of customs will afford security to U. S. bankers assuming foreign debt of Honduras. Senate refuses consent and bankers refuse to proceed.

Jan 17 Woodrow Wilson inaugurated governor of New Jersey. Under his leadership, Jan. to Apr., the state adopts election reform, utilities regulation, employer's liability and a corrupt practices act, thus placing itself in forefront of progressive states.

Jan 21 National Progressive Republi-can League organized at Washington residence of Senator LaFollette. Senator Jonathan Bourne of Oregon elected president.

Jan 21 Reciprocity agreement with Canada signed. Submitted to Congress by President Taft in special message Jan. 26. House passes bill Apr. 21. Senate consents June 21. Later rejected by Canada.

Feb 14 Champ Clark, Democratic leader of House, debating Canadian reciprocity agreement says, "I am for it, because I hope to see the day when the American flag will float over every square foot of the British-North American possessions clear to the North Pole."

Feb 21 Treaty of commerce and navi-gation, including Gentlemen's Agreement of 1908, signed with Japan at Washington. Senate consents Feb. 24.

Mar 1 Appalachian Forest Reserve Act provides for purchase of forest lands, controlling sources of important streams in White Mountains and southern Appalachians.

Mar 7 President Taft accepts resignation of Secretary of Interior Ballinger who, though exonerated by Congressional committee, is still object of criticism.

Mar 7 Twenty thousand U. S. troops ordered to Mexican border, in Texas, because of Mexican revolution.

Mar 13 Corporation tax, included in Payne-Aldrich Tariff Act, 1909, upheld by Supreme Court.

Mar 18 Roosevelt Dam on Salt River, Ariz., dedicated. Theodore Roosevelt present.

Mar 23 Theodore Roosevelt speaking at University of California says, "I took the Isthmus, started the canal, and then left Congress—not to debate the canal, but to debate me."

May 5 Woodrow Wilson, speaking in Kansas City, takes friendly stand on initiative, referendum and recall.

May 8 First direct telephone conversation between New York and Denver made.

May 15 In *Standard Oil Company of New Jersey et al v. United States,* Standard Oil Company ordered dissolved by Supreme Court. The "rule of reason," says Chief Justice White, should determine the Court's decision.

May 15 Henry L. Stimson nominated Secretary of War, replacing J. M. Dickinson.

May 25 President Porfirio Diaz of Mexico overthrown in revolution headed by Francisco Madero.

May 29 In *United States v. American Tobacco Company,* American Tobacco Company ordered dissolved by Supreme Court. As a monopoly, it has violated Sherman Anti-Trust Act.

June 3 U. S. gunboat *Yorktown* ordered to proceed to Nicaraguan waters to protect U. S. interests.

June 5 Illinois adopts system of mothers' pensions. First state to do so.

June 6 Knox-Castrillo Convention signed with Nicaragua providing for customs control by U. S. and loans by U. S. bankers, a case of Taft's "dollar diplomacy." Creating in fact a protectorate, it goes into practical operation though consent is refused by Senate.

July 7 North Pacific Sealing Convention, regulating all pelagic sealing industry in North Pacific, signed in Washington by Russia, Japan, Great Britain and U. S. Senate consents July 24.

Aug President Taft vetoes new Woolens Tariff Bill, Farmer's Free List Bill and Cotton Bill, revisions of Payne-Aldrich Tariff passed by Democratic House and Senate insurgents.

Aug 22 President Taft vetoes New Mexico-Arizona Enabling Resolution because Arizona constitution provides for recall of judges.

Sept 17–Nov 5 First transcontinental air flight made by Calbraith P. Rodgers from New York to Pasadena, actual flying time, 3½ days.

Oct 10 California adopts woman suffrage by constitutional amendment.

Oct 16 National Conference of Progressive Republicans meets in Chicago. Endorses Senator Robert LaFollette for Republican Presidential candidate.

Nov 1 Naval pageant opens. Atlantic fleet mobilizes at New York, Pacific fleet at San Diego, with much ceremony and publicity.

Nov 11 George Harvey places at masthead of *Harper's Weekly,* "For President: Woodrow Wilson." Slogan appears for last time Dec. 9, following break between Wilson and Harvey.

Dec 4 John D. Rockefeller resigns as president of Standard Oil Company.

Dec 21 Treaty of Commerce with Russia (1832) terminated by joint resolution of Congress, in protest against Russia's refusal to honor passports granted to American Jews.

Dec 23 Theodore Roosevelt in letter to William B. Howland reveals intention to stand for Republican Presidential nomination.

1912

Massachusetts adopts minimum wage for women and children, first such legislation in country.

Elihu Root awarded Nobel Peace Prize.

Commerce Court, established by Mann-Elkins Act, comes to an end when Congress refuses to appropriate funds.

Woolworth Building, highest inhabitable building in the world, completed in New York.

The New Democracy by Walter Weyl published. Outline for political reform.

Jan 6 New Mexico enters the Union.

Jan 8 Jackson Day dinner in Washington, Woodrow Wilson and William J. Bryan among speakers.

Jan 12 Textile workers' strike under I.W.W. begins at Lawrence, Mass. Won by strikers. I.W.W. comes into prominence in the East among textile workers this year.

Feb U. S. marines arrive in Honduras to protect property of Americans.

Feb 2 Senator Robert LaFollette in speech before Periodical Publishers' Association in Philadelphia indulges in tirade against pundits of publishing world, losing support for Presidential nomination.

Feb 10 Seven Republican governors address letter to Theodore Roosevelt requesting him to be candidate for Presidency.

Feb 12 President Taft makes inept speech before Republican Club of New York, designating Progressives as "emotionalists and neurotics."

Feb 14 Arizona enters the Union.

Feb 21 Theodore Roosevelt before Ohio Constitutional Convention at Columbus, Ohio, delivers address, "A Charter of Democracy," advocating recall of judicial decisions.

Feb 23 Secretary of State Knox sails from Key West for tour of Central American capitals. Before Nicaragua Congress he states, "My government does not covet an inch of territory south of the Rio Grande."

Feb 24 Theodore Roosevelt, replying to letter of the 7 governors of Feb. 10, says, "I will accept nomination for President if it is tendered to me."

Mar 12 Girl Scouts founded by Juliette Low.

Mar 14 President Taft declares embargo on arms for Mexico.

Mar 16 Battleship *Maine*, raised from bottom of Havana Harbor, is sunk 3 miles out at sea.

Apr 7–10 Socialist Labor party convention meets at New York. Nominates Arthur E. Reimer of Massachusetts for President and August Gilhaus of New York for Vice-President.

Apr 9 Children's Bureau in Department of Commerce and Labor created by act of Congress. Miss Julia C. Lathrop its first Chief.

Apr 15 Sinking of the *Titanic*, of the Royal Mail Line, on its maiden voyage. Many prominent Americans among 1,500 lost.

Apr 17 Congress sends congratulatory resolution to people of China upon their adoption of republican form of government.

May House Committee on Banking and Currency, Arsene P. Pujo of Louisiana chairman, begins investigation of money powers in U. S.

May 11 Pension Act grants pensions of $30 a month to veterans of Mexican War, and from $13 to $30 to veterans of Civil War.

May 12–18 Socialist party convention meets at Indianapolis. Nominates Eugene V. Debs for President and Emil Seidel of Wisconsin for Vice-President.

May 15 Congress submits to states for ratification proposed amendment (17th) to the Constitution, providing for popular election of Senators.

June U. S. marines land in Cuba to protect American interests.

June 3 German warships on friendly visit welcomed by the President at Hampton Roads, Va.

June 6 Three-Year Homestead Act reduces period of residence required of homesteaders from 5 years to 3.

June 18–22 Republican National Convention meets in Coliseum at Chicago. President Taft and Vice-President Sherman renominated.

June 19 Eight-hour labor law extended to all Federal service by act of Congress.

June 22 Progressive party launched in Orchestra Hall, Chicago, on evening of adjournment of Republican Convention. Presidential nomination offered to Theodore Roosevelt who accepts conditionally.

June 25–July 2 Democratic National Convention meets at Baltimore. On 46th ballot, Woodrow Wilson nominated for President, Thomas R. Marshall of Indiana for Vice-President.

July 10–12 Prohibition party convention meets at Atlantic City. Nominates Eugene W. Chafin and Aaron S. Watkins, candidates of 1908.

July 13 Seat of Senator William L. Lorimer declared vacant by Senate following investigation of bribery charges in his election in Illinois 2 years earlier.

Aug U. S. lands 2,500 marines in Nicaragua to protect American interests during revolution.

Aug 2 Lodge Corollary to Monroe Doctrine, a resolution introduced by Henry Cabot Lodge, July 31, extending scope of Monroe Doctrine to non-European powers, adopted by Senate. Consequence of rumored move by a Japanese company to buy land on strategic Magdalena Bay, Lower California.

Aug 5–7 Progressive party convention meets at Chicago. Theodore Roosevelt nominated for President and Hiram Johnson of California for Vice-President.

Aug 13 Communications Act gives Department of Labor and Commerce control of wireless communication.

Aug 24 Alaska given territorial legislature of 2 houses by act of Congress. First legislature opens at Juneau Mar. 3, 1913.

Aug 24 Panama Canal Act exempts U. S. coastwise shipping from payment of tolls.

Sept U. S. marines land in Santo Domingo to restore order and protect customs service.

Sept 2 President Taft orders 38,000 acres of oil lands in Elk Hills region, Cal., set aside as Naval Petroleum Reserve No. 1. In 1915 President Wilson adds Teapot Dome, Wyo., to naval reserves.

Nov 5 Presidential election. Wilson and Marshall elected by electoral vote of 435, to 88 for Roosevelt and Johnson, 8 for Taft and Butler. Popular vote: Wilson, Democrat, 6,293,454; Roosevelt, Progressive, 4,119,538; Taft, Republican, 3,484,980; Debs, Socialist, 900,672; Chafin, Prohibition, 206,275; Reimer, Socialist Labor, 28,750.

Nov 5 Colorado adopts recall of judicial decisions, by constitutional amendment.

Dec 2 In *United States v. Union Pacific Railroad Co.*, Supreme Court orders Union Pacific and Southern Pacific railroad merger dissolved for violation of Sherman Anti-Trust Act.

Dec 9 Ambassador Bryce, for Great Britain, formally protests against exemption from tolls of U. S. coastwise shipping passing through Panama Canal, as contrary to Hay-Pauncefote Treaty of 1901.

1913

Assembly line technique in manufacturing adopted in plant of Ford Motor Company.

Rockefeller Foundation chartered in New York.

Armory Show in New York puts on International Exhibition of Modern Art, introducing modern movement in America.

Peace Palace at the Hague dedicated, gift of Andrew Carnegie.

Keokuk Dam opened, hydroelectric project on Mississippi River.

George W. Norris of Nebraska enters the Senate.

The New Freedom by Woodrow Wilson, containing major portions of his campaign speeches, published. "An attempt to express the new spirit of our politics."

An Economic Interpretation of the Constitution by Charles A. Beard published.

Jan 1 Parcel post system, established by act of Congress Aug. 24, 1912, put into operation throughout U. S.

Jan 11 President-elect Woodrow Wilson, speaking before Chicago Commercial Club, declares "The business of the United States [must be] set absolutely free of every feature of monopoly."

Feb 13 "Seven Sisters" laws, aimed at better regulation of trusts in New Jersey, signed by Governor Woodrow Wilson.

Feb 14 Immigration Bill, containing literacy test, vetoed by President Taft.

Feb 16 President Taft reaffirms his policy of non-intervention in letter to President Madero of Mexico.

Feb 22 Mobilization of 4,000 troops on Mexican border ordered by War Department.

Feb 23 President Madero shot by fol- lowers of Victoriano Huerta.

Feb 25 Sixteenth Amendment to Con- stitution, permitting Federal income tax,

proclaimed in force by Secretary of State Knox.

Feb 25 Silk workers' strike against improved machinery begins, Paterson, N. J., under I.W.W. Continues for 5 months.

Feb 28 Pujo Committee of House pub- lishes sensational report on the "money trust."

Mar 1 Webb-Kenyon Interstate Liquor Shipment Bill passed over President Taft's veto. First Federal victory of Anti-Saloon League, it forbids interstate shipping of liquor into states where its sale is illegal.

Mar 1 Physical Valuation Act pro- vides that Interstate Commerce Commission shall investigate physical valuation of railroads as basis for rate-making.

Mar 4 Department of Commerce and Labor separated by act of Congress into 2 departments, Commerce and Labor, secretary of each to have Cabinet status.

Mar 4 Protection of migratory game and insectivorous birds provided by act of Congress.

Mar 4 Woodrow Wilson inaugurated President and Thomas R. Marshall Vice-President.

[President Wilson's Cabinet: William J. Bryan, Secretary of State; William G. McAdoo, Secretary of Treasury; Lindley M. Garrison, Secretary of War; Josephus Daniels, Secretary of Navy; Franklin K. Lane, Secretary of Interior; David F. Houston, Secretary of Agriculture; William C. Redfield, Secretary of Commerce; William B. Wilson, Secretary of Labor; Albert S. Burleson, Postmaster General; James C. McReynolds, Attorney General.]

Mar 11 President Wilson announces he will not recognize government of Huerta in Mexico, because of its origin in force and intrigue.

Mar 18 President Wilson refuses gov- ernment endorsement of participation by U. S. bankers in reorganization loan to new Republic of China.

Mar 28 Walter Hines Page offered ambassadorship to Great Britain by President Wilson.

Apr 7 Congress convenes in special session to consider tariff. President Wilson delivers message in person Apr. 8, first President to do so since John Adams.

Apr 22 Underwood Tariff Bill reported from House Committee on Ways and Means, debate in House begins. Bill passes House May 8.

Apr 24 Secretary Bryan's proposed Treaties for Advancement of Peace, socalled "cooling-off treaties," submitted to all governments with diplomatic representatives at Washington. 21 treaties negotiated and ratified.

May 2 President Wilson recognizes Republic of China.

May 19 Webb Alien Land-Holding Bill signed by governor of California in spite of protests by Japan and President Wilson. Prohibits ownership of land in the state by aliens.

May 26 President Wilson makes public attack upon "insidious" tariff lobby seeking changes in Underwood Bill in interest of certain manufacturers.

May 31 Seventeenth Amendment to the Constitution (popular election of Senators) proclaimed in effect by Secretary of State Bryan.

June 23 President Wilson appears be- fore Congress with message urging banking and currency reform.

June 26 Carter Glass introduces bank- ing and currency bill in House. Passes House Sept. 17.

July 1–5 Civil War veterans of Union and Confederate armies meet in reunion at Gettysburg, 50th anniversary of the battle.

July 15 Newlands Act, replacing Erd- man Act of June 1, 1898, sets up Board of Mediation and Conciliation to adjust disputes between interstate railroads and employees.

Aug 27 President Wilson, under pres- sure for intervention, in message to Congress sets forth his "watchful waiting" policy toward Mexico. "We can afford to exercise the self-restraint of a really great nation which realizes its own strength and scorns to misuse it."

Sept   Coal miners' strike begins in southern Colorado. Dec. 1914, it is called off by UMW after unusual violence and Federal intervention.

Oct 3 Underwood-Simmons Tariff Act. Still protectionist in principle, schedules are 10 per cent lower than in Payne-Aldrich Tariff and 100 new items are added to free list.

Oct 10 President Wilson presses but- ton which blows up last obstruction in Panama Canal, the Gamboa Dike.

Oct 27 President Wilson in Mobile address declares his Latin-American policy. U. S. will not meddle in Latin-American affairs in name of Monroe Doctrine nor "again seek one additional foot of territory by conquest."

Nov 1 President Wilson sends ulti- matum to President Huerta of Mexico, demanding his retirement from Mexican government.

Dec 10 Prohibition amendment to the Constitution introduced in House by Representative Richard P. Hobson and in Senate by Senator Morris Sheppard, while a great demonstration by 3,000 persons takes place before the Capitol. Subsequently, amendment dies in committee.

Dec 23 Glass-Owen Federal Reserve Bill, providing for Federal Reserve system, signed by President Wilson.

1914

Cape Cod Canal opened to traffic.

Mount Whitney in California flown over by Silas Christofferson, who sets altitude record of 15,728 feet.

Last known passenger pigeon dies in Cincinnati zoo.

The *New Republic* first published.

Other People's Money by Louis D. Brandeis published.

Jan 5 Henry Ford announces adoption of minimum wage of $5 a day, 8-hour day and profit sharing plan.

Jan 20 President Wilson before joint session of Congress recommends strengthening of anti-trust laws. "Private monopoly is indefensible and intolerable."

Jan 28 Direct wireless communication between Germany and U. S. established.

Feb 3 Embargo on shipment of arms to Mexico revoked by President Wilson in favor of Carranza and Constitutionalists.

Feb 12 Lincoln Memorial in Potomac Park, Washington, begun with breaking of ground.

Mar 5 Repeal of provisions of Panama Canal Act, Aug. 24, 1912, exempting U. S. coastwise vessels from tolls, urged upon Congress in joint session by President Wilson.

Mar 12 Alaska Railroad Act author-izes construction and operation of railroads in territory of Alaska by the government.

Apr 6 Treaty with Colombia signed, expressing "sincere regret" of U. S. that relations between the 2 countries were marred in 1903 and agreeing to pay Colombia $25,000,000 for loss of Panama. Senate does not consent until Apr. 20, 1921.

Apr 9 U. S. marines land at Tampico, Mexico, for supplies and are arrested. [Rear Admiral Mayo, commander, demands apology and salute of U. S. flag. Huerta refuses.]

Apr 20 President Wilson before joint session of Congress asks approval to use armed forces as may be necessary to bring Huerta to terms. By Apr. 22 both houses give assent.

Apr 21 U. S. Marines and sailors seize Vera Cruz and prevent landing of munitions for Huerta from a German ship. U. S. holds Vera Cruz until Nov. 23.

Apr 25 Congress provides for raising of volunteer forces in case of actual or threatened war.

Apr 25 President Wilson accepts offer of Argentina, Brazil and Chile to mediate in dispute with Mexico.

May 8 Smith-Lever Act provides agri-cultural extension work under Department of Agriculture, working through land-grant colleges.

May 15 Colonel Edward M. House sails for Europe on his "Great Adventure," to promote reduction of land and sea armament. Contemplates using armies of Germany, England, Japan and U. S. to develop waste areas of the world. War has come to Europe before he returns, July 29.

May 20–June 30 Niagara Falls Con-ference of representatives of Argentina, Brazil and Chile, with representatives of U. S. and Mexican factions, to solve U. S.-Mexican problem. No positive results other than postponement of military action and elimination of President Huerta who leaves for Spain in July.

June 1 Secretary of Navy Josephus Daniels issues order prohibiting use of alcoholic liquors in the Navy.

June 15 Panama Tolls Act repeals clause in Panama Canal Act of Aug. 24, 1912, exempting U. S. coastwise vessels from tolls.

June 28 Archduke Franz Ferdinand, heir to Austrian throne, assassinated at Sarajevo by young Serb nationalist.

June 28 "Suffragettes march on Capi-tol," newspaper headline of June 29, rivals news of assassination of an Austrian archduke at Sarajevo.

July 15 President Huerta forced from office in Mexico by Carranza.

July 28 Austria-Hungary declares war on Serbia.

July 30 Czar of Russia orders general mobilization.

July 31 New York Stock Exchange closes to avoid panic because of conditions in Europe.

Aug 1 Germany declares war on Rus-sia.

Aug 3 Germany declares war on France.

Aug 4 Formal proclamation by U. S. of neutrality in war between Austria and Serbia, Germany and Russia, Germany and France.

Aug 4 Great Britain declares war on Germany.

Aug 4 German troops invade Belgium.

Aug 5 Formal proclamation by U. S. of neutrality in war between Great Britain and Germany.

Aug 5 U. S. offers mediation to European belligerents.

Aug 5 Bryan-Chamorro Treaty signed with Nicaragua, giving U. S. a right of way for an interoceanic canal, a 99-year lease on Great Corn and Little Corn Islands, and naval base on Gulf of Fonseca for $3,000,000. Senate consents Feb. 18, 1916.

Aug 6 Austria-Hungary declares war on Russia.

Aug 6 U. S. cruiser *Tennessee* leaves New York with $5,000,000 in gold for use of Americans stranded in Europe.

Aug 6 U. S. suggests to European belligerents in identical notes that they adopt Declaration of London, 1909, as code to be applied in all matters of naval warfare.

Aug 6 Death of Mrs. Woodrow Wilson (Ellen Axson Wilson).

Aug 6 President Charles W. Eliot of Harvard proposes in letter to President Wilson "an offensive and defensive alliance with the entente powers, including Japan."

Aug 10 *The Fatherland,* a weekly by German-Americans, George Sylvester Viereck editor, begins publication in New York.

Aug 15 U. S. government declares loans to belligerent powers inconsistent with our neutrality, in letter of Secretary of State Bryan to J. P. Morgan.

Aug 15 Panama Canal formally opened to traffic.

Aug 18 Cotton Futures Act.

Aug 19 President Wilson in message to Senate appeals to the American people to be "neutral in fact as well as in name during these days that are to try men's souls."

Aug 20 British Order in Council makes exceptions to contraband provisions of Declaration of London, striking severe blow at U. S. trade.

Aug 23 Japan declares war on Germany.

Sept 2 Bureau of War Risk Insurance set up in Treasury Department, backed by $5,000,000, to provide insurance for merchant vessels and crews.

Sept 5 Naval operation of one or more wireless stations for transatlantic communication provided for by executive order.

Sept 26 U. S. makes vigorous protest to British Order in Council of Aug. 20.

Sept 26 Federal Trade Commission Act provides machinery for regulation of corporations engaged in commerce.

Oct 15 U. S. government announces it will not forbid extension of credits or shipment of gold by banks to the belligerents, despite Secretary Bryan's letter of Aug. 15.

Oct 15 Clayton Anti-Trust Act.

Oct 22 Revenue Act imposes special taxes to offset decline in import duties brought on by war in Europe.

Oct 22 U. S. formally withdraws insistence upon Great Britain's adherence to Declaration of London, but bases American rights upon existing rules of international law.

Nov 2 Great Britain declares whole of North Sea a military area into which neutral ships will sail at their own risk.

Nov 3 Rockefeller Foundation relief ship *Massapequa* sails with cargo of food for Belgium.

Nov 14 "Christmas ship" *Jason* sails from New York with $3,000,000 worth of gifts for victims of war in Europe.

Nov 16 Federal Reserve System goes into effect with Federal Reserve Bank at head of each of 12 Federal Reserve regions.

Nov 23 U. S. forces withdrawn from Vera Cruz.

Dec 1 National Security League, a preparedness group, organized in New York.

Dec 26 U. S. sends vigorous protest to Great Britain because of her interference with U. S. trade. Protest deflated by German action of same day.

Dec 26 Germany places food supply of empire under government control. [Britain then declares all food stuffs contraband.]

1915

1915–1918, war prosperity in U. S.

AFL numbers 2,000,000 members.

Nonpartisan League organized among farmers of North Dakota under Arthur C. Townley.

"The Birth of a Nation," motion picture, produced by David Wark Griffith. Heightens racial tension.

The Woman Rebel, birth control magazine, first published by Margaret Sanger.

Jan 1 Panama-California Exposition opens at San Diego, Cal.

Jan 12 Proposed woman suffrage amendment defeated in House.

Jan 25 Long distance telephone service between New York and San Francisco inaugurated by Alexander Graham Bell. "Hello Frisco" is song of the year.

Jan 26 Rocky Mountain National Park established by act of Congress.

Jan 28 Immigration Bill with literacy test vetoed by President Wilson.

Jan 28 U. S. vessel *William P. Frye,* loaded with wheat for Great Britain, sunk in South Atlantic by German cruiser.

Jan 30 Colonel Edward M. House sails on *Lusitania* for Europe, as agent of President Wilson in interest of peace.

Feb 4 Germany proclaims war zone about British Isles, which neutral shipping will enter at own peril from submarines. Blockade to begin Feb. 18.

Feb 10 U. S. protests German proclamation of proposed war zone about British Isles: Germany will be held to "strict accountability" if American lives are lost.

Feb 10 U. S. protests Great Britain's use of U. S. flag on British merchant ships. Foreign Minister Sir Edward Grey replies Feb. 20 that the flying of neutral flags to escape enemy action is common practice, employed by Union ships during Civil War.

Feb 20 Panama-Pacific International Exposition at San Francisco opens. Closes Dec. 4.

Mar 4 LaFollette Seamen's Act, to bring order in labor relations in merchant marine.

Mar 11 British Order in Council proclaims blockade of German ports, to be enforced by stopping vessels before they enter North Sea or English Channel. Order also lists contraband.

Mar 28 British ship *Falaba,* carrying passengers and munitions, torpedoed and sunk in Irish Sea with loss of one American life.

Mar 30 U. S. protests British blockade of German ports as interfering with legitimate neutral trade.

Apr 4 German note condemns U. S. as unneutral and as failing to safeguard her legitimate commerce with Germany.

Apr 30 Wireless communication established between Washington and Canal Zone.

Apr 30 President Wilson by executive order creates Naval Petroleum Reserve No. 3, the Teapot Dome in Wyo., 9,481 acres.

May 1 U. S. tanker *Gulflight* torpedoed by German submarine off Scilly Islands, 2 of crew drowned, captain dies from shock.

May 1   German Embassy publishes in New York newspaper a warning to travelers sailing in war zone on ships under British flag that they do so at own risk.

May 7   British Cunard liner *Lusitania* sunk by German submarine off Irish coast. 1,198 lives lost, of which 124 are American.

May 10   President Wilson in address at Philadelphia says, "There is such a thing as a man being too proud to fight. There is such a thing as a nation being so right that it does not need to convince others by force that it is right."

May 13   First *Lusitania* note sent by Secretary of State Bryan to Ambassador Gerard in Germany. It calls upon Germany to disavow the sinking and to make indemnity. U. S. "must hold the Imperial German Government to a strict accountability for any infringements" of rights of U. S. citizens.

May 24   Pan-American Financial Con-ference opens at Washington under presidency of Secretary of Treasury William G. McAdoo.

May 28   Germany's reply to first *Lusi-*tania* note noncommittal, alleging that the *Lusitania* was carrying munitions and was armed, thus justifying the sinking.

June 8   Secretary of State Bryan re-signs, unwilling to sign second *Lusitania* note.

June 9   President Wilson sends second *Lusitania* note to Germany, signed by Acting Secretary Robert Lansing. Takes issue with Germany's contentions and demands definite pledges.

June 17   League to Enforce Peace or-ganized at Independence Hall, Philadelphia, with William H. Taft president. Embraces plan for a league of nations.

June 21   "Grandfather clause" in con-stitutions of Oklahoma and Maryland declared unconstitutional by Supreme Court.

June 23   Robert Lansing appointed Secretary of State.

July 8   Germany replies to President Wilson's second *Lusitania* note that Americans may cross seas safely in well-marked neutral ships, but fails to give definite pledges asked.

July 11   Secretary of State Lansing in memorandum: "Germany must not be allowed to win this war, or to break even, though, to prevent it, this country is forced to take an active part."

July 21   President Wilson's third *Lusi-*tania* note practically an ultimatum. Warns that a repetition of acts in contravention of U. S. rights will be regarded as "deliberately unfriendly."

July 23   Great Britain defends her blockade of German ports as matter of necessity and such as U. S. used in the Civil War.

July 24   Briefcase of Dr. Heinrich Al-bert, director of German propaganda in U. S., containing documents signed by Ambassador Bernstorff and Captain Franz von Papen, when left on New York subway train is snatched up by member of U. S. secret service. Aug. 15, New York *World* begins publication of the documents, revealing German sabotage in U. S.

July 25   U. S. steamship *Leelanaw*, carrying flax, sunk off coast of Scotland by German submarine, which first removed the crew.

July 27   Direct wireless communication completed between U. S. and Japan.

July 28   U. S. Marines land in Haiti to quell revolution. Begins a 19-year occupation.

Aug 5   Latin-American   conference opens at Washington. Representatives of Argentina, Brazil, Chile, Bolivia, Uruguay and Guatemala meet with President Wilson to consider ways of ending chaos in Mexico.

Aug 10   Plattsburg, N. Y., military training camp for civilians inaugurated by General Leonard Wood.

Aug 19 British White Star liner *Arabic,* out from Liverpool for New York, sunk by German submarine without warning. Two Americans lose lives.

Aug 20 Great Britain declares cotton to be absolute contraband of war. October estimate of year's cotton crop in U. S. is 11,000,000 bales.

Sept 1 *Arabic* **pledge given to U. S. by** German Ambassador von Bernstorff: "Liners will not be sunk by our submarines without warning and without safety of the lives of noncombatants, provided that the liners do not try to escape or offer resistance."

Sept 8 Recall of Dr. Constantin Dum-ba, Austro-Hungarian ambassador, demanded by U. S.

Sept 16 Treaty signed with Haiti con-verts that country into a protectorate of U. S. Senate consents Feb. 28, 1916.

Oct 15 A $500,000,000 loan at 5 per cent to British and French governments arranged with U. S. bankers.

Oct 19 U. S. formally recognizes Car-ranza government in Mexico, following Latin-American conference opening Aug. 5.

Oct 21 Secretary of State Lansing in note to Great Britain protests her interference with U. S. shipping and stands for neutral rights.

Nov 7 Italian liner *Ancona* **sunk with-**out warning by Austrian submarine. Among 272 lives lost, 27 are Americans. [Austria assumes responsibility.]

Nov 25 Ku Klux Klan of Civil War days revived under Colonel William J. Simmons of Atlanta, Ga.

Nov 30 Explosion at DuPont powder plant, Wilmington, Del., with death of 31. Sabotage suspected.

Dec 1 Recall of Captain Franz von Papen, military attaché to German Embassy, and Captain Karl Boy-Ed, naval attaché, requested by U. S.

Dec 4 Henry Ford peace ship *Oscar II* sails for Europe, "to get the boys out of the trenches by Christmas."

Dec 7 President Wilson in annual message to Congress recommends standing army of 142,000 and reserve of 400,-000 "disciplined citizens."

Dec 17 Emergency Internal Revenue Act extends for one year Revenue Act of Oct. 22, 1914.

Dec 27 Second Pan-American Scientific Congress opens at Washington.

Dec 27 Iron and steel workers at East Youngstown, Ohio, strike for increase of wages. Jan. 13, 1916, strike ends with 10 per cent wage increase.

Dec 28 Colonel Edward M. House, as representative of President Wilson, sails for Europe for conferences with British, German and French officials.

1916

Over 2,000 strikes and lockouts recorded during first 7 months of the year.

University of Wisconsin establishes model extension service throughout the state.

National Research Council organized by National Academy of Sciences.

Jan 4 U. S. protests British seizure of mail to and from Scandinavian countries.

Jan 6 President Wilson addresses second Pan-American Scientific Congress urging "confidence and trust between the Americas."

Jan 10 General Francisco Villa, rival of Carranza, takes 18 young American mining engineers from train at Santa Ysabel, Mexico, and shoots them.

Jan 24 In *Brushaber v. Union Pacific Railroad Company,* Supreme Court upholds constitutionality of Federal income tax.

Jan 27 President Wilson starts on speaking tour into the West to urge preparedness, ending tour at St. Louis Feb. 3.

Jan 28 Louis D. Brandeis nominated Justice of the Supreme Court by President Wilson. Confirmed by Senate June 1.

Feb 11 Formal notification of intention of Germany and Austria-Hungary to sink armed enemy merchant ships without warning, after Mar. 1, given Ambassador Gerard in Berlin.

Feb 16 German liability for indemnity for American lives lost on *Lusitania* formally announced by Ambassador Bernstorff to Secretary of State Lansing.

Feb 22 Grey Memorandum drafted in London by Colonel E. M. House and Foreign Minister Sir Edward Grey: "Should the Allies accept [the proposal of a conference to put an end to the war] and should Germany refuse it, the United States would probably enter the war against Germany. . . ."

Mar 3 Gore-McLemore Resolution, to prohibit issuance of passports to Americans traveling on ships of belligerent nations, tabled by Senate. Mar. 7, tabled by House. Resolution opposed by President Wilson because it would restrict U. S. rights.

Mar 6 Newton D. Baker appointed Secretary of War to succeed Lindley M. Garrison, resigned.

Mar 9 General Villa with force of Mexican soldiers makes raid upon Columbus, N. Mex., killing 17 Americans.

Mar 15 General John J. Pershing leads punitive raid into Mexico, "to capture Villa dead or alive," with grudging consent of Carranza.

Mar 24 Unarmed French steamer *Sussex* torpedoed in English Channel, 3 American lives lost.

Apr 18 Secretary of State Lansing sends *Sussex* note to Germany: Unless Germany abandons her "submarine warfare against passenger and freight-carrying vessels, the Government of the United States can have no choice but to sever diplomatic relations with the German Empire. . . ."

Apr 19 President Wilson before joint session of Congress reports ultimatum sent to Germany the evening before and asks approval.

Apr 23 Socialist Labor party meets at New York. Nominates 1912 candidate Arthur E. Reimer for President, and Caleb Harrison of Illinois for Vice-President.

May U. S. Marines land in Santo Domingo to restore order. U. S. occupation continues until 1924.

May 4 Germany replies to U. S. note of Apr. 18, in the *Sussex* pledge, that merchant ships "shall not be sunk without warning and without saving human lives unless they attempt to escape or offer resistance," but reserves "complete liberty of decision" unless U. S. insists that Great Britain observe international law regarding the blockade.

May 8 Secretary of State Lansing ac-cepts assurances contained in German note of May 4, but refuses its qualifications.

May 13 Citizens' preparedness parade held in New York.

May 27 President Wilson addresses League to Enforce Peace at Washington, making his first public commitment to league of nations idea.

May 29 U. S. protests Great Britain's refusal to allow importation of German knitting needles needed for manufacture. Feb. 15, 1917, importation allowed.

June 3 National Defense Act provides increase of standing Army by 5 annual stages to 175,000, National Guard to 450,000. National Guard to be federalized and officers' reserve corps created.

June 7–10 Republican National Con-vention meets at Chicago. Nominates Charles Evans Hughes of New York on first ballot for President and Charles Warren Fairbanks of Indiana for Vice-President.

June 7 Progressive party convention meets at Chicago. Nominates Theodore Roosevelt for President, who withdraws in favor of Charles Evans Hughes and Republican party. John M. Parker of Louisiana nominated for Vice-President.

June 14–16 Democratic National Convention meets at St. Louis. Renominates by acclamation Woodrow Wilson for President and Thomas R. Marshall for Vice-President.

June 14 President Wilson leads a preparedness parade down Pennsylvania Avenue in Washington.

June 18 Call issued for mobilization of substantially all state militia for service on Mexican border.

July 9 German submarine *Deutschland* arrives at Baltimore with cargo of dyestuffs. In November, arrives at New London, Conn., with valuable cargo of chemicals, gems and securities.

July 11 Federal Highway Act authorizes Federal aid for 5 years to the states on 50–50 basis in construction of rural post roads.

July 17 Federal Farm Loan Act provides Farm Loan Banks throughout the country and Federal Farm Loan Board.

July 18 Blacklist containing names of about 30 U. S. firms, under British Trading with the Enemy Act, published by London *Official Gazette*. Sharp protest by U. S.

July 19–21 Prohibition party convention meets at St. Paul. Nominates Frank Hanly of Indiana for President and Ira D. Landrith of Massachusetts for Vice-President.

July 22 Preparedness parade in San Francisco marred by explosion of a bomb, killing many. Thomas J. Mooney and Warren K. Billings, radical labor leaders arrested as implicated and finally given life imprisonment.

July 30 Munitions explosion on Black Tom Island, N. J., with property loss of $22,000,000. Sabotage suspected.

Aug 4 Treaty concluded with Denmark by which U. S. acquires Danish West Indies (Virgin Islands) for $25,-000,000. Senate consents Sept. 7.

Aug 14 Railroad operators and employees, in White House conference, begin negotiations on 8-hour day demanded by the latter.

Aug 18 Loans to belligerents by Americans neither approved nor disapproved by the government, according to State Department note.

Aug 25 National Park Service in Department of Interior established by act of Congress.

Aug 29 President Wilson urges before joint session of Congress immediate legislation for 8-hour day to prevent threatened railroad strike scheduled for Sept. 4.

Aug 29 Jones Act grants to Philippines territorial government with promise of independence when ability to govern themselves is demonstrated.

Aug 29 Naval Appropriation Act authorizes appropriation of $313,000,000 for naval purposes and a 3-year building program. Battle of Jutland, May 31, showed value of both dreadnoughts and light cruisers.

Aug 29 Army Appropriation Act authorizes appropriation of $267,000,000 for Army, and creates Council of National Defense, with power to "coordinate industries and resources for national security and welfare."

Sept 1 Keating-Owen Act bars from interstate commerce products of child labor.

Sept 3 Adamson Bill signed by President Wilson. Provides for 8-hour day and time and a half for overtime on interstate railroads. Strike for Labor Day, Sept. 4, called off by railroad brotherhoods on Sept. 2 because the President said he would sign the bill.

Sept 7 U. S. Shipping Board created by act of Congress.

Sept 7 Workmen's Compensation Act brings the 500,000 Federal employees under the system.

Sept 8 Emergency Revenue Act doubles normal rate of income tax and adds inheritance and munitions profits taxes; establishes bi-partisan Tariff Commission to investigate fiscal, administrative and industrial effects of tariff laws. [Frank W. Taussig appointed chairman.]

Fall   U. S. has reached a state of benevolent neutrality toward British blockade of Germany and the North Sea.

Oct 7 German submarine *U-53* arrives in Newport Harbor. Without violation of international law, it sinks 9 British merchant vessels off Nantucket Oct. 8–9.

Oct 26 President Wilson in address before Chamber of Commerce at Cincinnati says, "I believe that the business of neutrality is over. The nature of modern war leaves no state untouched."

Nov 7 Presidential election. Wilson and Marshall re-elected by electoral vote of 277, to 254 for Hughes and Fairbanks. Popular vote: Wilson, Democrat, 9,129,606; Hughes, Republican, 8,538,221; Allan L. Benson, Socialist, 585,113; Hanly, Prohibition, 220,506; Reimer, Socialist Labor, 13,403.

Nov 7 Democrats continue control in both houses in Congressional elections.

Nov 7 Jeanette Rankin of Montana elected to House, first Congresswoman.

Nov 24 Protocol signed with Mexico by joint commissioners of Mexico and U. S. by which General Pershing's troops would be withdrawn and border guarded by the 2 armies, acting independently. [Carranza refuses to accept protocol.]

Nov 27 Federal Reserve Board cautions member banks against further purchase of bonds of warring powers.

Dec 12 Germany publishes note indicating willingness to enter into peace negotiations, but specifying no terms.

Dec 18 President Wilson sends identical note to each of the 14 warring powers asking for their statement of "terms upon which the war might be concluded." Earlier drafting of the note having been prevented by illness, his action is received by the Allies now, following German note, as playing into hands of Germany.

Dec 26 Alfred Zimmermann of German Foreign Office delivers to Ambassador James W. Gerard in Berlin a note

formally accepting invitation of U. S. of Dec. 18, but containing no statement of terms.

Dec 30 German advances toward negotiation of peace of Dec. 12 rejected by the Allies in joint reply.

1917

Motion picture audiences pay over $175,000,000 in admissions.

Jan 8 Webb-Kenyon Act of 1913, prohibiting shipment of liquor to dry states, upheld by Supreme Court as constitutional.

Jan 10 The White House picketed by Congressional Union for Woman Suffrage, to persuade President Wilson to support woman suffrage amendment in Congress.

Jan 10 Allied powers reply to U. S. note of Dec. 18, 1916, stating their war aims.

Jan 22 "Peace without victory" speech by President Wilson before Senate states essential terms of peace in Europe.

Jan 29 President Wilson vetoes for second time Immigration Bill containing literacy test. Feb. 5, it becomes law over the veto.

Jan 31 Germany announces unrestricted submarine warfare to become effective next day.

Jan 31 Mexico adopts a new constitution.

Feb 2 Theodore Roosevelt in letter to Secretary Baker asks permission of War Department to raise a division of volunteers for service in Europe if war breaks out with Germany. Apr. 9, Roosevelt calls at White House to press request. May 11, he is officially informed by Secretary Baker that his services cannot be used.

Feb 3 U. S. steamship *Housatonic* sunk by German submarine after warning is given.

Feb 3 Diplomatic relations cut with Germany, Ambassador Gerard recalled, and Ambassador Bernstorff given his passports.

Feb 5 Pacifist organizations unite under name of Emergency Peace Federation with headquarters in New York.

Feb 5 General Pershing and last 10,-ooo cavalrymen leave Mexico.

Feb 23 Smith-Hughes Act creates Federal Board of Vocational Education for promotion of vocational education in cooperation with the states.

Feb 26 President Wilson asks Congress for legislation authorizing arming of merchant ships.

Feb 28 Armed Merchant Ship Bill introduced. Filibuster by "little group of willful men," as President Wilson calls them, begins in Senate, lasting until Mar. 3, when session closes without action.

Mar 1 Zimmermann note, addressed to German minister in Mexico and intercepted by British Naval Intelligence, Jan. 16, published by Department of State: German Foreign Secretary offers Mexico aid in recovery of states of Texas, New Mexico and Arizona, plus financial assistance in exchange for Mexican aid in case of war between Germany and U. S. Also, Mexico is to urge Japan to shift to German side.

Mar 2 Puerto Ricans granted citizenship and manhood suffrage by Puerto Rican Civil Government Act, the Jones Act.

Mar 3 Special Preparedness Fund Act provides for special fund for military and naval purposes to be raised by excess-profits and increased inheritance taxes.

Mar 3 Ambassador Henry P. Fletcher presents credentials at Mexico City. Diplomatic relations renewed with Mexico.

Mar 5 Woodrow Wilson and Thomas R. Marshall inaugurated for second terms. Wilson maintains Cabinet of first term.

Mar 5 Ambassador Walter H. Page cables President Wilson from London that "France and England must have a large enough credit in the United States to prevent collapse of world trade."

Mar 8 Senate cloture rule adopted by special session of the Senate, permitting a majority to terminate debate.

Mar 11 Carranza elected president of Mexico. President Wilson hastily recognizes the new government.

Mar 12 President Wilson by executive order authorizes arming of merchant ships bound for submarine zone.

Mar 12 U.S. unarmed merchant ship *Algonquin* sunk by German submarine, without warning.

Mar 15 News of Russian Revolution reaches Washington. Mar. 15, Czar Nicholas II abdicates; Mar. 16, Provisional Government assumes power.

Mar 18 News arrives of sinking of 3 more American ships by German submarines.

Mar 19 In *Wilson v. New,* Supreme Court, 5–4, declares Adamson Act, Sept. 3, 1916, constitutional.

Mar 20 Members of Cabinet, in regular session, all agree war is inevitable.

Mar 21 President Wilson calls special session of Congress for Apr. 2 to receive message on "grave questions of national policy."

Mar 21 Standard Oil steamer *Healdton* sunk by submarine, without warning, in safety zone off coast of Holland.

Mar 22 New government in Russia recognized by U. S., first nation to do so.

Mar 24 Commercial Economy Board created by Council of National Defense.

Apr 2 President Wilson before special session of Congress asks for declaration of war against Germany. "The world must be made safe for democracy."

Apr 4 Senate passes war resolution, 82–6.

Apr 6 House at 3 A.M. concurs in war resolution, 373–50.

Apr 6 President Wilson shortly after 1 P.M., signs proclamation that a "state of war exists between the United States and the Imperial German Government."

Apr 7 Socialist party in convention at Chicago passes resolutions against participation in the war, causing split in Party. John Spargo and Upton Sinclair among seceders.

Apr 8 Samuel Gompers pledges support of AFL to the war effort.

Apr 8 Austria-Hungary severs diplomatic relations with U. S.; Turkey follows Apr. 20.

Apr 9 General Munitions Board created by Council of National Defense, Frank A. Scott chairman.

Apr 14 Committee on Public Information, consisting of Secretaries of State, War and Navy, and George Creel, chairman, appointed by the President.

Apr 16 Emergency Fleet Corporation of U. S. Shipping Board chartered under laws of District of Columbia, Charles M. Schwab chairman.

Apr 19 Steamship *Mongolia* of American Line, with first shot of the war, repels submarine attack off English coast.

Apr 22 British War Mission headed by Foreign Secretary Arthur J. Balfour arrives in Washington.

Apr 24 Emergency Loan Act, the "Liberty Loan Act," authorizes bond issue of $5,000,000,000 at 3.5 per cent, $2,000,000,000, earmarked for costs of war, $3,000,000,000 for loans to Allies.

Apr 25 French War Mission headed by M. Viviani and including Marshall Joffre arrives in Washington.

Apr 25 Loan of $200,000,000 made to Great Britain under Liberty Loan Act. By Nov. 30, 1918, over $7,000,000,000, loaned to governments of Allies.

May 2 First Liberty Loan, to secure $2,000,000,000, offered to public. Oversubscribed by one-half when closed June 15.

May 4 Flotilla of U. S. destroyers reaches Queenstown, Ireland, to aid Admiral William S. Sims in blockade of Germany.

May 10 Red Cross War Council established, Henry P. Davison chairman. One week's campaign in June, for $100,000,000, over-subscribed.

May 15 Officers' training camps opened. First class of 1st and 2nd lieutenants graduates in August.

May 16 Aircraft Production Board established, Howard E. Coffin, chairman.

May 18 Selective Service Act provides for enrollment of all men between 21 and 31, from which men shall be drafted for the Army.

May 18 First of the American Expeditionary Forces, under command of General Pershing, ordered by the President to proceed to France.

May 23 Italian War Mission under Prince Udine reaches Washington.

May 30 People's Council for Democracy and Terms of Peace organized in New York by Pacifists and Socialists.

June 5 Registration Day. 9,586,508 registered for military service in local draft boards.

June 13 General John J. Pershing and his staff arrive in Paris.

June 13 U. S. 1st Division embarks for France. Begins landing at San Nazaire June 26.

June 15 Espionage Act provides penalties for obstruction of war operations.

July 2 Race riots in East St. Louis, Ill., 37 killed.

July 4 General Pershing, with initial command of 14,500 troops, parades through streets of Paris.

July 4 First government training field for aviators opened at Rantoul, Ill.

July 6 General Pershing informs War Department that 1,000,000 men should be sent to Europe by May 1918.

July 9 President Wilson issues embargo proclamation, placing export of fuel, foodstuffs, iron, steel and war materials under government control.

July 20 First drawing of numbers for draft under Selective Service Act made by Secretary of War Baker, first number being 258.

July 24 Congress appropriates $640,000,000 for military aviation.

July 28 War Industries Board created, Frank A. Scott chairman. A reorganization of General Munitions Board, to have charge of all war purchases.

Aug 5 National Guard drafted en masse into U. S. Army.

Aug 6 Mrs. James (Ma) Ferguson elected governor of Texas, first woman governor in the country.

Aug 10 Lever Act establishes control over food and fuel.

Aug 10 Herbert Hoover appointed Food Administrator by President Wilson. "Food will win the war," the slogan.

Aug 23 Harry A. Garfield appointed Fuel Administrator by President Wilson.

Sept 1 General Pershing establishes general headquarters at Chaumont, adjacent to the Toul sector.

Sept 1 Grain Corporation of the Food Administration goes into operation. It buys, stores, transports and sells grain, fixes price of wheat, and prohibits use of food products in making of distilled beverages. Wheat crop of 1917 bought at $2.20 a bushel, $2.00 guaranteed for 1918.

Sept 5 Draftees for new national Army begin assembling at training camps.

Sept 12 The Liberty Motor, America's chief contribution to war in the air, announced by Secretary of War Baker as having passed perfection test.

Sept 21 Major General Tasker H. Bliss appointed Chief of Staff, U. S. Army.

Oct 1 Second Liberty Loan drive begins, offering $3,000,000,000 at 4 per cent. Over-subscribed by half at end of drive, Oct. 27.

Oct 3 War Revenue Act doubles income tax of 1916 and widely extends the excise to nearly everything in sight. Letter postage raised to 3 cents, postcards to 2.

Oct 6 Bureau of War Risk Insurance of Treasury Department enlarged by act of Congress to provide war risk insurance for members of all armed forces and their dependents.

Oct 6 Trading with the Enemy Act provides for control of U. S. imports and exports and allows seizure of property of enemy aliens.

Oct 12 Censorship Board created by executive order to administer censorship of communications between U. S. and any foreign country, by authority of Trading with the Enemy Act.

Oct 12 War Trade Board created by executive order, with Vance McCormick chairman, by authority of Trading with the Enemy Act.

Oct 12 A. Mitchell Palmer appointed Alien Property Custodian by executive order.

Oct 15 Shipping Board requisitions all privately owned ocean-going ships for government use.

Oct 17 Transport *Antilles,* returning from France, torpedoed by German submarine with loss of 67 lives.

Oct 21 First U. S. detachments enter front line trenches under French supervision in Sommerviller sector, northeast of Lunéville.

Oct 25 Equal Suffrage as a state issue endorsed by President Wilson in address at the White House before group of New York State Woman Suffrage Party.

Oct 27 Twenty thousand women march in suffrage parade in New York.

Oct 27 U. S. soldiers in France fire their first shots in trench warfare.

Nov 2 Lansing-Ishii Agreement signed in which U. S. admits that "territorial propinquity" gives Japan special interests in China.

Nov 6 New York adopts constitutional amendment granting equality of suffrage, first eastern seaboard state to do so.

Nov 6–7 Bolshevist *coup d'état* overthrows Provisional Government, puts extreme Left in control of Russian revolution and Lenin and Trotsky into power. [U. S. refuses recognition.]

Nov 15 Electric signs restricted throughout the country by order of Fuel Administrator Nov. 13.

Nov 16 Enemy alien registration required by Presidential proclamation.

Nov 29–Dec 3 Inter-Allied Conference meets at Paris to formulate statement of war aims. Fails in agreement. Colonel House and delegation represent U. S.

Dec 3 War Savings and Thrift Stamps go on sale.

Dec 7 Forty-second or Rainbow Division, made up of picked units from National Guard of all states, has arrived in France. Colonel Douglas MacArthur a member.

Dec 7 U. S. declares war against Austria-Hungary.

Dec 15 War Council created in War Department.

Dec 18 Eighteenth Amendment to Constitution approved by Congress and sent to states for ratification.

Dec 28 President Wilson takes over control of all railroads, appointing William G. McAdoo Director General.

1918

Economic prosperity continues.

Jan 7 Constitutionality of Selective Service Act upheld by Supreme Court in *Selective Draft Law Cases.*

Jan 8 President Wilson announces the war aims of U. S. in Fourteen Points speech before Congress.

Jan 16 Harry A. Garfield, Fuel Administrator, to conserve coal for ships, orders closing of all manufacturing plants east of the Mississippi, not making war essentials, for 5 days and 9 subsequent Mondays.

Jan 26 Herbert C. Hoover, Food Administrator, asks voluntary observance of wheatless Mondays and Wednesdays, meatless Tuesdays, porkless Thursdays and Saturdays, and use of Victory bread.

Feb 5 British ship *Tuscania*, carrying 2,000 U. S. troops, sunk by submarine off coast of Ireland, 210 lives lost. Only transport lost with U. S. troops during the war.

Feb 8 First issue of *Stars and Stripes*, official weekly publication of American Expeditionary Forces in France, appears.

Feb 11 President Wilson before joint session of Congress announces the Four Principles, supplementary to the Fourteen Points, as basis for peace with the enemy.

Feb 12 All Broadway theaters in New York closed to save coal.

Feb 21 Price of 1918 wheat crop proclaimed at $2.20 by the President. Sept. 2, he sets price of $2.26 for 1919 crop.

Feb 25 President Wilson orders construction of Muscle Shoals dam on the Tennessee to produce power for manufacture of explosives and nitrates.

Mar U. S. troops reported in action on 4 sectors of Western front in France: Lorraine, Champagne, Alsace and near the Chemin des Dames.

Mar 3 Bolshevists sign Brest-Litovsk Treaty with Germany.

Mar 4 Bernard Baruch takes over chairmanship of reorganized War Industries Board.

Mar 6 All Army canteen work in France taken over by YMCA.

Mar 6 Dry zones extending 5 miles around naval training stations ordered by Secretary of Navy Josephus Daniels.

Mar 10 Secretary of War Baker arrives in France to get "complete view" of war situation.

Mar 20 War Cabinet begins weekly meetings, attended by Secretaries of War and Navy and the 6 War Board heads.

Mar 21 Railroad Control Act provides for Federal control of railroads, to end not later than 1 year and 9 months after ratification of a treaty of peace.

Mar 25 Karl Muck, German director of Boston Symphony Orchestra, arrested as enemy alien.

Mar 26 French General Ferdinand Foch placed in supreme command of Allied armies.

Mar 28 General Pershing offers to General Foch all U. S. forces ready for service, to be used where needed.

Mar 31 Daylight Saving Time goes into effect in U. S.

Apr 5 War Finance Corporation created, with fund of $500,000,000 for financing essential industries, by act of Congress.

Apr 6 Third Liberty Loan drive for $3,000,000,000, with interest at 4.5 per cent, begins.

Apr 8 National War Labor Board appointed by the President. The Board, with ex-President Taft and Frank P. Walsh co-chairmen, will act as court of last resort for labor disputes.

Apr 10 Webb-Pomerene Act exempts export associations from restraints of anti-trust law.

Apr 16 Charles M. Schwab named Director General of Emergency Fleet Corporation.

May Public reconciliation of William H. Taft and Theodore Roosevelt occurs in dining room of Hotel Blackstone, Chicago, notice to the world that Republican party is again united.

May 13 War Labor Policies Board appointed, with Felix Frankfurter chairman.

May 15 Daily airmail service between Washington and New York opens.

May 16 Sedition Act, amending Espionage Act of 1917, provides penalties for bringing into "contempt, scorn, contumely, or disrepute," by speech or publication, U. S. form of government, armed forces, flag or military uniform.

May 20 Overman Act gives to the President greatly expanded powers, act to remain in force until 6 months after end of the war.

May 20 Division of Military Aeronautics and Bureau of Aircraft Production created by President Wilson.

May 23 Work or Fight order given by War Department, effective July 1. New Jersey, New York and Rhode Island passed similar legislation earlier in year.

May 24 General Peyton C. March appointed Chief of Staff of U. S. Army.

May 25 Director General of Railroads McAdoo in General Order No. 27 announces increase of wages for 2,000,000 railroad employees.

May 28 U. S. 1st Division, operating with the French, wins first U. S. military success by taking village of Cantigny near Mondidier.

May 28 American Railway Express Company formed by merging 4 companies, and placed under Federal management by order of Director General of Railroads McAdoo.

May 31 Conscientious objectors may be furloughed, without pay, for agricultural service, by order of Secretary of War Baker.

June North Sea mine barrage begun by U. S. ships, laying mines between Orkney Islands and coast of Norway.

June 3 In *Hammer v. Dagenhart*, Supreme Court rules Keating-Owen child labor law of 1916 unconstitutional, as encroachment upon state rights.

June 4 U. S. 2nd Division, with the French, break German advance near Chateau-Thierry.

June 5 Second Registration Day adds another 750,000 to draft list, those who reached their 21st birthday since June 5, 1917.

June 25 Belleau Wood, after action of 2 weeks with 9,500 casualties, fully in American hands.

June 27 Smith-Sears Vocational Rehabilitation Act provides for vocational rehabilitation of disabled service men.

June 28 Military Board of Allied Supply meets for first time in Paris. Its U. S. member is Charles G. Dawes, General Purchasing Agent for the A.E.F.

June 30 Eugene V. Debs arrested in Cleveland on charge of interfering with recruiting. Sept. 14, sentenced to 10 years' imprisonment.

July U. S. Housing Corporation formed, under law of New York, by Secretary of Labor Wilson.

July 1 Secretary of War Baker reports to the President that 1,019,000 men have been embarked for France.

July 1 Sugar rationing system goes into effect, 2 pounds per month per person.

July 4 President Wilson in address at Mt. Vernon announces the Four Ends for which U. S. and the Allies are fighting. "What we seek is the reign of law, based upon the consent of the governed and sustained by the organized opinion of mankind."

July 4 Ninety-five ships launched in U. S. shipyards on this day.

July 16 Government control of telephone and telegraph authorized by joint resolution of Congress.

July 18–Aug 6 Second Battle of the Marne. U. S. force of 250,000 with French Army regain ground between Rheims and Soissons. Allied counteroffensive begun.

July 19 German retreat across the Marne begins.

July 21 U. S. and French forces retake Chateau-Thierry.

July 24 Four lightless nights of each week, beginning on this date, ordered by Fuel Administration to conserve winter fuel.

Aug Ten thousand Americans join with the Allies in armed occupation of Vladivostok and its hinterland in Siberia, lasting until Jan. 1920.

Aug 10 General Pershing, with consent of General Foch, assumes command of U. S. 1st Army at La Ferte-sous-Jouarre.

Aug 17 A hundred I.W.W. leaders found guilty of conspiracy against prosecution of war, in court of Judge Kenesaw Landis, Chicago. Heavy sentence of imprisonments and fines sustained by U. S. Circuit Court of Appeals, Chicago, Oct. 5, 1920.

Sept Archangel-Murmansk campaign in Northern Russia begins, lasting until May 1919. 5,000 Americans, with the Allies, intervene to protect ammunition depot; end by supporting White Russians against Bolsheviks.

Sept 10 Airmail carried from Chicago to New York in 12 hours, 55 minutes, completed in one day for first time.

Sept 12 Third draft registration held, for men between 18 and 45, under Man Power Act of Aug. 31. Brings total registration to 24,234,021.

Sept 12–14 Battle of St. Mihiel conducted succesfully by General Pershing's forces against German position, first independent operation of U. S. 1st Army. Eliminates St. Mihiel salient and opens up railroads between Verdun and Toul.

Sept 16 Austria-Hungary asks for peace conference in note to Great Britain and U. S. President Wilson in curt reply declares U. S. has already made its position clear.

Sept 26–Nov 11 Battle of the Meuse-Argonne, in which 1,200,000 U. S. troops are thrown against German position. 47 days in Meuse Valley and Argonne Forest cost more American lives than all the rest of the war, 120,000.

Sept 27 President Wilson, speaking at opening of Fourth Liberty Loan, New York City, commits himself to a league of nations as "indispensable instrument" of peace settlement, and adds Five Particulars to the Fourteen Points.

Sept 28 Fourth Liberty Loan campaign opens for $6,000,000,000 at 4.25 per cent interest. Campaign closes Oct. 19, loan oversubscribed.

Oct Epidemic of influenza spreads among armed forces and civilians in U. S. as in Europe.

Oct 1 Resolution providing for Woman Suffrage Amendment rejected by Senate for third time. Was passed by House Jan. 10.

Oct 1 Student Army Training Corps opens in over 500 colleges.

Oct 3 Prince Maximilian of Baden, newly appointed German Chancellor, addresses request for armistice to President Wilson. Officially presented through Swiss chargé Oct. 7.

Oct 8 President Wilson replies to Germany with questions as to exact meaning of Chancellor's note of Oct. 3.

Oct 12 Prince Maximilian sends second peace note to President Wilson: German government accepts terms of President Wilson's Jan. 8 address and subsequent addresses.

Oct 14 President Wilson replies to second German note: Armistice must be determined by military advisers, German armies must cease their illegal and inhumane practices, and arbitrary government in Germany must be set aside.

Oct 20 Third German peace note accepts President Wilson's terms.

Oct 23 President Wilson in note to Germany consents to transmit armistice request to the Allies.

Oct 25 President Wilson calls for return of Democratic majority to both houses of Congress. [Republicans draft reply accusing President Wilson of using the war to party advantage.]

Nov 4 Austria-Hungary surrenders.

Nov 5 President Wilson informs German government of readiness of General Foch to deliver armistice terms to agents of the enemy if requested.

Nov 5 Republican majorities returned to both houses of Congress in mid-term election.

Nov 7 U. S. forces reach Sedan at far edge of Argonne Forest but are ordered not to take it.

Nov 7 False Armistice celebrated in U. S.

Nov 8 German envoys receive General Foch's terms of armistice in his train in Compiègne Forest.

Nov 9 Kaiser Wilhelm II abdicates and flees to Holland.

Nov 11 Armistice Day. Armistice signed at 5 A.M., Paris time, in General Foch's train in Forest of Compiègne. Hostilities cease at 11 A.M. President Wilson reads terms before joint session of Congress, announcing that the war is at an end. [Cost to U. S. of World War I, 1917–1918: numbers engaged, Army, Navy, Marines, 4,609,190; total deaths, 130,-274; total wounded, not mortal, 203,-460; total casualties, 333,734; cost in dollars, $41,755,000,000. *Source: Departments of Defense and Treasury.*]

Nov 21 War Prohibition Act prohibits, until demobilization is completed, manufacture of intoxicating liquors from May 1, 1919, and sale of intoxicating liquors from June 30, 1919.

Nov 22 Lightless nights ban lifted by Fuel Administrator.

Dec 1 First returning U. S. troops arrive in New York Harbor on British transport *Mauretania*.

Dec 2 President Wilson announces before joint session of Congress his intention of going to Europe.

Dec 4 President Wilson and U. S. delegates leave New York on the *George Washington* for the Peace Conference; arrive Dec. 14.

Dec 8 Submerged steel net, placed across the Narrows, New York Harbor, when U. S. entered the war, is lifted.

Dec 13 Units of U. S. 3rd Army cross the Rhine. As American occupation forces in Germany, set up headquarters tabloid, first published.

Dec 22 All food regulations suspended by Food Adminstration, effective Dec. 23.

Dec 25 President Wilson is with U. S. troops at Chaumont.

Dec 26 President Wilson arrives in England for 5-day sojourn.

1919

Year opens with business recession, but ends with post-war boom.

Turbulent year for industry. Some 4,-000,000 men are on strike or lockout during year.

Institute of International Education established under Carnegie Endowment for International Peace.

Dearborn *Independent* first published by Henry Ford, anti-semitic in tone.

New York *Daily News,* first illustrated tabloid, first published.

Jan 1 War Industries Board terminated, first of wartime agencies to end.

Jan 3 President Wilson arrives in Rome for 4-day sojourn in Italy.

Jan 6 Colonel Theodore Roosevelt, ex-President, dies at Sagamore Hill, Oyster Bay, N. Y.

Jan 12 President Wilson meets in Paris with representatives of principal Allies in preliminary caucus, the Council of Ten.

Jan 16 Eighteenth Amendment ratified by Nebraska, 36th state to ratify.

Jan 18 Peace Conference opens officially with first plenary session in Clock Room of the Quai d'Orsay. U. S. delegation consists of the President, Secretary of State Lansing, Colonel House, Henry White and General Tasker H. Bliss.

Jan 25 Second plenary session of Peace Conference. President Wilson's proposal that the matter of a league of nations receive priority is approved. He is appointed chairman of a committee to draft agreement for a league.

Jan 29 Eighteenth Amendment (Prohibition) proclaimed, to become effective Jan. 16, 1920.

Feb 7 Plumb plan for government ownership of railroads and their operation shared by employees presented before Senate Interstate Commerce Committee by Glenn E. Plumb, counsel for railroad brotherhoods.

Feb 14 President Wilson presents the Covenant of the League of Nations at third plenary session of Peace Conference.

Feb 15 President Wilson sails for U. S. from Brest for close of Congress. Opposition to proposed League of Nations appears in U. S. before he arrives.

Feb 20 Victor L. Berger, editor of Socialist *Milwaukee Leader,* indicted for conspiracy to violate Espionage Act, sentenced to 20 years imprisonment by Judge Kenesaw Landis. Sentence later set aside.

Feb 24 President Wilson lands at Boston. Delivers address in Mechanics' Hall, Governor Calvin Coolidge presiding. President Wilson declares, "Arrangements of the present peace cannot stand a generation unless they are guaranteed by the united forces of the civilized world."

Feb 24 War Revenue Act levies taxes on incomes, excess-profits, estates and products of child labor.

Feb 25 A hundred million dollars voted by Congress for European relief fund.

Feb 26 Grand Canyon National Park, Ariz., established by act of Congress.

Feb 26 President Wilson meets members of Senate and House committees on Foreign Relations at the White House for dinner and conference on proposed League of Nations.

Feb 28 Senator Henry Cabot Lodge delivers two and a half hour set oration in Senate against proposed Covenant of League of Nations. Senator Lodge spearhead of the opposition.

Mar 2 "Round robin," signed by 39 Senators and Senators-elect, declares that only after peace is established should the negotiators concern themselves with a League of Nations.

Mar 2 Herbert Hoover appointed Director General of American Relief Administration by President Wilson.

Mar 3 In *Schenck v. United States,* an espionage case, Supreme Court justifies exception to constitutional guarantee of freedom of speech. Justice Oliver W. Holmes says, "When a nation is at war, many things that might be said in times of peace are such a hindrance to its effort that their utterance will not be endured so long as men fight. . . ."

Mar 4 President Wilson addresses audience of 5,000 at Metropolitan Opera House, New York, on eve of return to Europe, and throws down the gauntlet to "round robin" signers. Ex-President William H. Taft also speaks in favor of League of Nations.

Mar 5 President Wilson sails again for Peace Conference in Paris. Arrives Mar. 14.

Mar 5 A. Mitchell Palmer becomes Attorney General.

Mar 10 Supreme Court unanimously sustains constitutionality of conviction of Eugene V. Debs under Espionage Act. [Debs sent to Atlanta Federal Prison.]

Mar 15 American Legion organized in Paris by Colonel Theodore Roosevelt, Jr. Incorporated by act of Congress Sept. 16.

Apr 21 Victory Loan campaign opens. $4,500,000,000 offered at 4.75 per cent. [Oversubscribed by $750,000,000.]

Apr 23 President issues statement opposing the ceding of Fiume to Italy.

Apr 28 Revised Covenant of League of Nations, containing amendments proposed by ex-President Taft and others, presented to plenary session of Peace Conference and voted into Treaty.

May 7 German delegates seated at Peace Conference for first time and presented with Treaty.

June 5 Woman Suffrage Amendment to Constitution (19th), adopted by joint resolution of Congress, is sent to states for ratification.

June 9 Draft of Peace Treaty, brought from Paris by *Tribune* correspondent, published in Chicago *Tribune.* Same day, Senator Borah presents draft in Senate.

June 28 Treaty of Peace signed by U. S. and Allies with Germany in Hall of Mirrors at Versailles.

June 28 Tripartite treaty of guarantee signed with France by President Wilson and Prime Minister Lloyd George promising aid against Germany if needed. Submitted to U. S. Senate July 29, never seriously considered by it.

June 29 President Wilson sails on the *George Washington* from Brest for U. S. Lands at Hoboken, N. J., July 8.

June 29 Prohibition under War Prohibition Act of Nov. 21, 1918, goes into effect at midnight, to continue until end of demobilization.

July 1 Daily airmail service inaugurated between New York and Chicago.

July 10 President Wilson submits to Senate for ratification the Versailles Treaty with League Covenant tied in. At this time public sentiment throughout the country is clearly in favor of acceptance of the Treaty.

July 11 Army reduced to average strength of 325,000 by act of Congress.

July 14 Trade relations with Germany resumed with authorization of Department of State.

July 14–Sept 10 Peace Treaty in Foreign Relations Committee of Senate for analysis, public hearings and purposeful delay.

July 19 Race riots in Washington break out with attacks by white soldiers and sailors upon Negro quarters.

July 27   Race riots in Chicago begin
upon Lake Michigan bathing beach and
spread into Black Belt; 15 whites and 23
Negroes killed. Such riots occur in 26
American cities during year.

July 31   Telephone and telegraph sys-
tems returned to private operation.

Aug 8   President Wilson appears be-
fore Congress to urge attack upon high
cost of living. Has increased in New
York City 79 per cent since 1914, according to Bureau of Labor Statistics.

Aug 19   Foreign Relations Committee
of Senate meets with President Wilson
at the White House at his invitation,
questioning him for three and a half
hours.

Sept 1   Communist party meets at Chi-
cago for first convention. Chiefly Rus-
sian-speaking, it forms American section
of Third or Russian International.

Sept 2   Communist Labor party organ-
ized at Chicago by Socialist left-wingers,
not accepted by organizing Communist
party.

Sept 3   President Wilson leaves for
Western speaking tour in support of
Versailles Treaty and League of Nations.

Sept 9   UMW, with 2,000 delegates,
meets in convention at Cleveland under
leadership of John L. Lewis, higher
wages their major concern.

Sept 9   Boston police go on strike. Sept.
12, Governor Calvin Coolidge sends
state militia to patrol Boston. Sept. 14,
he telegraphs Samuel Gompers, AFL
leader, "There is no right to strike
against the public safety by anybody,
anywhere, any time."

Sept 10   Senator Lodge submits to Sen-
ate report of Foreign Relations Committee on Versailles Treaty, presenting
45 amendments and 4 reservations. Sept.
11, Senator Gilbert M. Hitchcock presents minority report calling for ratification without change.

Sept 10   Republican Senators Hiram
W. Johnson and William E. Borah begin Western tour at Chicago, following
President Wilson and speaking against
ratification of Versailles Treaty.

Sept 10   U. S. 1st Division, back from
Europe, General Pershing at its head,
marches up Fifth Avenue, New York, in
greatest of 1919 parades.

Sept 22   Great steel strike starts in
Gary, Ind., to force U. S. Steel Corporation to recognize unions. Jan. 8, 1920,
strike called off, a failure.

Sept 26   President Wilson, after 40th
speech of his campaign in support of
Treaty of Versailles, at Pueblo, Colo.,
collapses as his train speeds toward
Wichita, Kan.

Oct 2   King Albert, Queen Elizabeth
and Crown Prince Leopold of Belgium
arrive in U. S. on good-will mission.

Oct 6   National Industrial Conference
called by President Wilson meets in
Washington. [With the President ill
and both labor and management un-
yielding, conference ends, a failure.]

Oct 8   Sixty-three army airplanes start
in first aerial derby from Long Island to
San Francisco and return. Eight complete the run after 10 days.

Oct 28   Prohibition Enforcement (Vol-
stead) Act passed by Congress over President's veto. To go into effect Jan. 1920,
it defines intoxicating beverages as those
containing a half of one per cent alco-
hol.

Oct 29   International Labor Confer-
ence, authorized by Versailles Treaty,
opens at Washington. [Creates International Labor Organization (ILO).]

Nov 1   Bituminous coal strike begins
under lead of John L. Lewis and UMW.
Nov. 9, Attorney General Palmer secures
injunction under wartime powers of
Lever Act, and strike ends.

Nov 10   In *Abrams v. United States,*
Supreme Court upholds conviction of
Russian propagandists endeavoring to
defeat American military plans in Europe. Justices Holmes and Brandeis dissent in defense of right of free speech.

Nov 10   Edward, Prince of Wales, ar-
rives in U. S. from Canada on friendly
visit.

Nov 10 Victor Berger, Socialist member of House of Representatives, unseated by House. Re-elected by his Wisconsin district in December, his seat again declared vacant by House, January 1920.

Nov 19 Versailles Treaty fails to receive two-thirds majority in Senate: with reservations of Senator Lodge, 55–39; on Senator Hitchcock's resolution with 5 reservations, 51–41; for Treaty as signed, 53–38.

Dec 21 Two hundred and forty-nine Russians deported on transport *Buford*, part of Attorney General Palmer's Red hunt of 1919–1920.

Dec 24 Railroads returned to private control by proclamation of President Wilson, to take effect Mar. 1, 1920.

1920

Population, 105,710,620. Urban population for first time outstrips rural.

Year opens with prosperity, followed by recession and depression.

National League of Women Voters organized.

American Farm Bureau Federation organized.

Jan 1 Red raids in scores of cities by Department of Justice agents result in thousands of arrests, mostly of Russians. Anti-Red hysteria continues.

Jan 4 French government grants permission for removal to U. S. of bodies of 20,000 American soldiers buried in France.

Jan 16 First meeting of Council of League of Nations, called by President Wilson, opens in Paris.

Jan 16 Prohibition Amendment (18th) goes into effect at midnight.

Feb 13 Resignation of Secretary of State Robert Lansing accepted by President Wilson. Bainbridge Colby succeeds him Mar. 23.

Feb 28 Esch-Cummins Transportation Act authorizes creation of Railroad Labor Board, promotion of railroad consolidation by Interstate Commerce Commission, and immediate return of railroads to private operation.

Mar 1 In *United States v. United States Steel Corporation*, Supreme Court decides that the Corporation does not constitute an illegal monopoly.

Mar 1 Commercial radio stations released by Navy from war-time control.

Mar 2 Manufacture of 3.5 per cent beer permitted by act of New Jersey Legislature.

Mar 19 Versailles Treaty fails second and final time in Senate, 49–35. To 14 reservations of Senator Lodge was added a 15th favoring self-determination of Ireland.

Mar 20 Senator Truman H. Newberry convicted for violation of Corrupt Practices Act in Senatorial election, 1918. Sentenced to 2 years' imprisonment and $10,000 fine. Conviction reversed by Supreme Court May 2, 1921. Senate votes him entitled to his seat Jan. 12, 1922.

Apr Last of American forces arrive home from Siberia.

Apr 1 Five members of New York Legislature expelled, being members of Socialist party. Re-elected, they are again unseated in September.

May Government guarantee on price of wheat removed by end of May. Steady fall of prices begins.

May Communist and Communist Labor parties unite in United Communist party. Name changed to Workers' Party Dec. 1921.

May 5 Nicola Sacco and Bartolomeo Vanzetti arrested, accused of murder of shoe factory paymaster in Braintree, Mass., in April. Convicted on flimsy evidence, 1921, they are executed Aug. 23, 1927. Part of anti-Red hysteria.

May 5–10 Socialist Labor party meets in convention at New York. Nominates W. W. Cox of St. Louis for President and August Gilhaus of Brooklyn for Vice-President.

May 8–14 Socialist party convention meets at New York. Nominates Eugene V. Debs for President for fifth time, and Seymour Stedman for Vice-President. Eugene Debs conducts campaign from Federal prison, Atlanta.

May 27 Joint resolution of Congress declaring war with Germany at an end vetoed by President Wilson.

June 1 U. S. mandate over Armenia, requested by League of Nations Council, voted down by Senate.

June 4 Army Reorganization Act provides for peace-time Army of 298,000.

June 5 Merchant Marine Act continues Shipping Board with authority to dispose of wartime merchant fleet to private owners and to operate those not sold.

June 7 In 7 *National Prohibition Cases,* Supreme Court rules validity of 18th Amendment and Volstead Act and declares invalid state laws defining intoxicating liquors.

June 8–12 Republican National Convention meets at Chicago. Nominates Warren Gamaliel Harding of Ohio for President on tenth ballot and Calvin Coolidge of Massachusetts for Vice-President.

June 10 Water Power Act creates Federal Water Power Commission to regulate power plants on navigable streams of public lands.

June 19 AFL in annual convention in Montreal votes support of League of Nations without reservations.

June 28–July 5 Democratic National Convention meets at San Francisco. Nominates James M. Cox of Ohio for President and Franklin D. Roosevelt of New York for Vice-President. Platform endorses League of Nations.

July 7 Restrictions on trade with Russia lifted by State Department. However, political recognition is neither granted nor implied, leaving trade by U. S. citizens without protection of government.

July 10–14 Single Tax Convention meets at Chicago. Nominates Robert C. Macauley of Philadelphia for President and Richard C. Barnum of Ohio for Vice-President.

July 13–16 Farmer-Labor party meets in first nominating convention at Chicago. Nominates Parley P. Christensen of Utah for President and Max S. Hayes of Ohio for Vice-President.

July 21–22 Prohibition party convention meets at Lincoln, Neb. Nominates Aaron S. Watkins of Ohio for President after William J. Bryan declines.

Aug 26 Nineteenth Amendment (Woman Suffrage) to Constitution proclaimed in effect. Tennessee was 36th state to ratify, Aug. 18.

Sept 8 Transcontinental airmail established between New York and San Francisco, airplane by day, train by night.

Sept 16 Explosion of bomb in Wall Street, New York, before offices of J. P. Morgan and Company, killing 30 and with property loss of $2,000,000. Those guilty never discovered.

Oct 3 President Wilson issues appeal to the American people to support League of Nations in November election.

Oct 16 Bonus parade staged in New York by ex-service men.

Nov 2 Presidential election. Harding and Coolidge elected by electoral vote of 404, to 127 for Cox and Roosevelt. Popular vote: Harding, Republican, 16,152,200; Cox, Democrat, 9,147,353; Debs, Socialist, 919,799; Christensen, Farmer-Labor, 265,411; Watkins, Prohibition, 189,408; W. W. Cox, Socialist Labor, 31,715; Macauley, Single Tax, 5,837.

Nov 2 California Alien-Land Tax, to prevent Japanese from owning farm lands, approved by popular referendum.

Nov 11 Raw sugar quoted at 6 cents a pound; was 30 cents in August.

Dec 7 President Wilson sends his eighth and last annual message to joint session of Congress. Quotes Abraham Lincoln: "Let us have faith that right makes might, and in that faith let us dare to do our duty as we understand it."

Dec 10 Woodrow Wilson receives Nobel Peace Prize for 1919.

Dec 21 Three-hundredth anniversary of Landing of the Pilgrims celebrated at Plymouth Rock.

1921

Nearly 20,000 business failures and severe unemployment during year. Wage cuts from 10 to 25 per cent are widespread. U. S. Steel Corporation cuts 3 times during year. Many strikes.

Eight hundred thousand immigrants arrive in year ending June 30.

Port of New York Authority established by New York and New Jersey.

American Birth Control League incorporated, Mrs. Margaret Sanger president.

Insulin discovered by Fred Banting (Canadian) and Dr. Charles H. Best.

Jan 4 Activities of War Finance Corporation revived by Congress over President's veto, Jan. 3, to relieve depression in farm areas.

Mar 3 President Wilson vetoes Emergency Tariff Bill.

Mar 4 Warren G. Harding and Calvin Coolidge inaugurated President and Vice-President. President Harding's inaugural address is first to be heard over radio. "Normalcy," President Harding's contribution to American idiom, characterizes his administration.
[President Harding's Cabinet: Charles E. Hughes, Secretary of State; Andrew W. Mellon, Secretary of Treasury; John W. Weeks, Secretary of War; Edwin Denby, Secretary of Navy; Albert B. Fall, Secretary of Interior; Henry C. Wallace, Secretary of Agriculture; Herbert C. Hoover, Secretary

of Commerce; J. J. Davis, Secretary of Labor; Will H. Hays, Postmaster General; Harry M. Daugherty, Attorney General.]

Mar 25 Russia's plea for resumption of trade relations with U. S. rejected by Secretary of State Hughes, so long as Communism prevails.

Apr 20 Treaty with Colombia, signed Apr. 6, 1914, given consent of Senate. "Apology clause" withdrawn but treaty provides for payment of $25,000,000 for Colombia's loss of Panama.

Apr 25 Nebraska law denies alien ownership of land.

May Bipartisan Farm Bloc organized in Congress.

May 19 Emergency Quota Act restricts immigration for any nationality to 3 per cent of persons of that nationality living in U. S. in 1910.

May 27 Emergency Tariff Act raises duties on farm products, with embargo on German dyestuffs.

May 31 Administration of naval oil land reserves at Elk Hills and Buena Vista, Cal., and Teapot Dome, Wyo., transferred from Navy Department to Department of Interior, by executive order.

May 31 State Department in memorandum to Japanese embassy protests Japan's increase of forces in Siberia following withdrawal of other powers.

June 10 Budget Act establishes Bureau of the Budget. Charles G. Dawes appointed director June 21.

June 25 Samuel Gompers at Denver elected for 40th time president of AFL.

June 30 William Howard Taft appointed Chief Justice of Supreme Court by President Harding.

July 1 Railroad employees' wages reduced 12 per cent by Railroad Labor Board.

July 2 War with Germany declared at an end with signing by President Harding of joint resolution of Congress.

July 25 Henry Ford's offer to take 100-year lease of Muscle Shoals rejected by War Department.

Aug 9 U. S. Veterans' Bureau established by act of Congress. [Colonel Charles R. Forbes appointed director by the President.]

Aug 11 U. S. formally invites Great Britain, France, Italy and Japan, and the 4 Minor Powers, Belgium, China, the Netherlands and Portugal, to conference at Washington for discussion of limitation of arms and problems of the Pacific.

Aug 15 Packers' and Stockyards Act provides for regulation of interstate and foreign commerce in livestock and poultry products.

Aug 18 William J. Burns appointed director of Bureau of Investigation of Department of Justice (FBI).

Aug 24 Peace treaty signed with Austria at Vienna. Senate consents Oct. 18.

Aug 25 Peace treaty with Germany signed at Berlin. Treaty omits League of Nations but incorporates those provisions of Versailles Treaty which serve interests of U. S. Senate consents Oct. 18.

Aug 29 Peace treaty signed with Hungary at Budapest. Senate consents Oct. 18.

Sept 14 John Bassett Moore elected member of World Court by League of Nations.

Sept 26 Unemployment Conference, called by the President, meets at Washington, Herbert Hoover chairman. Nearly 3,500,000 unemployed over the country.

Oct 15 General Leonard Wood sworn in as governor general of Philippines.

Nov 1 Sergeant Emil Chambers makes record parachute jump of 26,000 feet from army plane at American Legion flying meet, Kansas City.

Nov 9 Federal Highway Act amends and extends Federal Highway Act of 1919, expired June 30.

Nov 11 America's Unknown Soldier buried at Arlington National Cemetery.

Nov 12–Feb 6 Washington Conference for Limitation of Armaments.

Nov 23 Sheppard-Towner Maternity and Infancy Act.

Nov 23 Revenue Act repeals some nuisance wartime taxes but does not greatly change revenue acts of war years.

Dec 13 Four-Power Pacific Treaty signed at Washington Conference by U. S., Great Britain, France and Japan. Senate consents Mar. 24, 1922.

Dec 19 In *Truax v. Corrigan,* Supreme Court holds an Arizona picketing law invalid.

Dec 22 Russian Famine Relief Act authorizes expenditure of $20,000,000 for purchase of seed grain, corn and preserved milk for Russia.

1922

Business revival: U. S. enters upon 7 years of plenty; automobile is key industry.

Commercials introduced by radio: WEAF first utilizes advertising to pay for broadcasting.

Life and Letters of Walter H. Page by Burton Hendrick published. Pulitzer prize 1923.

Jan 19 Senator Borah presents resolution advocating outlawry of war.

Jan 30 Permanent Court of International Justice (World Court) holds first formal session in Palace of Peace at The Hague.

Feb 6 Nine-Power Treaty signed at Washington Conference, to respect the "sovereignty, the independence, and the territorial and administrative integrity of China." Gives formal recognition to Open Door. Senate consents Mar. 30.

Feb 6 Five-Power Naval Treaty, providing for 10-year naval holiday, signed at Washington Conference by U. S., Great Britain, France, Italy and Japan. Senate consents Mar. 29.

Feb 9 **World War Foreign Debt Commission**, to be appointed by the President, created by act of Congress. Andrew Mellon appointed chairman Feb. 21.

Feb 11 **Yap Treaty signed with Japan** at Washington Conference recognizes Japan's mandate over former German islands north of Equator but reserves for U. S. cable rights on island of Yap. Senate consents Mar. 1.

Feb 18 **Capper-Volstead Act** exempts agricultural cooperatives from anti-trust law restrictions.

Feb 19 **Joseph Cannon** announces his retirement from Congress at end of term, after 46 years' service.

Feb 27 **National conference of radio**, telegraph and telephone experts opens at Washington, called by Department of Commerce.

Mar 28 **New York prohibits aliens** from teaching in public schools.

Apr **Secretary of the Interior Albert B. Fall** secretly leases Teapot Dome, naval oil reserve district, Wyo., to Harry F. Sinclair, oil magnate; and Elk Hills, naval oil reserve in Cal., to Edward L. Doheny, oil magnate.

Apr 1 **Anthracite and bituminous coal miners' strike** begins in protest against reduction of wages. 500,000 miners out on strike, return with minor concessions in September.

May 15 **In *Bailey v. Drexel Furniture Co.*,** Supreme Court declares unconstitutional child labor clause in War Revenue Act of Feb. 24, 1919.

May 26 **Narcotics Control Board** established by act of Congress. Board to consist of Secretaries of State, Treasury and Commerce.

May 28 **Railroad Labor Board** orders wage reduction of 13 per cent to affect 400,000 railroad employees.

May 30 **Lincoln Memorial, Washington, D. C.,** dedicated, its statue the work of sculptor Daniel Chester French.

June 3 **Federal Reserve Act amended** by Congress to provide for agricultural representation on Federal Reserve Board.

June 21–22 **Herrin, Ill., coal miners** riot in protest against strike breakers.

July 1 **Railway shopmen's strike begins** in protest against reduction of wages ordered by Railroad Labor Board, May 28. 400,000 on strike, return in September, defeated.

July 20 **Chile and Peru submit Tacna-Arica dispute** to President of U. S. Settled satisfactorily 1929.

Sept 19 **Fordney-McCumber Tariff Act** raises import duties to higher level than in any preceding tariff act.

Sept 19 **Soldiers' Bonus Bill vetoed** by the President. Veto overruled by House but sustained by Senate, Sept. 20.

Sept 21 **Grain Futures Act** regulates trading in grain under interstate commerce power. Supersedes similar act of Aug. 1921, declared unconstitutional by Supreme Court.

Sept 21 **Congress in joint resolution** favors establishment in Palestine of national home for the Jews.

Sept 22 **Cable Act** grants a married woman her citizenship independent of her husband's status.

Oct 6 **Sale of liquor on U. S. ships** anywhere or on foreign ships within 3-mile limit forbidden by Attorney General Harry M. Daugherty.

Nov 20 **Official U. S. observers attend** opening of Lausanne Conference because of concern in oil interests in Near East.

Dec 1 **Progressive bloc of 32 representatives** and senators under leadership of Senator LaFollette meet in Washington, protesting Harding administration policies.

1923

Prosperity. Wage increases all along the line.

Grace Abbott, Chief of Children's Bureau, attends a League of Nations committee meeting, first "unofficial observer" from U. S.

Robert A. Millikan, first to isolate the electron, awarded Nobel Prize for physics.

First transatlantic radio communication takes place between New York and London.

First radio broadcasts of opera presented by Manhattan Opera Company.

Time first published.

Jan 10 American Army of Occupation on the Rhine ordered home by President Harding. U. S. flag hauled down Jan. 24.

Feb   Charles R. Forbes, director of Veterans' Bureau, resigns under charges of mismanagement. Senate directs investigation.

Feb 24 Adherence of U. S. to World Court urged by President Harding in message to Senate.

Feb 28 British Debt Refunding Act provides that Great Britain pay her $4,-600,000,000 debt in semi-annual installments over period of 62 years with interest of 3.3 per cent.

Mar 4 Secretary Albert B. Fall resigns from Department of Interior. His leases of Teapot Dome and Elk Hills to oil magnates already under Senate investigation. [Fall succeeded by Hubert Work.]

Mar 4 Agricultural Credits Act provides for 12 Federal Intermediate Credit Banks to assist agricultural and livestock industries.

Mar 25 Fifth International American Conference opens at Santiago, Chile. U. S. delegates support agreement for peaceful settlement of disputes.

Apr 9 In *Adkins v. Children's Hospital,* Supreme Court rules minimum wage law for women in District of Columbia is unconstitutional.

Apr 14 Public portions of Lansing-Ishii Agreement with Japan of Nov. 2, 1917, formally annulled by exchange of notes.

May 23 Flogging at convict labor camps abolished by Florida Legislature.

June 4 In *Robert T. Meyer v. State* *of Nebraska,* Supreme Court declares unconstitutional state laws forbidding teaching of foreign languages in public schools.

June 19 Debt Funding Agreement signed by Great Britain, accepting terms of act of Feb. 28. By 1930, 17 of 20 other wartime borrower nations accept varied terms.

June 20 President Harding and party leave Washington for the West coast and Alaska.

Aug 2 U. S. Steel Corporation abol-ishes 12-hour day, adopts 8-hour day.

Aug 2 President Harding dies at San Francisco.

Aug 3 Calvin Coolidge sworn in to the Presidency by his father, notary public, Plymouth, Vt., in early hours of the morning.

Aug 31 President Obregón of Mexico officially recognized by U. S.

Sept 10 Special claims convention be-tween U. S. and Mexico, for settlement of claims of U. S. citizens arising from Mexican revolution, signed at Mexico City. Senate consents Jan. 23, 1924.

Sept 15 Governor J. C. Walton of Oklahoma places state under martial law because of Ku Klux Klan activities. Reorganized Klan has become powerful force in Midwest politics.

Dec 6 President Coolidge declares in favor of World Court, in first annual message to Congress.

Dec 8 Treaty of friendship, commerce and consular rights signed with Germany at Washington. Senate consents with reservations Feb. 10, 1925.

Dec 15 Reparations Commission, meeting in Paris, announces appointment of Charles H. Dawes and Owen D. Young to serve as unofficial representatives of U. S. on expert committees to investigate finances of Germany.

Dec 18 Secretary of State Hughes rejects the Soviet's plea for diplomatic recognition.

1924

Duke University founded at Durham, N. C., when James B. Duke makes Trinity College beneficiary of Duke Endowment.

Saturday Review of Literature begins publication.

American Mercury, H. L. Mencken editor, begins publication.

Jan 16 McNary-Haugen Farm Relief Bill for price-fixing of farm products first introduced in Congress; fails to pass. Fails again, 1926. Passes in 1927 and again in 1928, but is vetoed by President Coolidge.

Feb 3 Woodrow Wilson dies at Washington.

Feb 21 Independence of Philippines opposed by President Coolidge in a letter: "The Philippine people are by no means equipped . . . for the heavy burden . . . of political independence."

Feb 29 Charles R. Forbes, ex-director of Veterans' Bureau, indicted for defrauding government of $250,000,000 in corrupt contracts and building abuses. Feb. 4, 1925, sentenced to 2 years' imprisonment, with $10,000 fine.

Mar U. S. government institutes proceedings to cancel leases of Teapot Dome to Harry F. Sinclair and of Elk Hills to Edward L. Doheny. Supreme Court declares Elk Hills lease invalid Feb. 28, 1927, Teapot Dome invalid, Oct. 10, 1927.

Mar 1 Investigation of administration of Harry M. Daugherty, Attorney General, ordered by Senate. Mar. 4, 1927, he is freed of charges by New York Federal District Court.

Mar 24 Archbishops Patrick Joseph Hayes of New York and George W. Mundelein of Chicago made cardinals by Pope Pius XI.

Apr 10 Japanese Ambassador Hanihara declares to Secretary of State Hughes that grave consequences might follow exclusion of Japanese and abandonment of Gentlemen's Agreement.

May 11–13 Socialist Labor party convention meets at New York. Nominates F. T. Johns of Oregon for President and Vernal L. Reynolds of Maryland for Vice-President.

May 19 Soldiers' Bonus Bill passed over President's veto, provides for 20-year endowment insurance.

May 24 Rogers Act reorganizes diplomatic and consular services, henceforth to be known as Foreign Service of U. S.

May 26 Immigration Act limits annual quota of immigrants for any country to 2 per cent of number of individuals born in that country and resident in U. S. in 1890. Japanese totally excluded; Canadians and Latin-Americans not restricted.

June 2 Child Labor Amendment to Constitution submitted to states for ratification. [Is not ratified.]

June 2 All Indians born in U. S. are declared to be citizens, by act of Congress.

June 2 Revenue Act reduces surtax, estate and income taxes, and abolishes most excise taxes. Provides for publication of individual tax returns.

June 5 Prohibition party convention meets at Columbus, Ohio. Nominates H. P. Faris of Missouri for President and Miss Marie C. Brehm of California for Vice-President.

June 10–12 Republican National Convention meets at Cleveland. Nominates Calvin Coolidge for President on first ballot and Charles G. Dawes of Illinois for Vice-President.

June 17–19 Farmer-Labor party meets in convention at St. Paul. Nominates Duncan MacDonald of Illinois for President and William Bouck of Washington for Vice-President.

June 24–July 10 Democratic National Convention meets at New York. Nominates John W. Davis of West Virginia for President and Charles W. Bryan, governor of Nebraska, for Vice-President.

June 30 Albert B. Fall, Harry F. Sin- clair and Edward L. Doheny indicted for bribery and conspiracy to defraud government in Teapot Dome and Elk Hills leases. Finally, 1929, all are freed of charge of conspiracy to defraud; Fall, convicted of bribery, sentenced to a year's imprisonment and $100,000 fine; Doheny and Sinclair acquitted of bribery; Sinclair, for contempt of court, sentenced to 9 months' imprisonment and $1,000 fine.

July 1 Regular day and night air mail service established between New York and San Francisco.

July 4 Conference for Progressive Po- litical Action meets in convention at Cleveland. Nominates Senator Robert M. LaFollette of Wisconsin for President and Burton K. Wheeler of Montana for Vice-President.

July 10 Workers' party (Communist) at Chicago nominates William Z. Foster of New York for President and Benjamin Gitlow of New York for Vice-President.

July 28 Secretary of State Hughes leaves for informal visit to London, Paris and Berlin.

Aug 16 Dawes Plan for payment of German reparations accepted by the Allies and Germany, formally signed Aug. 30.

Aug 29 Edward, Prince of Wales ar- rives in U. S. for month's visit.

Sept 18 Removal of U. S. Marines from Santo Domingo completed.

Oct 30 Seymour Parker Gilbert be- comes Agent General of Reparation Payments.

Nov 4 Presidential election. Coolidge and Dawes elected by electoral vote of 382, to 136 for Davis and Bryan, 13 for LaFollette and Wheeler. Popular vote: Coolidge, Republican, 15,725,016; Davis, Democrat, 8,386,503; LaFollette, Progressive, 4,822,856; Faris, Prohibition, 57,520; Johns, Socialist Labor, 36,428; Foster, Workers (Communist), 36,386. Republicans retain control of both houses of Congress. Two women elected governors: Mrs. Nellie G. Ross, Wyoming, and Mrs. Miriam Ferguson, Texas.

Nov 17 U. S. officially represented at Opium Conference, Geneva, called by League of Nations.

Nov 28 Regular Republican Senators read insurgents Robert M. LaFollette, Smith W. Brookhart, Edwin F. Ladd and Lynn J. Frazier out of the party.

Nov 30 Radio Corporation of America demonstrates technique of sending photographs by transatlantic wireless telegraphy.

Dec 19 William Green chosen presi- dent of AFL to succeed Samuel Gompers.

Dec 27 Treaty signed with Santo Do- mingo, superseding that of February 1907. Ends U. S. military government and authorizes Dominican government to borrow, not to exceed $25,000,000. Senate consents Jan. 21, 1925.

1925

National Committee on Cause and Cure of War founded.

Florida land boom is at its height.

Ford roadster selling at $260.00.

Al Capone begins 6 years of gang wars, representing debauchery of the "dry" era.

John Simon Guggenheim Foundation of $3,000,000 established for advancement of knowledge and fine arts by means of fellowships.

Feb 24 Purnell Act authorizes funds for economic research in agricultural experiment stations.

Mar 3 Adherence to World Court recommended by House in overwhelming vote.

Mar 4 Calvin Coolidge and Charles G. Dawes inaugurated President and Vice-President.
[President Coolidge's Cabinet: Frank B. Kellogg, Secretary of State; Andrew W. Mellon, Secretary of Treasury; Dwight F. Davis, Secretary of War; Curtis D. Wilbur, Secretary of Navy; Hubert Work, Secretary of Interior; W. M. Jardine, Secretary of Agriculture; Herbert C. Hoover, Secretary of Commerce; J. J. Davis, Secretary of Labor; Harry S. New, Postmaster General; John G. Sargent, Attorney General.]

Mar 9 President Coolidge announces his decision in Tacna-Arica dispute between Chile and Peru in favor of Chile and orders a plebiscite to be held in each country.

Mar 13 Tennessee legislature makes teaching of theory of evolution in public schools unlawful.

Apr 13 Scheduled commercial airplane service between Detroit and Chicago inaugurated by Henry Ford.

June 8 In *Gitlow v. New York*, Supreme Court upholds New York's verdict of guilty for publication of Left-Wing Manifesto, Justices Holmes and Brandeis dissenting.

June 17 Convention for Supervision of International Trade in Arms and Implements of War, and Protocol prohibiting use of poisonous gases and bacteria in warfare signed by U. S. at League of Nations Conference, Geneva. Senate consents June 15, 1934.

July 10–21 Scopes trial at Dayton, Tenn. John T. Scopes, high school teacher, tried for teaching evolution in his classes. Defended by Clarence Darrow and Dudley Field Malone, opposed by William Jennings Bryan, Scopes is defeated legally and fined $100.

July 26 William Jennings Bryan dies of apoplexy at Dayton, Tenn., a casualty of Scopes trial.

Aug 3 Last U. S. Marines leave Nicaragua after 13 years of duty. Revolution ensuing, marines return 1926 to remain until January 1, 1933.

Aug 8 Ku Klux Klan stages parade in Washington with some 40,000 marching.

Aug 18 Debt Funding Agreement signed by Belgium. War debt of $417,-780,000 to be paid at interest rate of 1.8 per cent.

Sept 1 Federal income tax returns published according to Revenue Act of June 2, 1924, showing that John D. Rockefeller, Jr., paid largest personal tax, $6,277,699, and Henry Ford Company largest corporation tax, $16,493,-160.

Sept 3 U. S. Navy dirigible *Shenandoah* torn to pieces in thunder storm over Ava, Ohio.

Sept 12 National Aircraft Board appointed by the President, Dwight W. Morrow chairman.

Oct 16 Locarno Pact, a mutual guarantee to peace of western Europe, initialed by Germany, France, Belgium, Great Britain and Italy. Signed in London Dec. 1. Acclaimed with enthusiasm in U. S.

Nov 14 Debt Funding Agreement signed by Italy. War debt of $2,042,-000,000 to be paid at low interest rate of 0.4 per cent.

Dec Mexico adopts petroleum and land laws disadvantageous to American investors. Two years of State Department negotiation follow.

Dec 6 *Lusitania* claims of U. S. against Germany adjusted by German-American Claims Commission at $2,500,000.

Dec 8 President Coolidge again recommends adherence to World Court in message to Congress.

1926

Bootleg trade in U. S., in violation of Volstead Act, estimated at $3,600,000,-000 for year.

An original Gutenberg Bible sold in New York at auction for $106,000 and presented to Yale University.

Jan 27 Adherence to World Court, with 5 sweeping reservations, approved by Senate.

Feb 26 Revenue Act further reduces income tax, surtax and estate taxes, and repeals more nuisance taxes; publicity provision repealed.

Apr 29 Debt Funding Agreement with France finally signed. Payment of war debt of $4,025,000,000 to be extended over 62 years with interest at 1.6 per cent.

May 9 Rear Admiral Richard E. Byrd and Floyd Bennett fly over North Pole.

May 18 Preparatory Commission for Disarmament Conference opens at Geneva, with U. S. officially represented.

May 20 Air Commerce Act vests ex- tensive powers over commercial aviation in Department of Commerce.

May 25 Public Buildings Act author- izes expenditure of $165,000,000 on Federal buildings.

May 31–Nov 30 Philadelphia Sesqui- Centennial Exposition.

June 20–24 Eucharistic Congress of Roman Catholic Church held near Chicago; attracts 1,000,000 pilgrims.

July 2 Army Air Corps created by act of Congress.

July 3 Pension Act increases benefits for Civil War and Mexican War veterans and their widows.

July 26 Robert Todd Lincoln dies at Manchester, Vt., leaving papers of his father to Library of Congress, to be opened after 21 years.

Sept 1 Conference of signatories of World Court Protocol opens at Geneva

to consider the 5 reservations of U. S. Senate. Conference, accepting 4 reservations and part of the fifth, proposes supplementary agreement which Senate receives as rejection of her offer of adherence to the Court.

Sept 25 Henry Ford introduces 8-hour day and 5-day week in Ford Motor Company plants.

Sept 30 Charles E. Hughes appointed member of Permanent Court of Arbitration at The Hague by President Coolidge.

Nov 2 Congressional elections show swing to left: Smith Brookhart of Iowa returned, and Gerald Nye of North Dakota, Robert LaFollette, Jr., of Wisconsin and David Walsh of Massachusetts elected to Senate. Republican majorities cut in both houses.

Nov 11 President Coolidge in Armi- stice Day address says, "Unless the requirements of the Senate are met by the other nations, I can see no prospect of this country adhering to the Court."

Dec 4 Colonel Carmi A. Thompson, returning from tour of investigation in Philippines, reports to the President the islands are not yet ready for independence.

Dec 8 Liberia ratifies 99-year lease of 1,000,000 acres to Firestone Rubber Company.

1927

Restoration of colonial Williamsburg, Va., begins, through Rockefeller gift.

Mount Rushmore Memorial in Black Hills, S. D., begun by Gutzon Borglum, sculptor.

Mechanical cotton picker invented by John D. Rust.

William Hale Thompson, new mayor of Chicago, in effort to drive old King George out of the city, orders all pro-British books in public library removed and burned.

Nobel Prize for physics awarded Professor Arthur Compton of University of Chicago.

Motion pictures with dialogue, the talkies, begin with "The Jazz Singer," starring Al Jolson.

Main Currents in American Thought, first 2 vols., by Vernon L. Parrington, published.

Rise of American Civilization by Charles A. and Mary Beard published.

Jan 7 Radio telephone service opened between New York and London.

Feb 18 Hon. Charles Vincent Massey, Canada's first minister to the U. S., presents credentials at Washington. Diplomatic relations independent of Great Britain now established between Canada and U. S. [William Phillips first U. S. minister to Canada.]

Feb 23 Federal Radio Commission created by act of Congress.

Mar 3 Prohibition Bureau in Treasury Department created by Prohibition Reorganization Act.

Mar 4 Direct cable communication resumed with Germany, President Coolidge and President Von Hindenburg exchanging greetings of good will.

Mar 17 Naval oil reserves returned to control of Navy Department from Department of Interior, by executive order.

Apr Henry L. Stimson sent by President Coolidge to Nicaragua to reconcile quarreling factions. Arranges a new election and continuance of U. S. Marines, who remain until 1933.

Apr Mississippi River flood waters cover 4,000,000 acres in lower Mississippi Valley, property loss of $300,000,000. Demonstrates need of flood control.

Apr 6 Aristide Briand, Foreign Minister of France, proposes mutual agreement between France and U. S. for outlawry of war. [Plan publicly approved by President Nicholas Murray Butler and Professor James T. Shotwell of Columbia University.]

Apr 7 Television first successfully dem- onstrated in New York by Walter S. Gifford, president of American Telephone and Telegraph Company, showing Secretary of Commerce Herbert Hoover in Washington office.

May 3 Pan-American Commercial Conference at Washington welcomed by President Coolidge.

May 5 International Economic Con- ference of League of Nations opens at Geneva, with U. S. represented.

May 20–21 Charles A. Lindbergh makes non-stop solo flight in monoplane *Spirit of St. Louis* from New York airport to Le Bourget Field, outside Paris, in 33½ hours.

May 26 Henry Ford and son Edsel drive fifteen-millionth automobile produced in Ford plant.

May 26 Reduction in size of paper currency by about one-third authorized by Treasury Department. Goes into circulation July 10, 1929.

June 4 Clarence Chamberlain and Charles A. Levine leave New York for Europe in airplane *Colombia.* Arriving in Saxony, Germany, they make a new world non-stop record, 3,905 miles in 43 hours.

June 20 Limitation of Naval Arma- ment Conference called by President Coolidge opens at Geneva, U. S., Great Britain and Japan represented. France and Italy refuse invitation. Ends Aug. 4 in stalemate. Lobbyists of shipping and armament interests encouraged failure.

June 26 Radio communication opened between San Francisco and Philippines.

June 28 Two Army Air Corps pilots, Lts. Lester J. Maitland and Albert F. Hegenberger, make first successful flight from San Francisco to Honolulu.

Aug 2 President Coolidge at his sum- mer camp, Rapid City, S. D., announces, "I do not choose to run for President in 1928."

Aug 7 International Peace Bridge dedicated at Buffalo, with addresses by Vice-President Dawes and the Prince of Wales.

Sept 19 **American Legion Convention** opens in Paris.

Oct   **Dwight W. Morrow dispatched** by President Coolidge as ambassador to Mexico to restore good will.

Nov 12 **Holland vehicular tunnel** opened, under the Hudson between Manhattan and Jersey City.

Dec   **New Model-A Ford car viewed** by hundreds of thousands in New York Ford show rooms.

Dec   **Mexican legislature rescinds** petroleum law of Dec. 1925, objectionable to American capitalists.

Dec 8 **Senator Arthur Capper of Kansas** introduces resolution into Senate to outlaw war as instrument of public policy.

Dec 13 **Henry L. Stimson accepts appointment** as governor general of Philippine Islands, after death of General Leonard Wood in August.

Dec 13 **Charles A. Lindbergh leaves** Washington on good will flight to Mexico in his *Spirit of St. Louis.* Later in month, leaves Mexico on 6-week flight to Central and South American and Caribbean countries.

Dec 28 **Secretary of State Kellogg proposes** to Briand an extension of Briand's plan of Apr. 6 for outlawry of war, to include all nations of the world.

1928

Postwar prosperity approaches its crest; stocks dangerously high.

Technicolor motion pictures first shown by George Eastman at Rochester, N. Y.

Origins of the World War by Sidney B. Fay published. Explodes "myth" of Germany's war guilt.

Jan 16 **Sixth International American** Conference opened at Havana by President Coolidge. Ex-Secretary of State Charles E. Hughes heads U. S. delegation.

Feb 10 **Anti-third-term resolution carried** through Senate by opponents of President Coolidge.

Apr 13–18 **Socialist party convention** meets at New York. Nominates Norman Thomas of New York for President and James H. Maurer of Pennsylvania for Vice-President.

May 15 **Flood Control Act provides** for levee work on lower Mississippi at estimated cost of $325,000,000, over 10-year period.

May 17 **Air mail rate of 5 cents per** ounce established by act of Congress.

May 22 **Jones-White Merchant Marine Act** provides for Federal subsidies to private shipping concerns.

May 25 **Muscles Shoals Bill, providing** for government ownership of hydroelectric plant at Muscle Shoals in Tennessee River, passed by Congress. [Killed by pocket veto of President Coolidge.]

May 27 **Workers' party (Communist)** convention, at New York, nominates William Z. Foster and Benjamin Gitlow for President and Vice-President, the nominees of 1924.

June 3 **Amelia Earhart, first woman** to fly the Atlantic, hops off from Boston with 2 companions in monoplane "Friendship."

June 12–15 **Republican National convention** meets at Kansas City. Nominates Secretary of Commerce Herbert Hoover for President on first ballot and Senator Charles Curtis of Kansas for Vice-President.

June 26–29 **Democratic National convention** meets at Houston, Tex. On first ballot, nominates Governor Alfred E. Smith of New York for President and Senator Joseph T. Robinson of Arkansas for Vice-President.

July 12 **Prohibition party convention** meets at Chicago. Nominates William F. Varney of New York for President and James A. Edgerton of Virginia for Vice-President.

July 25 **Treaty signed with China at** Peiping, establishing principle of complete tariff autonomy for China. Senate consents Feb. 11, 1929.

Aug 11 Herbert Hoover at Palo Alto, Cal., accepting Republican nomination, says, "We in America today are nearer the final triumph over poverty than ever before in the history of any land."

Aug 25 Byrd Antarctic Expedition leaves New York in ice-ship *The City of New York.*

Aug 27 Kellogg-Briand Pact, Pact of Paris, for outlawry of war, signed in Paris by U. S., one of 15 nations. Sixty-three nations finally sign. U. S. Senate consents Jan. 15, 1929.

Sept 8 Charles Evans Hughes unanimously elected member of World Court by League of Nations. Succeeds John Bassett Moore.

Oct 15 The *Graf Zeppelin,* dirigible, Dr. Hugo Eckener commander, arrives at Lakehurst, N. J., from Friedrichschafen, Germany, on its first commercial flight, 6,630 miles in slightly more than 4½ days.

Nov 6 Presidential election. Herbert Hoover and Charles Curtis elected by electoral vote of 444, to 87 for Smith and Robinson. Popular vote: Hoover, Republican, 21,391,381; Smith, Democrat, 15,016,443; Thomas, Socialist, 267,835; Foster, Workers (Communist), 21,181; Varney, Prohibition, 20,106.

Nov 6 Franklin D. Roosevelt elected Democratic governor of New York.

Nov 19 President-elect Herbert Hoo-ver leaves San Pedro, Cal., on battleship *Maryland* on goodwill tour of Latin America.

Nov 26 International Conference on Economic Statistics of League of Nations opens at Geneva, with U. S. represented.

Dec 10 Pan-American Conference on Conciliation and Arbitration meets in Washington, called by President Coolidge. Conventions on conciliation and arbitration signed at its close, Jan. 5, 1929.

Dec 12 International Civil Aeronautics Conference opens in Washington with

address by President Coolidge. Delegates from 40 countries.

Dec 17 Clark Memorandum, drafted by Undersecretary of State J. Reuben Clark, is submitted to Secretary of State Kellogg, published 1930. U. S. will not again claim right to intervene in affairs of any Latin-American country as an "international policeman." Repudiates Roosevelt Corollary to Monroe Doctrine.

Dec 21 Boulder Dam Project Act commits government to participation in production of hydroelectric power.

1929

Delegation of 99 U. S. businessmen tour Soviet Russia.

Frank B. Kellogg awarded Nobel Peace Prize for Kellogg-Briand Pact.

Consumers' Research established, to furnish data on merits of advertised goods.

The trailer, invented by Glenn H. Curtiss, placed on display in New York in showrooms of Hudson Company.

Jan 15 Kellogg-Briand Pact consented to by U. S. Senate, 85–1.

Feb 2 Federal Reserve Board orders member banks not to make loans for stock speculation on margin.

Feb 11 Owen D. Young nominated chairman by a committee of financial experts meeting in Paris to revise Dawes Plan.

Feb 13 Cruiser Act provides for 15 cruisers and 1 airplane carrier, threatening new naval race.

Mar 4 Herbert Hoover inaugurated President and Charles Curtis Vice-President. In President Hoover's Inaugural address: "We have no desire for territorial expansion, for economic or other domination of other peoples."
[President Hoover's Cabinet: Henry L. Stimson, Secretary of State; Andrew W. Mellon, Secretary of Treasury; James W. Good, Secretary of War; Charles F. Adams, Secretary of Navy;

Ray L. Wilbur, Secretary of Interior; A. M. Hyde, Secretary of Agriculture; R. P. Lamont, Secretary of Commerce; J. J. Davis, Secretary of Labor; Walter F. Brown, Postmaster General; William D. Mitchell, Attorney General.]

May 17 Tacna-Arica boundary dis- pute between Chile and Peru announced as settled by President Hoover.

May 20 National Commission on Law Observance and Enforcement, George W. Wickersham chairman, appointed by President Hoover to conduct investigation on prohibition and related problems.

May 27 In *United States v. Schwimmer,* Supreme Court upholds refusal of citizenship to Rosika Schwimmer, pacifist from Hungary. Justice Oliver Wendell Holmes dissents, declaring most imperative principle of Constitution to be that of free thought.

June 7 Young Plan to supersede Dawes Plan for payment of German reparations announced by committee of experts in Paris. Acceptance of the Plan signed by Allies and Germany, January 1930.

June 14 Charles G. Dawes arrives in London, ambassador to Great Britain.

June 15 Agricultural Marketing Act provides for advisory Federal Farm Board with $500,000,000 revolving fund for encouragement of farmers' cooperatives; authorizes stabilization corporations to buy up farm surpluses to maintain prices: Grain Stabilization Corporation chartered Feb. 10, 1930; Cotton Stabilization Corporation chartered June 5, 1930.

July 1 "National origins" clause of Immigration Act of May 26, 1924, goes into effect. July 1, 1927, effective data provided for in act, postponed by complications until this date.

July 24 Kellogg-Briand Pact formally proclaimed in Washington by President Hoover.

Aug Steel and automobile produc- tion begins falling off.

Sept 8 League for Independent Po- litical Action formed, John Dewey chairman, to organize new political party.

Oct English money rates raised to 6.5 per cent, causing withdrawal of European capital from American market.

Oct 4 Prime Minister J. Ramsay MacDonald of Great Britain arrives in Washington, on invitation of President Hoover, to discuss naval parity. Oct. 9, MacDonald and President Hoover in joint statement reaffirm support of Kellogg-Briand Pact.

Oct 7 Great Britain issues invitation to naval disarmament conference in London, Jan. 1930. U. S. accepts Oct. 10.

Oct 22 Charles E. Mitchell of Na- tional City Bank of New York says, "I know of nothing fundamentally wrong with the stock market or with the underlying business and credit structure."

Oct 23 Minor panic develops in New York Stock Exchange.

Oct 24 Collapse of New York stock market. Over 19,000,000 shares change hands on Stock Exchange and Curb.

Oct 29 Blackest day in stock market history. Over 16,000,000 shares change hands on New York Stock Exchange. Market continues decline until Nov. 13, by which date $30,000,000,000 in capital values have been swept away.

Nov 11 Ambassador Bridge dedicated, built over Detroit River, connecting U. S. with Canada.

Nov 21 President Hoover holds con- fidential conference with representatives of big business at the White House; same day holds conference with trade union officials. Two weeks later, the President's program of cooperation ratified in White House conference attended by several hundred representatives of employers and laborers.

Nov 29 Rear Admiral Richard E. Byrd flies over South Pole.

Dec 2 Secretary of State Stimson in identical notes appeals to U.S.S.R. and China, as signers of Kellogg-Briand Pact, to settle their dispute in Manchuria [U.S.S.R. objects to meddling by U. S.]

Dec 3 Edsel Ford announces increase in minimum wage for Ford Motor Company employees from $6 to $7 a day.

Dec 3 President Hoover in annual message to Congress declares his conviction that business confidence has been re-established.

Dec 9 Root formula, as basis for ad- herence to World Court by U. S., accepted by League of Nations, is signed by American chargé d'affaires at Berne, Switzerland. [Accepted by Secretary of State Stimson, refused by Senate.]

1930

Population, 122,775,046.

Depression dominates. Grain and cotton prices drop steadily through year. Copper reaches lowest price since 1895. National income drops to less than 68 billion from a high of 81 billion in 1929. Unemployment passes the 4,-000,000 mark.

Automobiles average one for every 4.9 persons in the country.

Motion pictures viewed by estimated 100,000,000 weekly.

123,000,000,000 cigarettes produced this year.

Institute for Advanced Study at Princeton, N. J., established, endowed by Louis Bamberger and his sister Mrs. Felix Fuld.

Nearly 4,000 Gold Star mothers and widows of World War service men now buried in European cemeteries make government-paid pilgrimage to the graves in Europe.

Ninth planet, Pluto, discovered and named at Lowell Observatory, Flagstaff, Ariz.

Dry ice, solid carbon dioxide, commercially adopted.

Planting of hybrid corn in Corn Belt becomes general.

Boston celebrates 300th anniversary of its founding.

Sinclair Lewis awarded Nobel Prize for literature.

Jan 2–10 President Hoover discusses increased public works program with Congressional leaders.

Jan 21–Apr 22 London Naval Con- ference. Secretary of State Stimson heads U. S. delegation.

Feb 3 Charles Evans Hughes ap- pointed Chief Justice of Supreme Court.

Mar 4 Coolidge Dam in Arizona dedi- cated.

Mar 31 Public Buildings Act, supple- menting act of 1926, extends appropriation by $230,000,000 for erection of public buildings.

Apr 4 Government aid to state road building continued by Congressional appropriation of $300,000,000.

Apr 22 London Naval Treaty signed in London by U. S., Great Britain and Japan. A partial victory for disarmament. U. S. Senate consents July 21.

May 4 Petition of 1,028 economists, protesting passage of pending Hawley-Smoot Tariff Bill and urging Presidential veto if passed, made public in Washington.

May 24 *Literary Digest* poll reports majority in favor of repeal of 18th Amendment.

May 26 In *Texas and New Orleans Railroad Company v. Brotherhood of Railway and Steamship Clerks,* Supreme Court decides that an employer's attempt to impose a company union upon his employees is interference with their rights.

June 2 Spanish War Pension Bill passed by Congress over President's veto.

June 17 Hawley-Smoot Tariff Bill signed by President Hoover. Act provides for rates higher than ever and a Tariff Commission with promise of flexibility.

Summer drought, unprecedented, in Midwestern and Southern states.

Aug 15 White House conference of governors of drought states meets with President Hoover.

Sept 3 Electric passenger train tried out by Thomas A. Edison on Lackawanna Railroad between Hoboken and Montclair, N. J.

Sept 17 Hoover Dam, originally Boul-der Dam, at Las Vegas, Nev., dedicated and work begun; completed, 1936.

Sept 17 Frank B. Kellogg elected mem-ber of World Court by League of Nations.

Oct   President's Committee for Un-employment Relief, Colonel Arthur Woods chairman, appointed by President Hoover. 4,500,000 unemployed, the President's statement.

Nov 4 Democrats win majority in House in mid-term elections.

Nov 4 Franklin D. Roosevelt again elected governor of New York.

Nov 19 White House Conference on Child Health and Protection opens, called by President Hoover. Adopts Children's Charter Nov. 21.

Dec 2 President Hoover in annual message to Congress asks appropriation of from $100,000,000 to $150,000,000 for construction of public works, to aid unemployment.

Dec 10 Elihu Root formula for ad-herence to World Court by U. S. submitted to Senate by President Hoover; again, Dec. 1931; Senate fails to act both times.

Dec 11 Bank of the United States, New York City, with 60 branches in the city and 400,000 depositors, closes its doors. Over 1,300 banks throughout the country have closed during the year.

Dec 20 Emergency construction of public works, to provide employment, and an appropriation of $116,000,000 for the project authorized by act of Congress.

Dec 20 Drought Relief Act authorizes appropriation of $45,000,000.

1931

Depression deepens. Flow of American capital to Europe checked. Financial storm breaks in Austria, soon spreads to Germany and Great Britain, threatening all plans of international debt payments.

The year is turning point between hopes raised by the Treaty of Versailles and shadow of a second World War.

Poll of 19,000 Protestant ministers registers 12,000 opposed to any future war.

Number of emigrants from U. S. exceeds that of immigrants for first time.

Yale drops Latin requirement for B.A. degree.

Harold C. Urey of Columbia discovers deuterium, the heavy isotope of hydrogen.

Jan 7 Unemployment between four and five million, according to report by Colonel Arthur Woods, chairman of President's Emergency Committee for Unemployment Relief.

Jan 20 Wickersham Commission, ap-pointed by President Hoover, May 1929, reports prohibition not working.

Feb 24 Eighteenth Amendment upheld as constitutional by Supreme Court.

Feb 27 Bonus Loan Bill, extending cash loans to veterans up to 50 per cent of their adjusted compensation certificates, passed over President's veto.

Mar 3 Muscle Shoals Bill, introduced by Senator Norris, is vetoed by President Hoover, "opposed to government entering any business . . . in competition with our citizens."

Mar 3 "Star-Spangled Banner" designated by act of Congress as national anthem.

Mar 20 Federal Council of Churches of Christ in America guardedly endorses birth control.

May 1 Empire State Building, world's tallest skyscraper, dedicated in New York.

May 25 Dr. Douglass Clyde Macintosh, professor in Yale Divinity School, and Miss Marie Averill Bland, army nurse, conscientious objectors, held ineligible for citizenship by Supreme Court.

June 6 Guam, the Government decides, is to be dropped as military base, as no longer of military value.

June 16 Tomb of President Harding dedicated at Marion, Ohio. President Hoover and ex-President Coolidge give addresses.

June 20 Moratorium for a year on all intergovernmental debts and reparations proposed by President Hoover. Accepted by interested nations, goes into operation in July.

June 23 Wiley Post and Harold Gatty take off on round-the-world flight in the *Winnie Mae*. Trip lasts 8 days, 15 hours, 51 minutes.

July 22 Many Kansas counties declare moratorium on taxes to assist farmers, in year of largest wheat crop and lowest prices.

July 27 Plague of grasshoppers reported in Iowa, Nebraska and South Dakota.

Aug 19 President Hoover appoints Walter S. Gifford to succeed Colonel Arthur Woods as chairman of President's Committee for Unemployment Relief.

Sept 18 Japan marches into Manchuria, violating Kellogg-Briand Pact.

Sept 18 American Bar Association, in convention at Atlantic City, urges Senate to ratify Root formula for adherence to World Court as step toward world peace and business recovery.

Sept 21 Great Britain abandons gold standard.

Oct 1 Eastern railroad systems, Pennsylvania, New York Central, Baltimore and Ohio, Chesapeake and Ohio-Nickel Plate, agree upon plan of consolidation. Approved by Interstate Commerce Commission July 21, 1932.

Oct 5–13 Fourth Pan-American Commercial Congress at Washington.

Oct 16 Council of League of Nations invites U. S. to send representative to participate in its discussion of Japan's invasion of Manchuria. Secretary of State Stimson appoints Prentiss B. Gilbert, U. S. Consul General at Geneva.

Oct 17 Al Capone found guilty of income tax evasion in Federal Court at Chicago. [Sentenced to 11 years' imprisonment and $50,000 fine.]

Oct 24 George Washington Bridge over Hudson River formally opened.

Oct 25 President Hoover and French Premier Laval at close of conference in Washington issue joint statement of agreement to continue gold standard in France and U. S.

Oct 28 Treaty with reference to establishment and sojourn signed with Turkey. Senate consents May 3, 1932.

Dec 7 Hunger marchers, with petition for guarantee of employment at minimum wage, denied admission to White House.

Dec 8 President Hoover in annual message to Congress recommends an emergency reconstruction finance corporation and a public works administration.

1932

Depth of depression. Stocks fall to 10 per cent of their 1929 peak value, prices for farm products to 40 per cent, exports to one-third their total, industrial production to 50 per cent. Unemployment steadily increases, reaching 15,-

000,000 by end of year. National income has dropped from $81 billion in 1929 to $42 billion.

Ernest O. Lawrence of University of California builds first practical cyclotron. Receives Nobel Physics Prize 1939.

Vitamin C isolated by Dr. C. C. King, University of Pittsburgh.

Technocracy, pseudo-scientific plan for reshaping the state, enjoys a few months' vogue.

Jan 7 Stimson Doctrine announced in identical notes to Japan and China, as result of Japan's occupation of Manchuria: U. S. will not recognize any territory acquired by means contrary to obligations of Kellogg-Briand Pact, 1928.

Jan 12 Hattie W. Caraway, Arkansas, elected to Senate, first woman Senator.

Jan 22 Reconstruction Finance Cor- poration authorized by act of Congress, to aid in financing agriculture and industry, thus to increase employment. [Charles G. Dawes appointed chairman by President Hoover.]

Jan 29 Japan attacks Shanghai. [U. S. protests.]

Feb 2 World Disarmament Confer- ence opens at Geneva under League of Nations auspices. U. S. participates with 60 other nations, with little result.

Feb 4 Olympic Winter Games open at Lake Placid, N. Y. First big exhibition of skiing in U. S.

Feb 5 Andrew W. Mellon appointed ambassador to Great Britain.

Feb 10 Secretary of War Patrick J. Hurley, following tour of investigation, reports time is not ripe for Philippine independence.

Feb 27 Glass-Steagall Banking Act authorizes expansion of credit by Federal Reserve Banks.

Mar 1 Charles A. Lindbergh, Jr., 19- month old son of Colonel Charles A. Lindbergh, kidnapped near Hopewell, N. J.

Mar 3 Twentieth ("Lame Duck") Amendment to Constitution submitted to states for ratification: Congress shall convene on Jan. 3 and terms of President and Vice-President shall begin on Jan. 20.

Mar 7 Distribution of 40,000,000 bush- els of wheat of Federal Farm Board, through the Red Cross, authorized by Congress. 45,000,000 bushels of wheat and 250,000,000 pounds of cotton added July 5.

Mar 23 Norris-La Guardia Anti-In- junction Act prohibits injunctions in labor disputes, except under defined conditions.

Apr 7 Franklin D. Roosevelt broad- casts "forgotten man" speech, keynote of his preconvention campaign.

Apr 30–May 2 Socialist Labor party convention meets at New York. Nominates Verne L. Reynolds of New York for President and J. W. Aiken of Massachusetts for Vice-President.

May 20 Amelia Earhart starts on first solo transatlantic flight made by a woman.

May 22–24 Socialist party convention meets at Milwaukee. Nominates Norman M. Thomas for President and James H. Maurer of Pennsylvania for Vice-President.

May 28 Communist party convention opens at Chicago. Nominates William Z. Foster for President and James W. Ford, Harlem Negro leader, for Vice-President.

June 14–16 Republican National con- vention meets at Chicago. Renominates Herbert Hoover for President on first ballot, and Charles Curtis for Vice-President.

June 16–July 9 Lausanne Conference. European governments agree virtually to cancellation of German reparations if equivalent cancellation of their war debts to U. S. can be arranged. President Hoover and U. S. public opinion opposed.

June 17 Patman Bonus Bill, to pay to veterans the balance of their bonus certificates, rejected by the Senate, 62–18. Was passed in House June 15, under pressure of Bonus Army of 11,000 veterans encamped on edge of Washington.

June 27–July 2 Democratic National convention meets at Chicago. Platform endorses repeal of 18th Amendment. Franklin D. Roosevelt nominated for President on fourth ballot, July 1. John Nance Garner of Texas unanimously nominated for Vice-President July 2.

July 2 Franklin D. Roosevelt flies from Albany to Chicago to accept nomination: "I pledge you, I pledge myself, to a new deal for the American people."

July 5–7 Prohibition party conven- tion meets at Indianapolis. Opposes repeal of 18th Amendment. Nominates William D. Upshaw of Georgia for President and Frank S. Regan of Illinois for Vice-President.

July 10 Farmer Labor party nomi- nates Jacob S. Coxey for President.

July 18 St. Lawrence Deep-Waterway Treaty signed with Canada, to build a Great Lakes-St. Lawrence seaway. Senate refuses consent.

July 21 British Imperial Economic Conference opens in Ottawa, Canada, a response to Hawley-Smoot tariff.

July 21 Emergency Relief and Con- struction Act empowers Reconstruction Finance Corporation to lend $1,800,-000,000 to states for relief and self-liquidating public works.

July 22 Home Loan Bank Act estab- lishes 12 Federal Home Loan Banks, authorized to make loans to mortgage-lending institutions, in effort to rescue the banks.

July 28 Last of Bonus Army driven out of Washington by Federal troops under General Douglas A. MacArthur, by President's orders.

Aug 26 Moratorium on first-mortgage foreclosures ordered by Controller of the Currency.

Aug 31 Total eclipse of the sun ob- served over New England.

Oct 2 Lytton Commission of League of Nations to investigate Japan's invasion of Manchuria, Major-General Frank R. McCoy, U. S. representative, publishes its report, branding Japan as aggressor.

Oct 15 War Memorial Opera House, San Francisco, dedicated with performance of "Tosca" by San Francisco Opera Company.

Oct 31 Nevada proclaims 12-day bank- ing holiday to save her banks.

Nov 7 In *Powell v. Alabama,* **first** Scottsboro case, retrial is granted by Supreme Court, declaring that Negroes on trial had not been properly represented by counsel.

Nov 8 Presidential election. Franklin D. Roosevelt and John N. Garner elected by electoral vote of 472, to 59 for Hoover and Curtis. Popular vote: Roosevelt, Democrat, 22,821,857; Hoover, Republican, 15,761,841; Thomas, Socialist, 881,951; Foster, Communist, 102,785; Reynolds, Socialist Labor, 33,276; Upshaw, Prohibition, 81,869; Coxey, Farmer Labor, 7,309.

Nov 8 House goes Democratic almost 3 to 1.

Nov 11 Tomb of Unknown Soldier in Arlington National Cemetery dedicated by Secretary of War Patrick J. Hurley.

Dec 15 Five debtor nations, including France, default in payments to U. S., 6 make payments due.

1933

The New Deal begins.

Average life expectancy has increased from 49 to 59 years since 1900.

Lynching wave spreads over the South with toll of 42 Negroes.

Minimum wage law for women in laundries passed by New York legislature. Invalidated by Supreme Court 1936.

American Newspaper Guild organized by Heywood Broun.

Newsweek begins publication.

Jan 2 Last U. S. Marines withdrawn from Nicaragua, ending 20-year occupation.

Jan 17 Hawes-Cutting Bill passed by Congress over the President's veto: Philippines are to be independent after 10 years' protectorate. [Unapproved by the Islands, the act never goes into effect.]

Feb 6 Twentieth ("Lame Duck") Amendment proclaimed in effect.

Feb 14 Governor W. A. Comstock of Michigan orders all banks of state closed for 8 days. Bank holidays proclaimed in a score of states by Mar. 4.

Feb 15 Franklin D. Roosevelt escapes assassin's bullet which fatally injures Mayor Anton J. Cermak of Chicago, at Miami, Fla.

Feb 20 Prohibition Repeal (21st) Amendment submitted to conventions in the several states for ratification.

Feb 24 Japanese delegates, having voted against Lytton Report, walk out of League Assembly.

Mar 4 4:30 A.M. Governor Herbert H. Lehman of New York declares a bank holiday.

Mar 4 Franklin D. Roosevelt inau- gurated President "Let me assert my firm belief that the only thing we have to fear is fear itself."

[President Roosevelt's Cabinet: Cordell Hull, Secretary of State; William H. Woodin, Secretary of Treasury; George H. Dern, Secretary of War; Claude A. Swanson, Secretary of Navy; Harold L. Ickes, Secretary of Interior; Henry A. Wallace, Secretary of Agriculture; D. C. Roper, Secretary of Commerce; Frances Perkins, Secretary of Labor; James A. Farley, Postmaster General; H. S. Cummings, Attorney General.]

Mar 5 President Roosevelt proclaims nation-wide bank holiday and places embargo upon exportation of gold.

Mar 9–June 16 The "Hundred Days." Congress, in special session called by President Roosevelt, enacts into law within 100 days principal policies of the New Deal.

Mar 9 Emergency Banking Act gives the President control over banking transactions and foreign exchange; forbids hoarding or export of gold; authorizes opening of banks as soon as determined solvent.

Mar 12 President Roosevelt broad- casts first fireside chat: "It is safer to keep your money in a reopened bank than under the mattress."

Mar 13 Banks begin to open. By Mar. 16 about 75 per cent of Federal Reserve banks are doing business again.

Mar 20 Economy Act reduces salary of Federal employees and reduces payments to veterans.

Mar 22 Beer and Wine Revenue Act legalizes beer and wine with alcoholic content of 3.2 per cent by weight, effective Apr. 7.

Mar 27 Japan formally resigns from League of Nations.

Mar 31 Unemployment Relief Act (Forestation) creates Civilian Conservation Corps.

Apr 4 U. S. Navy dirigible *Akron* beaten down in storm off Barnegat Bay, N. J., 73 persons drown.

Apr 5 The President orders all private holdings of gold surrendered to Federal Reserve banks in return for other coin or currency.

Apr 18 Minnesota Mortgage Morator- ium Law bans foreclosures on farms and homes.

Apr 19 U. S. abandons the gold stan- dard by Presidential proclamation.

Apr 21 British Prime Minister Mac- Donald arrives in Washington to discuss with President Roosevelt problems of forthcoming World Monetary and Economic Conference, London. Ex-Premier Herriot of France and Prime Minister Bennett of Canada, with representatives of other governments, join in discussions shortly.

Apr 24 Five thousand Chicago teachers, paid in scrip, storm banks for 10 months' back pay.

May 12 Federal Emergency Relief Act provides for cooperation between Federal government and the states in economic emergency; provides for Federal Emergency Relief Administration (FERA).

May 12 Agricultural Adjustment Act authorizes establishment of Agricultural Adjustment Administration (AAA) within Department of Agriculture.

May 16 President Roosevelt sends message to other 54 nations invited to World Monetary and Economic Conference, London, urging international economic accord.

May 16 President Roosevelt urges delegations at Geneva Disarmament Conference to "enter into a solemn and definite pact of non-aggression."

May 18 Tennessee Valley Authority Act creates Tennessee Valley Authority (TVA) to maintain and operate power plant at Muscle Shoals.

May 22 Federal Emergency Relief Administration organized, Harry L. Hopkins administrator.

May 27 Securities Act requires registration of new security issues with Federal Trade Commission to protect the buyer.

May 27–Nov 12 Century of Progress Exposition at Chicago marks centennial of founding of that city.

June 5 Gold Repeal Joint Resolution of Congress cancels gold clause in all Federal and private contracts.

June 6 Act creating U. S. Employment Service coordinates in Department of Labor all local, state and Federal employment agencies in one system.

June 12 World Monetary and Economic Conference opens at London. Secretary of State Cordell Hull heads U. S. delegation.

June 13 Home Owners' Refinancing Act creates Home Owners' Loan Corporation to refinance home mortgages.

June 16 National Industrial Recovery Act (NIRA) provides for "codes of fair competition" in industries and collective bargaining for labor under National Recovery Administration (NRA) [General Hugh S. Johnson administrator], and Public Works Administration (PWA) [Secretary of the Interior Harold L. Ickes administrator].

June 16 Farm Credit Act consolidates all rural credit agencies under Farm Credit Administration.

June 16 Emergency Railroad Transportation Act provides for Federal Coordinator of Transportation.

June 16 Glass-Steagall Banking Reform Act provides inter-bank control and protection of deposits and investments.

June 16 Seventy-third Congress, special session, adjourns at 1:22 A.M., ending the Hundred Days.

June 22 Illinois Waterway, linking Great Lakes with Gulf of Mexico, officially opened at Chicago.

July 3 President Roosevelt rejects currency stabilization plan proposed by gold standard countries at World Monetary and Economic Conference in London. Consequence, Conference ends in failure July 27.

Aug 1 Blue Eagle, sign of cooperation with National Recovery Administration (NRA), first appears in store and factory windows. "We Do Our Part."

Aug 5 National Labor Board established by the President under NRA to enforce right of collective bargaining, Senator Robert F. Wagner of New York chairman.

Aug 7 Agreement with Haiti signed, providing for withdrawal of U. S. Marines by Oct. 1, 1934.

Sept 30 U. S. Congress Against War, Communist dominated, ends its session, shortly to become League Against War and Fascism.

Oct Farm strike in Midwestern states withholds products from market for higher prices.

Oct 10 Antiwar Treaty of Non-aggression and Conciliation signed at Rio de Janeiro by the American states. U. S. Senate consents June 15, 1934.

Oct 14 Germany withdraws from Disarmament Conference at Geneva and resigns from League of Nations, effective 2 years hence.

Oct 17 Dr. Albert Einstein, German refugee, arrives in U. S. [Makes home in Princeton, N. J.]

Oct 25 President Roosevelt authorizes Reconstruction Finance Corporation to purchase newly mined gold at $31.36 an ounce, 27 cents above world market. Places value of the dollar at 66 cents in gold.

Nov 7 Fiorello H. La Guardia elected liberal reform mayor of New York.

Nov 9 The President by executive order establishes Civil Works Administration (CWA), Harry L. Hopkins administrator, to provide emergency jobs for 4,000,000 unemployed over the winter, until their absorption by Public Works Administration.

Nov 11 Great dust storm sweeps across South Dakota. In 2 days reaches Albany, N. Y.

Nov 16 Diplomatic relations with U.S.S.R. resumed after White House conference between President Roosevelt and Soviet Commissar for Foreign Affairs Litvinov.

Dec 3 Seventh International American Conference opens at Montevideo, Uruguay. Secretary of State Cordell Hull heads U. S. delegation and accepts policy of non-intervention in affairs of American states, recommended by Conference. Senate consents June 15, 1934.

Dec 5 Twenty-first Amendment, repealing 18th Amendment, goes into effect with ratification by Utah, 36th state.

Dec 28 President Roosevelt in address in Washington commits U. S. to doctrine formulated at Montevideo Conference: "The definite policy of the United States from now on is one opposed to armed intervention."

1934

National Archives created by Congress to preserve Federal records.

"Okies" and "Arkies" in their jalopies begin trek to California. Within next 5 years, 350,000 Dust Bowl farmers migrate to California.

Dr. Francis E. Townsend of Long Beach, Cal., announces his Old Age Revolving Pension plan. Would insure $200 monthly to every unemployed person over 60.

Father Charles Coughlin, radio priest of Royal Oak, Mich., organizes National Union for Social Justice, with demands for radical inflation.

Upton Sinclair, Democratic candidate for governor of California, announces plan, End Poverty in California, the EPIC.

Jan 4 President Roosevelt announces to Congress that cost of recovery program will reach $10,500,000,000 by June 20, 1935.

Jan 8 In *Home Building and Loan Association v. Blaisdell et al.*, Supreme Court upholds Minnesota Mortgage Moratorium Law as constitutional.

Jan 30 Gold Reserve Act authorizes President to revalue the dollar at 50 to 60 cents in terms of gold content. Jan. 31, Presidential proclamation fixes the dollar at 59.06 cents, gold value.

Jan 31 Farm Mortgage Refinancing Act creates Federal Farm Mortgage Corporation.

Feb 5 Senator Huey Pierce Long of Louisiana presents in the Senate his Share Our Wealth program, a plan of redistribution. "Every man a king."

Feb 12 Export-Import Bank of Washington incorporated with $11,000,000 capital, $10,000,000 subscribed by RFC.

Feb 15 Civil Works-Emergency Relief Act appropriates additional $950,000,000 for continuance of civil works program and for direct relief under Federal Emergency Relief Administration.

Feb 23 Crop Loan Act authorizes loans to farmers for crop production.

Mar 24 Tydings-McDuffie Philippine Independence Act promises independence after 10 years. Accepted by Philippine legislature May 1.

Apr 13 4,700,000 families on relief, as reported by Relief Administrator Harry L. Hopkins.

Apr 13 Johnson Debt Default Act prohibits additional loans to any country in default in debt to U. S.

Apr 19 Special committee to investigate munitions industry appointed by Senate, Senator Gerald P. Nye chairman.

Apr 21 Cotton Control Act empowers AAA to control cotton-planting quotas.

Apr 27 Argentine Anti-War Pact signed at Buenos Aires by U. S. with 12 Latin-American states. Senate consents June 15.

May 9 Jones-Costigan Sugar Act brings sugar beets and sugar cane under control of AAA.

May 10–11 Dust storm blows some 300,000,000 tons of topsoil from Texas, Oklahoma, Kansas and Colorado into Atlantic Ocean, aftermath of wartime plowing.

May 18 Six crime control bills signed on this day.

May 26 Century of Progress Exposition opens at Chicago for second year.

May 29 Treaty signed with Cuba releasing her from terms of Platt Amendment (May 22, 1903). Senate consents May 31.

May 31 U. S. Fleet of over 80 warships enters New York harbor from the Pacific via Panama Canal. Received by President Roosevelt.

June 6 Securities and Exchange Commission (SEC) established by act of Congress. Limits bank credit for speculative purposes.

June 7 Corporate Bankruptcy Act simplifies process of reorganization.

June 12 Air mail letter rate of 6 cents an ounce adopted by act of Congress.

June 12 Reciprocal Trade Agreements Act authorizes the President, for period of 3 years, to negotiate trade agreements with other countries without advice or consent of Senate. Secretary Hull concludes 18 treaties before end of Roosevelt's first term.

June 12 U. S. membership in International Telecommunication Union (ITC) becomes effective.

June 18 Indian Reorganization Act provides a more enlightened policy toward the Indians.

June 19 Silver Purchase Act, forced through Congress by silver bloc, authorizes the President to nationalize silver.

June 19 National Labor Relations Board, replacing National Labor Board 1933, created by joint resolution of Congress.

June 19 Federal Communications Commission (FCC), to supervise telephone, telegraph and radio industries, created by act of Congress.

June 27 Railway Pension Act.

June 28 Frazier-Lemke Farm Bankruptcy Act. Mortgage foreclosures may be postponed for 5 years under certain conditions.

June 28 Federal Housing Administration (FHA), to assist in financing building and improvements, created by National Housing Act.

June 28 Tobacco Control Act empowers AAA to control tobacco-planting quotas.

June 28 Taylor Grazing Act gives to Department of Interior power to regulate grazing on public domain of the West.

Summer Epidemic of strikes.

July 16 Country's first general strike called in San Francisco area, in sympathy with strike of 12,000 members of International Longshoremen's Association.

Aug American Liberty League formed to unseat President Roosevelt and the New Deal.

Aug 9 Silver nationalized and to be purchased at 50.01 cents an ounce, by Presidential proclamation.

Aug 15 Last of U. S. Marines with- drawn from Haiti, as ordered by President Roosevelt.

Aug 20 U. S. membership in Interna- tional Labor Organization (ILO), becomes effective.

Aug 24 Reciprocal trade agreement signed with Cuba, first of Secretary Hull's trade agreements.

Sept 18 U.S.S.R. admitted to League of Nations.

Nov 6 Nebraska adopts unicameral legislature.

Dec 3 Right of land-grant colleges to require military training upheld by Supreme Court in *Hamilton v. Regents of University of California.*

Dec 29 Japan renounces Washington Naval Treaty of 1922 and London Naval Treaty of 1930, withdrawal to take effect Dec. 1936.

1935

New Deal swings toward reform. 1933 emphasis was recovery.

Isolationist sentiment mounts with belief that the great blunder of U. S. was in entering World War I. Walter Millis' *Road to War; America, 1914–1917* (1935) reflects this temper.

American Student Union organized, "against war and fascism."

Alcoholics Anonymous organized.

Jan 4 President Roosevelt before joint session of Congress declares we "must quit this business of relief" by providing 3,500,000 jobs for idle "employables."

Jan 7 In *Panama Refining Company* *et al. v. Ryan et al.,* Supreme Court invalidates oil production control provi-

sions of National Industrial Recovery Act.

Jan 29 Senate again votes against ad- herence to World Court.

Feb 4 Issuance of "baby bonds" by Treasury Department authorized by act of Congress.

Feb 18 In *Norman v. Baltimore and* *Ohio Railroad Company,* Supreme Court upholds joint resolution of Congress eliminating gold clause from all public and private contracts, June 5, 1933.

Apr 1 In *Norris v. Alabama,* second Scottsboro case, Supreme Court calls for retrial, declaring accused Negroes were denied protection of laws before all-white jury.

Apr 8 Emergency Relief Appropria- tion Act authorizes expenditure of nearly $5,000,000,000 to provide "work relief and to increase employment by providing useful projects" under Works Progress Administration (WPA).

Apr 30 Resettlement Administration created by executive order of the President to move persons from poor lands to better, Rexford G. Tugwell administrator.

May 6 In *Railroad Retirement Board* *v. Alton Railway Company,* Supreme Court holds Railway Pension Act of June 27, 1934, unconstitutional.

May 6 Works Progress Administration (WPA) created by executive order of the President, Harry L. Hopkins administrator.

May 11 Rural Electrification Adminis- tration established by executive order of the President.

May 22 Soldiers' Bonus Bill vetoed by the President. Veto sustained.

May 27 National Recovery Adminis- tration invalidated in *Schechter Poultry Corporation v. United States* by unanimous decision of Supreme Court.

May 27 Frazier-Lemke Farm Bank- ruptcy Act invalidated by the Supreme Court in *Louisville Joint Stock Land Bank v. Radford.*

June 26 National Youth Administration (NYA), a division of Works Progress Administration, established by the President by executive order. Job-seeking youths estimated at 4,200,000.

July 4 National Education Association, at Denver convention, votes almost unanimously against military training in tax-supported schools.

July 5 Wagner-Connery or National Labor Relations Act creates new National Labor Relations Board and reasserts right of collective bargaining.

July 26 Works Progress Administration appoints directors of Writers', Art and Music projects.

July 29 Thomas E. Dewey made special prosecutor in drive against crime in New York.

Aug 9 Motor Carrier Act places interstate bus and truck lines under Interstate Commerce Commission.

Aug 14 Social Security Act provides system of old-age annuity and unemployment insurance.

Aug 26 UAW, at its first convention, Detroit, receives charter from AFL.

Aug 26 Public Utility Holding Company Act places all utility holding companies under supervision of Securities and Exchange Commission.

Aug 30 Bituminous Coal Conservation (Guffey Coal) Act. Designed to replace NRA code in bituminous industry.

Aug 30 Revenue Act provides for inheritance and gift taxes, the surtax and corporation income tax to achieve diffusion of wealth.

Aug 31 First Neutrality Act forbids transportation of munitions to any belligerents after the President has declared state of war, and authorizes the President to prohibit travel by American citizens on belligerent ships.

Sept 8 Senator Huey P. Long assassinated at Baton Rouge, La., dies Sept. 10.

Oct 5 President Roosevelt proclaims "that a state of war unhappily exists between Ethiopia and the Kingdom of Italy" and declares provisions of Neutrality Act of Aug. 31 in effect.

Oct 26 Farmers in 16 corn-hog states, in AAA sponsored referendums, vote 6–1 for continuance of Agricultural Adjustment Administration for 1936.

Nov 9 Committee for Industrial Organization (CIO), President John L. Lewis of UMW chairman, formed within AFL, at Washington.

Nov 11 Stratosphere flight made by army pilots in balloon *Explorer II* over South Dakota, reaching altitude of 14 miles.

Nov 15 Commonwealth of Philippines inaugurated under presidency of Manuel Quezon y Malina, elected Sept. 17.

Nov 22 *China Clipper* leaves Alameda, Cal., on first airmail trip across the Pacific, reaching Manila in 7 days.

Dec 9 Second London Naval Conference opens, Norman H. Davis U. S. delegate. Japan demands parity with U. S. and Great Britain and leaves Conference when refused.

1936

Sulfa drugs, discovered in Germany, are developed and used in U. S. from 1936.

Historical Records Survey set up by WPA.

Life, with name of earlier humor magazine, first published.

Jan 6 In *United States v. Butler,* Supreme Court invalidates Agricultural Adjustment Act.

Jan 27 Soldiers' Bonus Bill, providing for immediate payment of veterans' certificates, due in 1945, passed by Congress over the President's veto.

Feb 17 In *Ashwander v. Tennessee Valley Authority,* Supreme Court upholds right of TVA to dispose of surplus power, a victory for New Deal before Supreme Court.

Feb 29 Second Neutrality Act extends act of Aug. 31, 1935, to May 1, 1937, and amends it to prohibit loans or credits to belligerents.

Feb 29 Soil Conservation and Domestic Allotment Act, to circumvent invalidation of Agricultural Adjustment Act.

Mar 2 Treaty with Panama signed. U. S. ends its protectorate; Panama agrees to cooperate in defense of the Canal. Senate consents July 25, 1939.

Mar 20 Golden jubilee of establishment of alternating current system in America celebrated throughout the country under American Institute of Electrical Engineers.

Mar 25 New London Naval Treaty signed by France, Great Britain and U. S., providing cautious naval limitations. Senate consents May 18.

Apr 25–28 Socialist Labor party convention meets at New York. Nominates J. W. Aiken of Massachusetts for President and Emil F. Teichert of New York for Vice-President.

May 5–7 Prohibition party convention meets at Niagara Falls. Nominates Dr. D. Leigh Colvin of New York for President and Sergeant Alvin C. York of Tennessee for Vice-President.

May 9 Italy proclaims annexation of Ethiopia.

May 18 In *Carter v. Carter Coal Company et al.*, Supreme Court declares Bituminous Coal Conservation Act of Aug. 30, 1935, unconstitutional.

May 25 Norman M. Thomas nominated for President and George O. Nelson of Wisconsin for Vice-President, by Socialist party at Cleveland.

June 1 New York Minimum Wage Law for women, 1933, declared unconstitutional by Supreme Court in *Morehead v. New York ex rel. Tipaldo.*

June 9–12 Republican National Convention meets at Cleveland. Nominates Alfred M. Landon of Kansas for President and Frank Knox of Illinois for Vice-President.

June 19 William Lemke of North Dakota announces candidacy for Presidency on Union party ticket.

June 20 Robinson-Patman Price Discrimination Act prohibits price discrimination, advantageous to chain stores.

June 23–27 Democratic National Convention meets at Philadelphia. Renominates President Roosevelt and Vice-President Garner and endorses the New Deal.

June 24–28 Communist party convention meets at New York. Nominates Earl Browder for President and James W. Ford for Vice-President, both of New York.

June 27 Great Lakes Exposition opens at Cleveland.

June 29 Merchant Marine Act provides for development and maintenance of well-balanced merchant marine.

Aug   Unions associated with Committee for Industrial Organization (CIO) suspended by AFL.

Aug 7 U. S. announces policy of non-interference in Spanish civil war, which began July 17.

Sept 16 Harvard University Tercentenary opens.

Sept 16 President Roosevelt formally accepts invitation to become Presidential candidate of American Labor party.

Oct 8 Professor Manley O. Hudson elected to World Court by League Assembly.

Oct 25 Rome-Berlin Axis formed.

Oct 30 39,000 maritime workers go on strike, tying up all West Coast ports. Strike spreads to Eastern and Gulf ports. Ends Jan. 24, 1937, when seamen vote to accept tentative agreements.

Nov 3 Presidential election. Roosevelt and Garner elected by electoral vote of 523, to 8 for Landon and Knox. Popular vote: Roosevelt, Democrat, 27,751,597; Landon, Republican, 16,679,583; Lemke, Union, 882,479; Thomas, Socialist, 187,720; Browder, Communist, 80,159; Colvin, Prohibition, 37,847; Aiken, Socialist Labor, 12,777.

Nov 25 Japan signs Anti-Comintern Pact with Germany.

Dec 1 Inter-American Conference for the Maintenance of Peace opened by President Roosevelt at Buenos Aires, calling upon nations of New World to help Old World to avert war. [Conference adopts a consultative pact in interests of peace.]

Dec 30 Sit-down strike by UAW, backed by CIO, begins in General Motors plants at Flint, Mich. Strike ends Feb. 11, 1937, when UAW is recognized by General Motors as sole bargaining agency for all employees in its plants.

1937

Sharp drop in business activity sets in at mid-year, after 4 years of marked economic recovery.

4,470 strikes, mostly sit-down variety, recorded for year.

National Cancer Institute established.

Golden Gate Bridge, San Francisco, completed.

"Pins and Needles," musical show, presented by International Ladies' Garment Workers' Union Players at Labor State Theatre in New York. Breaks musical show records by 1939.

Road to Reunion by Paul H. Buck published. Pulitzer Prize 1938.

Jan 20 Franklin D. Roosevelt and John Nance Garner inaugurated for second term, on new date provided by 20th Amendment.
[President Roosevelt's Cabinet: Cordell Hull, Secretary of State; Henry Morgenthau, Jr., Secretary of Treasury; Harry A. Woodring, Secretary of War; Claude A. Swanson, Secretary of Navy; Harold L. Ickes, Secretary of Interior; Henry A. Wallace, Secretary of Agriculture; D. C. Roper, Secretary of Commerce; Frances Perkins, Secretary of Labor; James A. Farley, Postmaster General; H. S. Cummings, Attorney General.]

Feb 5 President Roosevelt in special message to Congress recommends reorganization of Federal judiciary. Asks legislation empowering him to appoint "additional judges in all Federal courts . . . where there are incumbent judges of retirement age who do not choose to retire or to resign."

Mar 1 Full pay to retiring Supreme Court Justices over 70 granted by act of Congress.

Mar 1 Reciprocal Trade Agreements Act extends Trade Agreements Act of 1934 for 3 years.

Mar 2 U. S. Steel Corporation, to avoid strike, grants unionization of employees under Steel Workers' Organizing Committee (CIO).

Mar 4 President Roosevelt, speaking at Democratic Victory Dinner, calls for party loyalty on Supreme Court reorganization proposals.

Mar 29 In *West Coast Hotel v. Parrish,* Supreme Court upholds principle of minimum wage for women, reversing its decisions in *Adkins v. Children's Hospital* (1923) and *Morehead v. New York* (1936).

Apr 12 National Labor Relations Act (1935) upheld by the Supreme Court in series of 5–4 decisions.

Apr 26 Bituminous Coal (Guffey-Vinson) Act, successor to Bituminous Coal Conservation (Guffey) Act (1935), provides for Bituminous Coal Commission.

May 1 Third Neutrality Act re-enacts neutrality legislation of 1935 and 1936, expiring at midnight, and authorizes the President to permit sale to belligerents of certain commodities, on cash-and-carry basis.

May 6 German dirigible *Hindenberg* explodes and burns at Lakehurst, N. J.

May 24 Social Security Act (1935) upheld by Supreme Court in 3 cases.

June 2 Justice Willis Van Devanter retires from Supreme Court at age of 78.

June 12 Pan-American Exposition at Dallas, Tex., opens. Closes Oct. 31.

June 14 Senate Judiciary Committee reports unfavorably on the President's Judiciary Reorganization Bill and his Supreme Court-packing plan.

July 14 Senator Joseph T. Robinson, Democratic leader in Senate, dies, signaling abandonment of the President's Court-packing plan.

July 22 Bankhead-Jones Farm Tenant Act provides for Farm Security Administration, replacing Resettlement Administration, with authority to make long term loans for purchase of farms.

Aug 12 Hugh L. Black of Alabama nominated to Supreme Court by the President, replacing Justice Willis Van Devanter.

Aug 26 Judiciary Reform Act makes only minor reforms in lower courts, without affecting Supreme Court in any way.

Sept 1 Wagner-Steagall Act establishes U. S. Housing Authority (USHA) to remedy housing shortage, by providing financial assistance to the states.

Sept 28 Bonneville Dam on Columbia River, Ore., dedicated by President Roosevelt.

Oct 5 President Roosevelt in his "quarantine speech" at Chicago pledges U. S., with other peace loving nations, to quarantine aggressor nations. Leads to bitter attacks by isolationists.

Nov 3 Brussels Conference of signatory powers of Nine Power Treaty (1922), except Japan, opens to negotiate an end to hostilities in China. Nov. 24 Conference ends, a failure.

Dec 11 Italy withdraws from League of Nations.

Dec 12 Japanese airmen sink U. S. gunboat *Panay* in Chinese waters. Demands for indemnity get quick results.

Dec 14 Amendment to the Constitution providing for popular referendum before war may be declared proposed by Congressman Louis L. Ludlow, Indiana. Shelved by vote of 209–188, Jan. 10.

1938

Year opens with recession in business. Unemployment increases: Government unemployment census reports 5,833,401 totally unemployed; 5,231,117 partially employed. Fewer strikes.

Increase in anti-Semitism observed.

Oxford group under Dr. Frank Buchman begins its "Moral Re-Armament" campaign.

Jan 14 Industrialists and labor leaders in White House conference tell the President he must do something about prices, taxation, utilities and money, to steady public nerves.

Jan 28 The President in national defense message asks Congress for appropriations to build up Army and Navy in face of possibility of war.

Feb 3 Conference of small business men, called by the President, presents resolutions calling for repeal or modification of New Deal measures.

Feb 11 Edison Tower, at Menlo Park, N. J., dedicated and lighted on 91st anniversary of inventor's birth.

Feb 16 Second Agricultural Adjustment Act includes the "ever-normal granary" in program.

Mar 16 U. S. Navy begins second war game in the Pacific within a year.

Mar 18 President Cárdenas of Mexico orders seizure of foreign-owned oil properties. Settlement not made with U. S. companies until 1941.

Mar 31 Herbert Hoover, guest of Council on Foreign Relations, warns U. S. to keep out of war, and to avoid alliance with other democratic nations against fascist countries. He asserts that planned economy and reciprocal tariff agreements are steps toward war.

Apr 14 President Roosevelt asks Congress for aid to stimulate further recovery.

May 17 Naval Construction Act authorizes billion-dollar expansion.

May 23 In *Helvering v. Gerhardt* Supreme Court holds that state employees are subject to Federal income tax.

May 27 Revenue Bill of 1938 reducing profits tax on corporations becomes law without the President's signature.

June 21 Emergency Relief Appropriation Act.

June 22 Basic Bankruptcy Act of July 1, 1898, amended by act of Congress.

June 23 Civil Aeronautics Authority (CAA) created by act of Congress to regulate air traffic.

June 25 Federal Food, Drug and Cosmetic Act safeguards the buyer.

June 25 Fair Labor Standards (Wages and Hours) Act. Culmination of New Deal effort for agriculture and labor.

June 28 Flood Control Act authorizes public works on rivers and harbors.

July 1–3 Reunion of the Blue and the Grey at 75th anniversary of Battle of Gettysburg. President Roosevelt dedicates memorial monument.

July 14 Howard Hughes completes record round-the-world flight in 3 days, 19 hours, 14 minutes, 28 seconds.

Aug 18 "Canada is part of the British Empire. . . . The United States will not stand idly by if" Canada is threatened "by any other Empire," so declares President Roosevelt at Queen's University, Kingston, Ontario.

Sept 21 Tropical hurricane strikes Atlantic Coast and New England without warning, taking 700 lives and destroying 2,000,000,000 trees.

Sept 26 President Roosevelt sends personal messages to governments of Czechoslovakia, France, Germany and Great Britain, urging settlement of the Sudetenland issue without war.

Sept 30 Munich Agreement signed by Hitler, Mussolini, Chamberlain and Daladier, averting war by allowing Nazis to take over the Sudetenland in Czechoslovakia.

Oct Majority of Americans express approval of Prime Minister Chamberlain's settlement at Munich, according to Gallup poll.

Oct 3 Hitler enters the Sudetenland, in Czechoslovakia, in triumph.

Oct 30 Orson Welles stages his "Invasion from Mars" over radio, causing widespread panic.

Nov Committee for Industrial Organization formally organizes as Congress of Industrial Organizations, adopts a constitution and, on Nov. 18, elects John L. Lewis president.

Nov 8 Mid-term elections reveal turning of the tide from New Deal. Republican membership in House increases from 89 to 172.

Nov 14 U. S. Ambassador Hugh R. Wilson recalled from Germany "for report and consultation."

Nov 18 Germany recalls her ambassador Dr. Hans Heinrich Dieckhoff from U. S.

Dec 12 In *Missouri ex rel. Gaines v. Canada*, Supreme Court rules that Missouri shall provide equal accommodations "within the state" for law students irrespective of race.

Dec 24 Declaration of Lima adopted by 21 American states at Eighth International American Conference, Lima, Peru. A reaffirmation of principle of consultation for defense of "peace, security, or territorial integrity" of the American republics (Buenos Aires, 1936).

1939

Clarence Streit, author of *Union Now*, advocates a merger of North Atlantic and Scandinavian democracies for self-defense.

Northern and Southern branches of Methodist Episcopal Church reunited.

Nylon, made from coal, air and water, becomes a commercial fabric.

Samuel H. Kress gives his collection of 375 Italian paintings to National Art Gallery, Washington.

Jan 4 President Roosevelt in annual message to Congress stresses need for revision of Neutrality Act of 1937.

Jan 5 President Roosevelt submits to Congress his budget message, including item of $1,319,558,000 for national defense.

Jan 5 Felix Frankfurter of Harvard Law School appointed to Supreme Court by President Roosevelt.

Jan 7 Thomas J. Mooney pardoned by Governor Olson of California after 23 years in prison. Was convicted of bombing preparedness parade, San Francisco, 1916.

Jan 12 President Roosevelt in special message to Congress recommends additional $535,000,000 for defense, to be spent during next 2 years.

Jan 30 In *Tennessee Electric Power Company v. Tennessee Valley Authority,* Supreme Court upholds TVA in competition with private companies.

Feb 13 Louis B. Brandeis, at 82, re- tires from Supreme Court.

Feb 18 Golden Gate Exposition opens at San Francisco. Closes Oct. 29.

Feb 27 In *National Labor Relations Board v. Fansteel Metallurgical Corporation,* Supreme Court outlaws sit-down strike.

Mar 14 Hitler invades Czechoslovakia, takes Bohemia and Moravia.

Mar 27 State income tax on Federal salaries upheld by Supreme Court in *Graves v. New York ex rel. O'Keefe.*

Apr 1 U. S. recognizes Franco's gov- ernment at end of Spanish civil war.

Apr 3 Reorganization Act empowers the President to investigate and reorganize executive agencies of the government.

Apr 7 Mussolini invades Albania.

Apr 14 President Roosevelt in identi- cal notes to Mussolini and Hitler asks

for 10-year guarantee of peace for 31 European and Near Eastern states, and offers participation in international discussion of world trade and limitation of armaments. No direct reply received.

Apr 17 Second Agricultural Adjust- ment Act of Feb. 16, 1938, upheld by Supreme Court in *Mulford v. Smith.*

Apr 30 New York World's Fair, The World of Tomorrow, opened by President Roosevelt in Court of Peace. Closes Oct. 31.

Apr 30 Television first publicly broad- cast from Empire State Building, New York.

May Food-Stamp Plan to dispense food surpluses to the needy tried out in Rochester, N. Y. Extended to some 150 cities within next 2 years.

May 23 U. S. submarine *Squalus* sinks off Portsmouth, N. H., 33 of her 59 men rescued by diving bell.

June 8 King George and Queen Eliza- beth of Great Britain arrive in Washington.

June 23 United States and Great Brit- ain sign agreement for exchange of 600,- 000 bales of American cotton for 85,000 tons of British rubber. Senate consents June 29.

June 28 Regular transatlantic pas- senger air service begins: 22 persons aboard Pan-American Airways' *Dixie Clipper* leave Port Washington, Long Island, reach Lisbon 23 hours and 52 minutes later.

July 1 Federal Security Agency, pro- vided for in Reorganization Act, Apr. 3, consolidating Federal welfare agencies, goes into effect.

July 14 President Roosevelt in special message to Congress asks repeal of arms embargo.

July 18 President Roosevelt and Sec- retary of State Hull urge Congress to act on neutrality revision.

July 26 Secretary of State Hull abro- gates trade treaty with Japan, signed in 1911.

Aug 2 Hatch Act, "to prevent pernicious political activities" of Federal employees. Outcome of campaigning by WPA administrators in certain states in 1938 elections.

Aug 23 Soviet-German Non-aggression Pact signed at Moscow.

Aug 24 President Roosevelt cables King Victor Emmanuel of Italy, Chancellor Hitler and President Moszicki of Poland, urging arbitration, conciliation or negotiation to avoid war.

Sept 1 Germany invades Poland without declaration of war, at dawn, beginning World War II.

Sept 3 Great Britain and France declare war on Germany.

Sept 3 President Roosevelt in fireside chat declares, "This nation will remain a neutral nation, but I cannot ask that every American remain neutral in thought as well."

Sept 3 British passenger ship *Athenia* torpedoed without warning off the Hebrides. Sinks the next day; 30 Americans drowned.

Sept 4 Secretary of State Hull issues order restricting travel by Americans to Europe to "imperative necessity."

Sept 5 U. S. proclaims neutrality in war in Europe.

Sept 17 U.S.S.R. invades Poland.

Sept 21 Congress convenes in special session upon call of the President, who urges repeal of embargo provisions of Neutrality Act of 1937 and return to neutral rights under international law.

Sept 28 Partition of Poland by Germany and U.S.S.R. in border and friendship treaty.

Oct 2 Secretary of State Hull announces U. S. does not recognize conquest of Poland by force, and will maintain diplomatic relations with new Polish government set up in Paris.

Oct 3 Declaration of Panama. Foreign ministers of the American Republics, meeting at Panama City, announce a sea safety zone around the Americas.

Oct 4 Secretary of State Hull warns American merchant ships to avoid shore waters of European belligerents.

Oct 9 U. S. *City of Flint* seized by German raider, taken to neutral port, Murmansk. Released Oct. 26.

Oct 11 AFL adopts resolutions opposing U. S. involvement in European War, and boycotting German, Russian and Japanese goods.

Oct 18 President Roosevelt issues proclamation closing U. S. ports and waters to submarines of belligerents.

Autumn Advisory Committee on Uranium appointed by President Roosevelt when it is disclosed that in Germany the uranium nucleus has been split by assault of neutrons.

Nov 4 Fourth Neutrality Act legalizes sale of munitions on basis of cash-and-carry.

Nov 30 U.S.S.R. invades Finland.

Dec 5 Ex-President Herbert Hoover organizes U. S. drive for Finnish relief.

Dec 10 Congress grants Finland $10,-000,000 credit for agricultural supplies.

Dec 23 Myron C. Taylor, Episcopal layman, appointed by President Roosevelt as personal representative to the Vatican.

1940

Population, 131,669,275.

Average life expectancy has reached 64 years, increased from 49 in 1900.

Radios are in 29,500,000 homes in U. S.

Average weekly attendance at movies reaches 54,000,000, according to Gallup poll.

Jan 2 U. S. protests British seizures of American mail.

Jan 3 President Roosevelt submits to Congress $8,400,000,000 budget, including $1,800,000,000 for national defense.

Feb 17 Undersecretary of State Sumner Welles departs to survey "present conditions in Europe." Visits Berlin, Paris, London, Rome. Sails for home Mar. 20.

Apr 7 Norman M. Thomas chosen Presidential nominee by Socialist party for fourth time.

Apr 10 President Roosevelt orders freezing of Danish and Norwegian assets in U. S. to prevent their falling into German hands. Denmark and Norway were invaded by Germany Apr. 9.

Apr 12 Reciprocal Trade Agreements Act re-enacted for 3 years.

Apr 28 Socialist Labor party in convention at New York nominates John W. Aiken of Massachusetts for President and Aaron M. Orange of New York for Vice-President.

Apr 29 President Roosevelt appeals to Premier Mussolini to exert influence for peace. Repeats appeal May 14, and May 26 and May 30. All rejected by Mussolini.

May 1 U. S. establishes provisional consulate in Greenland.

May 10 President Roosevelt orders freezing of assets in U. S. of Belgium, Luxemburg and the Netherlands, to prevent their falling into German hands. Germany invades these 3 countries this day.

May 10 Prohibition party in convention at Chicago nominates Roger W. Babson of Massachusetts for President and Edgar V. Moorman of Illinois for Vice-President.

May 11 New York World's Fair opens for second year. Closes Oct. 27.

May 16 President Roosevelt asks Congress for additional appropriation for defense. "I should like to see this nation geared . . . to production of 50,000 planes a year."

May 19 Committee to Defend America by Aiding the Allies organized by William Allen White.

May 25 Office for Emergency Management established by the President.

May 28 National Defense Advisory Commission of 7, headed by William S. Knudsen and Edward R. Stettinius, named by President Roosevelt to co-ordinate industry, finance, labor and consumer.

May 31 President Roosevelt requests of Congress additional defense appropriation of $1,275,000,000.

June 2 Communist party in convention at New York nominates Earl Browder for President and James W. Ford for Vice-President.

June 4 AFL and CIO pledge full support to national defense program.

June 10 Italy declares war against Great Britain and France.

June 10 President Roosevelt, speaking at University of Virginia, advocates "full speed ahead" in promotion of American defense and extension of material aid to "opponents of force."

June 11 Naval Supply Act authorizes appropriation of $1,490,000,000.

June 13 Military Supply Act authorizes appropriation of $1,800,000,000.

June 14 Germans enter Paris unopposed.

June 17 President Roosevelt orders freezing of all French assets in U. S.

June 18 Admiral Harold R. Stark, Chief of Naval Operations, recommends to Congress a 2-ocean navy in $4,000,000,000 expansion program.

June 18 U. S. notifies Germany and Italy that it will not recognize any territorial transfers in Western Hemisphere from one non-American power to another.

June 20 President Roosevelt appoints Henry L. Stimson Secretary of War and Frank Knox Secretary of Navy, both Republicans.

June 22 France signs armistice with Germany at Compiegne.

June 24–28 Republican National Convention meets at Philadelphia. Nominates Wendell L. Willkie of Indiana for President and Charles L. McNary of Oregon for Vice-President.

June 25 Revenue Act increases income taxes to yield $994,300,000 a year.

June 26 First Supplemental Defense Appropriation Act authorizes $1,762,-513,908 for defense.

June 27 Espionage Act of June 15, 1917, revised by proclamation of the President.

June 29 Alien Registration Act. Registration closed Dec. 26, numbering approximately 5,000,000 aliens.

July 2 Export Control Act empowers the President to stop or curtail export of material vital to American defense program.

July 10 Battle of Britain begins. First large-scale German air attack.

July 10 President Roosevelt submits to Congress additional $4,800,000,000 program for defense, including naval expansion and equipment for land force of 2,000,000.

July 13 President Roosevelt orders freezing of assets in U. S. of Estonia, Lithuania and Latvia. U.S.S.R. annexes these 3 countries July 21.

July 15–19 Democratic National Convention meets at Chicago. Franklin D. Roosevelt renominated on first ballot, and Henry A. Wallace nominated for Vice-President.

July 19 Hatch Act of Aug. 2, 1939 extended to curb election activities of employees of state agencies receiving Federal funds.

July 20 Congress authorizes appropriation of $4,000,000,000 for 2-ocean navy.

July 30 Declaration of Havana, plan for joint trusteeship of European colonies in Western Hemisphere in danger of being transferred to Germany, adopted by foreign ministers meeting at Havana in Pan-American Conference called by U. S. Senate consents Sept. 27.

July 31 U. S. embargoes aviation gasoline beyond Western Hemisphere.

Aug 17 Germany announces total blockade of waters around Great Britain.

Aug 18 U. S. and Canada announce Joint Board of Defense.

Aug 21 English children, to avoid German air raids over England, begin to arrive in America.

Aug 27 President Roosevelt authorized by Congress to call out National Guard because of "increasing seriousness of the international situation."

Sept America First Committee organized for avoidance of war at any price.

Sept 2 U. S.-British destroyer-bases deal completed: 50 American destroyers to be exchanged for right to build air and naval bases on British possessions in Western Hemisphere.

Sept 6 U. S. announces proposed use of leased naval and air bases by other American republics "for common defense of the Hemisphere."

Sept 9 Second Supplemental Defense Appropriation Act authorizes $5,251,-486,392 for Army and Navy.

Sept 16 Burke-Wadsworth Selective Training and Service Act.

Sept 27 German-Italian-Japanese 10-year military-economic alliance signed at Berlin.

Oct 8 Second Revenue Act of 1940 provides for excess-profits tax upon earnings of corporations.

Oct 8 Third Supplemental Defense Appropriation Act authorizes $1,482,-693,636 for defense.

Oct 16 U. S. embargoes exports of scrap iron and steel to Japan.

Oct 16 Selective Service Registration Day. Approximately 16,400,000 men between 21 and 36 register for year of military training and service.

Oct 24 Forty-hour week, provided for by Fair Labor Standards Act, 1938, goes into effect.

Oct 29 Serial number 158 drawn by Secretary of War Stimson, inaugurating first peacetime military draft in U. S.

Nov Radiation Laboratory set up at Massachusetts Institute of Technology for experimentation in radar.

Nov 5 Presidential election. Roosevelt and Wallace elected by electoral vote of 449, to 82 for Willkie and McNary. Popular vote: Roosevelt, Democrat, 27,-244,160; Willkie, Republican, 22,305,-198; Thomas, Socialist, 99,557; Babson, Prohibition, 57,812; Browder, Communist, 46,251; Aiken, Socialist Labor, 10,164.

Nov 15 Twelve-day airplane plant strike begins at Downey, Cal., halting $50,000,000 plane construction.

Nov 22 Philip Murray elected president of CIO, succeeding John L. Lewis.

Nov 28 Inter-American Coffee Marketing Agreement between U. S. and other American republics signed at Washington. Senate consents Feb. 3, 1941.

Dec Gallup poll indicates 39 per cent of Americans still think U. S. in error in entering World War I, drop from 64 per cent in 1937.

Dec President Roosevelt appoints Admiral William D. Leahy ambassador to Vichy France.

Dec 17 President Roosevelt in press conference suggests lending arms to Great Britain (lend-lease): "The best defense of Great Britain is the best defense of the United States."

Dec 29 President Roosevelt in fireside chat: "We must be the great arsenal of democracy."

1941

College and university enrollment declines sharply.

National Art Gallery in Washington, and $35,000,000 art collection, gift of Andrew W. Mellon, dedicated.

American Red Cross Blood Donor Service established, 13,000,000 blood donations received by end of hostilities, 1945.

Jan 6 President Roosevelt recommends to Congress lend-lease for the Allies and enunciates the Four Freedoms: freedom of speech and expression, freedom of religion, freedom from want, and freedom from fear.

Jan 7 Office of Production Management created by executive order. William S. Knudsen appointed director-general and Sidney Hillman associate director-general.

Jan 8 President Roosevelt submits to Congress budget of $17,485,529,000, of which $10,811,000,000 is for defense: it is "a reflection of a world at war."

Jan 10 Lend-Lease Bill, to extend lend-lease aid to countries whose defense is vital to that of U. S., introduced in both houses of Congress. Becomes law Mar. 11.

Jan 20 President Roosevelt's third inauguration. Henry A. Wallace becomes Vice-President.

[President Roosevelt's Cabinet: Cordell Hull, Secretary of State; Henry Morgenthau, Jr., Secretary of Treasury; Henry L. Stimson, Secretary of War; Frank Knox, Secretary of Navy; Harold L. Ickes, Secretary of Interior; Claude R. Wickard, Secretary of Agriculture; Jesse Jones, Secretary of Commerce; Frances Perkins, Secretary of Labor; Frank C. Walker, Postmaster General; Francis Biddle, Attorney General.]

Jan 23 Colonel Charles A. Lindbergh, reflecting isolationist sentiment in U. S., tells House Foreign Affairs Committee that aid to Britain will not affect outcome of the war.

Feb 3 In *United States v. Darby Lumber Company*, Fair Labor Standards Act (June 25, 1938) upheld by Supreme Court.

Feb 4 United Service Organizations (USO) organized. Brings together 6 national non-profit organizations to serve religious, welfare, educational and social needs of armed forces and defense industries of U. S.

Feb 6 John G. Winant appointed ambassador to Great Britain.

Mar 19 National Defense Mediation Board created by executive order to cope with strikes in defense industries.

Mar 27 Congress authorizes appropriation of $7,000,000,000 to carry out Lend-Lease Act.

Mar 30 U. S. Coast Guard takes over 28 Italian and 2 German merchant ships and 35 Danish freighters lying in American harbors.

Apr 8 President Roosevelt cables "all material aid possible" to Yugoslavia, invaded by Germany Apr. 6.

Apr 9 Agreement signed with Danish minister permitting establishment of air bases in Greenland.

Apr 10 President Roosevelt proclaims Red Sea open to U. S. ships and aircraft.

Apr 11 Office of Price Administration created by executive order, Leon Henderson director.

Apr 25 The President praises heroic resistance of Greek people upon German invasion, Apr. 6.

May 4 Naval chiefs of 11 Latin-American countries begin coast-to-coast tour of U. S. naval establishments.

May 15 President Roosevelt rebukes France for collaboration with Germany.

May 15 U. S. government takes into protective custody French ships in American harbors, including the *Normandie*.

May 20 Office of Civilian Defense created by executive order. Mayor Fiorello La Guardia of New York director.

May 21 U. S. merchant vessel *Robin Moor*, en route to Capetown, sunk by German submarine without warning. President Roosevelt to Congress, June 20: "An act of intimidation, to which we do not propose to yield."

May 27 President Roosevelt proclaims that "an unlimited national emergency confronts this country."

June 6 Congress authorizes seizure of all foreign ships in U. S. ports for needs of commerce and national defense.

June 9 North American Aviation Company, Inglewood, Cal., by executive order of the President, seized by U. S. troops when strike of UAW interferes with production.

June 10 Mussolini charges that U. S. is already in the war.

June 12 Associate Justice Harlan Fiske Stone nominated Chief Justice of Supreme Court, to succeed Charles Evans Hughes. Senator James F. Byrnes and Attorney General Robert H. Jackson nominated to associate justiceships.

June 14 President Roosevelt orders freezing of all Axis funds in U. S.

June 16 U. S. orders all German consulates closed and their staffs withdrawn by July 10.

June 19 Germany and Italy expel U. S. consular officials.

June 20 U. S. orders Italian consulates closed.

June 22 Germany invades U.S.S.R. in violation of non-aggression pact of 1939.

June 23 Undersecretary of State Sumner Welles, endorsing British policy, says, "Any defense against Hitlerism" must be supported.

June 24 President Roosevelt promises aid to U.S.S.R. June 25, refuses to apply neutrality statute to U.S.S.R.

June 25 Fair Employment Practice Committee (FEPC) created by executive order, to prevent discrimination on account of race, creed or color, in defense plants.

June 28 Office of Scientific Research and Development created by executive order.

July 4 President Roosevelt in broadcast: "The United States will never survive as a happy and fertile oasis of liberty, surrounded by a cruel desert of dictatorship."

July 7 Iceland occupied by U. S. marines to relieve British troops.

July 17 Harry L. Hopkins, President Roosevelt's personal representative, arrives in London.

July 24   U. S. denounces Japan's move into Indo-China.

July 25   President Roosevelt freezes all Japanese assets in U. S., in effect an embargo upon her trade. By same executive order, Chinese assets frozen at request of Chinese government.

July 30   U. S. gunboat *Tutuila* bombed by Japanese at Chungking, China.

July 30   Economic Defense Board created by executive order to coordinate wartime trade policies in interest of national defense, Vice-President Henry Wallace chairman.

July 30   Harry L. Hopkins arrives in Moscow as President Roosevelt's representative. Confers with Stalin about U. S. aid.

Aug 1   Export of aviation oil to Japan banned by U. S.

Aug 14   Atlantic Charter, an 8-point declaration of principles for post-war world, announced by President Roosevelt and Mr. Churchill after meeting in North Atlantic, Aug. 9–12.

Aug 17   U. S. ship *Sessa*, under flag of Panama, torpedoed by German submarine near Greenland.

Aug 18   President Roosevelt announces ferry service for planes to British forces in Middle East by way of West Africa.

Aug 18   Selective Service Extension Act extends service to 18 months.

Aug 28   Japanese ambassador presents note from Premier Konoye to President Roosevelt: Japan desires "to pursue courses of peace in harmony with the fundamental principles to which the people and government of the United States are committed."

Sept 1   President Roosevelt in Labor Day broadcast pledges every effort to defeat Germany: "Our effort is not yet enough."

Sept 4   U. S. destroyer *Greer* attacked off Ireland by German submarine.

Sept 4   U. S. extends lend-lease aid to Poland.

Sept 7   U. S. freighter *Steel Seafarer* sunk by German airplane in Red Sea.

Sept 11   U. S. ship *Montana* torpedoed off Iceland.

Sept 11   President Roosevelt announces shoot-on-sight order to U. S. Navy in American defense waters.

Sept 15   U. S. ships may carry war material to British possessions in Near and Far East and Western Hemisphere, under Neutrality Act, as ruled by Attorney General.

Sept 16   U. S. Navy takes over protection of all shipping as far as Iceland.

Sept 20   Revenue Act of 1941 provides sharp increases in tax rates in nearly all categories to raise $3,553,400,000 for wartime expenditures.

Sept 29   Conference of U. S. and British delegates on aid to U.S.S.R. opens in Moscow. W. Averell Harriman heads U. S. delegation.

Oct 17   U. S. destroyer *Kearney* torpedoed off Iceland by German submarine, but not sunk. Eleven lives lost.

Oct 18   General Hideki Tojo appointed Premier of Japan. New cabinet hostile to U. S. Oct. 20, Premier Tojo addresses War Office staff in Tokyo: "Japan stands at the crossroads of its rise or fall."

Oct 24   Office of Facts and Figures established by executive order, Archibald MacLeish director.

Oct 27   Strike called in "captive" coal mines by John L. Lewis. President Roosevelt's proposal for arbitration accepted by UMW Nov. 22.

Oct 27   President Roosevelt in Navy Day broadcast: "America has been attacked, the shooting has started."

Oct 28   Second Supplemental Defense Appropriation Act adds $6,000,000,000 to lend-lease.

Oct 28   Office of Lend-Lease Administration established by executive order, Edward R. Stettinius director.

Oct 30   U. S. destroyer *Reuben James*, on convoy duty, torpedoed and sunk off Iceland, 100 of crew lost.

Oct 30 President Roosevelt offers lend-lease of $1,000,000,000 to U.S.S.R.

Nov 3 Ambassador Joseph C. Grew warns U. S. of possible sudden attack by Japan.

Nov 4 Fiorello La Guardia elected mayor of New York for third term.

Nov 7 Secretary of State Hull warns President and Cabinet that relations with Japan are extremely critical: imminent possibility of attack at any time.

Nov 15 Saburo Kurusu, special Japanese envoy, joins Ambassador Kichisaburo Nomura in Washington.

Nov 17 Kurusu and Nomura begin prolonged negotiation with State Department in apparent effort to settle differences between the 2 countries.

Nov 17 Premier Tojo declares in the Diet that Japanese foreign policy aims at peace in East Asia.

Nov 17 Ambassador Grew warns U. S. that Embassy in Japan may be unable to give advance notice of possible attack by Japan.

Nov 17 Neutrality Act amended to allow arming of merchant ships and their entrance into combat zones.

Nov 19 U. S.-Mexico economic agreement signed. Mexico agrees to full settlement of expropriation of Mar. 18, 1938. U. S. agrees to buy newly mined silver.

Nov 20 Japanese proposals for peaceful settlement presented to Secretary Hull.

Nov 24 In *Edwards v. California*, Supreme Court holds California's "Anti-Okie Law" invalid, being a barrier to interstate commerce.

Nov 24 U. S. occupies Dutch Guiana, by agreement with the Netherlands and Brazil, to protect aluminum sources.

Nov 26 U. S. replies to Japanese demands of Nov. 20 with Outline of Proposed Basis for Agreement.

Nov 29 Premier Tojo declares American and British exploitation of Orient must be purged with vengeance.

Dec Basic food stuffs have risen 61 per cent over pre-war prices.

Dec 2 President Roosevelt in note to Japanese envoys requests reasons for massing of Japanese troops in Indo-China.

Dec 3 Japanese consulates in U. S. begin burning secret documents.

Dec 6 President Roosevelt makes personal appeal to Emperor Hirohito to avoid conflict in Pacific.

Dec 7 **1:20 P.M., Washington time** (7:50 A.M., Honolulu time), Japanese bombers attack Pearl Harbor, Hawaii, without declaration of war.

2:15 P.M., Washington time, Ambassador Nomura and Mr. Kurusu deliver reply to Secretary Hull's note of Nov. 26. Delivery timed to take place after Pearl Harbor attack.

Japan makes air attacks on Manila, International Settlement at Shanghai, Malaya, Thailand, Hongkong and U. S. island possessions.

9 P.M., Washington time (11 A.M. December 8, Tokyo time), Japanese Foreign Minister advises U. S. Embassy at Tokyo that a state of war exists between U. S. and Japan.

Dec 8 U. S. declares war on Japan: Senate, 82–0, House 388–1. The President approves, 4:10 P.M.

Dec 10 Japanese land on Luzon in Philippines.

Dec 11 Guam falls to Japanese.

Dec 11 Germany and Italy declare war on U. S.

Dec 11 U. S. declares war on Germany and Italy.

Dec 12 Rumania declares war on U. S.

Dec 13 Bulgaria declares war on U. S.

Dec 15 Third Supplemental Defense Appropriation Act authorizes appropriation of $10,000,000,000 for armed forces and lend-lease.

Dec 16 French steamship *Normandie*, in New York Harbor, requisitioned by U. S. Navy Department.

Dec 17 Admiral Chester W. Nimitz placed in command of Pacific Fleet, succeeding Admiral H. E. Kimmel.

Dec 17–23 Management-Labor Conference in Washington called by President Roosevelt. President Roosevelt accepts its decision of no strikes or lockouts during the war and recommendation of a war labor board to handle disputes.

Dec 18 Office of Defense Transportation established by executive order.

Dec 18 Congressional Pearl Harbor Investigating committee appointed by President Roosevelt, Associate Justice Owen J. Roberts chairman.

Dec 18 First War Powers Act authorizes the President to redistribute duties of executive boards and agencies.

Dec 19 Office of Censorship established by executive order, Byron Price director.

Dec 19 Lieutenant General Douglas MacArthur made full general; Admiral Ernest Joseph King made Commander-in-Chief of U. S. Fleet Dec. 20.

Dec 20 Draft Act calls for registration of all men between ages of 18 and 65, with liability for military service for all between 20 and 45.

Dec 22 Japanese launch major attack on Philippines. Land 80,000 to 100,000 troops in Gulf of Lingayen.

Dec 22 Mr. Churchill and President Roosevelt begin war conferences at Washington.

Dec 23 Wake Island falls to Japanese.

Dec 25 Hongkong falls to Japanese.

1942

"Remember Pearl Harbor" is rallying cry for nation in a year of defeats unparalleled since the Revolution.

Jan 1 United Nations Declaration pledging cooperation for victory signed in Washington by U. S. and 25 Allied Nations.

Jan 2 Manila falls to Japanese. General MacArthur withdraws to Bataan.

Jan 3 Unified command in Southwest Pacific under General Archibald Wavell announced by President Roosevelt and Mr. Churchill.

Jan 6 President Roosevelt in State of Union message calls for production in 1942 of 60,000 planes, 45,000 tanks, 20,000 anti-aircraft guns, 6,000,000 deadweight tons of merchant ships.

Jan 7 Budget of $58,927,902,000 submitted to Congress by President Roosevelt, over 52 billion for war effort.

Jan 12 National War Labor Board, to replace National Defense Mediation Board, established by executive order.

Jan 14 German submarines go into action along U. S. Atlantic Coast.

Jan 14 Alien registration ordered by proclamation of the President.

Jan 15–28 Rio de Janeiro Conference of Foreign Ministers of all 21 American republics. Resolution to sever relations with Germany, Italy and Japan adopted Jan. 28.

Jan 16 War Production Board set up by executive order, Donald Nelson director.

Jan 23–28 Battle of Macassar Strait. U. S. and Dutch air and naval forces attack Japanese convoy. Japan suffers first great sea losses.

Jan 25 Thailand declares war on U. S.

Jan 26 First U. S. troops sent to European theater land in North Ireland.

Jan 26 Three Anglo-American joint boards announced: Combined Raw Materials, Munitions Assignments and Shipping Adjustment.

Jan 30 Emergency Price Control Act authorizes Office of Price Administration to set ceilings of prices and rents.

Feb 1 U. S. naval and air raid on Japanese naval bases in Marshall and Gilbert Islands.

Feb 2 Appropriation by Congress of $26,500,000,000 for Navy brings total war costs since June 1940 to $116,000,000,000.

Feb 6 Combined Chiefs of Staff established by U. S. and Great Britain to ensure coordination of effort, announced by War Department.

Feb 7 War Shipping Administration established by executive order.

Feb 9 Clocks turned ahead one hour for Daylight Saving Time for duration.

Feb 9 Former French liner *Normandie*, under conversion for transport service, burns and capsizes in her berth in New York Harbor.

Feb 20 Relocation of West-Coast Japanese-Americans authorized by President Roosevelt from fear of aid to enemy.

Feb 24 National Housing Agency created by executive order.

Feb 27–Mar 1 Battle of Java Sea won by Japanese. Allied squadron wiped out.

Mar 10 General Joseph Stilwell made Chief of Staff of Allied Armies in Chinese theater of operations. Mar. 19, assumes command of 5th and 6th Chinese Armies in Burma.

Mar 11 Office of Alien Property Custodian established by executive order, Leo T. Crowley custodian.

Mar 12 U. S. troops land on New Caledonia, on supply route to Australia.

Mar 13 Japanese land in Solomons, threatening vital route to Australia.

Mar 17 General MacArthur arrives in Australia from Philippines, to assume command of Allied forces in Southwest Pacific.

Mar 27 Second War Powers Act authorizes President to allocate materials and facilities as necessary for defense.

Apr 1 Pacific War Council to sit in Washington, representing Australia, Canada, China, Netherlands, New Zealand, Great Britain and U. S., holds first meeting.

Apr 3 Carlton J. H. Hayes appointed ambassador to Spain by President Roosevelt.

Apr 8 General George C. Marshall and Harry L. Hopkins arrive in London for discussions on strategy and supply.

Apr 8 War Production Board halts all non-essential building to conserve materials.

Apr 9 Bataan, after 3-months siege, falls to Japanese. General Wainwright and remnant of forces escape to Corregidor.

Apr 18 War Manpower Commission established by executive order. [Paul V. McNutt director.]

Apr 18 American bombing raid over Japan led by Major James H. Doolittle, taking off from deck of *Hornet,* hits Tokyo, Kobe, Nagoya, Yokohama.

Apr 21 Alien Property Custodian ordered by the President to seize all patents owned or controlled by enemy nations.

Apr 27 President Roosevelt outlines drastic 7-point economic program to combat inflation, including control of incomes, wages, prices and distribution.

Apr 28 Dim-out, 15 miles in depth along Atlantic coast, put into effect to combat sinkings by submarines.

Apr 29 Burma Road cut with capture of Lashio by Japanese. In few days, American forces are driven toward India.

May U. S. Transport Command establishes air routes from India to China, called Himalayan Hump.

May 4–8 Battle of Coral Sea. U. S. Navy inflicts great losses upon Japanese fleet. U. S. loses carrier *Lexington.*

May 5 Sugar rationing begins, because of shipping shortage.

May 6 Corregidor surrendered to Japanese by General Wainwright.

May 8 President Quezon of Philippines arrives in San Francisco from Australia.

May 14 Women's Auxiliary Army Corps (WAAC) established by act of Congress. May 16, Mrs. W. P. Hobby sworn in as director.

May 15 Gas rationing goes into effect in 17 Eastern states.

May 18 Retail price ceilings go into effect.

May 29 Vyacheslav Molotov, People's Commissar of Foreign Affairs of U.S.S.R., arrives in Washington for talks on second military front in Europe and lend-lease aid.

June 2 Lend-Lease agreement signed with China at Washington.

June 3–6 Battle of Midway turns back Japanese in crushing defeat by carrier-borne planes. With battle of Coral Sea, it stops Japanese advance in Pacific.

June 5 U. S. declares war on Bulgaria, Hungary and Rumania.

June 7 Japanese occupy Attu and Kiska in Aleutian Islands.

June 9 Two Anglo-American Combined Boards announced by President Roosevelt: Production and Resources, and Food.

June 11 Smaller War Plants Corporation, to mobilize production facilities, authorized by act of Congress.

June 13 Office of War Information (OWI) created by executive order. [Elmer Davis director.]

June 13 Office of Strategic Services (OSS), William J. Donovan director, created by executive order.

June 13–17 Eight German saboteurs landed by submarine on coasts of Long Island and Florida. Captured and tried before a military commission, 6 electrocuted Aug. 8, 2 imprisoned.

June 15–30 Scrap rubber drive.

June 16 Soldier Pay Readjustment Act.

June 17 *Yank*, the Army newspaper, first published.

June 19 Mr. Churchill and President Roosevelt begin conferences in Washington to formulate plans for North African invasion.

June 23 Servicemen's Dependents Allowance Act.

June 24 Royal Family of Netherlands arrives in U. S.

June 25 Major General Dwight D. Eisenhower appointed commander of U. S. forces in European theater.

June 30 Civilian Conservation Corps (CCC) comes to end from lack of appropriations.

June 30 Appropriation of $42,800,-000,000 for Army made by Congress.

July 1 U. S. expenditures now averaging $150,000,000 a day, Washington reports.

July 4 First U. S. fliers participate with RAF in assault on Nazi targets on Continent.

July 9 Naval Expansion Act.

July 16 Little Steel Formula. War Labor Board grants 15 per cent increase in wages for certain steel workers, equivalent to rise of living costs between Jan. 1, 1941 and May 1, 1942.

July 30 Women Accepted for Voluntary Emergency Service (WAVES), women's branch of Naval Reserve, authorized by act of Congress. [Lieutenant Commander Mildred McAfee in command.]

Aug 7 U. S. forces land on Guadalcanal in first successful invasion of Solomon Islands.

Aug 8 General Mark W. Clark, Commander of U. S. ground forces, establishes headquarters in England.

Aug 12 Moscow Conference begins. W. Averell Harriman, U. S. representative, and Mr. Churchill confer with Mr. Stalin on war against Germany.

Aug 17 U. S. Marines make successful raid on Makin Island in the Gilberts.

Aug 17 First all-American bombing raid made on Nazi arsenals in occupied France.

Aug 26 Wendell Willkie, special envoy of President Roosevelt, leaves New York for round-the-world tour to explain U. S. war effort and to report on conditions. Returns to Minneapolis Oct. 14.

Late Summer War in Europe reaches turning point: Germany put on defensive.

Sept 10 Baruch-Compton-Conant Commission reports on rubber emergency: "Unless corrective measures are taken immediately, this country will face both a military and civilian collapse."

Sept 11 U. S. signs rubber agreement with Mexico, Mexico to sell entire production of guayule to U. S. until end of 1946.

Sept 14 U. S. fliers raid Kiska in the Aleutians.

Sept 15 William M. Jeffers appointed head of nation's rubber program.

Oct 2 Stabilization Act provides for stabilization of wages and salaries to curb inflation.

Oct 3 Office of Economic Stabilization created by executive order, James F. Byrnes director.

Oct 7 Plan to establish U.N. Commission for Investigation of War Crimes at end of war announced by President Roosevelt.

Oct, middle General Mark Clark and group of Commandos land secretly on North African coast to complete arrangements for invasion 3 weeks later.

Oct 21 Revenue Act of 1942 to produce $9,000,000,000, largest in nation's history. Contains provision for Victory Tax, a 5 per cent tax on all incomes over $624, for duration.

Oct 24 Vice Admiral William F. Halsey made Allied commander in South Pacific.

Oct 26 Battle of Santa Cruz Island, first battle of the Solomons. U. S. aircraft carrier *Hornet* sunk, but Japanese fleet suffers heavy losses.

Oct 27 Economic Director James F. Byrnes issues order to limit salaries to $25,000 a year, in effect Jan. 1, 1943.

Nov 2 General Montgomery and British 8th Army shatter Marshal Rommel's line at El Alamein. Axis forces begin retreat from Egypt next day.

Nov 3 Republicans make impressive gains in mid-term elections. Thomas E. Dewey elected governor of New York.

Nov 7–8 Allies land in North Africa. Armada of 500 British and U. S. transports, convoyed by 350 naval vessels, land 400,000 men at Casablanca, Oran and Algiers.

Nov 8 Vichy France breaks diplomatic relations with U. S.

Nov 13 Teenage Draft Act, an amendment to Selective Training and Service Act of 1940, makes 18- and 19-year-old boys subject to draft.

Nov 13–15 Admiral Halsey's fleet fights major battle in Solomons, smashing Japan's greatest naval effort to recapture Guadalcanal-Tulagi area. Japan loses 28 warships and transports.

Nov 21 Governor Herbert H. Lehman of New York announced as Director of Foreign Relief and Rehabilitation.

Nov 21 Alcan International Highway, built by U. S. from Alberta to Alaska, officially opened.

Nov 23 Women's division of Coast Guard Reserve (SPARS) created by act of Congress.

Nov 27 French fleet scuttled at Toulon by its crews to balk German seizure.

Nov 28 Coffee rationing goes into effect.

Nov 28 Boston's Coconut Grove night club fire, 492 reported killed.

Nov 30 Third naval battle in Solomons, American victory. Japanese troop transports meet heavy losses.

Dec 1 Nationwide gas rationing goes into effect to save tires.

Dec 2 Petroleum Administration for War established, Secretary of Interior Harold Ickes administrator.

Dec 4 Works Progress Administration (WPA) given "honorable discharge" by President Roosevelt.

Dec 6 Secretary of Agriculture Claude A. Wickard given control of nation's food program.

Dec 8 President Roosevelt and Mr. Churchill pledge their nations to complete defeat of Japan.

Dec 11 William C. Phillips appointed President Roosevelt's personal representative in India.

Dec 16 Seventy-seventh Congress, sec-ond session, adjourns after 346 days, longest session in nation's history.

Dec 17 Army and Navy announce plan to take over 200 to 300 colleges and universities as training grounds for men in armed forces.

Dec 18 Settlement of Mexican Claims Act provides for commission to render decisions in expropriation claims by American nationals against government of Mexico.

Dec 21 Supreme Court rules that Ne-vada's 6-weeks notice divorces are valid.

1943

Army Specialized Training Program (ASTP) and Navy college programs have 100,000 uniformed students on American college campuses by end of year.

V-mail letters from Europe and the Pacific appear in home post boxes.

Streptomycin discovered by Dr. Selman Waksman, research specialist in microbiology, and associates at Rutgers University.

One World by Wendell Willkie, account of his world tour, 1942, published. Sells 2,000,000 copies in 2 years.

Jan 2 Buna in New Guinea falls to Allies after 2 weeks' resistance.

Jan 5 U. S. 5th Army constituted in Tunisia under General Mark W. Clark.

Jan 11 President Roosevelt submits to Congress budget of $108,903,047,923, of which $100,000,000,000 is for war.

Jan 11 U. S. relinquishes extraterri-torial rights in treaty with China. Senate assents Feb. 11.

Jan 14–24 Casablanca Conference. President Roosevelt and Mr. Churchill meet to consider invasion of Sicily and cross-Channel invasion of Europe. Agree on necessity of unconditional surrender.

Jan 22 Sanananda, captured by Aus-tralians and Americans, completes conquest of Southeastern tip of New Guinea, assuring safety of Australia and start on road back to Philippines.

Jan 27 First all-American bombing as-sault on Germany, in daylight attack on Wilhelmshaven. 1943 is year of continuous Allied heavy bombing of industrial centers in Germany and occupied France.

Feb Wiley B. Rutledge appointed asso-ciate justice of Supreme Court. Since Supreme Court dispute, 1937, President Roosevelt has appointed 8 justices and one Chief Justice.

Feb 6 General Eisenhower appointed Commander-in-Chief of Allied Expeditionary Forces in North Africa.

Feb 7 Shoes added to rationed com-modities.

Feb 8 Japanese resistance on Guadal-canal ends after 4 sea battles for control.

Feb 25 Kasserine Pass in Tunisia re-gained by Allies.

Mar 1 Point rationing system set up for processed foods, using ration coupon books.

Mar 2–4 Battle of Bismarck Sea. Estimated 21 Japanese ships with 15,000 troops aboard, bound for New Guinea, sunk by Liberators and Flying Fortresses.

Mar 8 Admiral W. H. Standley, U. S. ambassador to U.S.S.R., states that Russian people are not informed of U. S. aid. Mar. 11, Ambassador Litvinov in Washington publicly thanks U. S. for lend-lease supplies.

Mar 12 Anthony Eden arrives in Washington for discussions on war situation and post-war problems. Mar. 29, discussions concluded with general agreement.

Mar 16 Ball-Burton-Hatch-Hill Res-olution, the B_2H_2, favoring postwar peace organization, introduced in Senate. Tabled later.

Mar 26 War Food Administration established by executive order.

Apr 1 Rationing of meats, fats and cheese instituted.

Apr 6 Secretary of Treasury Morgenthau proposes a postwar currency stabilization plan.

Apr 7 British and U. S. forces join in North Tunisia.

Apr 10 Dr. Herbert V. Evatt, Australian foreign minister, arrives in Washington.

Apr 13 Thomas Jefferson memorial in Washington dedicated. President Roosevelt delivers address.

Apr 19 Anglo-American Conference on Refugees opens at Hamilton, Bermuda.

Apr 20 President Roosevelt confers with President Avila Comacho of Mexico at Monterrey, Mexico, on cooperating during and after the war.

May 1 Secretary of Interior Ickes ordered by President to take over soft coal mines, threatened by strikes.

May 7 President Roosevelt announces Joseph E. Davies is being sent to Moscow with letter to Mr. Stalin, to ease strained relations.

May 7 Bizerte taken by U. S. 2nd Corps under General Omar N. Bradley. Tunis taken by British 1st Army.

May 11–27 Second Washington Conference between President Roosevelt, Mr. Churchill and their chiefs of staff.

May 11 U. S. troops land on Attu in Aleutians. By May 31 all Japanese resistance ends on Attu.

May 12 German resistance ends in North Africa. General von Arnim taken prisoner.

May 18–June 3 U.N. Conference on Food and Agriculture at Hot Springs, Va., provides for U.N. Food and Agricultural Organization (FAO).

May 27 Office of War Mobilization created by executive order, James F. Byrnes director.

June 9 Current Tax Payment, "Pay-As-You-Go" Tax, Act provides for withholding of income tax at source of wages and salaries.

June 11 Island of Pantelleria, off Sicily, surrenders to Allies after 2-week aerial bombardment.

June 14 In *West Virginia Board of Education v. Bernette,* Supreme Court holds as invalid a state law requiring children to salute the flag, under penalty of expulsion.

June 20–22 Race riot in Detroit, Mich., involving thousands. Toll, 34 dead. Quelled by Federal troops.

June 23 American Commission for Protection and Salvage of Artistic and Historic Monuments in War Areas established by Secretary of State.

June 25 Smith-Connally War Labor Dispute Bill becomes law over President's veto.

July 6 Naval clash in Kula Gulf devastating to Japanese.

July 9–10 Invasion of Sicily begins with U. S. airborne troops and British paratroopers.

July 15 Office of Economic Warfare created by executive order, Leo T. Crowley director. Replaces Board of Economic Warfare and resolves dispute over policy between Henry A. Wallace and Jesse H. Jones.

July 16 President Roosevelt and Mr. Churchill in joint message call upon Italian people to surrender. Millions of leaflets dropped from planes carry message.

July 19 Rome attacked by over 500 U. S. bombers.

July 25 Fall of Mussolini; Marshal Badoglio named Prime Minister.

Aug 1 Race riot in Harlem, New York.

Aug 5 Munda, Japanese air base on New Georgia in Solomons, taken by U. S. forces.

Aug 11–24 Quebec Conference. President Roosevelt and Mr. Churchill survey "whole field of world operations."

Aug 15 Allied forces retake Kiska in Aleutians, find it evacuated.

Aug 17 Wewak airfields in New Guinea bombed in surprise attack, destroying over 300 Japanese planes by Aug. 21.

Aug 17 Messina taken, completing conquest of Sicily.

Aug 21 Andrei Gromyko announced in Moscow to succeed Litvinov as ambassador to U. S.

Autumn Ledo Road being constructed through jungle from Assam to Burma by Allied engineers.

Sept 1 Mr. Churchill arrives at White House to conclude Quebec talks with President Roosevelt.

Sept 3 Allied armies hurdle Straits of Messina, beginning invasion of Italy. Italy signs armistice.

Sept 8 Italy's unconditional surrender announced by General Eisenhower.

Sept 9 Salerno beachhead, near Naples, established by 5th U. S. Army under General Clark.

Sept 11 Salamaua, on New Guinea, taken by American and Australian forces. Sept. 16, Lae falls.

Sept 21 Fulbright Concurrent Resolution, favoring U. S. participation in a world organization to maintain peace, adopted by House, 360–29.

Sept 25 Edward Stettinius named Undersecretary of State to succeed Sumner Welles.

Oct 1 Army begins induction of pre-Pearl Harbor fathers.

Oct 1 Naples taken by 5th Army under General Clark.

Oct 12–Nov 2 Air raids on Rabaul, New Britain, by Allied bombers.

Oct 13 Italy declares war on Germany.

Oct 16 Chicago's first subway, 5 miles long, dedicated by Mayor Edward J. Kelly.

Oct 19–30 Moscow Conference of foreign secretaries of U. S., Great Britain and U.S.S.R. Moscow Declaration on postwar security and cooperation issued Nov. 30. China signs subsequently.

Nov 1 The President orders Secretary of Interior Ickes to take over soft coal mines upon threat of strike by John L. Lewis. Nov. 3, strike settled by negotiation.

Nov 1 U. S. forces land on Bougainville Island in Solomons.

Nov 2 State elections place in office 26 Republican governors and 22 Democratic.

Nov 5 Connally Resolution for U. S. support of postwar peace organization passed in Senate, 85–5.

Nov 9 U.N. Relief and Rehabilitation Administration (UNRRA) agreement signed by 44 Allied and Associated Nations at Washington. UNRRA begins first formal conference at Atlantic City, N. J., Nov. 10.

Nov 12 Prohibition party convention, held in Indianapolis, nominates Claude A. Watson of California for President and Andrew Johnson of Kentucky for Vice-President.

Nov 20–24 Tarawa and Makin Islands in the Gilberts taken by U. S. forces with 3,772 casualties.

Nov 22–26 Cairo Conference. President Roosevelt, Mr. Churchill and Generalissimo Chiang Kai-shek agree upon defeat of Japan and a free Korea.

Nov 28–Dec 1 Teheran Conference. President Roosevelt, Mr. Churchill and Mr. Stalin decide approximate date of invasion of Western Europe. First face to face meeting of Roosevelt and Stalin.

Dec 4–6 Second Cairo Conference. President Roosevelt, Mr. Churchill and President Ismet Inonu of Turkey discuss preliminaries of Turkey's entrance into war.

Dec 17 Chinese Exclusion Acts repealed by act of Congress. Quotas established for admission of Chinese.

Dec 24 President Roosevelt in Christmas radio message announces that General Eisenhower will lead U. S.-British attack in Western Europe and General Carl D. Spaatz will command American strategic bombing against Germany.

Dec 24 Allied 3,000-plane attack (including 1,300 U. S. 8th Air Force planes) made upon Pas de Calais area.

Dec 26 Allied landing on Cape Gloucester, New Britain.

Dec 27 Railroads seized by government to avoid strike.

1944

The war has reached highest pitch."This nation has become an active partner in the world's greatest war."—Roosevelt.

Jan 10 President Roosevelt submits to Congress $70,000,000,000 budget.

Jan 16 General Eisenhower arrives in England, Supreme Commander of Allied Expeditionary Forces.

Jan 17 General Omar Bradley named to command U. S. armies in the field under General Eisenhower.

Jan 22 Allied troops land on Anzio beachhead 25 miles south of Rome.

Jan 22 War Refugee Board created by executive order.

Jan 26 U.S.S.R. declines U. S. offer of mediation in her relations with Poland.

Jan 31 U. S. forces launch amphibious attack on Marshall Islands, establishing bridgehead on Kwajalein Island, captured Feb. 6.

Feb 3 Paramushiru, in Kuriles, shelled by U. S. warships, first attack on Japanese home territory.

Feb 3 Agreement signed with Mexico on utilization of waters of Rio Grande, Colorado and Tijuana rivers.

Feb 3 Mustering-out Payment Act.

Feb 16–17 U. S. naval task force attacks Truk in Carolines, main Japanese base in Central Pacific: 201 Japanese planes and 26 ships destroyed, 17 U. S. planes lost.

Feb 17 U. S. troops land on Eniwetok, Japanese air-base. By end of March, U. S. position in Marshalls is secure.

Feb 29 U. S. troops land at Los Negros in Admiralty Islands, seize airfield.

Mar U. S. troops in action in Burma for first time as a unit.

Mar 4 Non-recognition of Argentine government declared by Acting Secretary of State Stettinius, because of her non-cooperation with U.N.

Mar 6 Berlin bombed by 800 U. S. planes in daylight raid, beginning of round-the-clock bombing.

Mar 21 Secretary of State Hull issues 17-point program of U. S. foreign policy, aimed at postwar world of international cooperation.

Mar 22 General Tojo informs Japanese Diet that war situation is "truly grave."

Mar 29 House Joint Resolution approved, authorizing appropriation not exceeding $1,350,000,000 for UNRRA.

Mar 30 U. S. bombers from Mediterranean base begin series of heavy bombings in Balkans.

Apr 1 Soldier Vote Bill, authorizing absentee soldier votes, becomes law without the President's signature.

Apr 3 In *Smith v. Allwright*, "White Primary" case, Supreme Court holds that a man cannot be denied right to vote in Democratic primary in Texas because of color.

Apr 4 Wendell Willkie defeated in Wisconsin primaries for Republican Presidential nomination. Apr. 6, withdraws from contest.

Apr 22 Allies land at Hollandia in New Guinea.

Apr 24 Financial Conference in Cairo, called by Middle Eastern Supply Center, attended by U. S. Treasury officials and delegates from Great Britain and Middle East.

Apr 26   Montgomery Ward and Company, defying order of National Labor Relations Board, seized by U. S. troops.

Apr 29–30   Socialist Labor party convention meets at New York City. Nominates Edward A. Teichert of Pennsylvania for President and Alva A. Albaugh of Ohio for Vice-President.

Apr 30   General MacArthur declares he does not covet Presidential nomination and would refuse it if offered.

May 1   "General" Jacob S. Coxey, at 90, from steps of Capitol in Washington delivers address which he, as leader of Coxey's Army, was barred from giving just 50 years before.

May 10   James Forrestal appointed Secretary of Navy to succeed Secretary Frank Knox, died Apr. 28.

May 18   Cassino, town and monastery, captured by Allies.

May 19–22   Communist party convention meets at New York City. Endorses candidacy of President Roosevelt.

May 23   Allies, with tremendous air support, launch offensive from Anzio beachhead.

June 3–4   Socialist party convention meets at Reading, Pa. Nominates Norman M. Thomas for President and Darlington Hoopes of Reading for Vice-President.

June 4   Rome is taken by U. S. 5th Army.

June 5–6   Night. Allied airborne troops, using over 1,000 troop carriers and gliders, land behind German lines in Normandy.

June 6   D-Day. Allies land in Normandy between Cherbourg and LeHavre. News of invasion reaches America over morning broadcast.

June 9   General George C. Marshall, Chief of Staff, Admiral Ernest J. King, Chief of Naval Operations, and General Henry H. Arnold, Commander of Army Air Forces, arrive in London.

June 13   First German flying bombs land in England.

June 15   First superfortress raid on Japan: B-29's bomb Yawata, on Kyushu Island.

June 15   Admiral Nimitz's forces land on Saipan in the Marianas. Conquest completed July 8.

June 19   Battle of Philippine Sea. Losses, 402 Japanese planes, 27 American.

June 20   Vice-President Henry Wallace, on mission for President Roosevelt, arrives in Chungking to confer with Chiang Kai-shek.

June 22   Servicemen's Readjustment Act, G.I. Bill of Rights, extends wide educational opportunities to veterans.

June 26–28   Republican National Convention meets at Chicago. Nominates Governor Thomas E. Dewey of New York for President and Governor John Bricker of Ohio for Vice-President.

June 26   Cherbourg, city and port, falls to U. S. forces.

June 30   U. S. severs diplomatic relations with Finland.

July 1   Contract Settlement Act provides for settlement of claims arising from termination of war contracts.

July 1–22   U.N. Monetary and Financial Conference meets at Bretton Woods, N. H., 44 nations represented. International Bank for Reconstruction and International Monetary Fund agreed upon.

July 6   General Charles de Gaulle arrives in Washington for conference with President Roosevelt.

July 6   Disastrous Ringling Brothers and Barnum and Bailey Circus fire at Hartford, Conn., 168 killed, 250 injured.

July 19–21   Democratic National Convention meets at Chicago. Nominates President Roosevelt for 4th term and Senator Harry S. Truman for Vice-President.

July 20   U. S. forces land on Guam in Marianas, after 17-day aerial attack. Twenty days of hard fighting quell organized resistance.

July 20   Attempt by German generals to assassinate Hitler.

July 24   Marine divisions invade island of Tinian in the Marianas. Aug. 1, all Japanese resistance ended.

July 25   Allies launch offensive from Normandy beachhead between St. Lo and Lessay, General Bradley in charge of U. S. forces.

July 28   General George S. Patton placed in command of U. S. 3rd Army.

Aug 11   U. S. forces cross Loire River.

Aug 12   Germans start general retreat from Normandy.

Aug 14   U.S.S.R. proposes to U. S. and Great Britain creation of world organization, backed by "international military air corps."

Aug 15   U. S. 7th Army under General Patch lands in south France from Mediterranean, to proceed up Rhone Valley.

Aug 19   General Patton's 3rd Army reaches River Seine.

Aug 21–Oct 7   Dumbarton Oaks Con-ference of U. S., Great Britain and U.S.S.R. meets at Washington. During last 10 days, Chinese delegates replace Russian. Oct. 9, Conference publishes "Proposals for Establishment of a General International Organization."

Aug 23   Rumania accepts Russian ar-mistice terms and Aug. 25, declares war upon Germany.

Aug 23   Marseilles retaken by French troops.

Aug 25   Paris liberated by U. S. and French troops. Unconditional surrender signed by German General Dietrich von Scholtitz.

Aug 28   U. S. 3rd Army crosses the Marne, takes Chateau-Thierry and closes in on Rheims.

Aug 29   U. S. 3rd Army takes Soissons.

Aug 30   U. S. 1st Army crosses River Marne and reaches Rheims.

Aug 31   Allies take Amiens and Ver-dun, crossing the Somme and the Meuse.

Sept 2   U. S. 5th Army in Italy takes Pisa and crosses River Arno.

Sept 2   Allied troops cross into Bel-gium; Sept. 3, Brussels liberated.

Sept 8   U. S. 1st Army captures Liege and pushes to within 20 miles of Germany.

Sept 9   Bulgaria signs armistice with Allies.

Sept 10   U. S. 1st Army units enter Luxembourg.

Sept 11–16   Second Quebec Conference. President Roosevelt and Mr. Churchill shape plans for war and peace in Europe and Pacific areas.

Sept 11   U. S. 7th Army, General Patch, from the south and 3rd Army, General Patton, make contact near Dijon.

Sept 11   U. S. 1st Army units cross Ger-man frontier, north of Trier.

Sept 15   U. S. Marines land on Pelelieu Island in the Palaus, last Japanese bases in open Pacific. Oct. 13, organized resistance ends.

Sept 17   Allied airborne troops land behind enemy lines at Arnhem, Holland. Sept. 25, evacuation begins after heavy losses.

Oct 3   Surplus War Property Act pro-vides for distribution of government surplus.

Oct 3   War Mobilization and Recon-version Act provides for removal of emergency war controls.

Oct 12   U. S. begins 3-day carrier raid on Formosa. Over 300 Japanese planes destroyed first day.

Oct 20   General MacArthur begins in-vasion of Philippines, landing on Leyte after 7-week aerial preliminary. Oct. 23–26, Battle of Leyte Gulf, series of naval and air engagements, ending in overwhelming U. S. victory. Dec. 25, Japanese resistance ends on Leyte.

Oct 21 **Aachen captured by U. S. 1st Army**, first large German city to fall into Allied hands.

Oct 23 **Provisional Government of French Republic** under General de Gaulle recognized by Allies.

Nov 1 **International Civil Aviation Conference** opens at Chicago, 52 countries represented.

Nov 7 **Presidential election. Roosevelt** and Truman elected by electoral vote of 432, to 99 for Dewey and Bricker. Popular vote: Roosevelt, Democrat, 25,602,504; Dewey, Republican, 22,006,285; Thomas, Socialist, 80,518; Watson, Prohibition, 74,758; Teichert, Socialist Labor, 45,336.

Nov 19 **President Roosevelt opens 6th War Loan drive** for $14,000,000,000, stating that the war is costing $250,000,000 a day.

Nov 24 **First superfortress raid on Tokyo** made from air base on Saipan in the Marianas.

Nov 27 **Edward R. Stettinius** appointed Secretary of State, succeeding Cordell Hull, resigned.

Dec 15 **General MacArthur's forces** land on Mindoro, 150 miles from Manila.

Dec 16 **Battle of the Bulge:** German counteroffensive launched in Ardennes Forest.

Dec 26 **Allies begin counterattack** against German Ardennes offensive. Salient eliminated by end of January 1945.

Dec 26 **Bastogne,** held against overwhelming odds by 101st Airborne Division, relieved by U. S. 3rd Army. General Anthony C. McAuliffe replies "Nuts" to German demand of surrender, Dec. 22.

1945

"Fighting all over the globe reaches climax of fury." — Roosevelt in Budget Message.

Jan 9 **President Roosevelt submits** budget for $83,000,000,000 to Congress.

Jan 9 **American forces invade Luzon** at Lingayen Gulf. Land 68,000 men and establish 15-mile beach first day.

Jan 20 **Franklin D. Roosevelt inaugurated** for fourth term. In his inaugural, "We have learned that we cannot live alone. . . . We have learned to be citizens of the world, members of the human community."
[President Roosevelt's Cabinet: E. R. Stettinius, Secretary of State; Henry Morgenthau, Jr., Secretary of Treasury; Henry L. Stimson, Secretary of War; James Forrestal, Secretary of Navy; Harold L. Ickes, Secretary of Interior; Claude R. Wickard, Secretary of Agriculture; Henry A. Wallace, Secretary of Commerce; Frances Perkins, Secretary of Labor; Frank C. Walker, Postmaster General; Francis Biddle, Attorney General.]

Jan 20 **Hungary signs armistice with Allies.**

Jan 28 **First U. S. trucks reach China** over newly opened Ledo-Burma Road.

Feb 1 **U. S. Rangers liberate over 500** from Japanese prison camp in Bataan.

Feb 3 **A thousand U. S. planes make** heavy raid on Berlin.

Feb 4–11 **Crimea Conference (Yalta).** President Roosevelt, Mr. Churchill and Mr. Stalin meet at Yalta in Crimea to plan final blows against Germany and her subsequent occupation and control; decide to call U.N. Conference at San Francisco Apr. 25; U.S.S.R. to enter war against Japan 2 or 3 months after end of war in Europe.

Feb 4 **U. S. troops enter Manila.** Feb. 24, recovery of Manila completed.

Feb 19–Mar 16 **Battle for Iwo Jima,** "toughest Pacific Island," by U. S. Marines. Feb. 23, reach summit of Surabachi and raise U. S. flag. Marine casualties: 4,189 killed, 15,305 wounded, 441 missing.

Feb 21–Mar 8 **Inter-American Conference on Problems of War and Peace at**

Mexico City, including all American republics except Argentina. Act of Chapultepec signed Mar. 3 to strengthen Pan-American system against aggression; signed by Argentina Apr. 4. Dumbarton Oaks proposals endorsed.

Feb 23 U. S. 1st and 9th Armies break River Roer line. Final Allied drive to Rhine begins.

Mar 2 U. S. 9th Army reaches Rhine, opposite Düsseldorf.

Mar 7 Cologne occupied by U. S. 1st Army.

Mar 7 U. S. 1st Army crosses Rhine at Remagen over Ludendorff bridge left by enemy.

Mar 10 U. S. troops land on southwest tip of Mindanao in Philippines.

Mar 10 U. S. B-29's begin incendiary raids on Tokyo.

Mar 10 Allied armies close gap on Rhine near Andernach. Allies now control west bank of Rhine from Nijmegen, Holland, to Coblenz.

Mar 12 Anti-discrimination law enacted by New York legislature.

Mar 15 U. S. 3rd and 7th Armies begin assault on Saar Basin. Last German forces withdraw beyond the Rhine Mar. 25.

Mar 23 U. S. 9th and British 2nd Armies cross Lower Rhine toward Ruhr, joined by 40,000 airborne troops.

Mar 25 U. S. 1st Army breaks out of Remagen bridgehead to encircle the Ruhr.

Apr 1–June 21 Battle for Okinawa in Ryukyu Islands, by U. S. 10th Army supported by large fleet. Casualties: U. S., 79,500; Japanese, nearly 120,000.

Apr 1–18 Battle of the Ruhr. U. S. 1st and 9th Armies encircle Ruhr pocket Apr. 1, pocket wiped out Apr. 18. German prisoners number 325,000.

Apr 9 Gallup poll reports 81 per cent in favor of a world organization with police power; 1937, 26 per cent favored joining a new league; 1944, 72 per cent favored it.

Apr 12 U. S. 9th Army crosses the Elbe south of Magdeburg.

Apr 12 Death of President Roosevelt, of cerebral hemorrhage, at Warm Springs, Ga., at 4:35 P.M. Vice-President Truman sworn in as President at 7:09 P.M.

President Truman's Cabinet: By Sept. 18 Mr. Truman has made these appointments: May 2, Robert E. Hannegan, Postmaster General; May 23, Tom C. Clark, Attorney General, Lewis B. Schwellenbach, Labor, and Clinton P. Anderson, Agriculture; July 2, James F. Byrnes, State; July 6, Fred Vinson, Treasury; Sept. 18, Robert P. Patterson, War.

Retains of Roosevelt's Cabinet: James Forrestal, Navy; Harold L. Ickes, Interior; and Henry A. Wallace, Commerce.

Apr 13 Buchenwald concentration camp liberated by U. S. 3rd Army; Dachau concentration camp Apr. 24.

Apr 21 Nuremberg, Nazi shrine, finally taken by U. S. 7th Army.

Apr 21 Russians reach suburbs of Berlin.

Apr 25 U. S. and Russian patrols meet at Torgau on the Elbe below Berlin.

Apr 24–June 26 U. N. Conference, with delegates from 50 nations, at San Francisco, opens with broadcast from Washington by President Truman. U.N. Charter signed June 26. Secretary of State Stettinius at Conference: "The sovereignty of no nation, not even the most powerful, is absolute. There is no such thing as complete freedom of decision for any nation." America's good will toward U.S.S.R. is at high point.

Apr 28 Mussolini and 12 members of his Cabinet shot to death at Lake Como. Next day Mussolini hanged in Milan Square.

Apr 29 German armies in Italy surrender unconditionally to Allies, effective May 2.

Apr 30 Hitler commits suicide in Reich Chancellery, Berlin, according to evidence of British Intelligence published Nov. 1, 1945.

May 1 Hitler reported dead by Admiral Karl Doenitz, who assumes command.

May 2 Berlin surrenders to Russian and Ukrainian armies.

May 4 German forces in Holland, Denmark and northwest Germany surrender.

May 6 German forces surrender in Austria.

May 7 2:41 A.M., Paris time, Germany makes unconditional surrender to Western Allies and U.S.S.R. at General Eisenhower's headquarters at Rheims. General Jodl signs for Germany. Surrender ratified in Berlin by Field Marshal Keitel, 12:01 A.M., May 9 (6:01 P.M., May 8, New York time).

May 8 V-E Day. President Truman announces end of war in Europe over radio at 9 A.M.

May 10 Point system for discharge of enlisted men announced by Secretary of War Stimson. By December, 5,000,000 have been discharged from Army, 1,-500,000 from Navy.

May 13 U. S. opposes occupation of Trieste by Yugoslavia.

June 4 Office of Civilian Defense ter-minated by executive order.

June 5 Allied Control Council organ-ized in Berlin, with authority to exercise supreme control over Germany. Germany to be divided into 4 zones, each to be governed by one of victor powers, U. S., Great Britain, France and U.S.S.R.

June 18 General Eisenhower arrives in Washington from Europe, greeted by cheering thousands.

June 21 First meeting of Allied Repa-rations Commission at Moscow.

June 26 U.N. Charter signed at San Francisco by delegates of 50 nations.

June 30 Office of Price Administration extended to June 30, 1946, by act of Congress.

July 3 First unit of U. S. occupation forces enter Berlin.

July 5 General MacArthur announces reconquest of Philippines. Philippine campaign has cost 60,628 killed, wounded and missing.

July 5 U. S. and Great Britain recog-nize Provisional Government of Poland.

July 10 A thousand carrier-borne planes, with planes from the Marianas and Okinawa, raid Kyushu and Honshu, beginning full stride of air war against Japan.

July 16 First atom bomb test made in desert near Los Alamos, N. Mex.

July 17–Aug 2 Potsdam Conference. President Truman, Mr. Churchill, Mr. Stalin meet to consider treatment of Germany in control period. Council of Foreign Ministers provided for. Mr. Attlee, new British premier elected July 26, arrives at Conference July 29.

July 17 British carrier forces join with U. S. 3rd Fleet in air attack on Tokyo area.

July 19 Bretton Woods agreements ap-proved by Senate, 61–16. July 31, Congress provides for U. S. participation.

July 26 Japan warned by joint note issued from Potsdam by U. S., Great Britain and China, of complete destruction unless she surrenders unconditionally. Next day, thousands of leaflets dropped over cities by B-29's threaten destruction by air.

July 28 U.N. Charter approved by U. S. Senate, 89–2.

July 30 Allied Control Council holds first meeting in Berlin, General Eisenhower chairman.

July 31 U. S. accepts membership in U.N. Food and Agricultural Organization (FAO).

July 31 Tax Adjustment Act designed to facilitate economic reconversion.

Aug 2 King George visits President Truman on board U. S. Cruiser *Augusta* in Plymouth Sound.

Aug 6 Hiroshima blasted by first atomic bomb, dropped by a B-29 of U. S. Army Air Force. Estimated killed and injured, 180,000.

Aug 8 U.S.S.R. declares war upon Japan.

Aug 8 Agreement creating International War Crimes Tribunal signed by U. S., Great Britain, France and U.S.S.R.

Aug 8 Allied Commission for Austria and its division into 4 zones agreed upon by U. S., Great Britain, France and U.S.S.R.

Aug 9 Nagasaki hit by second atomic bomb. Leaflets from U. S. aircraft had given warning. Estimated killed and injured, 80,000.

Aug 10 Japan sues for peace.

Aug 14 Japan's surrender announced by President Truman at 7 P.M.

Aug 15 Gasoline and fuel oil ration- ing ends by order of Price Administrator.

Aug 19 Preliminary surrender docu- ment signed by Japanese delegates at Manila before General MacArthur.

Aug 21 Termination of Lend-Lease announced by President Truman.

Sept 2 Japan formally surrenders on battleship *Missouri* in Tokyo Bay 9:08 A.M. Tokyo time (8:08 P.M. Eastern War Time). President Truman proclaims Sept. 2 official V-J Day.
[Cost to U. S. of World War II, 1941–1945: numbers engaged, Army, Navy, Marines, 15,493,657; total deaths, 325,-464; total wounded, not mortal, 669,-429; total casualties, 994,893; direct cost in dollars, $330,500,000,000; Lend-Lease to June 30, 1945, $46,070,-000,000. *Source: Departments of Defense, Treasury and Commerce.*]

Sept 6 President Truman sends to Congress 21-point domestic program, extension of New Deal.

Sept 8 General MacArthur enters Tokyo.

Sept 9 General John R. Hodge re- ceives formal surrender of Japanese troops in southern zone in Korea.

Sept 11 Council of Foreign Ministers (China, France, Great Britain, U.S.S.R. and U. S.) meets for first time in London to prepare draft treaties of peace. Oct. 2, ends in failure.

Sept 14 Ford Motor Company closes plants for 3 weeks, 50,000 idle, result of strikes in supplier plants.

Sept 21–Oct 17 Bituminous coal strike, 200,000 out.

Oct 4 War Production Board termi- nated and a Civil Production Administration created by executive order to aid in reconversion to peacetime economy.

Oct 23 President Truman before Con- gress calls for universal peacetime military training.[Stormy debate in Congress and country.]

Oct 24 U.N. Charter goes into effect upon ratification by 29 nations.

Oct 27 President Truman in Navy Day address in New York lays down 12 fundamentals of U. S. foreign policy.

Nov 5 Labor-Management Conference called by the President opens in Washington. Closes Nov. 30 without success.

Nov 8 Revenue Act provides for re- duction of taxes. Estimated reduction, nearly $6,000,000,000.

Nov 15 President Truman, Prime Min- isters Attlee and Mackenzie King of Great Britain and Canada, meeting in Washington, issue joint statement advocating U.N. Atomic Energy Commission.

Nov 20 International War Crimes Tribunal opens trial of 24 top Nazi leaders at Nuremberg, Associate Justice Robert H. Jackson of U. S. Supreme Court, prosecutor. Sentence pronounced Oct. 1, 1946: 18 convicted, 11 sentenced to hanging, 7 to imprisonment. Hermann Goering escapes hanging by sui-cide.

Nov 21 General Motors strike, with 200,000 out, begins in plants in 20 different states. Mar. 13, 1946, strike settled with pay raise of 18.5 cents per hour and liberal vacation allowances.

Nov 23 Food rationing ends on all items except sugar.

Nov 27 Major General Patrick Hur-ley resigns as ambassador to China, denouncing career diplomats. [Replaced by General George C. Marshall.]

Dec 500,000 idle in labor disputes at beginning of this month.

Dec 16–27 Council of Foreign Min-isters meets for second time, in Moscow, with ministers of U. S., Great Britain and U.S.S.R. present. Disagrees on treaty procedure but recommends Atomic Energy Commission.

Dec 17 Congress appropriates $1,350,-000,000 for UNRRA in 1946.

Dec 20 Reorganization Act provides for reorganization of Federal government agencies.

Dec 27 Joint Commission of U. S. and U.S.S.R. representatives provided for by Moscow Conference of Foreign Ministers to assist in establishment of provisional Korean government.

Dec 28 Pledge of allegiance to U. S. flag given official recognition by Congress.

1946

Strikes during year involve 4,600,000 workers, with loss of 116,000,000 mandays, greatest work stoppage since 1919, following World War I.

Rising living costs lead to new wage demands and wage increases lead to higher prices; housing shortage and insatiable demand for goods mark the year.

Teacher shortage, 60,000 public school positions unfilled, 1945–1946.

Jan 7 Committee on Atomic Energy, Dean Acheson chairman, established by State Department.

Jan 10 U.N. General Assembly, first part of first session, opens at London. U. S. delegation consists of Secretary of State Byrnes, former Secretary Stettinius,

Senators Connally and Vandenberg, and Mrs. Eleanor Roosevelt.

Jan 15 Strike of 200,000 electrical workers in General Electric, Westinghouse and General Motors; 263,000 meat packers strike Jan. 16; 750,000 steel workers strike Jan. 20.

Jan 17 U.N. Security Council meets for first time, in London. Mar. 25, meets at Hunter College in New York.

Jan 24 Atomic Energy Commission created by U.N. General Assembly for limitation of field of atomic energy to peaceful purposes only.

Jan 25 John L. Lewis and UMW re-turn to AFL which they left in 1936.

Feb Fair Employment Practices Commission Bill for permanent FEPC killed in Senate by long filibuster.

Feb 6 Provisional government estab-lished in Korea with 10-man council, 5 Russians, 5 Americans, with 38th parallel dividing Korea into 2 zones: Soviet-controlled North Korea, and American-controlled South Korea.

Feb 11 Anglo-American air agreement signed at Hamilton, Bermuda.

Feb 13 Secretary of Interior Ickes re-signs. [Replaced by J. A. Krug.]

Feb 14 President Truman announces wage-pattern formula: Labor entitled to 33 per cent wage increase to equal the rise in cost of living since Jan. 1941.

Feb 20 Employment Act declares max-imum employment is government policy.

Feb 21 Office of Economic Stabiliza-tion, to assure control of prices, re-established by executive order. Chester Bowles appointed director.

Feb 28 "Getting tough with Russia" policy announced by Secretary of State Byrnes at dinner of Overseas Press Club, New York: "We cannot allow aggression . . . by coercion or . . . political infiltration."

Mar 5 Winston Churchill, speaking at Westminster College, Fulton, Mo., proposes "a fraternal association of English-speaking peoples" to stem encroaching power of Soviet Union.

Mar 6 Japan drafts new constitution, with approval of General MacArthur, military governor.

Apr United Negro and Allied Vet-erans of America organize to secure "full measure of rights."

Apr 1 Strike of 400,000 bituminous coal miners begins.

Apr 8 League of Nations Assembly meets for last time in Geneva, to transfer assets and powers to U.N. Apr. 18, adjourns, *sine die.*

Apr 22 In *Girouard v. United States,* Supreme Court reverses McIntosh decision, 1931, and holds applicant for naturalization need no longer swear willingness to take up arms for U. S., if against his religious scruples.

Apr 25 Council of Foreign Ministers meets in Paris to draft peace terms for Italy, Hungary, Rumania, Bulgaria and Finland, without success. Adjourns in June, calling peace conference at Paris in July.

May 17 Government seizes country's railroads in face of imminent strike.

May 22 Government seizes soft coal mines. Week later, contract signed by John L. Lewis and Secretary Krug giving miners wage increase of 18.5 cents an hour, vacation pay and safety rules.

May 23 Railroad trainmen and engi-neer brotherhoods go on strike.

May 24 President Truman asserts de-termination to end railroad strike by 5 o'clock next afternoon.

May 25 Railroad strike ends with ac-ceptance of President's recommendations of wage increases.

June 3 Trial of 28 Japanese war crim-inals opens at Tokyo; Nov. 12, 1948, 25 sentenced; Dec. 23, 1948, former Premier Tojo and 6 others hanged in Tokyo.

June 5 Senator Warren R. Austin of Vermont appointed U. S. representative on U.N. Security Council, to succeed Edward R. Stettinius, resigned.

June 11 Federal Mediation Bill ve-toed by President Truman as insufficient in major strikes.

June 14 U.N. Atomic Energy Commis-sion meets for first time, in New York, Bernard M. Baruch U. S. representative.

June 29 Selective Service Act extend-ed to Mar. 31, 1947, to induct men from 19 to 45, excepting fathers.

June 29 Compromise Price Control Bill, continuing OPA until June 30, 1947, vetoed by President Truman; Office of Price Administration expires.

July 1 First Bikini Atoll test of atom bomb; second, July 25.

July 4 Philippine Islands achieve in-dependence under provisions of McDuffie-Tydings Act of Mar. 1934.

July 15 Loan of $3,750,000,000, plus $650,000,000 to finance lend-lease payments, to Great Britain signed by President Truman. To be paid in 50 annual installments, at 2 per cent interest.

July 20 Congressional Pearl Harbor Investigating Committee makes public its report: failures were of judgment, not dereliction in duty.

July 25 New Price Control Act revives OPA.

July 29–Oct 15 Paris Peace Confer-ence of 21 nations to draft terms of peace for Italy, Rumania, Hungary, Bulgaria and Finland. With disagreement between U. S., backing demands of 17 small nations, and U.S.S.R., declaring peace terms are concern of only the Big Four, Conference adjourns with disputed points referred to Council of Foreign Ministers.

July 30 U. S. accepts membership in U.N. Educational, Scientific and Cultural Organization (UNESCO).

Aug 1 McMahon Act authorizes civil-ian 5-man U. S. Atomic Energy Commission. David E. Lilienthal sworn in as chairman Nov. 1.

Aug 2 Senate votes adherence to International Court of Justice, 60–2.

Aug 2 Legislative Reorganization Act designed to improve Congressional procedure.

Aug 6 U. S. accepts membership in International Civil Aviation Organization (ICAO).

Aug 14 Domestic air mail rate reduced to 5 cents per ounce by act of Congress, effective Oct. 1.

Sept 6 Secretary of State Byrnes in address at Stuttgart, Germany, declares policy of U. S. toward Germany is one of helping "the German people to win their way back to an honorable place among the free and peace-loving nations of the world."

Sept 12 Secretary of Commerce Wallace in political speech in New York criticizes Secretary of State Byrnes and U. S. policy toward U.S.S.R.

Sept 20 President Truman requests resignation of Secretary Wallace, to be replaced by W. Averell Harriman.

Oct College and university enrollment reaches all-time high of over 2,000,000. Veterans make up majority.

Oct 15 Meat price controls end.

Oct 23–Dec 15 U.N. General Assembly, second part of first session, meets at Flushing Meadows Park, New York.

Nov 4–Dec 11 Council of Foreign Ministers meets in New York. Agrees upon peace treaties for Finland, Italy and the Balkans.

Nov 5 New Jersey adopts new constitution, first change since 1844.

Nov 5 Mid-term elections return Republican majorities to Senate, 51 to 45, and House, 246 to 188.

Nov 9 All wage and price controls, save on rents, sugar and rice, lifted by executive order. Steep rise in prices sets in.

Nov 21 Soft coal miners go on strike, John L. Lewis defying government injunction.

Dec 2 U. S. and Great Britain sign agreement for economic fusion of their zones in Germany.

Dec 2 Rear Admiral Richard E. Byrd's second Antarctic Expedition sails from Norfolk, Va.

Dec 4 John L. Lewis fined $10,000 for contempt of court in soft coal strike, and UMW $3,500,000, by Federal District Court.

Dec 7 John L. Lewis orders soft coal miners back to work.

Dec 14 Curbs on housing priorities and sales prices lifted by executive order.

Dec 14 U.N. accepts gift of $8,500,000 from John D. Rockefeller, Jr., toward purchase of property on East River, New York, as site of permanent headquarters.

Dec 30 U.N. Atomic Energy Commission, with U.S.S.R. and Poland abstaining, approves U. S. atomic control plan for strict international control of atomic energy and outlawing of the bomb with penalty for violation.

Dec 31 President Truman in surprise proclamation formally declares end of hostilities for World War II, effective as of noon this day.

1947

A year of confusion and disappointment, of political and economic strife and over-all, "cold war" between Soviet Union and the West.

About 100 northern Civil War veterans remain on Veterans Administration pension rolls. Less than 80 Confederate veterans are living.

Jan 6 Lieutenant General Lucius D. Clay appointed commander of U. S. forces in Europe and U. S. military governor.

Jan 7 James F. Byrnes resigns as Secretary of State, succeeded by General George C. Marshall Jan. 21.

Jan 29 U. S. announces its withdrawal from effort to mediate between Chiang Kai-shek and Chinese Communists.

Feb 2 Herbert Hoover leaves New York to make survey of food problems in Europe.

Feb 10 Peace treaties with Italy, Hun- gary, Rumania, Bulgaria and Finland signed in Paris by U. S., Great Britain, France and U.S.S.R. U. S. Senate consents to all but Finland, June 5.

Feb 24–Mar 3 Buffalo, N. Y., teachers strike for cost-of-living bonus. Result, salary increases, $300 to $625 per year.

Feb 26 Lewis W. Douglas appointed ambassador to Great Britain.

Mar 3 President Truman arrives in Mexico City, reaffirms Good Neighbor policy. President Aleman of Mexico returns visit in April.

Mar 6 Supreme Court upholds District Court's ruling in contempt conviction of John L. Lewis and UMW Dec. 4, 1946.

Mar 10 Council of Foreign Ministers meets in Moscow, in fourth major session, to consider peace terms for Germany and Austria. Ends in failure after 7 weeks.

Mar 12 Truman Doctrine announced before joint session of Congress as the President requests appropriation of $400,000,000 for military and economic aid to Greece and Turkey: "I believe that it must be the policy of the United States to support free peoples who are resisting attempted subjugation by armed minorities or by outside pressures."

Mar 21 Loyalty investigation of all Federal government employees ordered by President Truman.

Mar 25 Centralia, Ill., mine disaster, 111 miners trapped and killed.

Mar 31 Selective Service Law expires.

Apr 2 U.N. Security Council awards Japanese mandated islands in the Pacific to trusteeship of U. S.

Apr 12 Henry Wallace speaking at Manchester, England, blasts U. S. administration policy as imperialistic.

Apr 14 General Motors Corporation settles UEW strike with 15-cent-an-hour raise, part of second round of wage increases.

May 2 AFL and CIO deny report of a merger.

May 14 Portal-to-portal Act outlaws approximately $5,000,000,000 of union portal-to-portal back pay suits.

May 22 Greek-Turkish Aid Act au- thorizes appropriation of $400,000,000 for relief.

May 31 $350,000,000 relief for coun- tries abroad devastated by war, approved by the President.

June 1 President Truman's Advisory Commission on Universal Training makes first report, urging compulsory military training for youths of 18.

June 3 President Truman announces 5-year U. S.-Argentina estrangement at end.

June 5 Marshall Plan. Secretary of State Marshall in address at Harvard University outlines basis for U. S. aid to European recovery.

June 5 President Truman denounces Communist coup in Hungary.

June 11 President Truman in address before Canadian Parliament outlines U. S. foreign policy.

June 11 Sugar rationing ends at mid- night after 5 years' duration.

June 16 Four-billion-dollar Income Tax Reduction Bill vetoed by the President as discriminating against small taxpayers.

June 23 Taft-Hartley Labor Bill passed by Congress over President's veto of June 20. Act provides protection for employer as well as employee, limits use of closed shop, provides for union responsibility under negotiated contracts.

June 24 General Eisenhower accepts appointment as president of Columbia University, effective early in 1948.

June 26–28 Prohibition party convention meets at Winona Lake, Ind. Nominates Claude A. Watson of California for President.

June 30 Coal mines restored to private operation after government operation since May 22, 1946.

July 1 U. S. accepts membership in International Refugee Organization (IRO).

July 7 UMW, using threat of strike, win wage boost of 44.375 cents an hour.

July 7 Hoover Commission on organization of executive branch of the government provided for by act of Congress.

July 12–Sept 22 Conference on European Economic Cooperation, with delegates from 16 nations, meets in Paris to work out program under Marshall Plan. U.S.S.R. has rejected it.

July 25 Act of Congress terminates about 175 war statutes.

July 26 Abraham Lincoln papers, gift of Robert Todd Lincoln to Library of Congress, opened to public.

July 26 National Security Act coordinates Army, Navy and Air forces in single National Military Establishment under Secretary of Defense with Cabinet status. James Forrestal appointed Secretary.

July 26 Veterans permitted to cash their terminal leave bonds by act of Congress.

Aug 10 William P. Odum arrives at Douglas Airport, Chicago, completing record round-the-world flight in 73 hours, 5 minutes, 11 seconds.

Aug 15–Sept 2 Inter-American Conference for Maintenance of Continental Peace and Security at Rio de Janeiro. Inter-American Treaty of Reciprocal Assistance (Treaty of Rio de Janeiro) signed by 19 American republics Sept. 2. U. S. Senate consents Dec. 8. Presi-

dent Truman addresses closing session of Conference.

Sept 17 U. S. submits problem of independence of Korea to General Assembly of U.N. after stalemate between U. S. and U.S.S.R. on all major issues of problem.

Sept 17 Secretary of State Marshall proposes to U.N. General Assembly establishment of an Interim Committee, so-called "Little Assembly," in face of Soviet obstruction in Security Council. Interim Committee established by General Assembly Nov. 13.

Sept 17 Freedom Train dedicated at Philadelphia, on 160th anniversary of signing of Constitution, before its departure on 33,000-mile tour of country. Symbolic of revived nationalism.

Sept 18 Deputy Foreign Minister Andrei Vishinsky of U.S.S.R. in U.N. General Assembly attacks U. S. policy as leading to war and many of its high officials as warmongers.

Sept 22 Conference on European Economic Cooperation at Paris reports to Washington Europe's need of over $22,000,000,000 in next 4 years for recovery.

Oct 5 President Truman urges meatless and eggless days to save grain for Europe.

Oct 9 Pilotless rocket planes with speed of 1,500 miles an hour announced by National Advisory Committee for Aeronautics.

Oct 20 House Committee on Un-American Activities begins hearings to ferret out Communists in Hollywood. Dec. 5, 10 Hollywood figures indicted by Federal grand jury for contempt of Congress.

Nov 8 Friendship Train leaves Los Angeles for cross-country tour to collect food for Europe.

Nov 17 Special session of Congress opens, called by the President to consider high cost of living in U. S. and provide interim aid to Europe. President Truman asks immediate appropriation of $597,000,000 for France, Italy and Austria.

Nov 21 General Omar N. Bradley appointed to succeed General Eisenhower as Chief of Staff of Army.

Nov 25 Council of Foreign Ministers meets in London for second attempt to frame peace treaty for Germany and Austria. Dec. 15, breaks up in utter failure.

Dec 12 UMW again withdraws from AFL. Message: "Green AFL We disaffiliate Lewis."

Dec 17 Foreign Aid Act authorizes interim aid to Europe.

Dec 23 Congress authorizes appropriation of $540,000,000 for interim aid to France, Italy, Austria and China.

Dec 26 Snowfall of 25.8 inches, worst in 60 years, cripples New York City and vicinity.

Dec 29 Henry A. Wallace announces his candidacy for President on third party ticket. Immediately favored by Moscow.

1948

Production, employment and national income all at new high levels. Nationwide strikes continue, resulting in third round of wage increases, followed by higher prices and further wage demands in the inflation spiral.

World's largest telescope, with a 200-inch mirror, installed at Mt. Palomar, Cal.

Jan 15 Secretary of Interior Krug urges voluntary reduction in use of gasoline, fuel, oil and gas to meet oil shortage.

Jan 23 General Eisenhower declares he could not accept nomination for Presidency even if tendered.

Jan 27 Mundt Act authorizes overseas information program, including Voice of America.

Mar 8 In *Illinois ex rel. McCallum v. Board of Education of School District No. 71, Champaign Co., Illinois et al.,* Supreme Court holds that use of state's tax-supported school equipment to enable sectarian groups to give religious instruction violates 1st Amendment of Constitution.

Mar 15 360,000 soft coal miners strike, demanding from operators retirement pension of $100 a month at age of 62. Apr. 12, strike ends with tentative agreement on pension.

Mar 17 Brussels Pact. Great Britain, France, Belgium, the Netherlands and Luxembourg enter into 50-year alliance for military cooperation.

Mar 19 U. S. abandons support of partition of Palestine and urges its trusteeship under U.N.

Mar 30 Ninth International American Conference of 21 nations opens at Bogotá.

Apr 2 Income Tax Reduction Act becomes law over President's veto.

Apr 3 Foreign Assistance Act creates European Recovery Program (ERP), implementing Marshall Plan, establishes Economic Cooperation Administration (ECA), and authorizes $5,300,000,000 for first year of economic assistance to 16 European countries.

Apr 6 Paul G. Hoffman appointed Economic Cooperation Administrator for ERP by President Truman.

May 2 Socialist Labor party convention at New York nominates Edward A. Teichert for President.

May 9 Socialist party convention at Reading, Pa., nominates Norman M. Thomas for President, for sixth consecutive time.

May 10 Government operation of nation's railroads under Secretary of Army ordered by President to prevent nationwide strike.

May 14 State of Israel recognized by U. S.

May 21 Air Force and Navy Aircraft Act authorizes $3,000,000,000 for 70-group Air Force.

May 21 Statehood for Alaska requested by President Truman in special message to Congress.

May 25 General Motors grants 11-cent increase to UAW to avert strike.

June 5 Trade Agreements Act extended for 3 years.

June 9 President Truman in speech at Spokane, Wash., declares the 80th Congress "the worst we've ever had."

June 11 Vandenberg Resolution, affirming U. S. support of such security pacts as that adopted at Brussels, passed by Senate.

June 12 Women's Armed Services Integration Act establishes Women's Army Corps in Regular Army.

June 14 U. S. accepts membership in World Health Organization (WHO).

June 21–25 Republican National Convention meets at Philadelphia. Governor Thomas E. Dewey of New York nominated for President; Governor Earl Warren of California for Vice-President.

June 24 Berlin blockade set up by U.S.S.R. bans all land traffic between Western Germany and Berlin.

June 24 New Selective Service Act provides for registration of all men between 18 and 25, with induction restricted to those between 19 and 25, for 21 months' service.

June 25 Berlin airlift put in operation by U. S. and British planes, bringing supplies to over 2,000,000 people in Western sector of Berlin. By September, it is carrying 4,500 tons per day.

June 25 Displaced Persons Act authorizes admission of 205,000 European displaced persons within next 2 years.

June 28 Foreign Aid Appropriations Act authorizes appropriation of over $6,000,000,000 for European Recovery Program (ERP) and other foreign aid.

June 29 Panama Railroad Company reincorporated by act of Congress.

July 2 National Industrial Reserve Act provides for maintenance of reserve of industrial productivity for common defense.

July 6 U. S., Great Britain and France send separate notes to U.S.S.R. demanding end of Berlin blockade. July 14, U.S.S.R. refuses demand.

July 6 U. S. begins informal talks with Brussels Pact nations and Canada on security of North Atlantic region.

July 12–15 Democratic National Convention meets at Philadelphia. President Truman renominated, and Senator Alben W. Barkley of Kentucky nominated for Vice-President.

July 17 Southern delegates of 13 states, the Dixiecrats, having bolted Democratic Convention, meet at Birmingham, Ala., and nominate Governor J. Strom Thurmond of South Carolina for President and Governor Fielding L. Wright of Mississippi for Vice-President.

July 23–25 Progressive party convention meets at Philadelphia. Nominates Henry A. Wallace for President and Senator Glen H. Taylor of Idaho for Vice-President.

July 26 Eightieth Congress meets in special session, called by President to act on housing, civil rights and price controls to end inflation. Adjourns Aug. 7, after half-hearted 11-day session.

July 31 International Airport at Idlewild, New York, largest commercial airport in world, dedicated by President Truman.

Aug Cost of living at new all-time high. Prewar dollar now has a 58-cent purchase value.

Aug Alger Hiss, president of Carnegie Endowment for International Peace, charged before House Un-American Activities Committee of having been a Communist agent while working for State Department. Dec. 15, Hiss indicted for perjury by Federal Grand Jury in New York. Jan. 25, 1950, sentenced to 5 years in prison.

Aug 2–6 Communist party convention at New York gives support to Henry Wallace as Presidential nominee.

Aug 10 Housing Act authorizes Federal loans for private construction of low-cost homes.

Aug 11 U.N. Loan Act authorizes loan of $65,000,000 for building of United Nations' permanent headquarters, New York.

Aug 15 South Korea proclaims a Republic.

Aug 16 Anti-inflation Act to "protect Nation's economy against inflationary pressures."

Aug 17 Installment buying curbs or-dered by Board of Governors of Federal Reserve System.

Aug 22 First International assembly of World Council of Churches opens at Amsterdam, Holland.

Aug 24 U.S.S.R. closes consulates in U. S. Aug. 25, U. S. closes consulate at Vladivostok.

Aug 27 Four Powers (U. S., Great Britain, France and U.S.S.R.) at Moscow reach agreement on issues of currency and Berlin blockade: Soviet mark to be sole currency in Berlin and blockade to be lifted. Neither carried out.

Aug 30 Second peacetime draft opens with registration of men between 18 and 25.

Sept 17 Dr. Ralph J. Bunche, grand-son of a slave, appointed by U.N. Security Council as Acting U.N. Mediator in Palestine to succeed Count Bernadotte of Sweden, assassinated in Jerusalem.

Sept 22 U. S., Great Britain and France in identical notes ask U.S.S.R. if she is ready to recognize their rights in Berlin, as pledged at Potsdam.

Sept 25 U.S.S.R. replies to Western Powers that she has recognized their rights in Berlin as pledged at Potsdam, but that they have broken their agreement.

Sept 26 U. S., Great Britain and France break off negotiations with U.S.S.R. over Berlin blockade and, Sept. 29, refer matter to U.N. Security Council.

Oct 5 Russia's Foreign Minister Vishin-sky refuses to participate in Security Council discussion of Berlin situation, declaring it a matter for Council of Foreign Ministers.

Oct 30 First shipload of displaced per-sons reaches New York on army transport *General William Black.*

Nov 1 Landslide for Dewey in coming election predicted by most experts by this date.

Nov 2 Presidential election: Truman and Barkley elected by electoral vote of 303, to 189 for Dewey and Warren, 39 for Thurmond and Wright. Popular vote: Truman, Democrat, 24,105,695; Dewey, Republican, 21,969,170; Thurmond, State Rights Democrat, 1,169,-021; Wallace, Progressive, 1,158,103; Thomas, Socialist, 139,009; Watson, Prohibition, 103,216; Teichert, Socialist Labor, 29,061.

Nov 2 Democrats regain control of both houses of Congress.

Nov 13 Berlin situation referred back to Four Powers for negotiation by U.N. [U.S.S.R. agrees to hold conversations but declares she will not lift blockade. U. S. and Great Britain refuse to confer until it is lifted.]

Dec 1 Madame Chiang Kai-shek ar-rives in Washington to seek financial and military aid against Chinese Communists.

1949

Jan 1 U. S. recognizes government of Republic of Korea, headed by Dr. Syngman Rhee.

Jan 2 Puerto Rico inaugurates Luis Muñoz Marin, first elected governor.

Jan 5 President Truman in State of the Union message to Congress gives name to his administration: the "Fair Deal."

Jan 7 General George C. Marshall's resignation as Secretary of State accepted by President Truman, who nominates Dean G. Acheson to post Jan. 10. Senate confirms nomination, 83–6, Jan. 18.

Jan 19   The President's salary increased to $100,000, with tax-free expense allowance of $50,000, by act of Congress. Salary of Vice-President and Speaker of the House raised to $30,000.

Jan 20   Inauguration of Harry S. Truman, President, and Alben Barkley, Vice-President. Point Four, "a bold new program for making the benefits of our scientific advances and industrial progress available for the improvement and growth of underprivileged areas," is the fourth of "four major courses of action" in a U. S. program for peace and freedom, announced by President Truman in his inaugural address.

[President Truman's Cabinet: Dean Acheson, Secretary of State; John W. Snyder, Secretary of Treasury; James Forrestal, Secretary of Defense; Oscar L. Chapman, Secretary of Interior; Charles F. Brannan, Secretary of Agriculture; Charles Sawyer, Secretary of Commerce; Maurice J. Tobin, Secretary of Labor; Jesse M. Donaldson, Postmaster General; J. Howard McGrath, Attorney General.]

Jan 31   U. S. recognizes governments of Israel and Trans-Jordan.

Feb 8   Air Force XB-47 jet bomber crosses U. S. in 3 hours, 46 minutes at rate of 607 miles per hour, fastest transcontinental flight yet made.

Mar 2   Air Force B-50 Superfortress, *Lucky Lady II,* arrives Fort Worth, Tex., from first non-stop, round-the-world flight ever made. Taking fuel in mid-air, made 23,452 miles in 94 hours, 1 minute.

Mar 4   President Truman nominates Louis A. Johnson Secretary of Defense, to succeed James Forrestal, resigned. Senate confirms nomination Mar. 23.

Mar 11   President John L. Lewis of UMW orders 2-week stoppage of work in coal mines east of the Mississippi in protest against appointment of Dr. James Boyd, new director of U. S. Bureau of Mines.

Mar 24   Special contribution of $16,-000,000 for Palestine refugees authorized by Congress.

Mar 25   Leftist so-called "Cultural and Scientific Conference for World Peace" meets in New York. Sessions end Mar. 27 with denunciations of North Atlantic Pact.

Apr 1   Dismissal of teachers and other employees in public school system who are Communists is directed by act of New York legislature.

Apr 4   North Atlantic Pact signed by 12 nations, including U. S., at Washington. "Article V: . . . an armed attack against one or more of them in Europe or North America shall be considered an attack against them all." Senate consents, 82–13, July 21. President Truman proclaims Pact in effect Aug. 24.

Apr 8   U. S., France and Great Britain sign agreement to merge the 3 Western German zones of occupation.

Apr 14   Commission on Renovation of the Executive Mansion established by Congress.

Apr 23   Secretary of Defense orders all work stopped on Navy's super-aircraft-carrier, 65,000-ton *United States.* Secretary of Navy Sullivan resigns in protest Apr. 26.

May 12   Soviet blockade of Berlin for-mally lifted.

May 18   President Truman welcomes General Enrico Gaspar Dutra, President of Brazil, on arrival for 10-day state visit to U. S.

June 6   President Truman by executive order establishes office of U. S. High Commissioner for Germany. June 7, he nominates John J. McCloy to office.

June 20   Reorganization Act authorizes the President to reorganize executive branch of the government, subject to disapproval of either house of Congress.

June 20   Council of Foreign Ministers, meeting in Paris (May 23–June 20) on unification of Germany, adjourns without agreement.

June 20 Charter of tripartite Allied High Commission for Germany signed in Paris by representatives of U. S., Great Britain and France.

June 24 President Truman requests of Congress specific measures to implement his Point Four program.

June 29 Last U. S. combat troops leave Korea.

June 30 Virgin Islands Corporation Act establishes a body corporate to promote economic development of Virgin Islands.

July 8–10 Three-power talks by U. S., Canada and Great Britain on sterling area's dollar crisis, in London, conclude with agreement to maintain currency equality for time being.

July 15 Housing Act establishes national housing policy and provides Federal aid to slum-clearance and low-rent public housing projects.

Aug 3 Flag Day designated by act of Congress to be June 14 of each year.

Aug 5 U. S. issues White Paper, placing responsibility for seizure of China by Communists upon the Nationalists, absolving U. S. of responsibility.

Aug 8 President Truman welcomes Elpidio Quirino, first president of Philippine Republic to visit U. S. while in office.

Aug 10 National Security Act of 1947 amended: National Military Establishment renamed Department of Defense and reorganized; non-voting chairman of Joint Chiefs of Staff established. Aug. 11, President Truman nominates General Omar Nelson Bradley to this office.

Aug 24 Alaska Public Works Act authorizes program to foster settlement and development of the Territory.

Aug 31 Grand Army of the Republic holds final meeting, Indianapolis, 6 delegates, each over 100 years old, attending. 16 G.A.R. members still living, 1951.

Sept 2 General MacArthur, on fourth anniversary of surrender of Japan, declares it merits right to a peace treaty.

Sept 7 Island of Guam transferred by the President from administration of Secretary of Navy to that of Interior, effective July 1, 1950.

Sept 8 U. S. Export-Import Bank extends loan of $20,000,000 to Yugoslavia to help her avoid Soviet domination.

Sept 23 President Truman announces "we have evidence that within recent weeks an atomic explosion occurred in the U.S.S.R."

Sept 26 Trade Agreements Extension Act authorizes President to extend reciprocal trade agreements for 3 years, from June 12, 1948.

Oct 1–Nov 11 Nation-wide steel strike, involving 500,000 workers. Results without wage increases but with provision for company-paid pensions.

Oct 6 Mutual Defense Assistance Act authorizes appropriation of funds for military assistance under North Atlantic Pact.

Oct 11 Expenditure to provide continuing program for reforestation and revegetation of national forest and range lands authorized by Congress.

Oct 13 Jawaharlal Nehru, prime minister of India, on visit to U. S., addresses joint session of Congress: India stands for peace, but will not remain neutral where freedom is endangered.

Oct 14 Eleven Communist leaders after 7-month trial are found guilty by Federal court in New York of conspiring to overthrow U. S. government. Oct. 21, sentenced to prison terms.

Oct 24 Consul General Angus Ward and 4 others of U. S. Embassy staff at Mukden, Manchuria, arrested by Chinese Communist authorities. Released and dismissed from country Nov. 22.

Oct 24 President Truman pledges continued U. S. support of U.N. at ceremonies dedicating its new site, New York.

Oct 26 Minimum Wage Act raises minimum wage from 40 cents to 75 cents an hour, amending Fair Labor Standards Act, 1938.

Oct 28 Military Assistance Program Act authorizes appropriation of $1,314,-010,000 in military aid for North Atlantic Pact countries and other countries resisting communism.

Nov 4 U. S. imposes stringent controls on exports of strategic commodities to all countries save Canada, to forestall their reshipment to Soviet bloc.

Dec 15 Bilateral Economic Coopera-tion Administration agreement signed at Bonn, making Western Germany a full partner in ECA.

Dec 20 State Department in stern note to Hungary calls for immediate release of Robert A. Vogeler, official of International Telephone and Telegraph Corporation, arrested Nov. 18, and bars American travel in Hungary. Feb. 18, 1950, Vogeler convicted of espionage for U. S. Intelligence in Vienna, sentenced to 15 years in prison. Apr. 28, 1951, released.

Dec 24 Yugoslav and U. S. representa-tives sign civil air transport agreement, granting U. S. civil air transport planes right to use of Yugoslav civilian airfields and transit over Yugoslav territory.

Dec 26 Albert Einstein's "generalized theory of gravitation" announced.

1950

Population, 150,697,361.

Foreign policy and national defense are chief political issues of year.

AFL membership approximates 8,000,-000; CIO, 6,000,000.

Television sets in U. S., 8,000,000. Radios in 45,000,000 homes.

Jan 2 Ex-President Hoover and Sena-tor Robert A. Taft call for military protection of Formosa, haven of Chinese Nationalists.

Jan 5 President Truman bars any form of military aid to Formosa and limits U. S. aid to Chinese Nationalists to the current ECA program.

Jan 14 Secretary of State Acheson or-ders withdrawal of U. S. official personnel from Peking, as result of seizure of U. S. Consulate by Chinese Communists.

Jan 31 President Truman announces he has ordered Atomic Energy Commission to develop hydrogen bomb.

Feb 21 U. S. breaks diplomatic rela-tions with Bulgaria because of her violations of the international diplomatic code.

Feb 27 U. S. and Canada sign 50-year treaty to increase power output of Niagara River and protect beauty of the Falls.

Mar 5 Soft coal operators and UMW sign new contract, ending 8 months' dispute.

Mar 8 French aircraft carrier *Dixmude* begins loading at Norfolk, Va., first shipment in the $1,000,000,000 arms-aid program for North Atlantic Pact nations.

Mar 13 General Motors Corporation reports its 1949 net profits to be $656,-434,232, greatest ever recorded by an American corporation.

Mar 16 Federal taxes on oleomarga-rine repealed by act of Congress.

Mar 16 Secretary of State Acheson in address at University of California outlines 7-point program to permit U. S. and U.S.S.R. to coexist "in reasonable security," without armed conflict.

Mar 28 Chiefs of Staff of North At-lantic Pact nations, meeting at the Hague, agree upon 5-year "integrated defense plan" for North Atlantic Pact area.

Mar 29 General Eisenhower warns against cut in budget for armed forces.

Apr 6 President Truman appoints John Foster Dulles as foreign policy adviser to Secretary of State Acheson.

Apr 18 Postmaster General Jesse M. Donaldson orders restriction of residential mail deliveries to one a day and other reductions in postal service, to curtail rising deficit.

Apr 19 Rehabilitation of Navajo and Hopi Indian tribes authorized by act of Congress.

May 10 Senate Subcommittee to Investigate Interstate Crime appointed by Vice-President Barkley: Senators Kefauver (Tennessee), chairman, O'Conor (Maryland), Hunt (Wyoming), Tobey (New Hampshire), Wiley (Wisconsin).

May 20 Armed Forces Day first observed, emphasizing unification of the services.

May 23 General Motors Corporation, in 5-year no-strike contract with UAW, grants pensions and wage increases.

June 5 Foreign Economic Assistance Act authorizes appropriations for 5 foreign aid programs, one of which is Point Four, thus approved by Congress.

June 5 Supreme Court bars segregation of Negroes in 2 Southern universities, in *Sweatt v. Painter* (Texas) and in *McLaurin v. Oklahoma State Regents.*

June 16 Displaced Persons Act of 1948 amended to admit larger number of displaced persons to U. S.

June 23 Board of Regents of University of California votes unanimously to discharge 157 staff members for failure to sign non-Communist affirmation.

June 25 Communist North Korea invades Republic of South Korea. Attack begins 4 A.M. (1 P.M. Eastern Standard Time), June 24.

June 25 U. S. representative on U.N. Security Council presents "cease-fire" resolution to an emergency meeting of Security Council. Council calls upon U.N. members to render assistance to U.N. in execution of the resolution. Passed 9–0, U.S.S.R. delegate boycotting.

June 26 Severe stock market drop.

June 27 President Truman orders U. S. air and sea forces "to give Korean government troops cover and support."

June 27 U. S. resolution that members of the U.N. use armed force in repelling invasion of South Korea approved by U.N. Security Council.

June 30 President Truman announces that he has ordered U. S. ground forces from Japan to repel invaders in Korea, and Navy to blockade Korean coast.

June 30 Selective Service Extension Act extends Act of 1948 until July 9, 1951, and authorizes calling reserves into service.

July 3 U. S. troops go into action against North Korean forces for first time.

July 3 Organization of constitutional government for Puerto Rico authorized by Congress.

July 7 U.N. Security Council authorizes U. S. to establish unified command for U.N. Armed Forces defending South Korea, paving way for appointment of General MacArthur, Commander-in-Chief, and use of U.N. flag. MacArthur appointed July 8.

July 19 President Truman asks Congress for $10,000,000,000 war fund, and internal economic controls.

Aug 1 Organic Act of Guam authorizes provision for a civil government for Island of Guam in the Marianas.

Aug 4 Return to Mexico of flags, standards and emblems captured in Mexican War authorized by act of Congress.

Aug 25 President Truman orders seizure of railroads, effective 4 P.M., Aug. 27, to avert scheduled strike.

Sept 6 Omnibus Appropriation Act to implement Foreign Economic Assistance Act of June 5, including $26,900,000 for Point Four.

Sept 8 Defense Production Act establishes system of priorities for materials, provides for price and wage stabilization, and curbs installment buying.

Sept 10 National Production Authority established to handle U. S. economy for war needs.

Sept 12 Secretary of Defense Louis A. Johnson resigns; succeeded by General George C. Marshall Sept. 20.

Sept 15 U.N. forces land at Inchon, port city for Seoul, on Korea's west coast.

Sept 19 Foreign ministers of U. S., Britain and France, meeting in New York, announce agreement to end state of war with Germany, to bring Western Germany into European family, and to defend Western Germany if attacked.

Sept 23 Revenue Act provides increase in income and corporation taxes.

Sept 23 Internal Security Act, requiring registration of Communist organizations, listing their memberships, passed by Congress over President's veto.

Sept 26 Capture of Seoul, capital of South Korea, from North Koreans, by U.N. forces announced by General MacArthur.

Sept 27 Emergency Defense Appropriation Act authorizes appropriation of $17,000,000,000.

Oct 7 U.N. General Assembly, 47–5, tacitly approves advance north of 38th parallel in Korea and charts plans for unification of Korea. U. S. troops cross parallel same day.

Oct 11 FCC authorizes Columbia Broadcasting System to begin commercial color television operations.

Oct 15 President Truman and General MacArthur confer at Wake Island on Far East policy.

Oct 17 President Truman in foreign policy address at San Francisco declares victory in Korea would not change U. S. hands-off policy in Asia.

Oct 19 State Department announces that Point Four program will start in Iran with $500,000 allotment for improving health, agriculture and education.

Oct 26 U. S. and Canada, at Washington, sign agreement of economic cooperation to strengthen continental defenses.

Nov 1 Two Puerto Rican nationalists attempt assassination of President Truman at Blair House, Washington.

Nov 6 General MacArthur announces that Chinese Communist troops have entered Korean war against U.N.

Nov 29 National Council of Churches constituted by 29 major American Protestant churches and 4 Eastern Orthodox churches.

Nov 30 President Truman warns atomic bomb would be used in Korean war if necessary for victory.

Dec 16 President Truman proclaims existence of a national emergency.

Dec 19 North Atlantic Council, meeting at Brussels, appoints General Eisenhower commander of defense forces of Western world.

Dec 20 Herbert Hoover, in radio-television address, urges foreign policy based on protecting the Americas, holding the Atlantic and Pacific, rearming Japan, and waiting for Europe to show united will to fight before sending more men or money.

Dec 25 Federal Reserve Board estimates that 4 out of 10 families are worth at least $5,000 and that one family in 10 has assets of $25,000 or more.

Dec 29 Yugoslav Emergency Relief Assistance Act authorizes use of $50,000,-000 of emergency relief funds for Yugoslavia.

Dec 29 John Foster Dulles before American Association for the United Nations in New York, in reply to Hoover's speech of Dec. 20, calls upon all free nations to make collective security effective by developing full power to counterattack any Communist aggression.

Dec 30 Secretary of State Acheson in year-end statement declares intention of U. S. to continue policy of creating "unity and security for the free world," to stand by her friends, and to build power to counter Communism. "American strength is the indispensable component of world peace."

INDEX

A

insurrection recognized 135
Lee's surrender 148
Northern army 134, 139, 141, 142, 143, 144
Northern army, Negroes in 139, 140, 143
Northern finances 135, 136, 139, 141, 144, 145, 147; *see also* Greenbacks, Internal Revenue Acts, Tariff, 1862, ff., Treasury notes
peace movements 145, 147
taxes, return to states 178
trade with enemy 135, 148
in the West 137
see also: Confederacy; specific battles; campaigns; generals
Civil Works Administration (CWA) 254
Civil Works-Emergency Act 254
Civilian Conservation Corps (CCC) 252, 272
Civilian Production Administration 283
Claiborne, William (c.1587–c.1677) 15, 16, 22
Clark, Champ (1850–1921) 209
Clark, Francis Edward (1851–1927) 167
Clark, George Rogers (1752–1818) 60
Clark, J. Reuben (1871–   ) 245
Clark, Mark Wayne (1896–   ) 272, 273, 274
Clark, Tom C. 281
Clark, William (1770–1838) 80
Clark Memorandum 245
Clarke, James Freeman (1810–1888) 157
Clay, Henry (1777–1852):
  "Alabama Letters" 114
  and American System 94, 101
  and annexation of Texas 113
  and censure of Jackson 91
  and Compromise of 1850, 121
  and distribution of land revenues 111
  duel with John Randolph 96
  and internal improvements 94
  and Latin America 90
  nomination for President, 1822, 93
  nomination for President, 1830, 99
  nomination for President, 1831, 101
  nomination for President, 1844, 113
  peace commissioner 87
  resigns from Senate 111
  Secretary of State 95
  and surplus revenue 102
  and tariff 103
  "War Hawk" 84
  and Whig program 110
Clay, Lucius D. (1897–   ) 286
Clayton, John Middleton (1796–1856) 120

Clayton Anti-Trust Act 216
Clayton-Bulwer Treaty 121, 169
Clayton Compromise 119
Cleopatra's Needle 167
Cleveland, Grover (1837–1908):
  Cabinet of, 1885, 172
  Cabinet of, 1893, 180
  governor of N. Y. 170
  on labor 173
  mayor of Buffalo 168
  operation for sarcoma of jaw 181
  and pensions 173, 174
  President 171, 172
  re-elected, 1892, 180
  renominated, 1888, 175
  renominated, 1892, 179
  and tariff 174
Cleveland, Ohio 75
Clinton, De Witt (1769–1828) 85, 86
Clinton, George (1739–1812) 81, 83
Clinton, Sir Henry 55, 57, 60, 61
Clipper ships 114, 122
Clocks 72, 78
Cloture in Senate 223
Clymer, George E. (1754–1834) 88
Coal:
  anthracite 51
  bituminous 27, 45
Coal mines:
  government control, 1946–1947, 285, 288
  in World War II 275, 276
Coast Guard 70
Cobb, Howell (1815–1868) 121, 128
Cochrane, Elizabeth, "Nelly Bly" 176
Cochrane, John (1813–1898) 145
Cocoanut Grove, Boston, fire 273
Coddington, William (1601–1678) 18
Coffee Marketing Agreement, Inter-American 266
Coffee rationing 273
Coffin, Howard Earle (1873–1937) 224
Cogswell, Joseph Green (1786–1871) 93
Cohens v. Virginia 92-93
Coinage, 162, 177; *see also* currency
Coinage Act:
  1834, 104
  1853, 124
  Fourth 160
Coit, Dr. Stanton 172
Coke, Thomas (1747–1814) 65
Colby, Bainbridge (1869–1950) 233
Cold Harbor, Va., battle 145
"Cold War" 286
Colden, Dr. Cadwallader David (1688–1776) 40
Cole, Thomas (1801–1848) 95

U

The text and index of this book are
set in 9 point Linotype Baskerville,
leaded one point, with headings
in 14 point Vogue Extra Bold.
Design by Marshall Lee
Eagle on cover by Lily Saarinen